POE DAMERON

STAR WARS

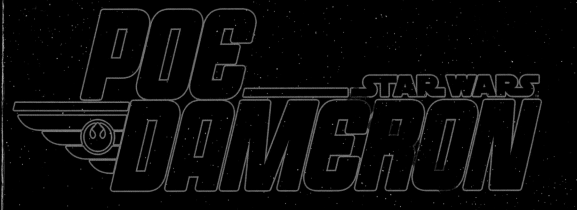

THE SPARK AND THE FIRE

THE SPARK AND THE FIRE

ISSUES #26-31

Writer	**CHARLES SOULE**
Artist	**ANGEL UNZUETA**
Color Artists	**ARIF PRIANTO** WITH
	RACHELLE ROSENBERG (#27)
Letterer	**VC'S JOE CARAMAGNA**
Cover Art	**PHIL NOTO**
Assistant Editors	**HEATHER ANTOS** & **TOM GRONEMAN** WITH
	CHRISTINA HARRINGTON & **EMILY NEWCOMEN**
Editors	**JORDAN D. WHITE** & **MARK PANICCIA**

ANNUAL #2

Writer	**JODY HOUSER**
Artist	**ANDREA BROCCARDO**
Color Artist	**STEFANI RENEE**
Letterer	**VC's JOE CARAMAGNA**
Cover Art	**ROD REIS**
Assistant Editor	**TOM GRONEMAN**
Editor	**MARK PANICCIA**

Editor in Chief	**C.B. CEBULSKI**
Chief Creative Officer	**JOE QUESADA**
President	**DAN BUCKLEY**

For Lucasfilm:

Assistant Editor	**NICK MARTINO**
Senior Editor	**ROBERT SIMPSON**
Executive Editor	**JENNIFER HEDDLE**
Creative Director	**MICHAEL SIGLAIN**
Lucasfilm Story Group	**JAMES WAUGH, LELAND CHEE, MATT MARTIN**

Collection Editor	JENNIFER GRÜNWALD	VP Production & Special Projects	JEFF YOUNGQUIST
Assistant Editor	CAITLIN O'CONNELL	SVP Print, Sales & Marketing	DAVID GABRIEL
Associate Managing Editor	KATERI WOODY	Book Designer	ADAM DEL RE
Editor, Special Projects	MARK D. BEAZLEY		

STAR WARS: POE DAMERON VOL. 5 — THE SPARK AND THE FIRE. Contains material originally published in magazine form as STAR WARS: POE DAMERON #26-31, and ANNUAL #2. First printing 2018. ISBN 978-1-302-91170-6. Published by MARVEL WORLDWIDE, INC., a subsidiary of MARVEL ENTERTAINMENT, LLC. OFFICE OF PUBLICATION: 135 West 50th Street, New York, NY 10020. STAR WARS and related text and illustrations are trademarks and/or copyrights, in the United States and other countries, of Lucasfilm Ltd. and/or its affiliates. © & TM Lucasfilm Ltd. No similarity between any of the names, characters, persons, and/or institutions in this magazine with those of any living or dead person or institution is intended, and any such similarity which may exist is purely coincidental. Marvel and its logos are TM Marvel Characters, Inc. Printed in the U.S.A. DAN BUCKLEY, President, Marvel Entertainment; JOHN NEE, Publisher; JOE QUESADA, Chief Creative Officer; TOM BREVOORT, SVP of Publishing; DAVID BOGART, SVP of Business Affairs & Operations, Publishing & Partnership, DAVID GABRIEL, SVP of Sales & Marketing, Publishing; JEFF YOUNGQUIST, VP of Production & Special Projects; DAN CARR, Executive Director of Publishing Technology; ALEX MORALES, Director of Publishing Operations; DAN EDINGTON, Managing Editor; SUSAN CRESPI, Production Manager; STAN LEE, Chairman Emeritus. For information regarding advertising in Marvel Comics or on Marvel.com, please contact Vit DeBellis, Custom Solutions & Integrated Advertising Manager, at vdebellis@marvel.com. For Marvel subscription inquiries, please call 888-511-5480. Manufactured between 9/28/2018 and 10/30/2018 by LSC COMMUNICATIONS INC., KENDALLVILLE, IN, USA.

10 9 8 7 6 5 4 3 2 1

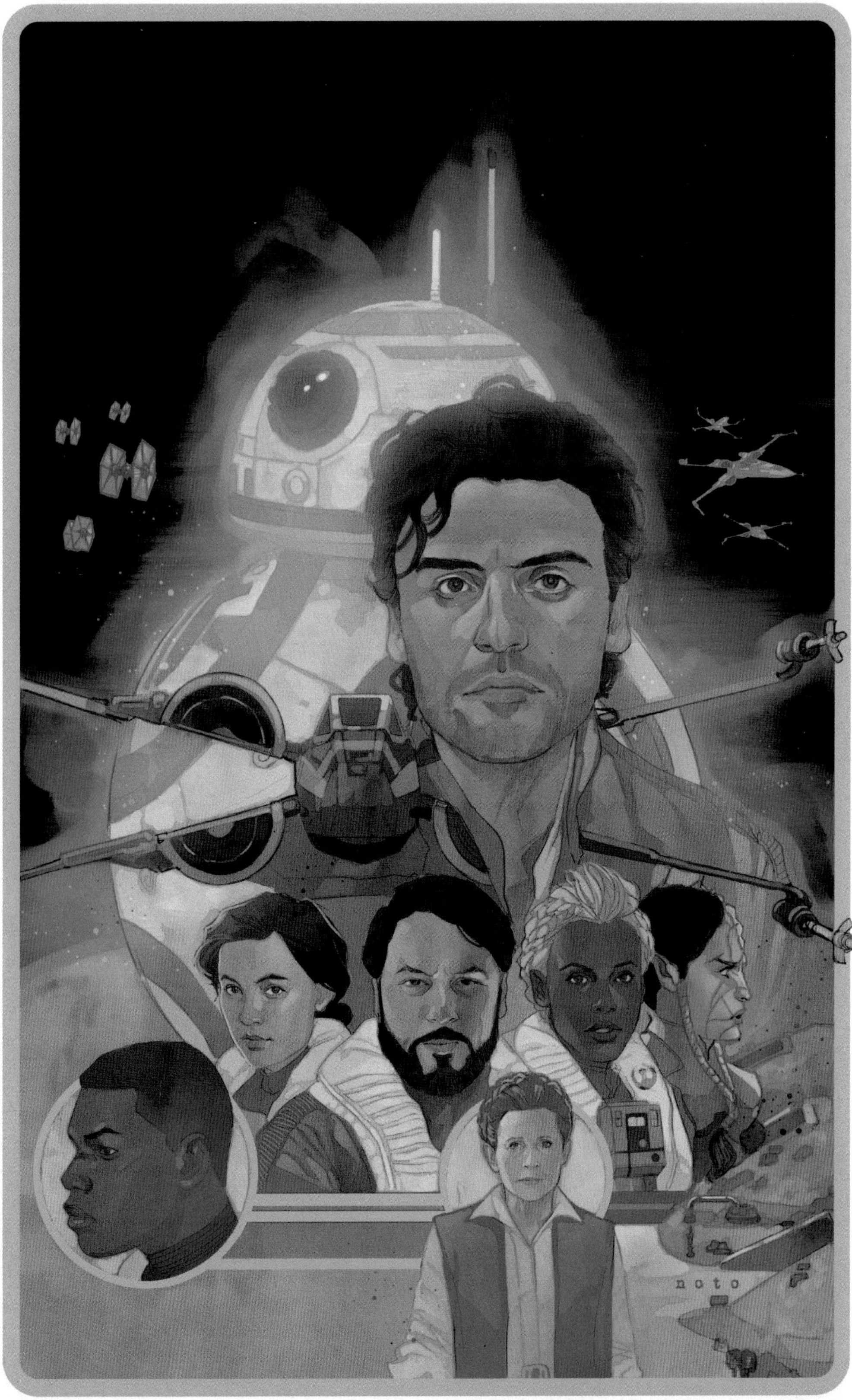
noto

THE AWAKENING

The Resistance has barely escaped total destruction at the hands of the evil First Order during the Battle of Crait. Their survival depended on sacrifices made by many brave heroes, Jedi Master Luke Skywalker among them.

Now, the remnants of General Leia Organa's Resistance flee through hyperspace aboard the *Millennium Falcon*, seeking refuge.

In this rare moment of peace, Poe Dameron takes the opportunity to reflect upon the journey that brought him and the rest of the Resistance to this point....

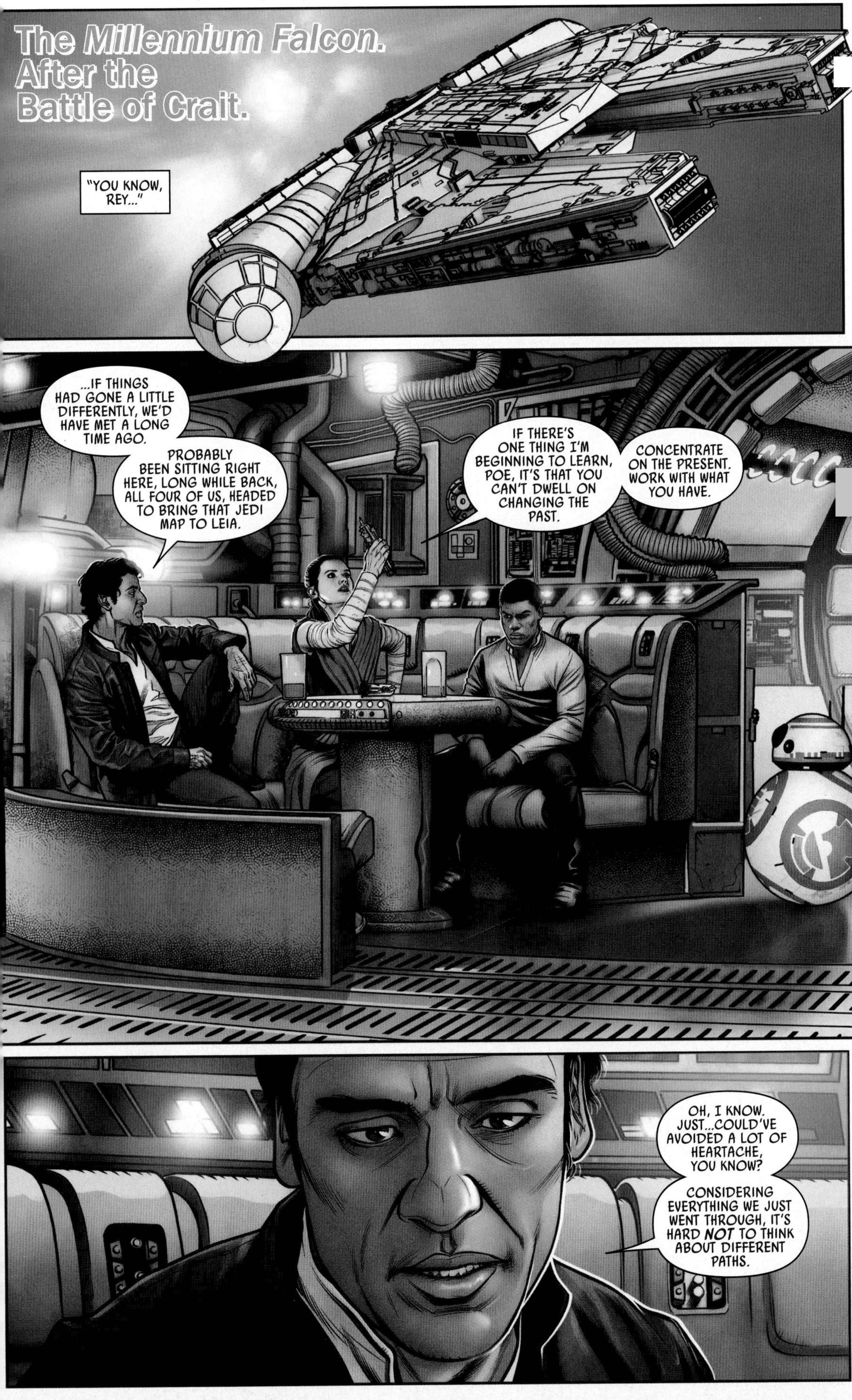
The Millennium Falcon. After the Battle of Crait.
"YOU KNOW, REY..."
...IF THINGS HAD GONE A LITTLE DIFFERENTLY, WE'D HAVE MET A LONG TIME AGO.
PROBABLY BEEN SITTING RIGHT HERE, LONG WHILE BACK, ALL FOUR OF US, HEADED TO BRING THAT JEDI MAP TO LEIA.
IF THERE'S ONE THING I'M BEGINNING TO LEARN, POE, IT'S THAT YOU CAN'T DWELL ON CHANGING THE PAST.
CONCENTRATE ON THE PRESENT. WORK WITH WHAT YOU HAVE.
OH, I KNOW. JUST...COULD'VE AVOIDED A LOT OF HEARTACHE, YOU KNOW?
CONSIDERING EVERYTHING WE JUST WENT THROUGH, IT'S HARD NOT TO THINK ABOUT DIFFERENT PATHS.

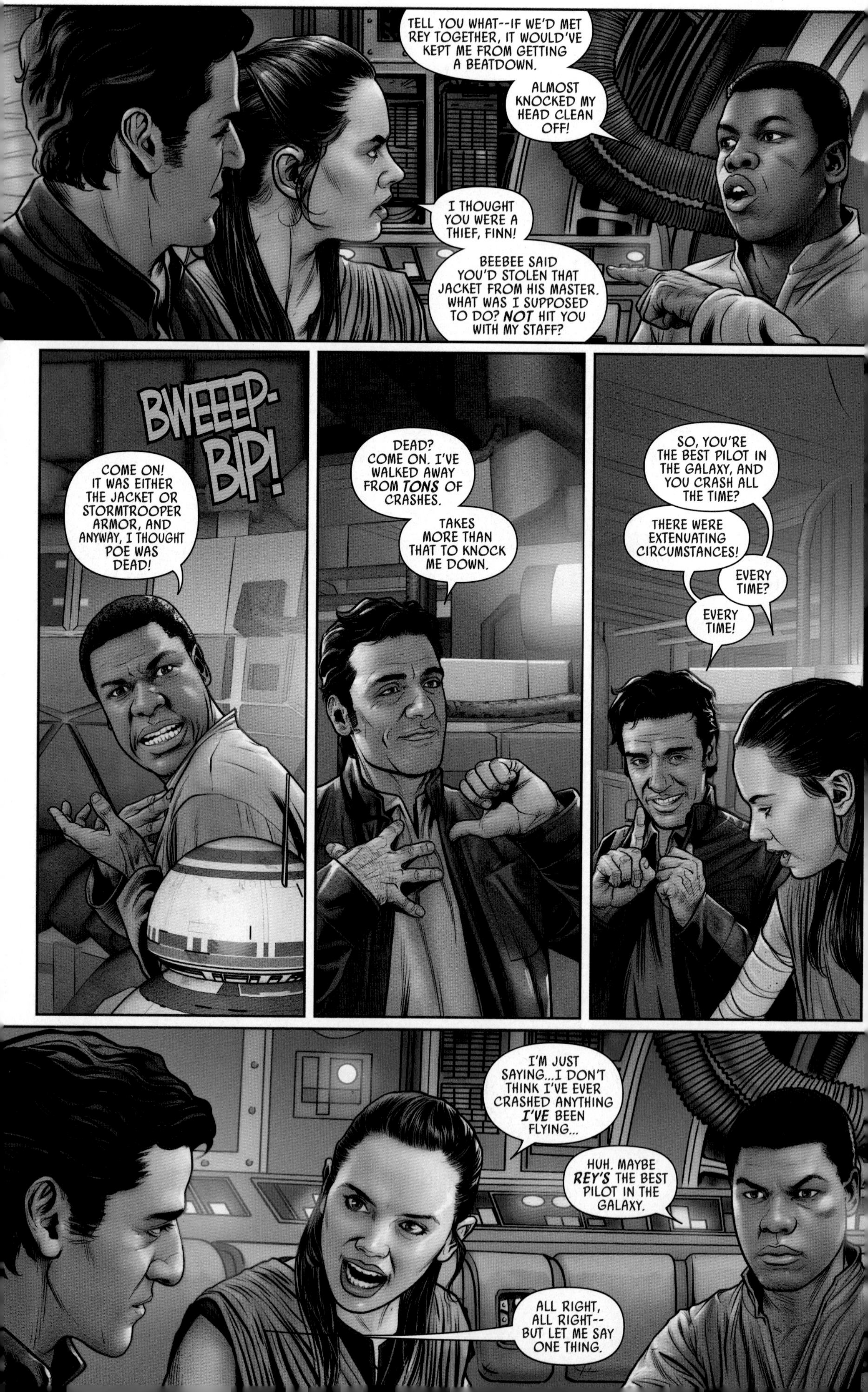

TELL YOU WHAT--IF WE'D MET REY TOGETHER, IT WOULD'VE KEPT ME FROM GETTING A BEATDOWN.
ALMOST KNOCKED MY HEAD CLEAN OFF!
I THOUGHT YOU WERE A THIEF, FINN!
BEEBEE SAID YOU'D STOLEN THAT JACKET FROM HIS MASTER. WHAT WAS I SUPPOSED TO DO? NOT HIT YOU WITH MY STAFF?
BWEEEP-BIP!
COME ON! IT WAS EITHER THE JACKET OR STORMTROOPER ARMOR, AND ANYWAY, I THOUGHT POE WAS DEAD!
DEAD? COME ON. I'VE WALKED AWAY FROM TONS OF CRASHES.
TAKES MORE THAN THAT TO KNOCK ME DOWN.
SO, YOU'RE THE BEST PILOT IN THE GALAXY, AND YOU CRASH ALL THE TIME?
THERE WERE EXTENUATING CIRCUMSTANCES!
EVERY TIME?
EVERY TIME!
I'M JUST SAYING... I DON'T THINK I'VE EVER CRASHED ANYTHING I'VE BEEN FLYING...
HUH. MAYBE REY'S THE BEST PILOT IN THE GALAXY.
ALL RIGHT, ALL RIGHT-- BUT LET ME SAY ONE THING.

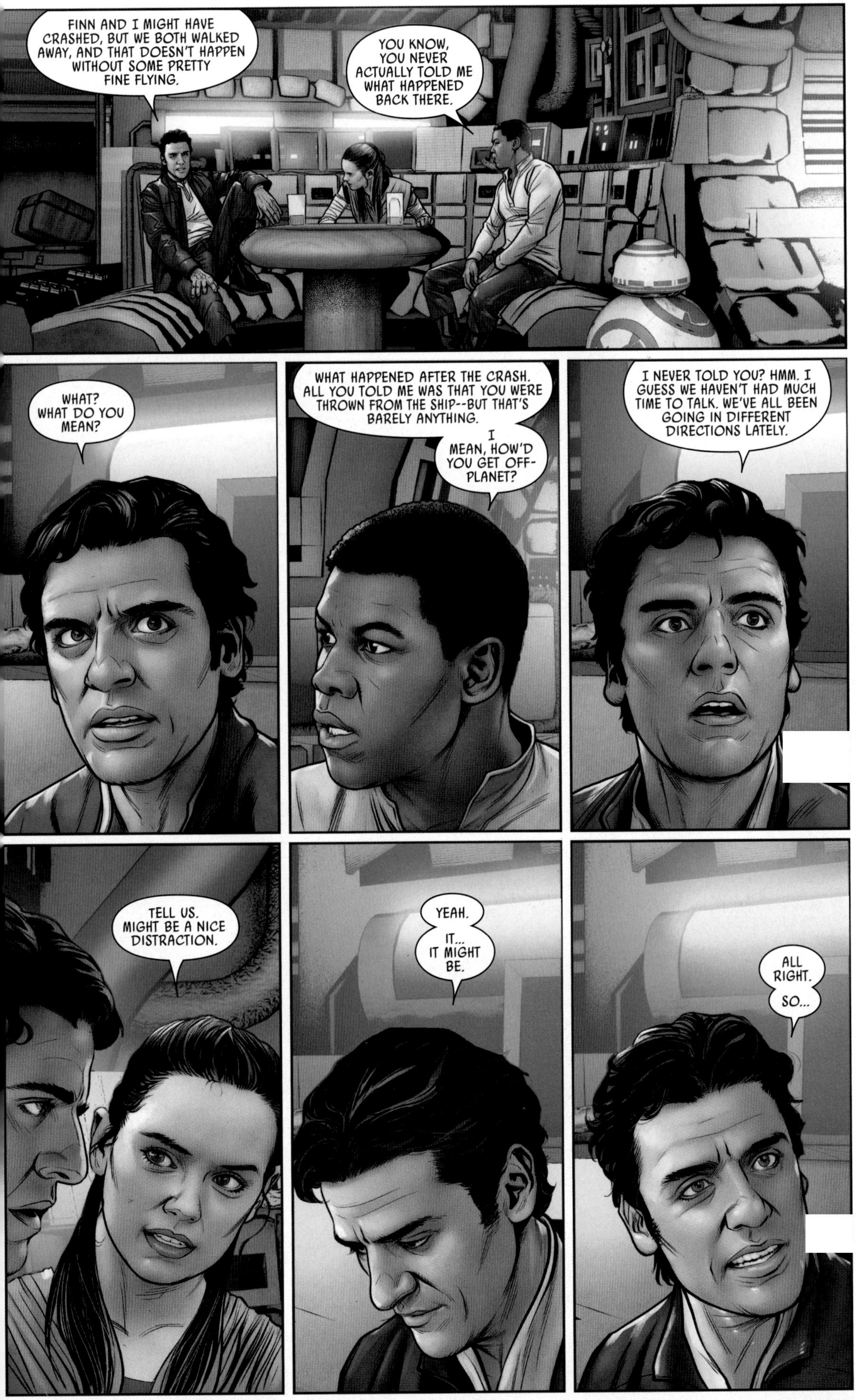
FINN AND I MIGHT HAVE CRASHED, BUT WE BOTH WALKED AWAY, AND THAT DOESN'T HAPPEN WITHOUT SOME PRETTY FINE FLYING.
YOU KNOW, YOU NEVER ACTUALLY TOLD ME WHAT HAPPENED BACK THERE.
WHAT? WHAT DO YOU MEAN?
WHAT HAPPENED AFTER THE CRASH. ALL YOU TOLD ME WAS THAT YOU WERE THROWN FROM THE SHIP--BUT THAT'S BARELY ANYTHING.
I MEAN, HOW'D YOU GET OFF-PLANET?
I NEVER TOLD YOU? HMM. I GUESS WE HAVEN'T HAD MUCH TIME TO TALK. WE'VE ALL BEEN GOING IN DIFFERENT DIRECTIONS LATELY.
TELL US. MIGHT BE A NICE DISTRACTION.
YEAH.
IT... IT MIGHT BE.
ALL RIGHT.
SO...

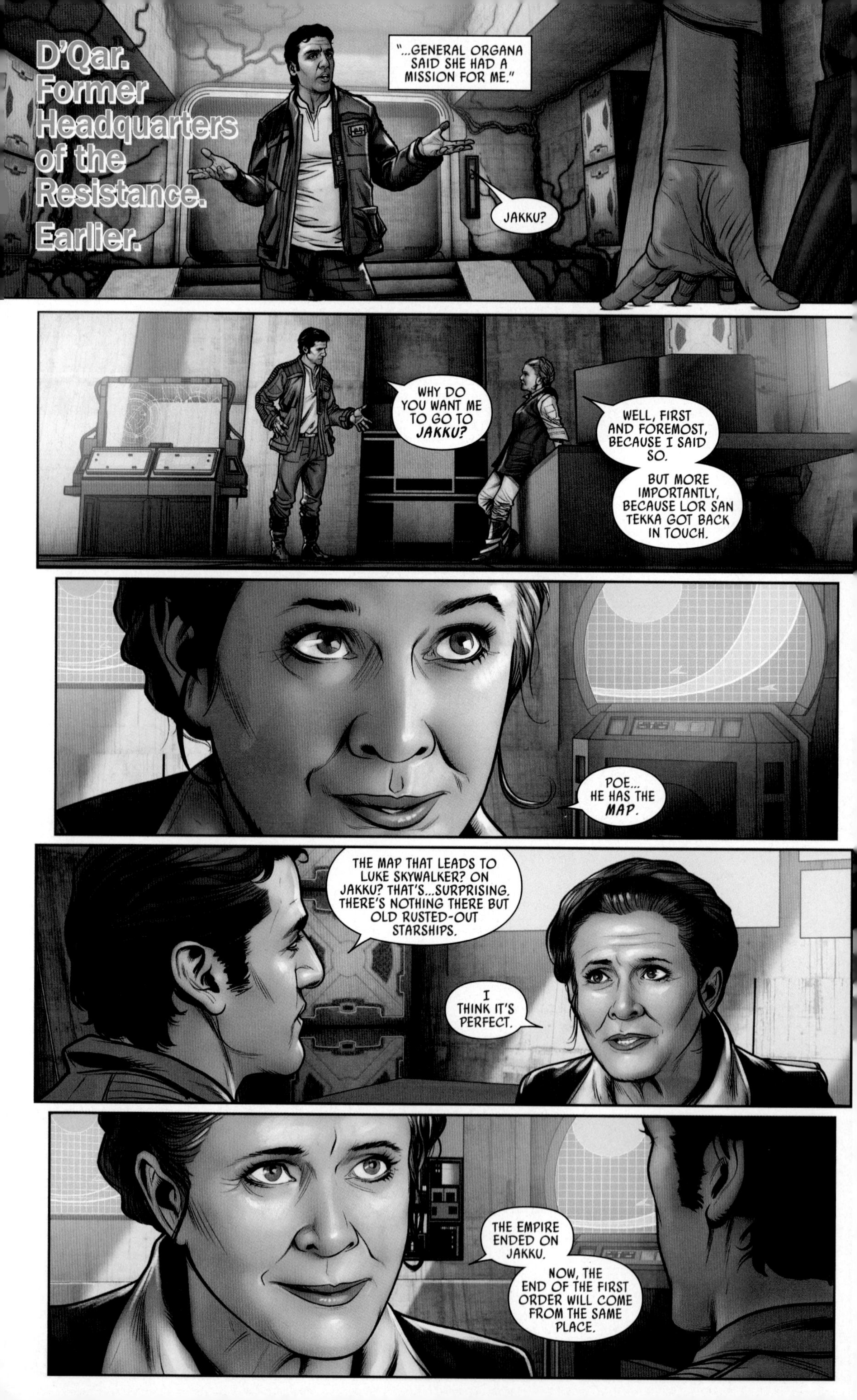
D'Qar. Former Headquarters of the Resistance.
Earlier.
"...GENERAL ORGANA SAID SHE HAD A MISSION FOR ME."
JAKKU?
WHY DO YOU WANT ME TO GO TO JAKKU?
WELL, FIRST AND FOREMOST, BECAUSE I SAID SO.
BUT MORE IMPORTANTLY, BECAUSE LOR SAN TEKKA GOT BACK IN TOUCH.
POE... HE HAS THE MAP.
THE MAP THAT LEADS TO LUKE SKYWALKER? ON JAKKU? THAT'S...SURPRISING. THERE'S NOTHING THERE BUT OLD RUSTED-OUT STARSHIPS.
I THINK IT'S PERFECT.
THE EMPIRE ENDED ON JAKKU.
NOW, THE END OF THE FIRST ORDER WILL COME FROM THE SAME PLACE.

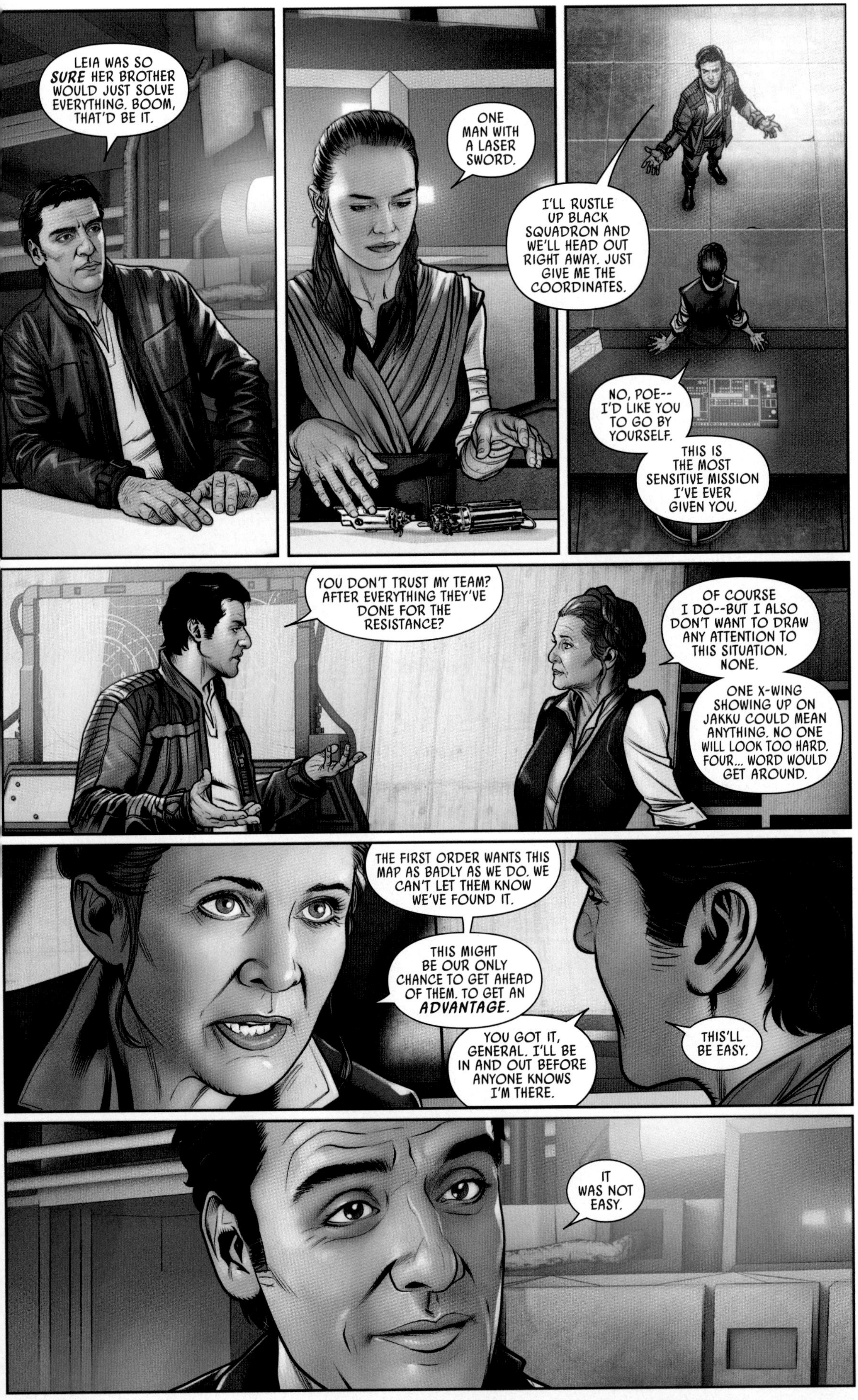
LEIA WAS SO SURE HER BROTHER WOULD JUST SOLVE EVERYTHING. BOOM, THAT'D BE IT.
ONE MAN WITH A LASER SWORD.
I'LL RUSTLE UP BLACK SQUADRON AND WE'LL HEAD OUT RIGHT AWAY. JUST GIVE ME THE COORDINATES.
NO, POE-- I'D LIKE YOU TO GO BY YOURSELF.
THIS IS THE MOST SENSITIVE MISSION I'VE EVER GIVEN YOU.
YOU DON'T TRUST MY TEAM? AFTER EVERYTHING THEY'VE DONE FOR THE RESISTANCE?
OF COURSE I DO--BUT I ALSO DON'T WANT TO DRAW ANY ATTENTION TO THIS SITUATION. NONE.
ONE X-WING SHOWING UP ON JAKKU COULD MEAN ANYTHING. NO ONE WILL LOOK TOO HARD. FOUR... WORD WOULD GET AROUND.
THE FIRST ORDER WANTS THIS MAP AS BADLY AS WE DO. WE CAN'T LET THEM KNOW WE'VE FOUND IT.
THIS MIGHT BE OUR ONLY CHANCE TO GET AHEAD OF THEM. TO GET AN ADVANTAGE.
YOU GOT IT, GENERAL. I'LL BE IN AND OUT BEFORE ANYONE KNOWS I'M THERE.
THIS'LL BE EASY.
IT WAS NOT EASY.

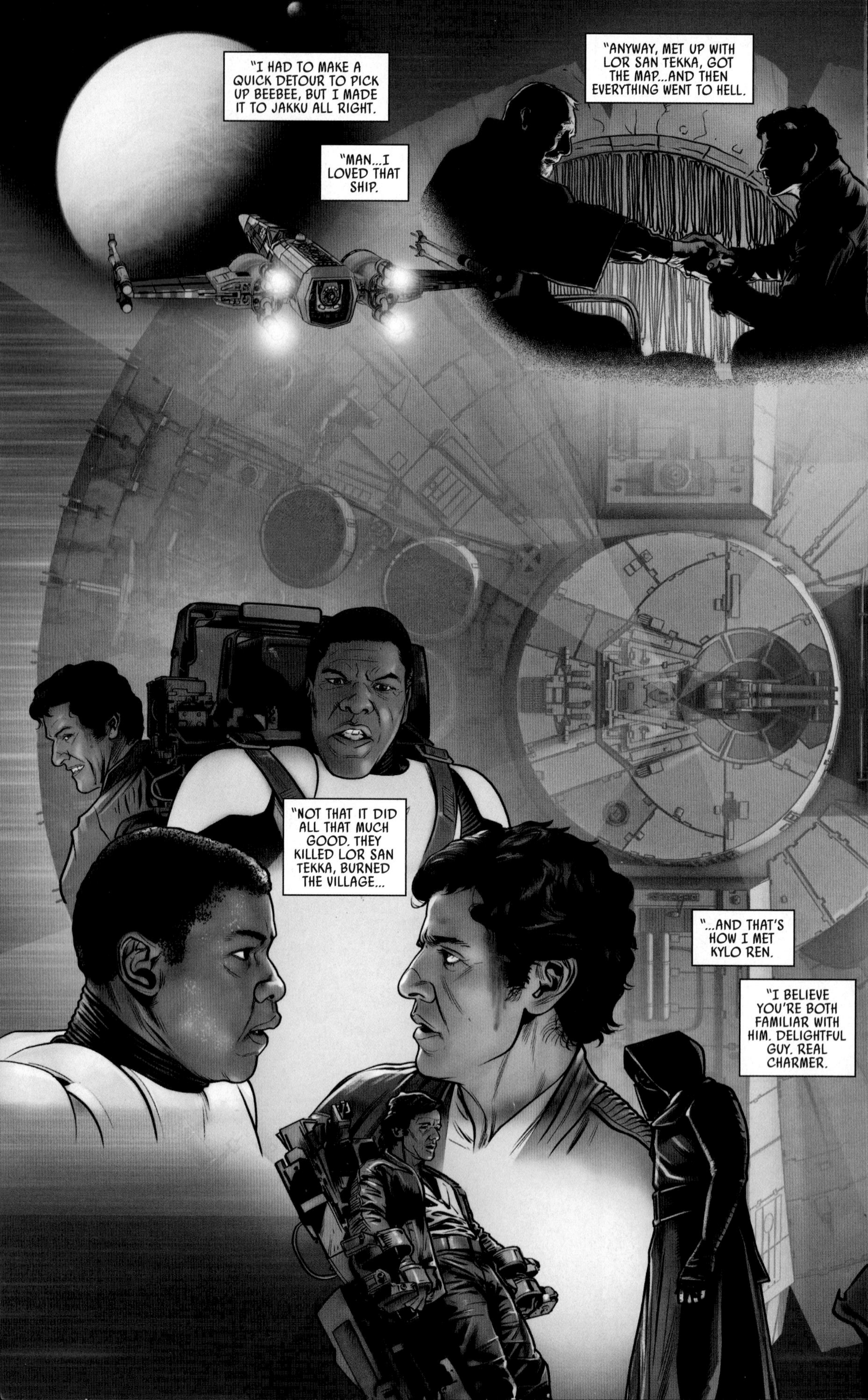
"I HAD TO MAKE A QUICK DETOUR TO PICK UP BEEBEE, BUT I MADE IT TO JAKKU ALL RIGHT.
"MAN...I LOVED THAT SHIP.
"ANYWAY, MET UP WITH LOR SAN TEKKA, GOT THE MAP...AND THEN EVERYTHING WENT TO HELL.
"NOT THAT IT DID ALL THAT MUCH GOOD. THEY KILLED LOR SAN TEKKA, BURNED THE VILLAGE...
"...AND THAT'S HOW I MET KYLO REN.
"I BELIEVE YOU'RE BOTH FAMILIAR WITH HIM. DELIGHTFUL GUY. REAL CHARMER.

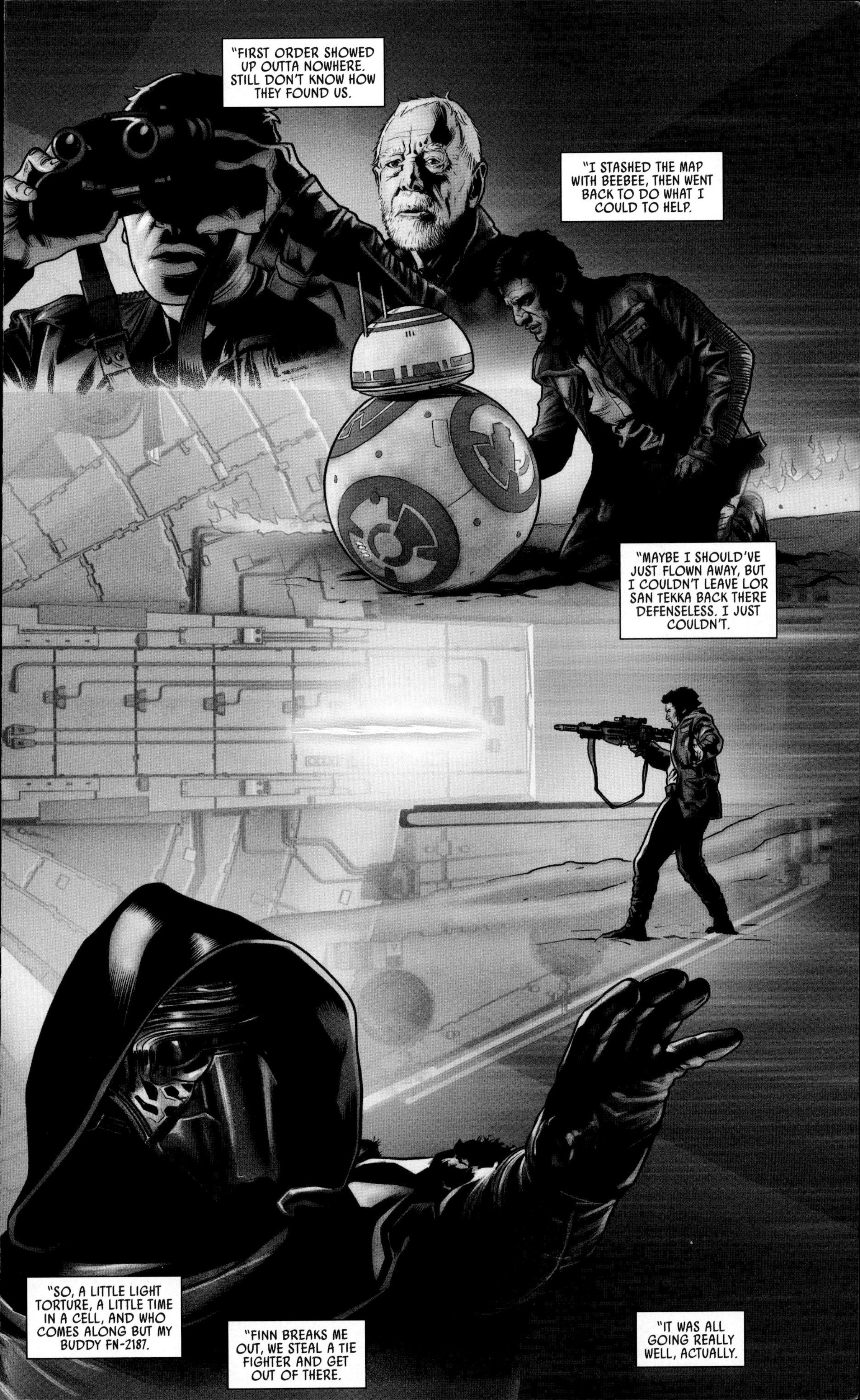
"FIRST ORDER SHOWED UP OUTTA NOWHERE. STILL DON'T KNOW HOW THEY FOUND US.
"I STASHED THE MAP WITH BEEBEE, THEN WENT BACK TO DO WHAT I COULD TO HELP.
"MAYBE I SHOULD'VE JUST FLOWN AWAY, BUT I COULDN'T LEAVE LOR SAN TEKKA BACK THERE DEFENSELESS. I JUST COULDN'T.
"SO, A LITTLE LIGHT TORTURE, A LITTLE TIME IN A CELL, AND WHO COMES ALONG BUT MY BUDDY FN-2187.
"FINN BREAKS ME OUT, WE STEAL A TIE FIGHTER AND GET OUT OF THERE.
"IT WAS ALL GOING REALLY WELL, ACTUALLY.

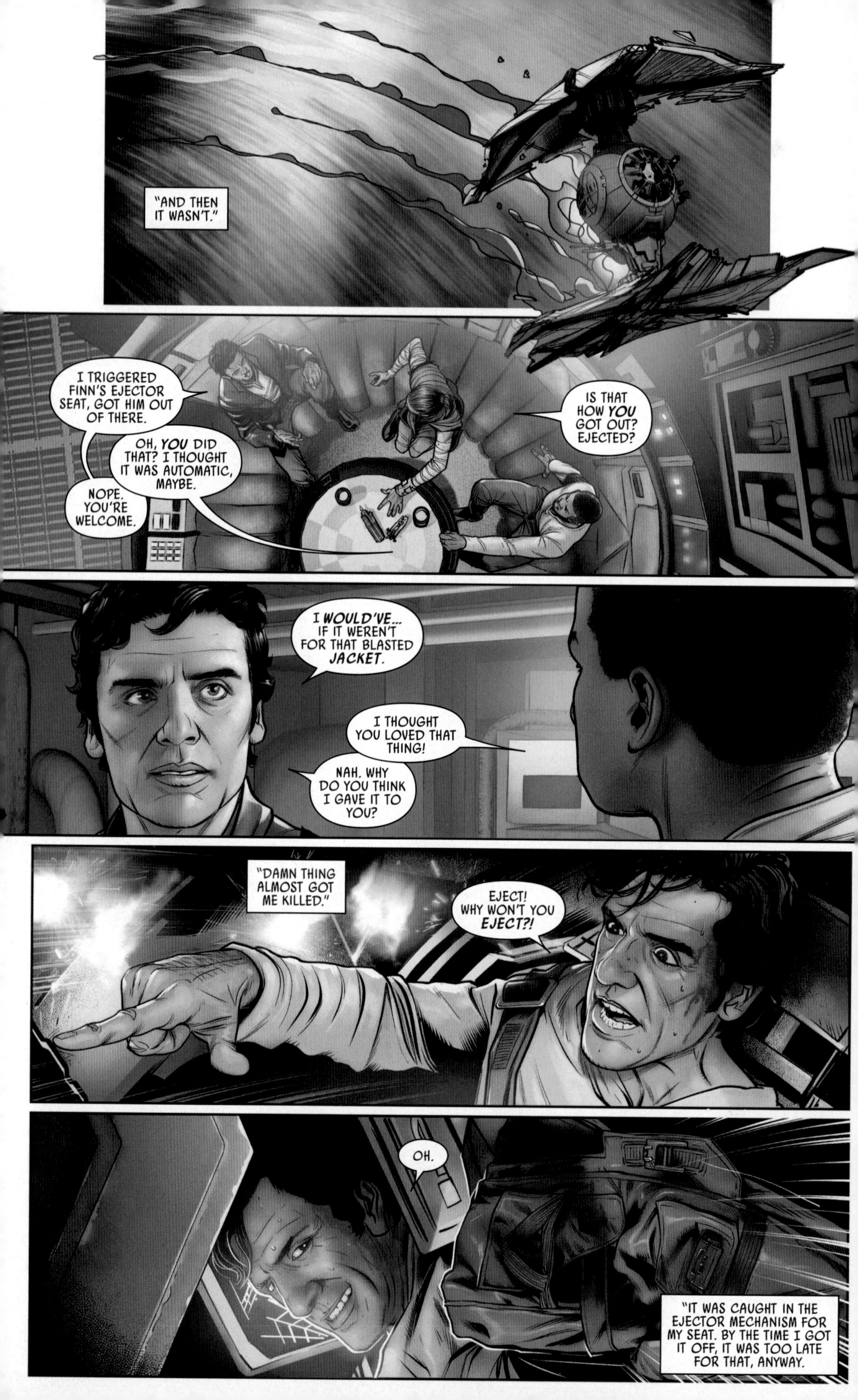
"AND THEN IT WASN'T."
I TRIGGERED FINN'S EJECTOR SEAT, GOT HIM OUT OF THERE.
OH, *YOU* DID THAT? I THOUGHT IT WAS AUTOMATIC, MAYBE.
NOPE. YOU'RE WELCOME.
IS THAT HOW *YOU* GOT OUT? EJECTED?
I *WOULD'VE*... IF IT WEREN'T FOR THAT BLASTED *JACKET*.
I THOUGHT YOU LOVED THAT THING!
NAH. WHY DO YOU THINK I GAVE IT TO YOU?
"DAMN THING ALMOST GOT ME KILLED."
EJECT! WHY WON'T YOU *EJECT?!*
OH.
"IT WAS CAUGHT IN THE EJECTOR MECHANISM FOR MY SEAT. BY THE TIME I GOT IT OFF, IT WAS TOO LATE FOR THAT, ANYWAY.

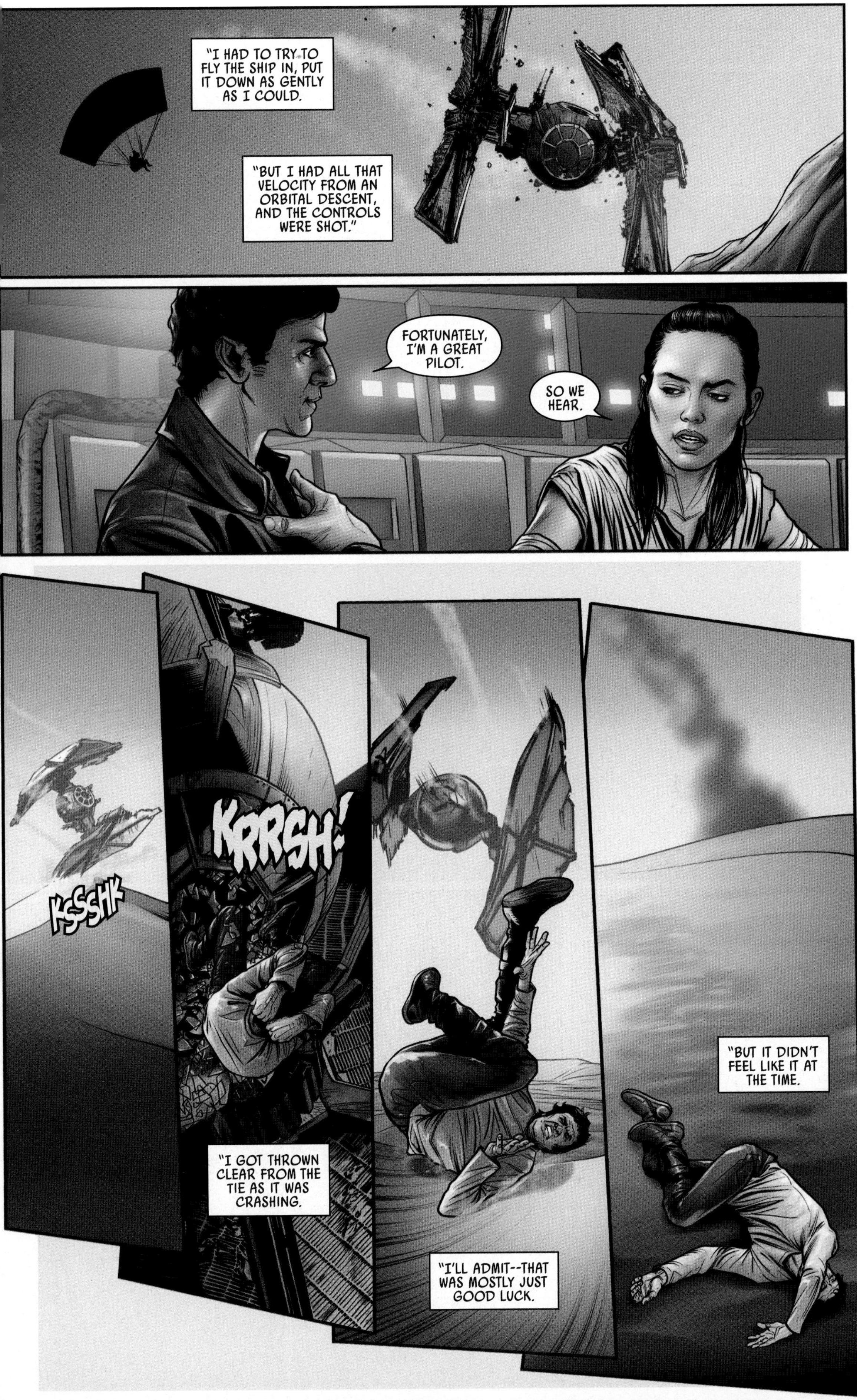
"I HAD TO TRY TO FLY THE SHIP IN, PUT IT DOWN AS GENTLY AS I COULD.
"BUT I HAD ALL THAT VELOCITY FROM AN ORBITAL DESCENT, AND THE CONTROLS WERE SHOT."
FORTUNATELY, I'M A GREAT PILOT.
SO WE HEAR.
KSSSHK
KRRSH!
"I GOT THROWN CLEAR FROM THE TIE AS IT WAS CRASHING.
"I'LL ADMIT--THAT WAS MOSTLY JUST GOOD LUCK.
"BUT IT DIDN'T FEEL LIKE IT AT THE TIME.

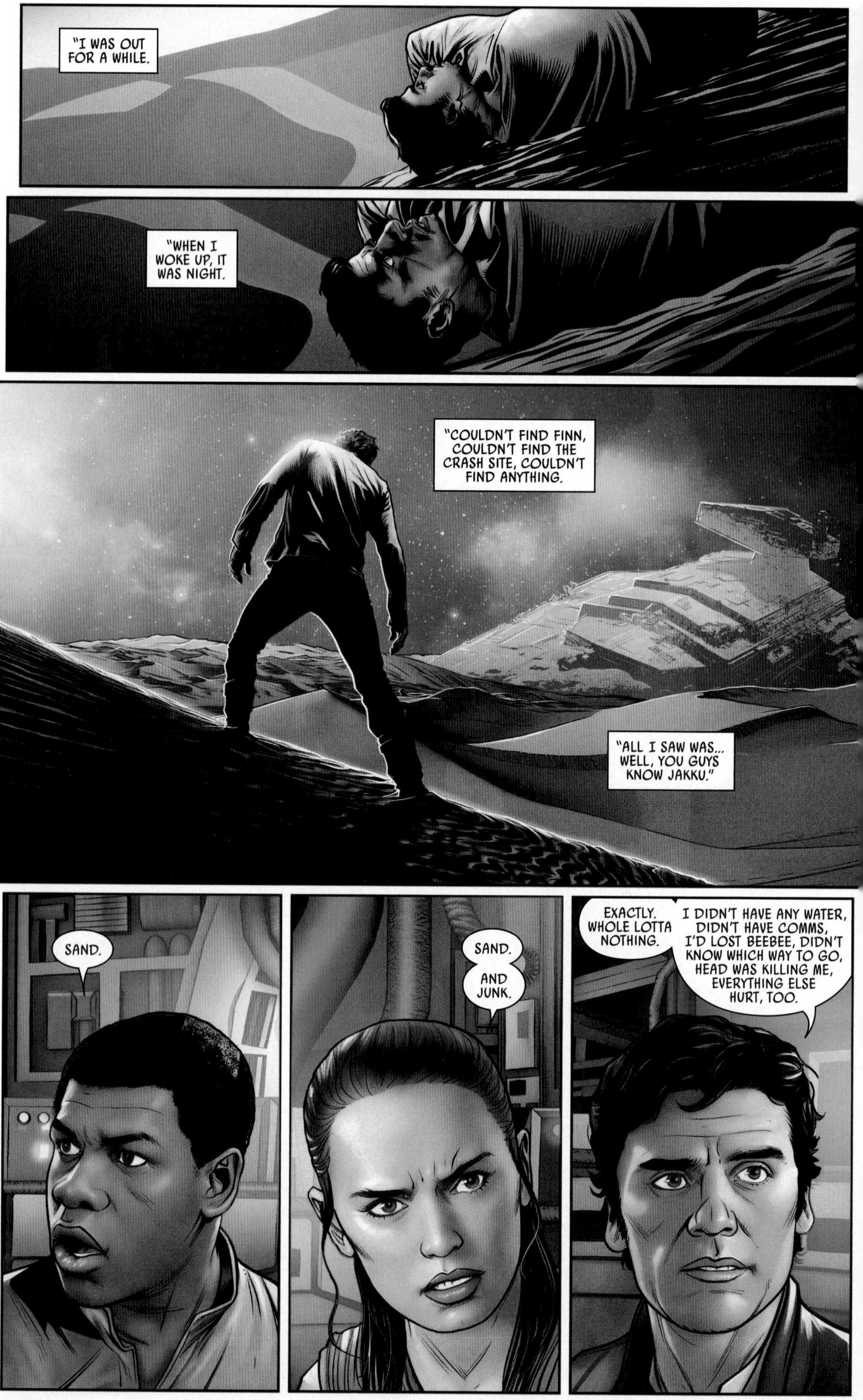
"I WAS OUT FOR A WHILE.
"WHEN I WOKE UP, IT WAS NIGHT.
"COULDN'T FIND FINN, COULDN'T FIND THE CRASH SITE, COULDN'T FIND ANYTHING.
"ALL I SAW WAS... WELL, YOU GUYS KNOW JAKKU."
SAND.
SAND.
AND JUNK.
EXACTLY. WHOLE LOTTA NOTHING.
I DIDN'T HAVE ANY WATER, DIDN'T HAVE COMMS, I'D LOST BEEBEE, DIDN'T KNOW WHICH WAY TO GO, HEAD WAS KILLING ME, EVERYTHING ELSE HURT, TOO.

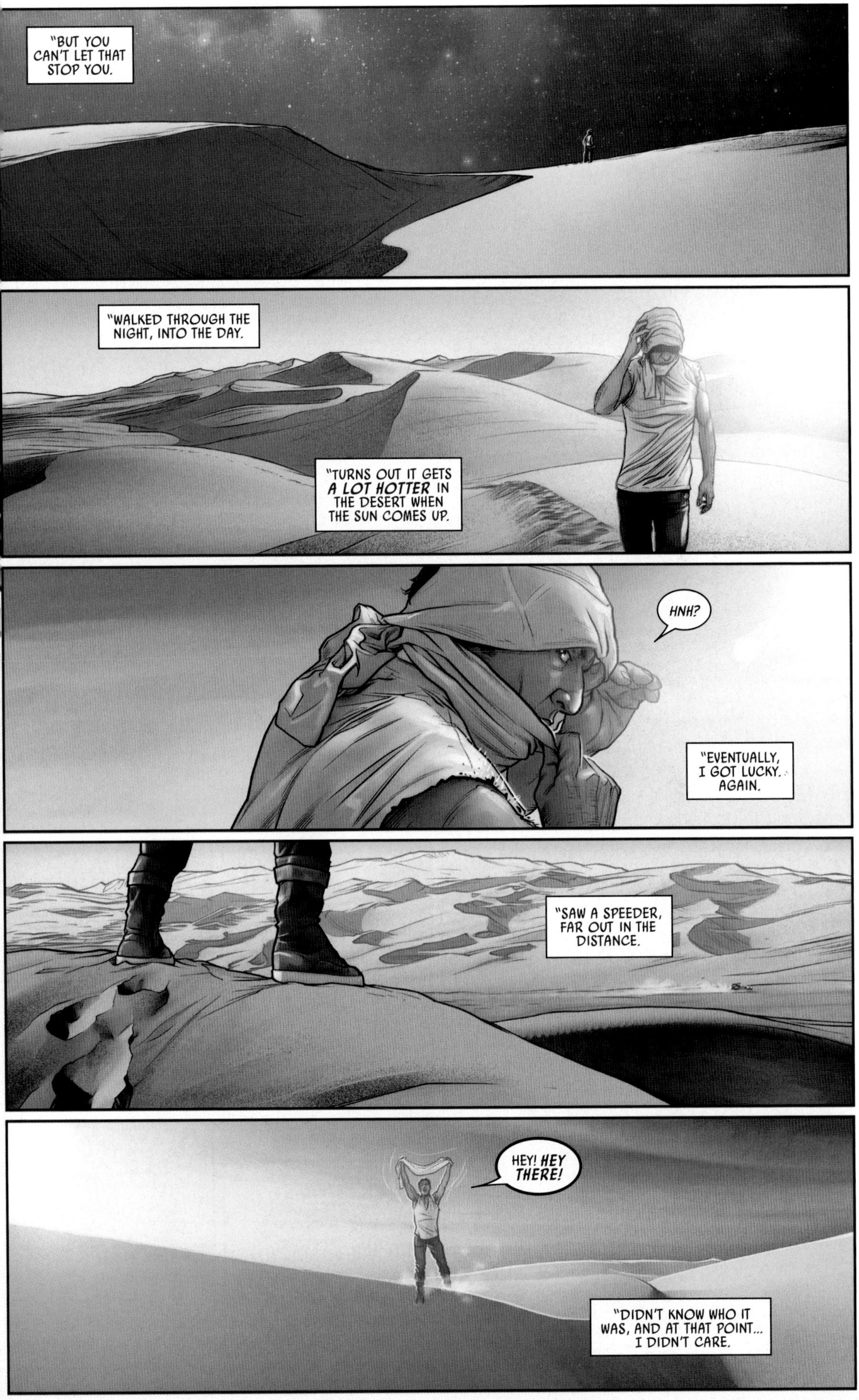

"BUT YOU CAN'T LET THAT STOP YOU.
"WALKED THROUGH THE NIGHT, INTO THE DAY.
"TURNS OUT IT GETS A LOT HOTTER IN THE DESERT WHEN THE SUN COMES UP.
HNH?
"EVENTUALLY, I GOT LUCKY. AGAIN.
"SAW A SPEEDER, FAR OUT IN THE DISTANCE.
HEY! HEY THERE!
"DIDN'T KNOW WHO IT WAS, AND AT THAT POINT... I DIDN'T CARE.

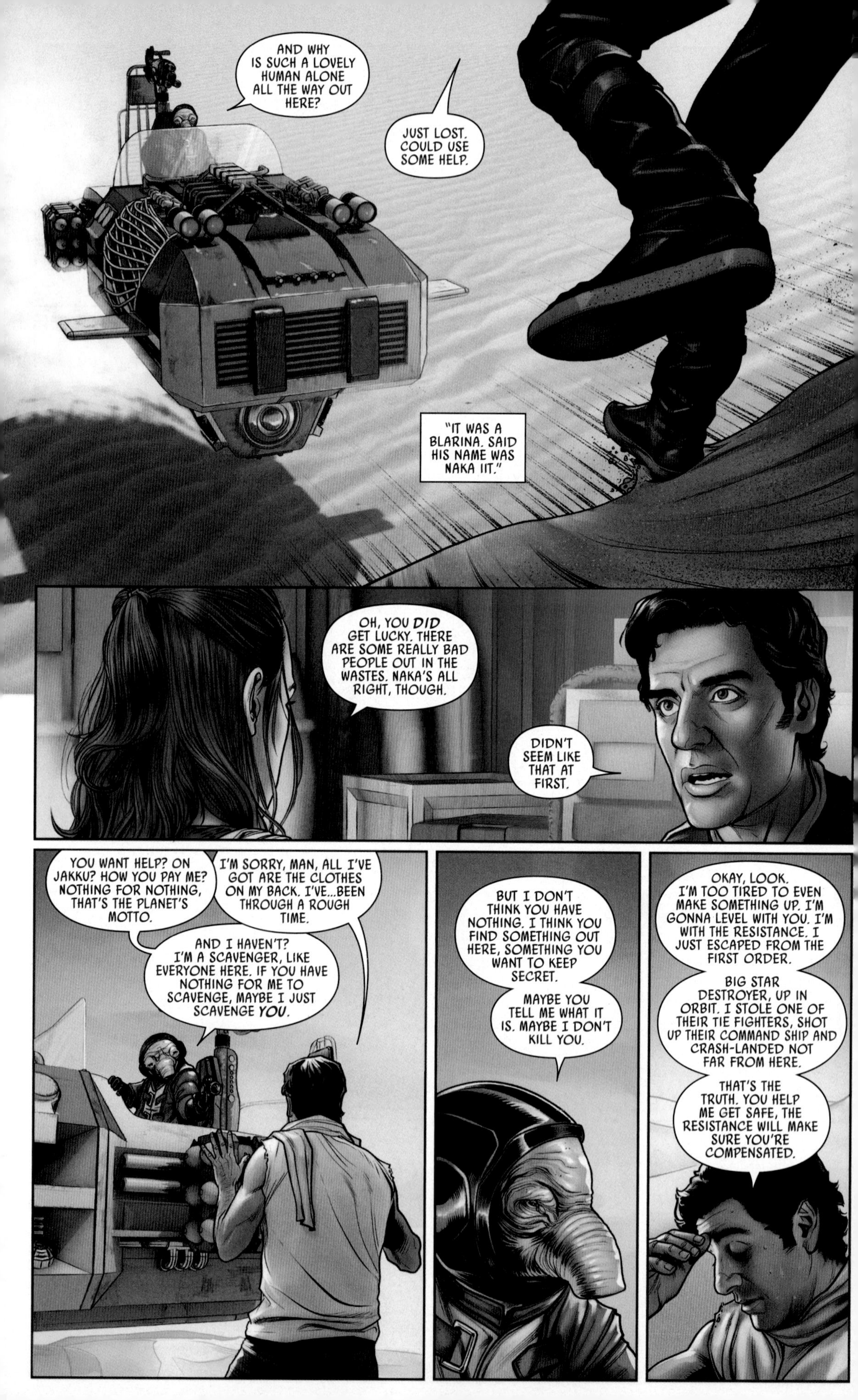
AND WHY IS SUCH A LOVELY HUMAN ALONE ALL THE WAY OUT HERE?
JUST LOST. COULD USE SOME HELP.
"IT WAS A BLARINA. SAID HIS NAME WAS NAKA IIT."
OH, YOU DID GET LUCKY. THERE ARE SOME REALLY BAD PEOPLE OUT IN THE WASTES. NAKA'S ALL RIGHT, THOUGH.
DIDN'T SEEM LIKE THAT AT FIRST.
YOU WANT HELP? ON JAKKU? HOW YOU PAY ME? NOTHING FOR NOTHING, THAT'S THE PLANET'S MOTTO.
I'M SORRY, MAN, ALL I'VE GOT ARE THE CLOTHES ON MY BACK. I'VE...BEEN THROUGH A ROUGH TIME.
AND I HAVEN'T? I'M A SCAVENGER, LIKE EVERYONE HERE. IF YOU HAVE NOTHING FOR ME TO SCAVENGE, MAYBE I JUST SCAVENGE YOU.
BUT I DON'T THINK YOU HAVE NOTHING. I THINK YOU FIND SOMETHING OUT HERE, SOMETHING YOU WANT TO KEEP SECRET.
MAYBE YOU TELL ME WHAT IT IS. MAYBE I DON'T KILL YOU.
OKAY, LOOK. I'M TOO TIRED TO EVEN MAKE SOMETHING UP. I'M GONNA LEVEL WITH YOU. I'M WITH THE RESISTANCE. I JUST ESCAPED FROM THE FIRST ORDER.
BIG STAR DESTROYER, UP IN ORBIT. I STOLE ONE OF THEIR TIE FIGHTERS, SHOT UP THEIR COMMAND SHIP AND CRASH-LANDED NOT FAR FROM HERE.
THAT'S THE TRUTH. YOU HELP ME GET SAFE, THE RESISTANCE WILL MAKE SURE YOU'RE COMPENSATED.

SURE, I DON'T BELIEVE ANY OF THAT.

AND EVEN IF IT *WERE* TRUE, SOUNDS LIKE AN AWFUL LOT OF TROUBLE.

OKAY, THEN HOW ABOUT THIS?

YOU HELP ME, MAYBE SOMETIME I CAN HELP YOU. OR MAYBE SOMEONE ELSE HELPS YOU WHEN YOU NEED IT.

MAYBE NOTHING FOR NOTHING ISN'T ACTUALLY THE BEST WAY TO LIVE, YOU KNOW?

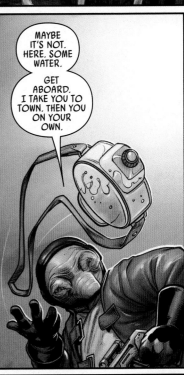

MAYBE IT'S NOT. HERE. SOME WATER.

GET ABOARD. I TAKE YOU TO TOWN, THEN YOU ON YOUR OWN.

BUT TELL ME MORE LIES ABOUT THE RESISTANCE. A FEW GOOD STORIES TO PASS THE TIME.

BETWEEN YOU AND ME...

...IT GETS BORING OUT HERE.

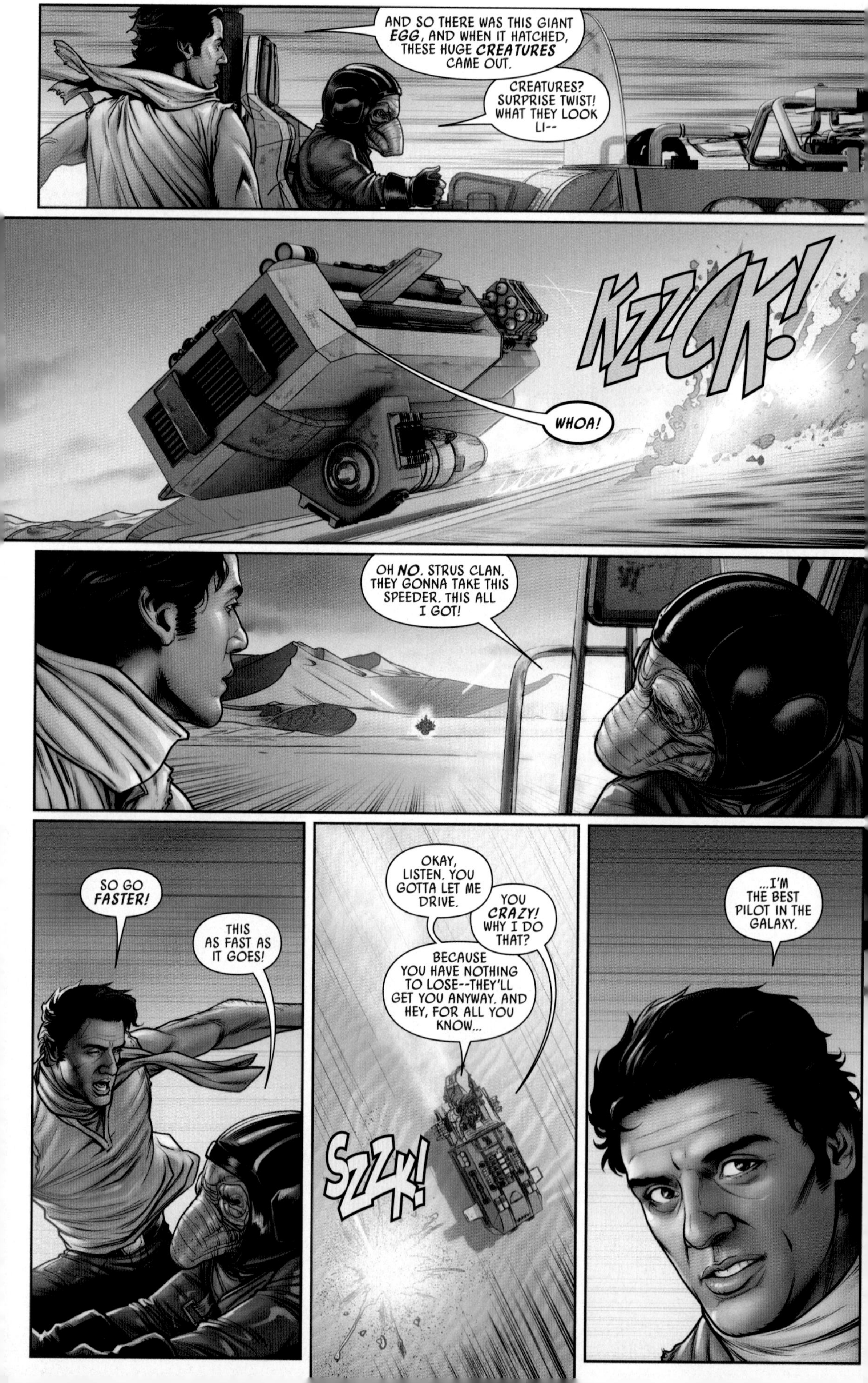
AND SO THERE WAS THIS GIANT EGG, AND WHEN IT HATCHED, THESE HUGE CREATURES CAME OUT.
CREATURES? SURPRISE TWIST! WHAT THEY LOOK LI--
KZZCK!
WHOA!
OH NO. STRUS CLAN. THEY GONNA TAKE THIS SPEEDER. THIS ALL I GOT!
SO GO FASTER!
THIS AS FAST AS IT GOES!
OKAY, LISTEN. YOU GOTTA LET ME DRIVE.
YOU CRAZY! WHY I DO THAT?
BECAUSE YOU HAVE NOTHING TO LOSE--THEY'LL GET YOU ANYWAY. AND HEY, FOR ALL YOU KNOW...
SZZK!
...I'M THE BEST PILOT IN THE GALAXY.

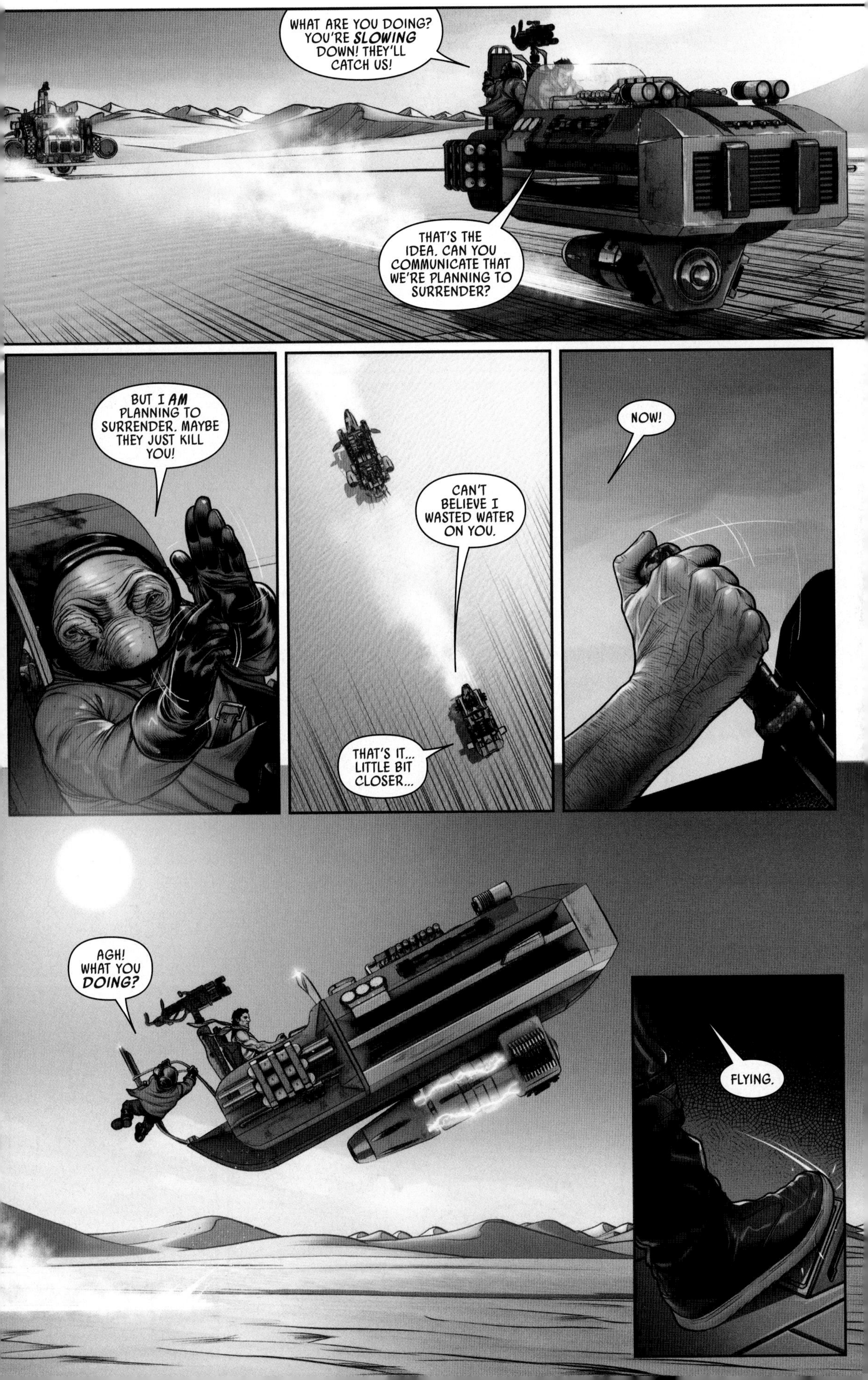
WHAT ARE YOU DOING? YOU'RE SLOWING DOWN! THEY'LL CATCH US!
THAT'S THE IDEA. CAN YOU COMMUNICATE THAT WE'RE PLANNING TO SURRENDER?
BUT I AM PLANNING TO SURRENDER. MAYBE THEY JUST KILL YOU!
CAN'T BELIEVE I WASTED WATER ON YOU.
THAT'S IT... LITTLE BIT CLOSER...
NOW!
AGH! WHAT YOU DOING?
FLYING.

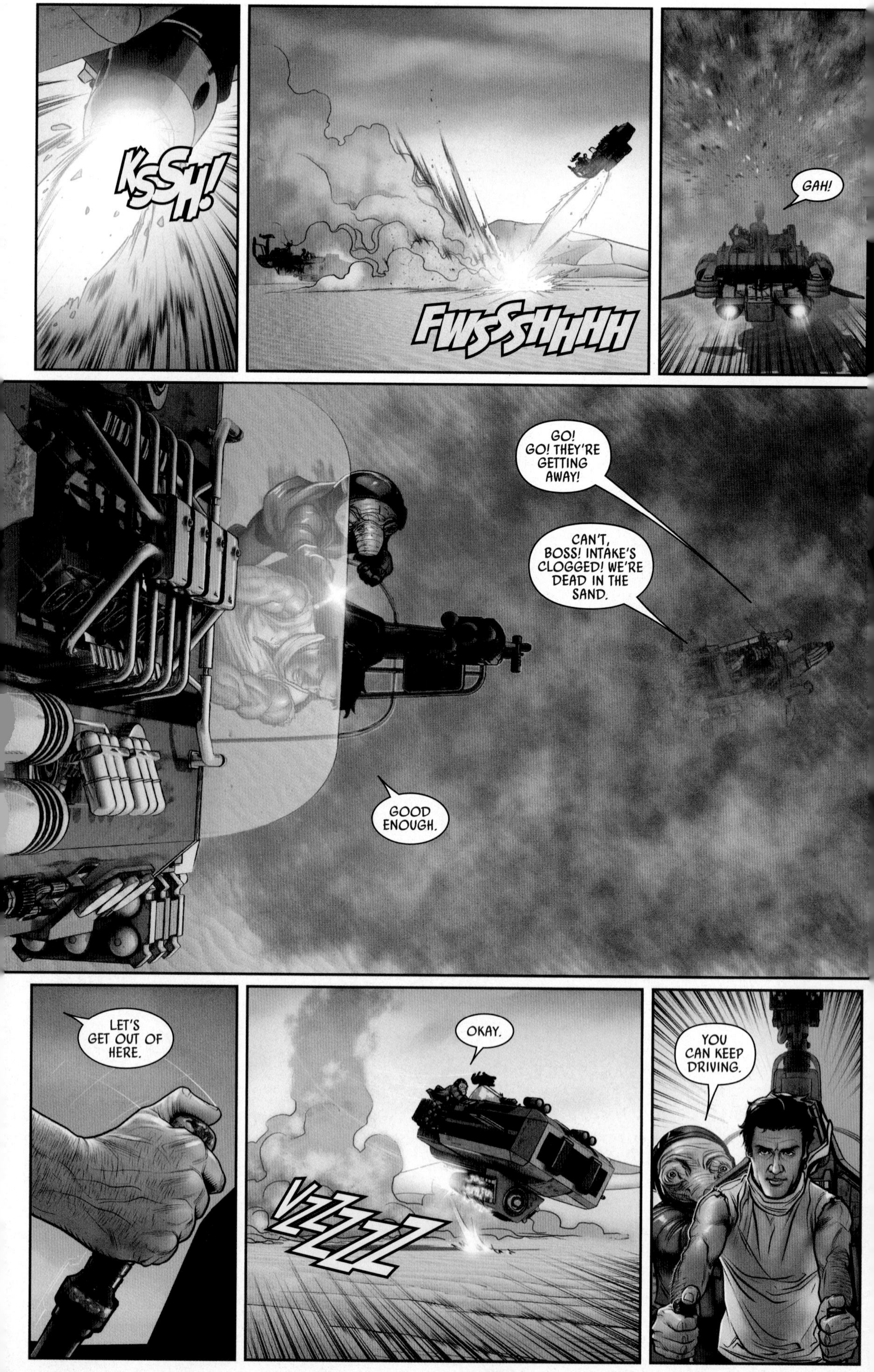
KSSH!
FWSSHHHH
GAH!
GO! GO! THEY'RE GETTING AWAY!
CAN'T, BOSS! INTAKE'S CLOGGED! WE'RE DEAD IN THE SAND.
GOOD ENOUGH.
LET'S GET OUT OF HERE.
OKAY.
VZZZZ
YOU CAN KEEP DRIVING.

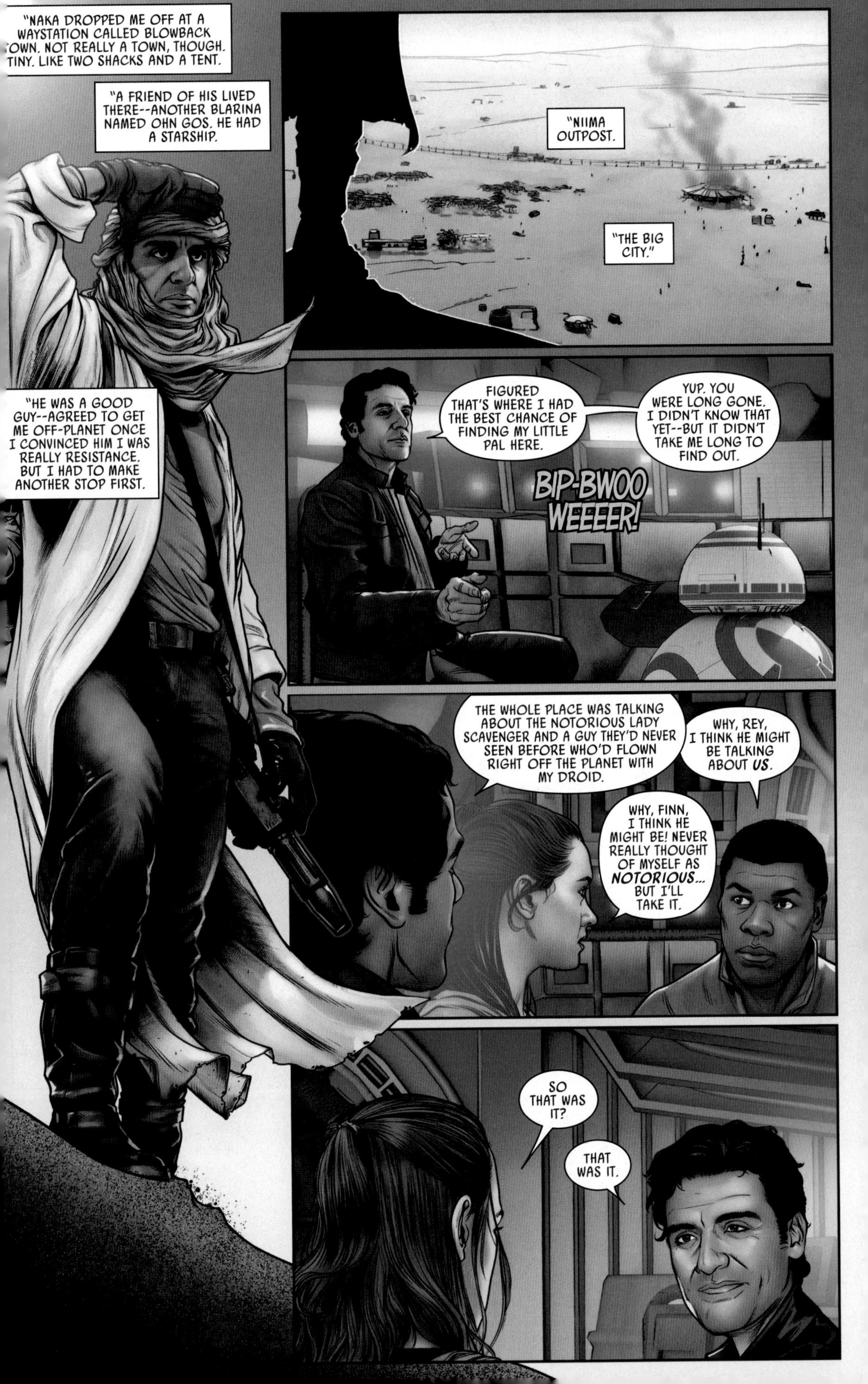
"NAKA DROPPED ME OFF AT A WAYSTATION CALLED BLOWBACK TOWN. NOT REALLY A TOWN, THOUGH. TINY. LIKE TWO SHACKS AND A TENT.
"A FRIEND OF HIS LIVED THERE--ANOTHER BLARINA NAMED OHN GOS. HE HAD A STARSHIP.
"HE WAS A GOOD GUY--AGREED TO GET ME OFF-PLANET ONCE I CONVINCED HIM I WAS REALLY RESISTANCE. BUT I HAD TO MAKE ANOTHER STOP FIRST.
"NIIMA OUTPOST.
"THE BIG CITY."
FIGURED THAT'S WHERE I HAD THE BEST CHANCE OF FINDING MY LITTLE PAL HERE.
YUP. YOU WERE LONG GONE. I DIDN'T KNOW THAT YET--BUT IT DIDN'T TAKE ME LONG TO FIND OUT.
BIP-BWOO WEEEER!
THE WHOLE PLACE WAS TALKING ABOUT THE NOTORIOUS LADY SCAVENGER AND A GUY THEY'D NEVER SEEN BEFORE WHO'D FLOWN RIGHT OFF THE PLANET WITH MY DROID.
WHY, REY, I THINK HE MIGHT BE TALKING ABOUT US.
WHY, FINN, I THINK HE MIGHT BE! NEVER REALLY THOUGHT OF MYSELF AS NOTORIOUS... BUT I'LL TAKE IT.
SO THAT WAS IT?
THAT WAS IT.

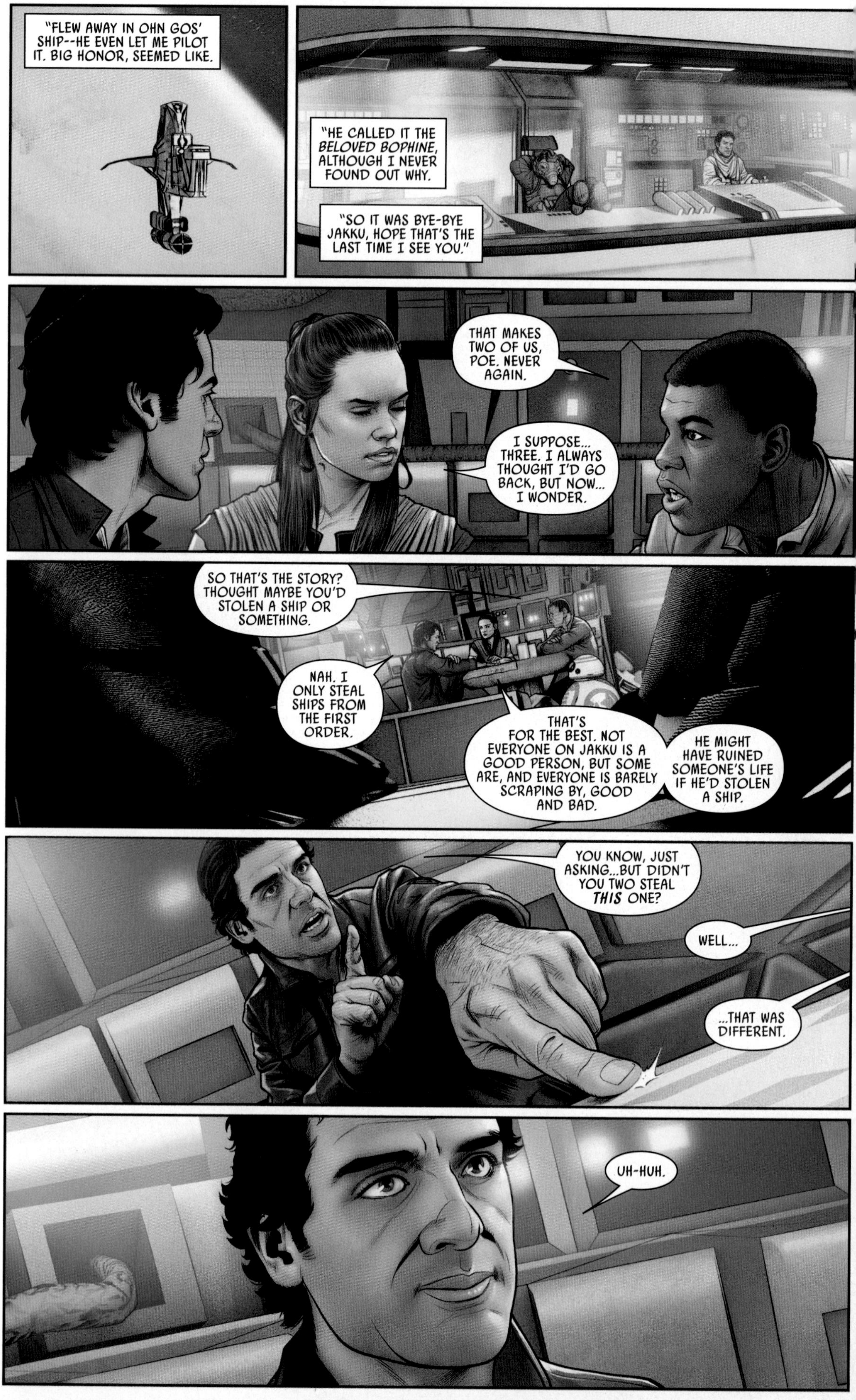
"FLEW AWAY IN OHN GOS' SHIP--HE EVEN LET ME PILOT IT. BIG HONOR, SEEMED LIKE.
"HE CALLED IT THE *BELOVED BOPHINE*, ALTHOUGH I NEVER FOUND OUT WHY.
"SO IT WAS BYE-BYE JAKKU, HOPE THAT'S THE LAST TIME I SEE YOU."
THAT MAKES TWO OF US, POE. NEVER AGAIN.
I SUPPOSE... THREE. I ALWAYS THOUGHT I'D GO BACK, BUT NOW... I WONDER.
SO THAT'S THE STORY? THOUGHT MAYBE YOU'D STOLEN A SHIP OR SOMETHING.
NAH. I ONLY STEAL SHIPS FROM THE FIRST ORDER.
THAT'S FOR THE BEST. NOT EVERYONE ON JAKKU IS A GOOD PERSON, BUT SOME ARE, AND EVERYONE IS BARELY SCRAPING BY, GOOD AND BAD.
HE MIGHT HAVE RUINED SOMEONE'S LIFE IF HE'D STOLEN A SHIP.
YOU KNOW, JUST ASKING...BUT DIDN'T YOU TWO STEAL **THIS** ONE?
WELL...
...THAT WAS DIFFERENT.
UH-HUH.

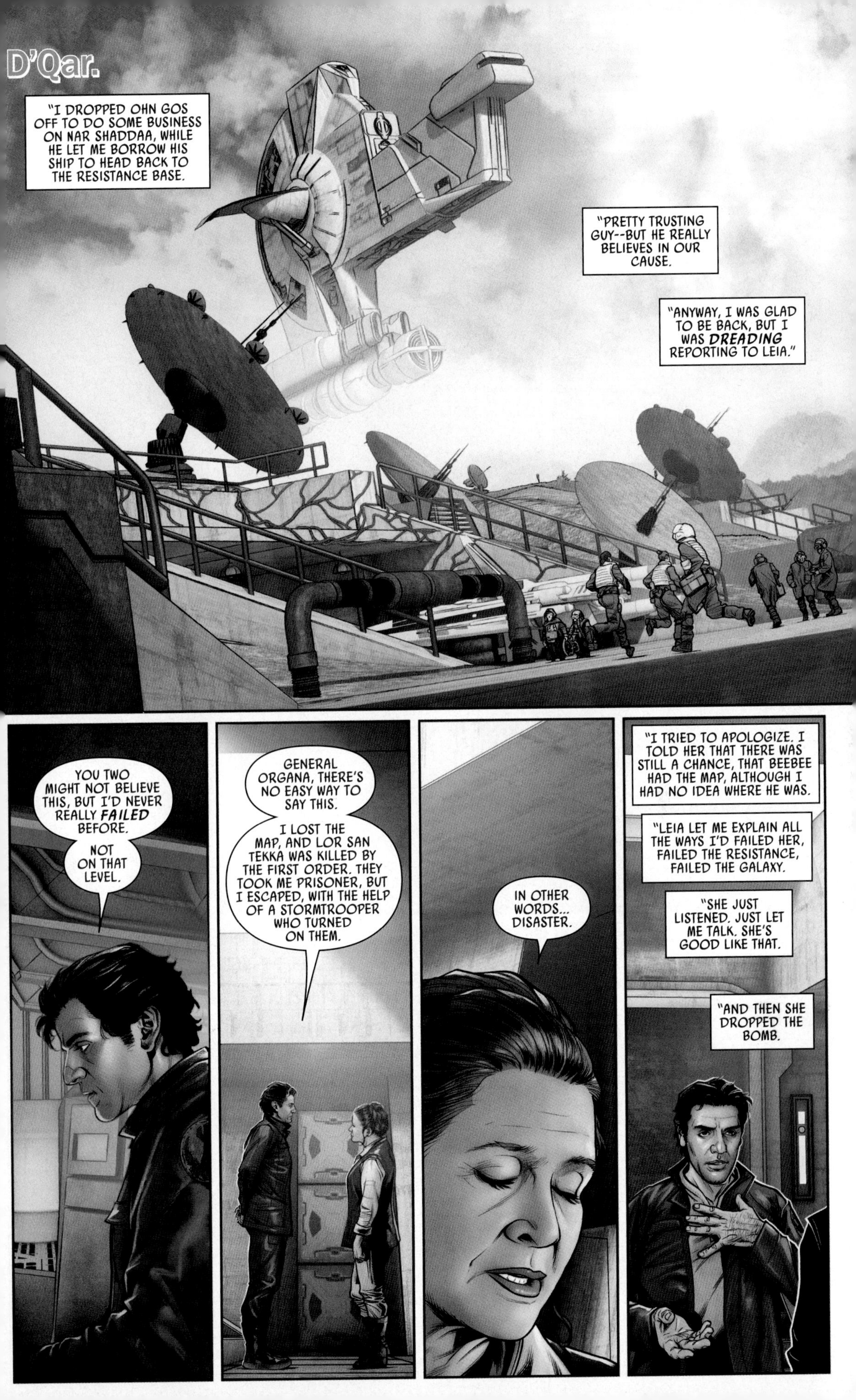

D'Qar.
"I DROPPED OHN GOS OFF TO DO SOME BUSINESS ON NAR SHADDAA, WHILE HE LET ME BORROW HIS SHIP TO HEAD BACK TO THE RESISTANCE BASE.
"PRETTY TRUSTING GUY--BUT HE REALLY BELIEVES IN OUR CAUSE.
"ANYWAY, I WAS GLAD TO BE BACK, BUT I WAS DREADING REPORTING TO LEIA."
YOU TWO MIGHT NOT BELIEVE THIS, BUT I'D NEVER REALLY FAILED BEFORE.
NOT ON THAT LEVEL.
GENERAL ORGANA, THERE'S NO EASY WAY TO SAY THIS.
I LOST THE MAP, AND LOR SAN TEKKA WAS KILLED BY THE FIRST ORDER. THEY TOOK ME PRISONER, BUT I ESCAPED, WITH THE HELP OF A STORMTROOPER WHO TURNED ON THEM.
IN OTHER WORDS... DISASTER.
"I TRIED TO APOLOGIZE. I TOLD HER THAT THERE WAS STILL A CHANCE, THAT BEEBEE HAD THE MAP, ALTHOUGH I HAD NO IDEA WHERE HE WAS.
"LEIA LET ME EXPLAIN ALL THE WAYS I'D FAILED HER, FAILED THE RESISTANCE, FAILED THE GALAXY.
"SHE JUST LISTENED. JUST LET ME TALK. SHE'S GOOD LIKE THAT.
"AND THEN SHE DROPPED THE BOMB.

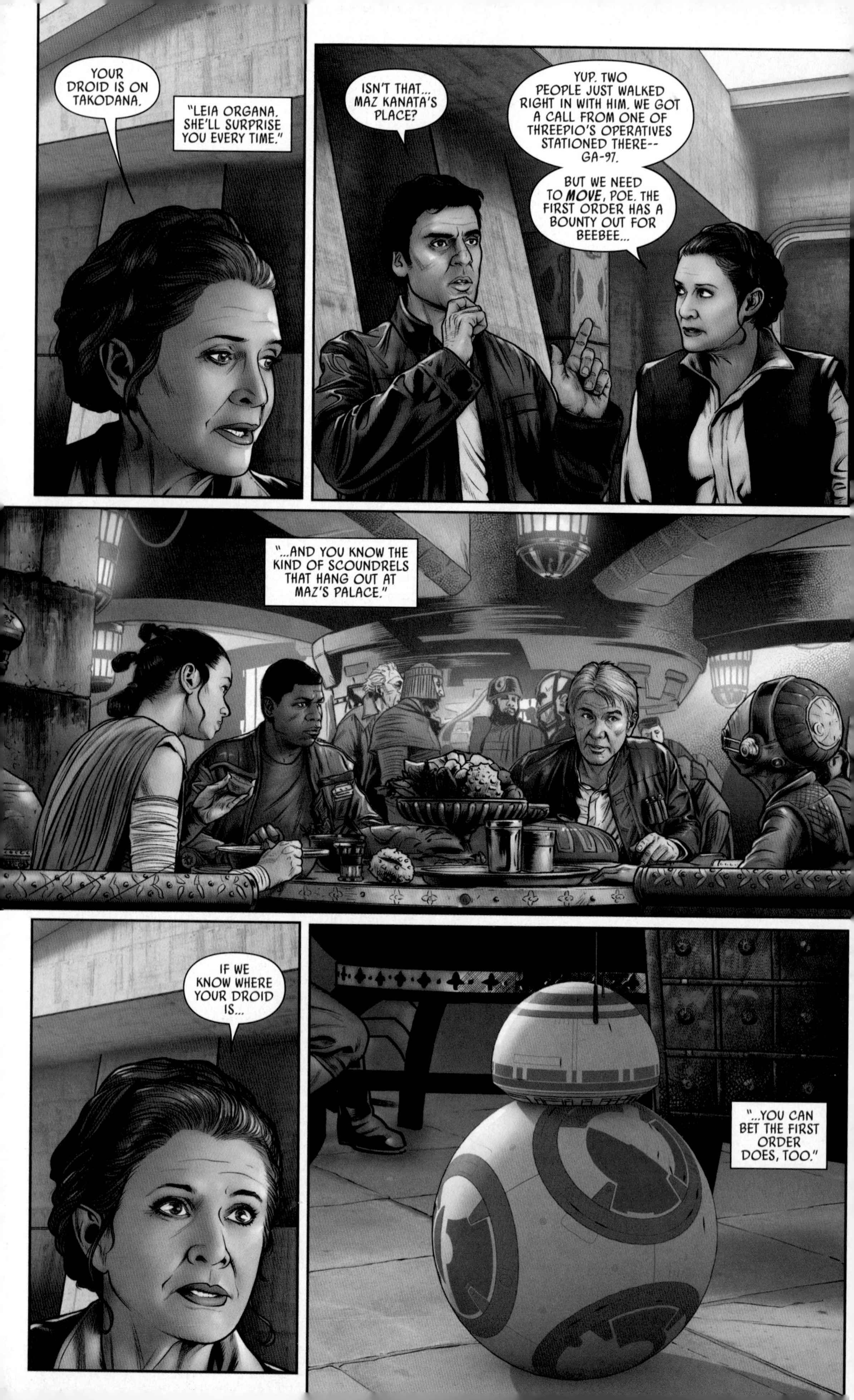
YOUR DROID IS ON TAKODANA.
"LEIA ORGANA. SHE'LL SURPRISE YOU EVERY TIME."
ISN'T THAT... MAZ KANATA'S PLACE?
YUP. TWO PEOPLE JUST WALKED RIGHT IN WITH HIM. WE GOT A CALL FROM ONE OF THREEPIO'S OPERATIVES STATIONED THERE-- GA-97.
BUT WE NEED TO MOVE, POE. THE FIRST ORDER HAS A BOUNTY OUT FOR BEEBEE...
"...AND YOU KNOW THE KIND OF SCOUNDRELS THAT HANG OUT AT MAZ'S PALACE."
IF WE KNOW WHERE YOUR DROID IS...
"...YOU CAN BET THE FIRST ORDER DOES, TOO."

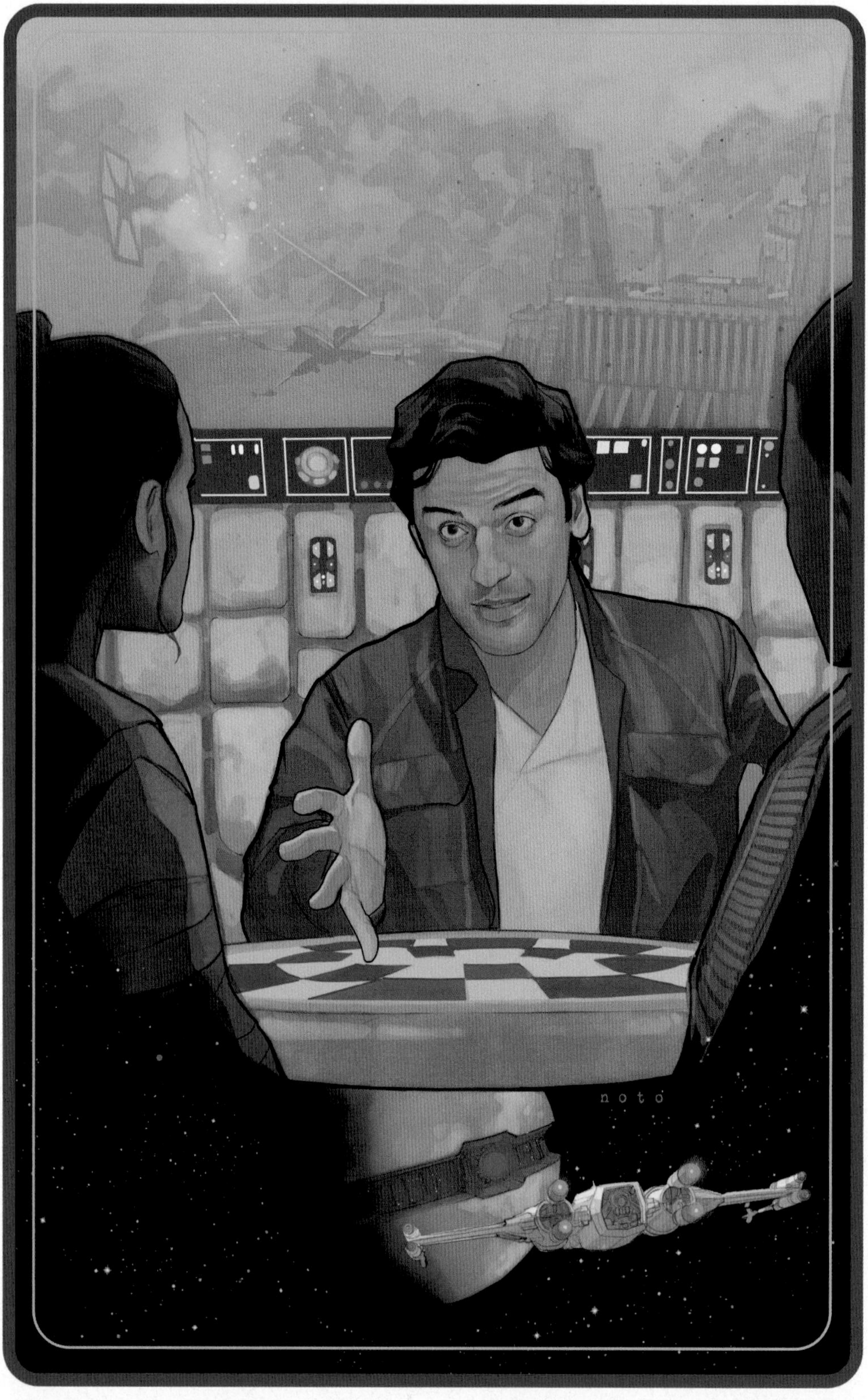
noto

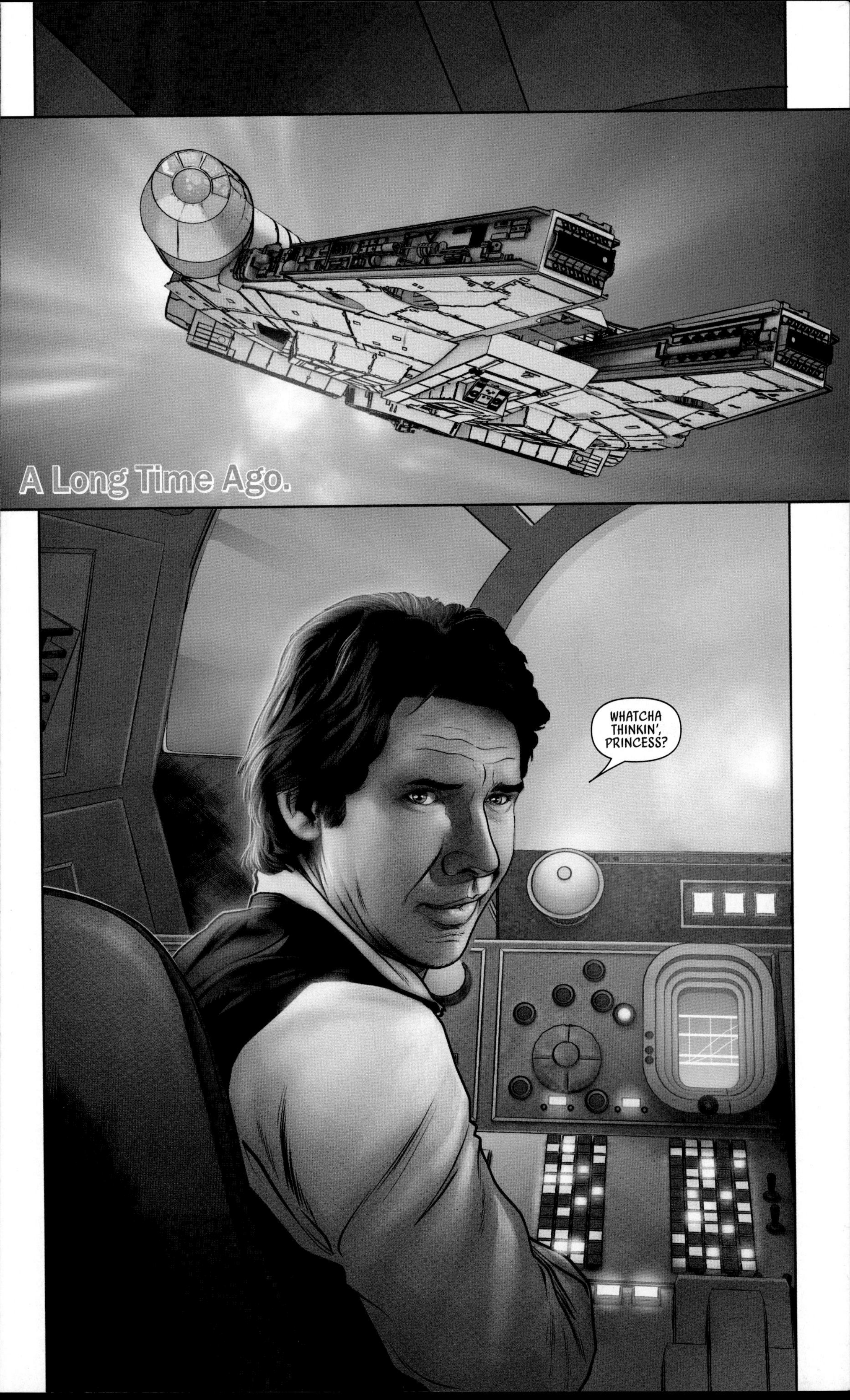
A Long Time Ago.
WHATCHA THINKIN', PRINCESS?

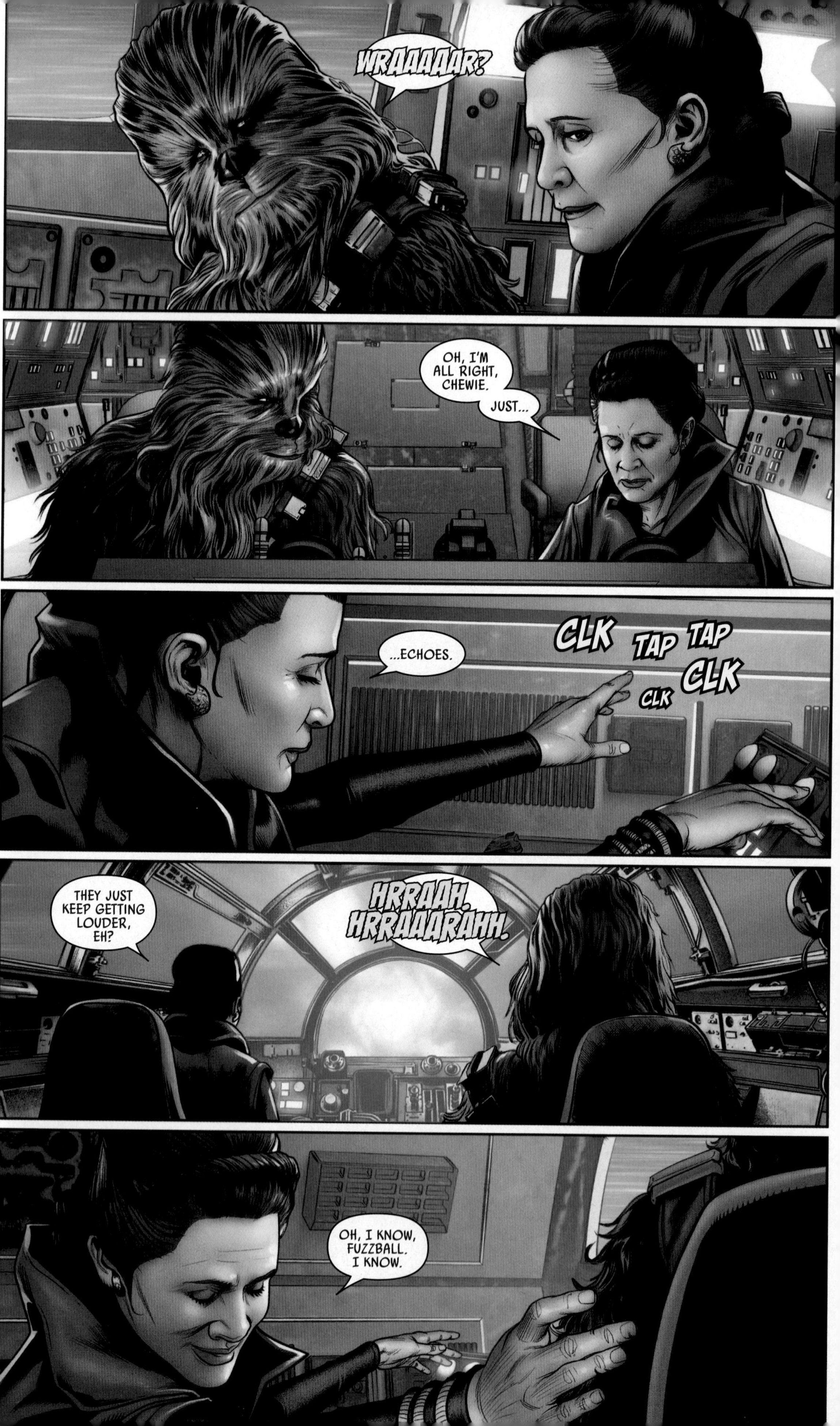
WRAAAAAR?
OH, I'M ALL RIGHT, CHEWIE.
JUST...
...ECHOES.
CLK TAP TAP CLK CLK
THEY JUST KEEP GETTING LOUDER, EH?
HRRAAH. HRRAAARAHH.
OH, I KNOW, FUZZBALL. I KNOW.

OH, HELLO, NIEN.

EETUU ACHAA DOO AHMTEE VEE AH...?

NO, NO, BE MY GUEST. I HAVE OTHER WORK TO DO.

AND FROM WHAT I RECALL, YOU HAVE AS MUCH RIGHT TO THE CO-PILOT'S SEAT ON THE *FALCON* AS ANYONE.

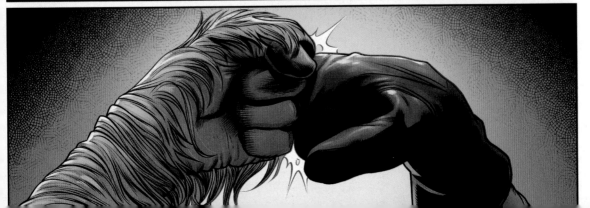

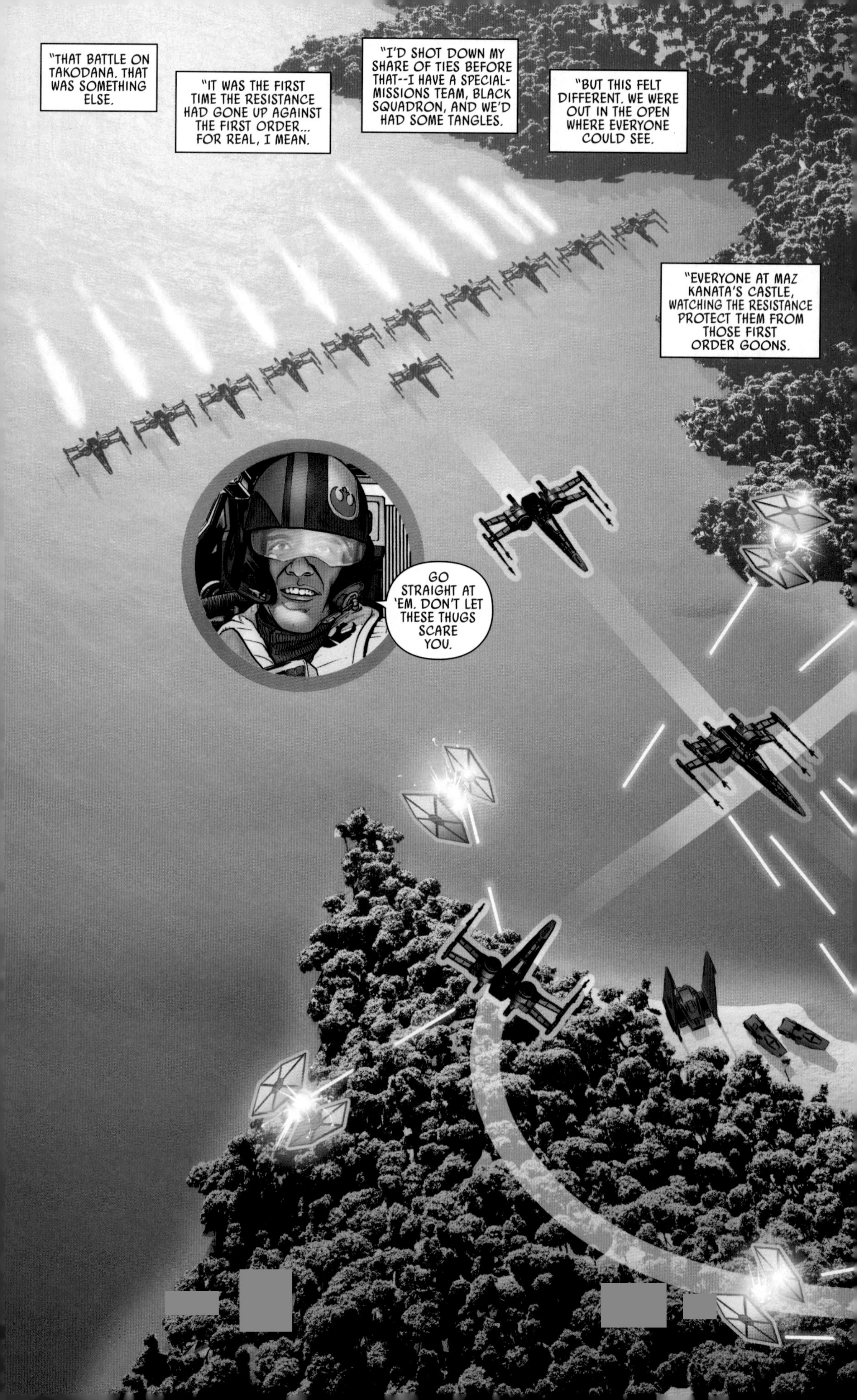
"THAT BATTLE ON TAKODANA. THAT WAS SOMETHING ELSE.
"IT WAS THE FIRST TIME THE RESISTANCE HAD GONE UP AGAINST THE FIRST ORDER... FOR REAL, I MEAN.
"I'D SHOT DOWN MY SHARE OF TIES BEFORE THAT--I HAVE A SPECIAL-MISSIONS TEAM, BLACK SQUADRON, AND WE'D HAD SOME TANGLES.
"BUT THIS FELT DIFFERENT. WE WERE OUT IN THE OPEN WHERE EVERYONE COULD SEE.
"EVERYONE AT MAZ KANATA'S CASTLE, WATCHING THE RESISTANCE PROTECT THEM FROM THOSE FIRST ORDER GOONS.
GO STRAIGHT AT 'EM. DON'T LET THESE THUGS SCARE YOU.

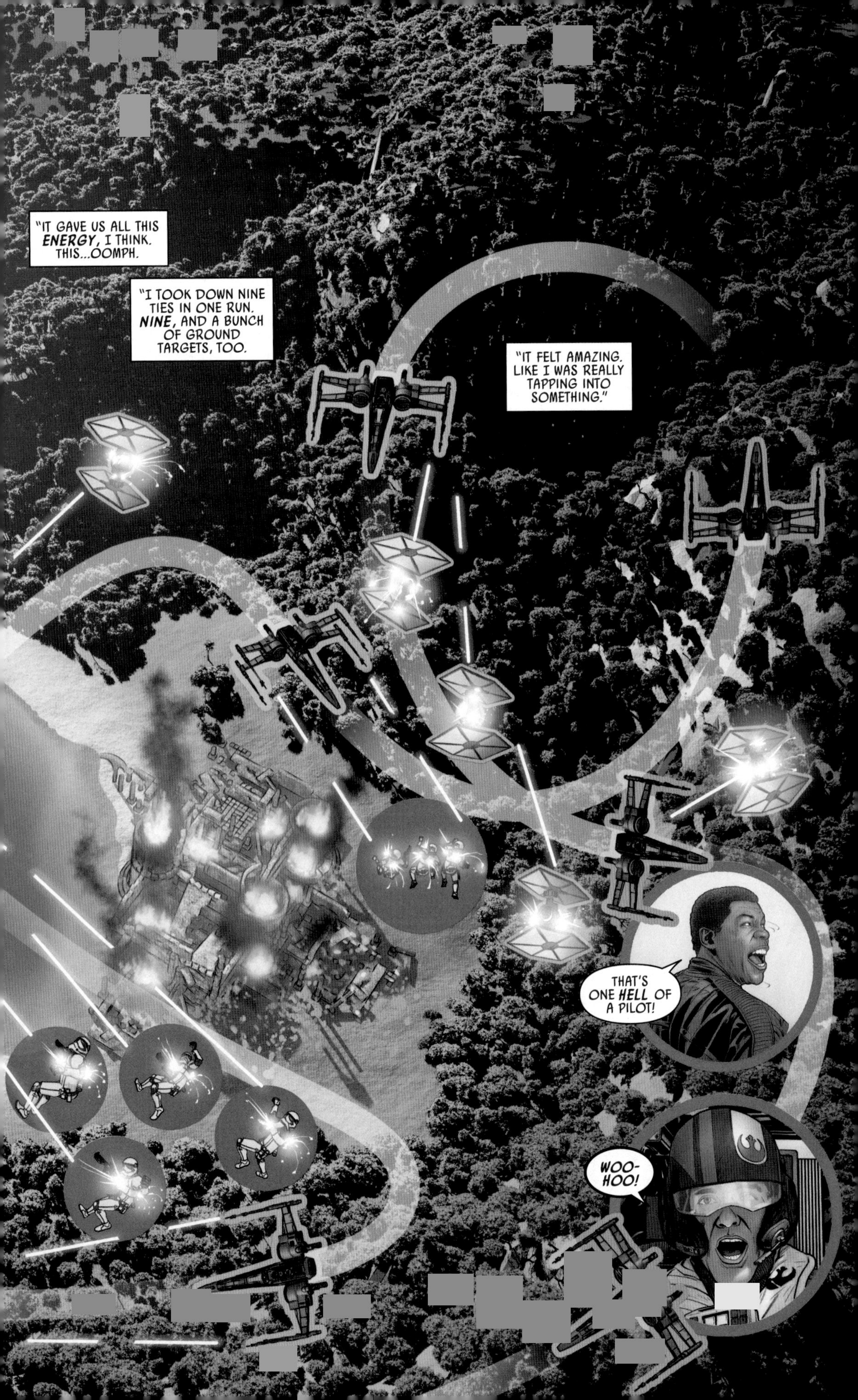
"IT GAVE US ALL THIS ENERGY, I THINK. THIS...OOMPH.
"I TOOK DOWN NINE TIES IN ONE RUN. NINE, AND A BUNCH OF GROUND TARGETS, TOO.
"IT FELT AMAZING. LIKE I WAS REALLY TAPPING INTO SOMETHING."
THAT'S ONE HELL OF A PILOT!
WOO-HOO!

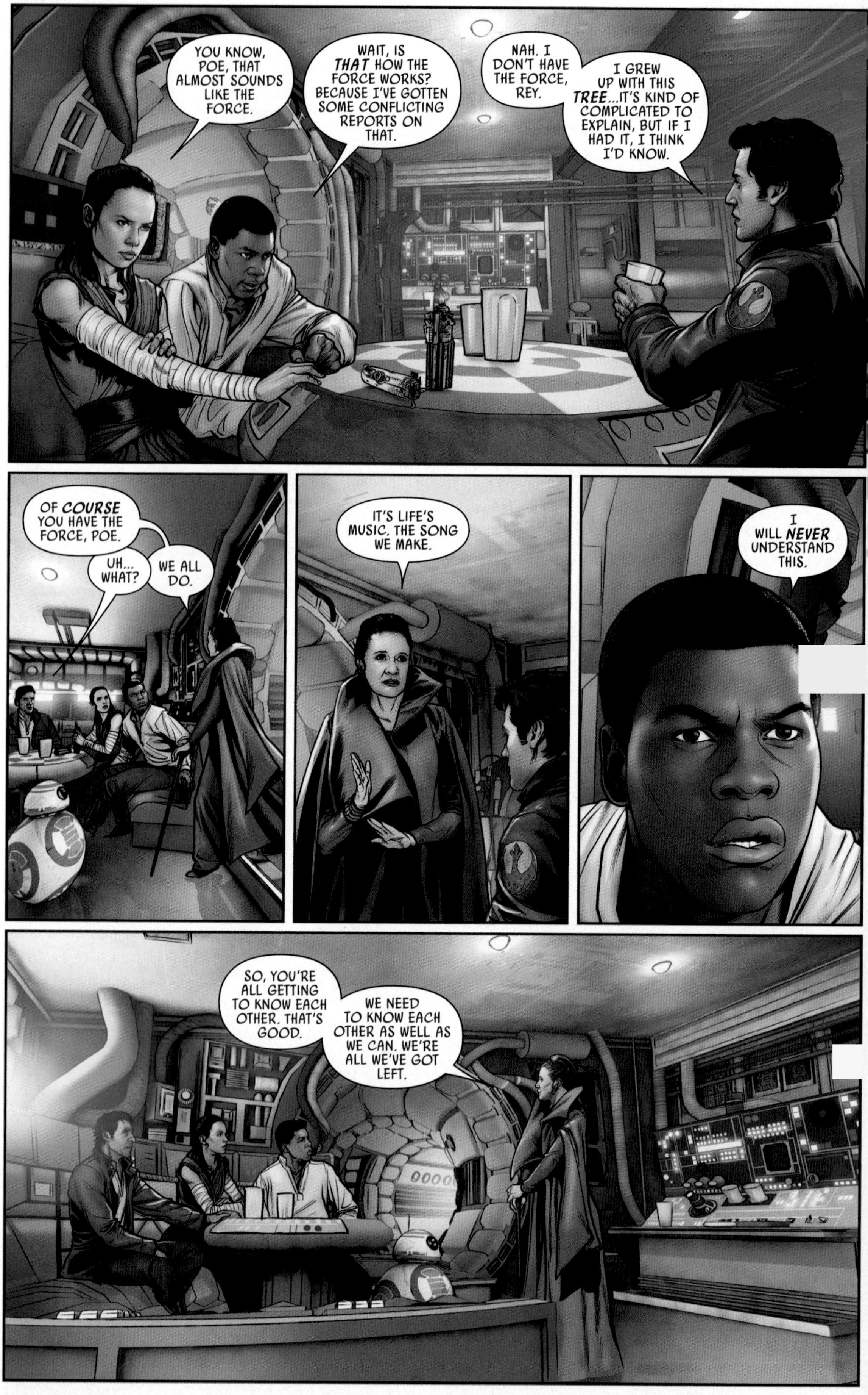
YOU KNOW, POE, THAT ALMOST SOUNDS LIKE THE FORCE.
WAIT, IS THAT HOW THE FORCE WORKS? BECAUSE I'VE GOTTEN SOME CONFLICTING REPORTS ON THAT.
NAH. I DON'T HAVE THE FORCE, REY.
I GREW UP WITH THIS TREE...IT'S KIND OF COMPLICATED TO EXPLAIN, BUT IF I HAD IT, I THINK I'D KNOW.
OF COURSE YOU HAVE THE FORCE, POE.
UH... WHAT?
WE ALL DO.
IT'S LIFE'S MUSIC. THE SONG WE MAKE.
I WILL NEVER UNDERSTAND THIS.
SO, YOU'RE ALL GETTING TO KNOW EACH OTHER. THAT'S GOOD.
WE NEED TO KNOW EACH OTHER AS WELL AS WE CAN. WE'RE ALL WE'VE GOT LEFT.

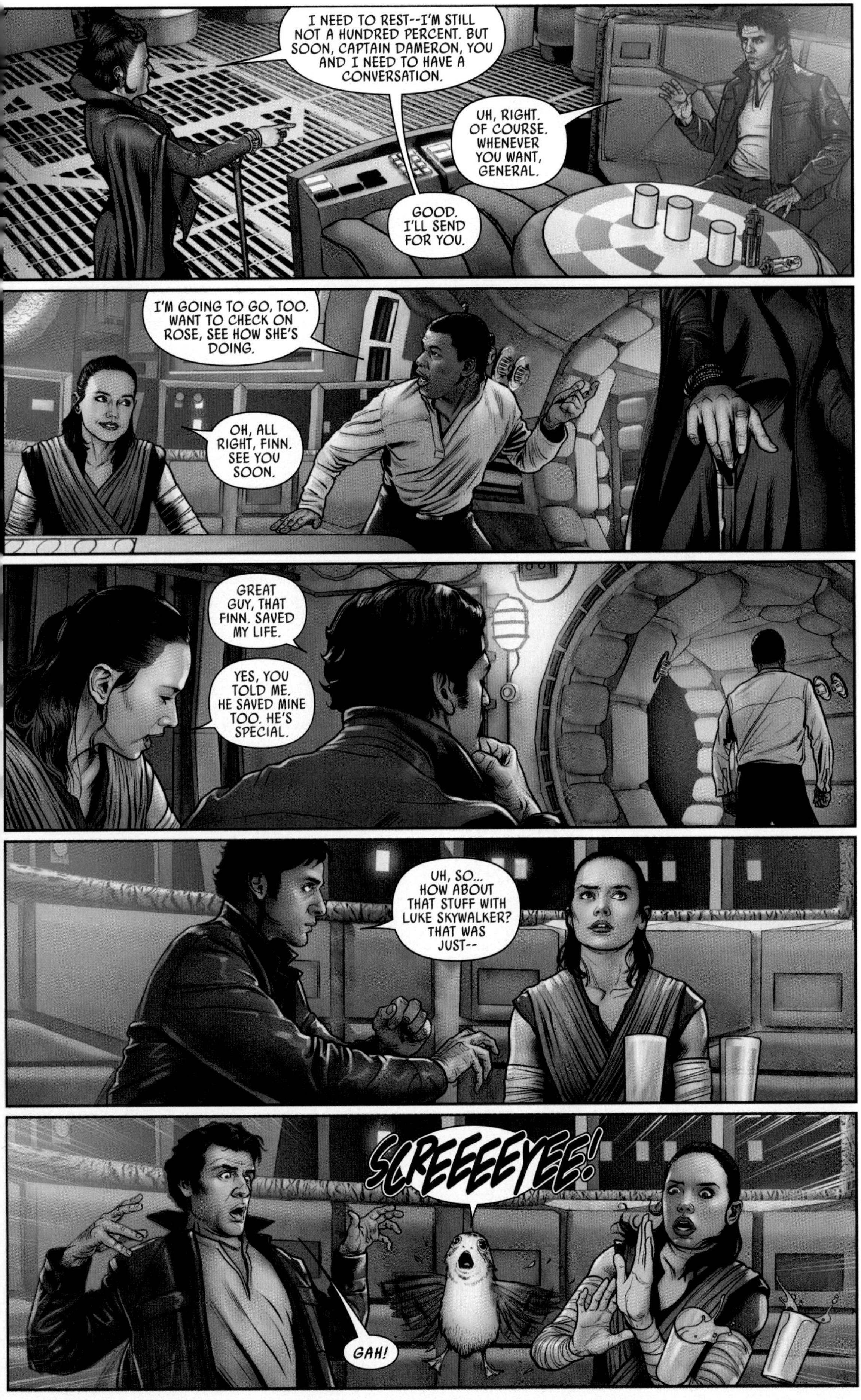
I NEED TO REST--I'M STILL NOT A HUNDRED PERCENT. BUT SOON, CAPTAIN DAMERON, YOU AND I NEED TO HAVE A CONVERSATION.
UH, RIGHT. OF COURSE. WHENEVER YOU WANT, GENERAL.
GOOD. I'LL SEND FOR YOU.
I'M GOING TO GO, TOO. WANT TO CHECK ON ROSE, SEE HOW SHE'S DOING.
OH, ALL RIGHT, FINN. SEE YOU SOON.
GREAT GUY, THAT FINN. SAVED MY LIFE.
YES, YOU TOLD ME. HE SAVED MINE TOO. HE'S SPECIAL.
UH, SO... HOW ABOUT THAT STUFF WITH LUKE SKYWALKER? THAT WAS JUST--
SCREEEEYEE!
GAH!

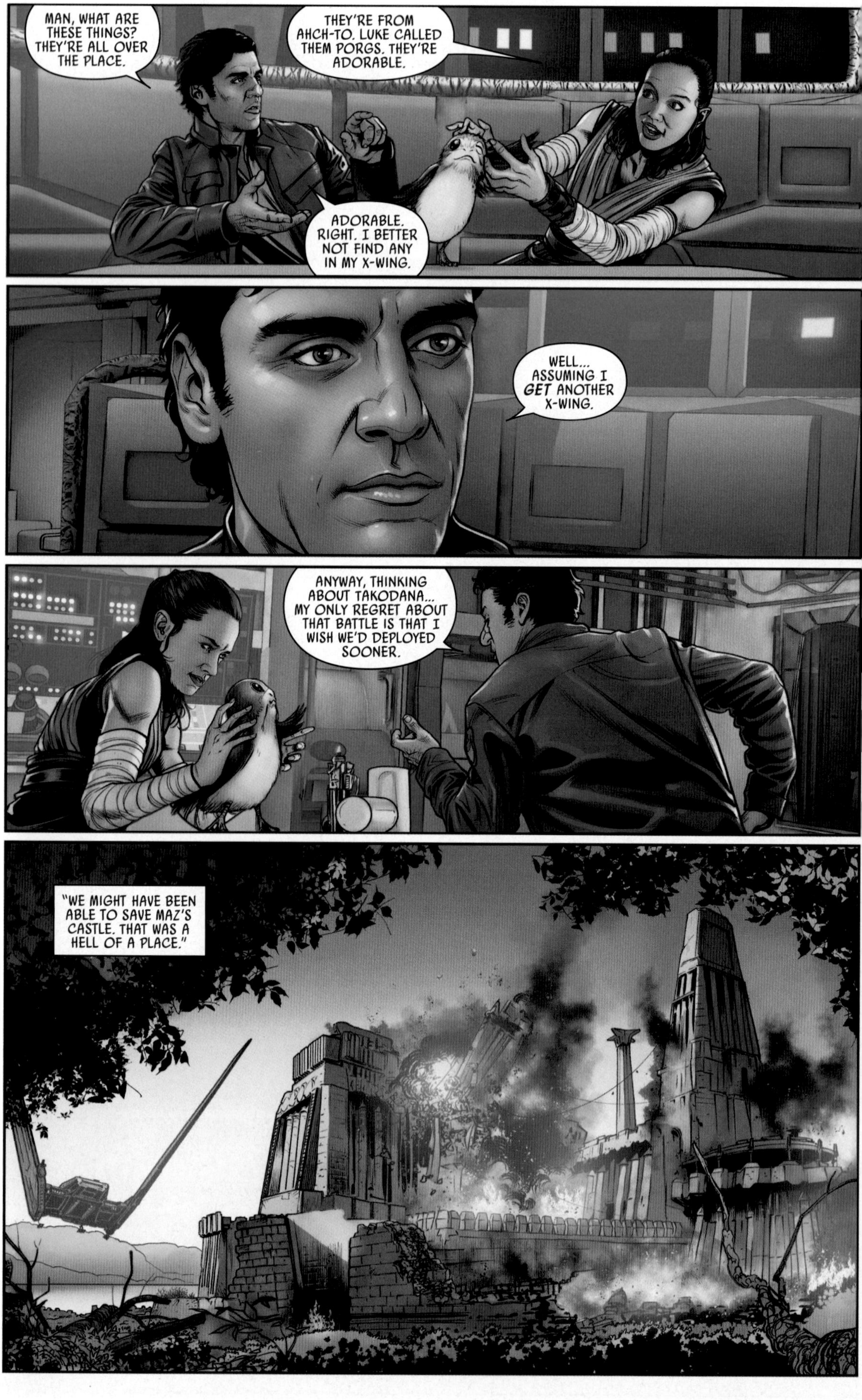
MAN, WHAT ARE THESE THINGS? THEY'RE ALL OVER THE PLACE.
THEY'RE FROM AHCH-TO. LUKE CALLED THEM PORGS. THEY'RE ADORABLE.
ADORABLE. RIGHT. I BETTER NOT FIND ANY IN MY X-WING.
WELL... ASSUMING I GET ANOTHER X-WING.
ANYWAY, THINKING ABOUT TAKODANA... MY ONLY REGRET ABOUT THAT BATTLE IS THAT I WISH WE'D DEPLOYED SOONER.
"WE MIGHT HAVE BEEN ABLE TO SAVE MAZ'S CASTLE. THAT WAS A HELL OF A PLACE."

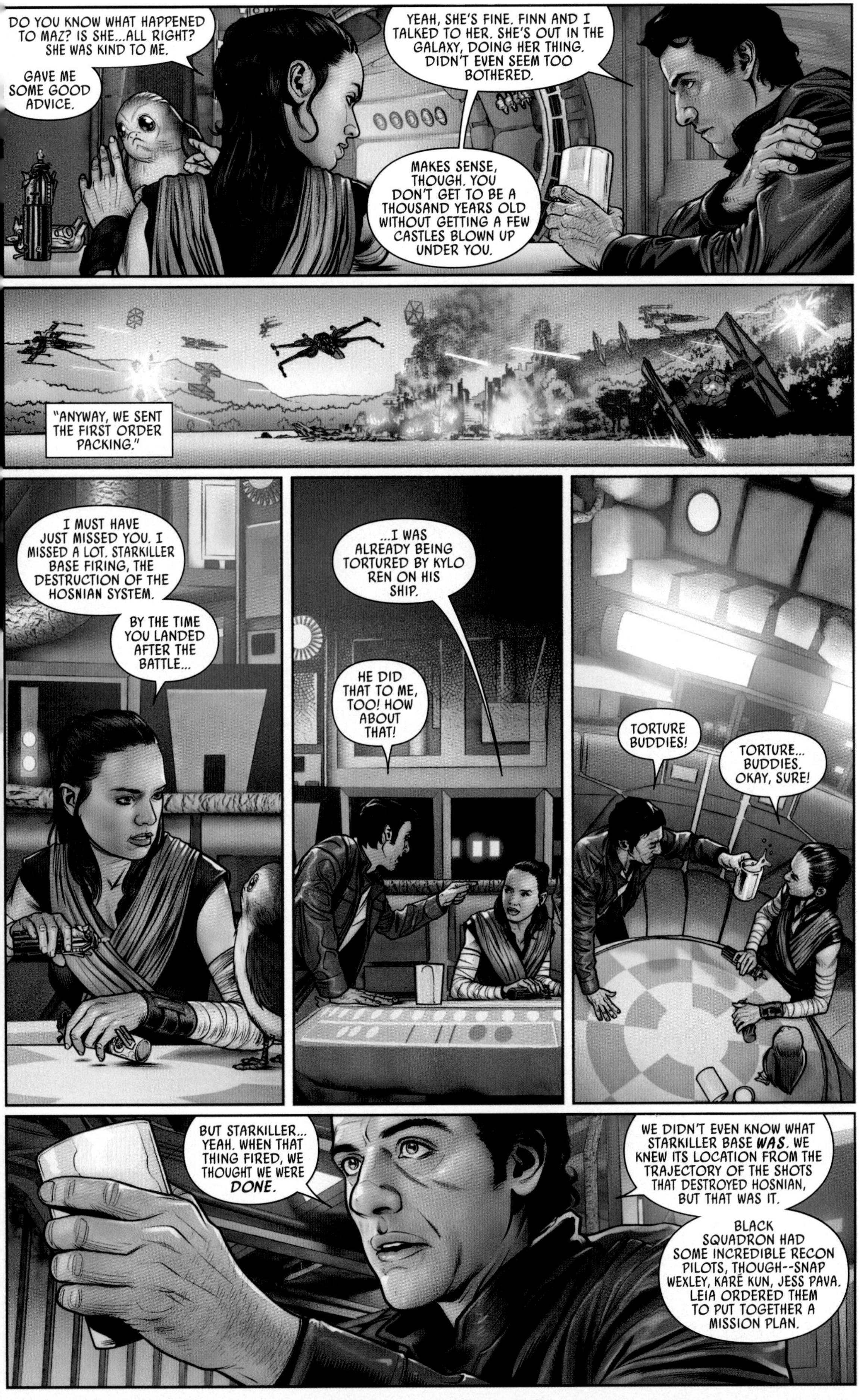
DO YOU KNOW WHAT HAPPENED TO MAZ? IS SHE...ALL RIGHT? SHE WAS KIND TO ME.
GAVE ME SOME GOOD ADVICE.
YEAH, SHE'S FINE. FINN AND I TALKED TO HER. SHE'S OUT IN THE GALAXY, DOING HER THING. DIDN'T EVEN SEEM TOO BOTHERED.
MAKES SENSE, THOUGH. YOU DON'T GET TO BE A THOUSAND YEARS OLD WITHOUT GETTING A FEW CASTLES BLOWN UP UNDER YOU.
"ANYWAY, WE SENT THE FIRST ORDER PACKING."
I MUST HAVE JUST MISSED YOU. I MISSED A LOT. STARKILLER BASE FIRING, THE DESTRUCTION OF THE HOSNIAN SYSTEM.
BY THE TIME YOU LANDED AFTER THE BATTLE...
...I WAS ALREADY BEING TORTURED BY KYLO REN ON HIS SHIP.
HE DID THAT TO ME, TOO! HOW ABOUT THAT!
TORTURE BUDDIES!
TORTURE... BUDDIES. OKAY, SURE!
BUT STARKILLER... YEAH. WHEN THAT THING FIRED, WE THOUGHT WE WERE ***DONE.***
WE DIDN'T EVEN KNOW WHAT STARKILLER BASE ***WAS.*** WE KNEW ITS LOCATION FROM THE TRAJECTORY OF THE SHOTS THAT DESTROYED HOSNIAN, BUT THAT WAS IT.
BLACK SQUADRON HAD SOME INCREDIBLE RECON PILOTS, THOUGH--SNAP WEXLEY, KARÉ KUN, JESS PAVA. LEIA ORDERED THEM TO PUT TOGETHER A MISSION PLAN.

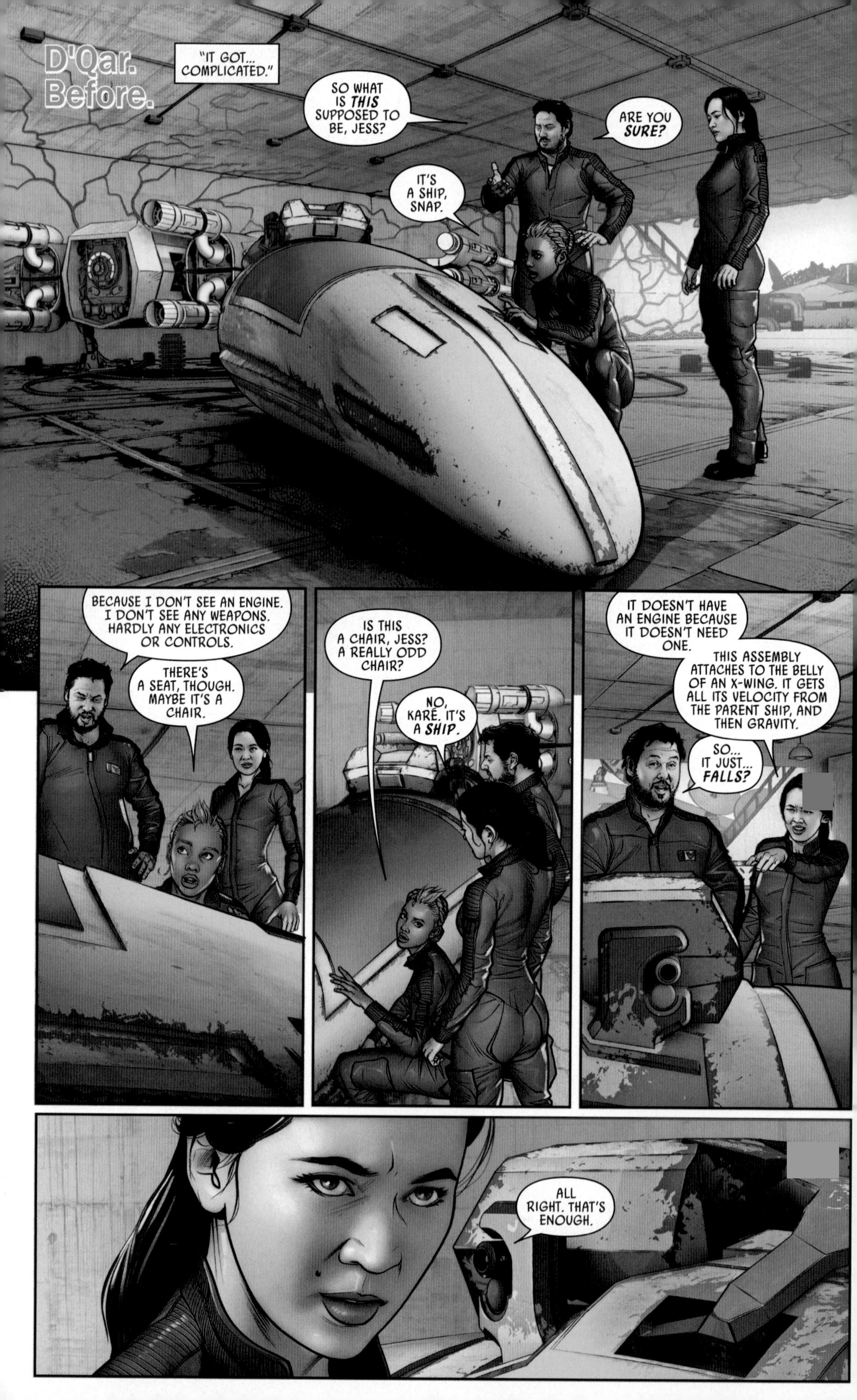
D'Qar. Before.
"IT GOT... COMPLICATED."
SO WHAT IS THIS SUPPOSED TO BE, JESS?
ARE YOU SURE?
IT'S A SHIP, SNAP.
BECAUSE I DON'T SEE AN ENGINE. I DON'T SEE ANY WEAPONS. HARDLY ANY ELECTRONICS OR CONTROLS.
THERE'S A SEAT, THOUGH. MAYBE IT'S A CHAIR.
IS THIS A CHAIR, JESS? A REALLY ODD CHAIR?
NO, KARÉ. IT'S A SHIP.
IT DOESN'T HAVE AN ENGINE BECAUSE IT DOESN'T NEED ONE.
THIS ASSEMBLY ATTACHES TO THE BELLY OF AN X-WING. IT GETS ALL ITS VELOCITY FROM THE PARENT SHIP, AND THEN GRAVITY.
SO... IT JUST... FALLS?
ALL RIGHT. THAT'S ENOUGH.

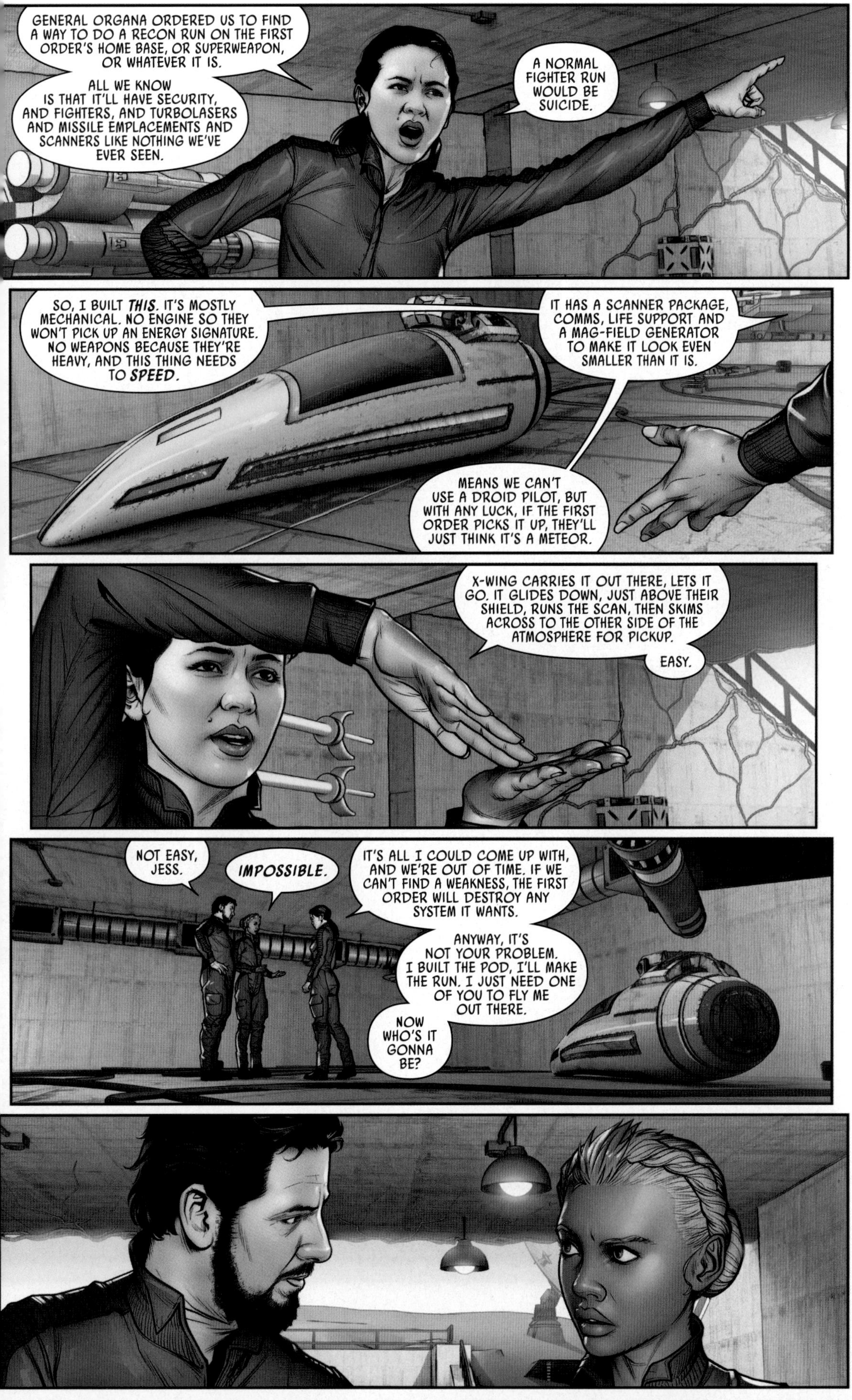
GENERAL ORGANA ORDERED US TO FIND A WAY TO DO A RECON RUN ON THE FIRST ORDER'S HOME BASE, OR SUPERWEAPON, OR WHATEVER IT IS.
ALL WE KNOW IS THAT IT'LL HAVE SECURITY, AND FIGHTERS, AND TURBOLASERS AND MISSILE EMPLACEMENTS AND SCANNERS LIKE NOTHING WE'VE EVER SEEN.
A NORMAL FIGHTER RUN WOULD BE SUICIDE.
SO, I BUILT **THIS**. IT'S MOSTLY MECHANICAL. NO ENGINE SO THEY WON'T PICK UP AN ENERGY SIGNATURE. NO WEAPONS BECAUSE THEY'RE HEAVY, AND THIS THING NEEDS TO **SPEED**.
IT HAS A SCANNER PACKAGE, COMMS, LIFE SUPPORT AND A MAG-FIELD GENERATOR TO MAKE IT LOOK EVEN SMALLER THAN IT IS.
MEANS WE CAN'T USE A DROID PILOT, BUT WITH ANY LUCK, IF THE FIRST ORDER PICKS IT UP, THEY'LL JUST THINK IT'S A METEOR.
X-WING CARRIES IT OUT THERE, LETS IT GO. IT GLIDES DOWN, JUST ABOVE THEIR SHIELD, RUNS THE SCAN, THEN SKIMS ACROSS TO THE OTHER SIDE OF THE ATMOSPHERE FOR PICKUP.
EASY.
NOT EASY, JESS.
IMPOSSIBLE.
IT'S ALL I COULD COME UP WITH, AND WE'RE OUT OF TIME. IF WE CAN'T FIND A WEAKNESS, THE FIRST ORDER WILL DESTROY ANY SYSTEM IT WANTS.
ANYWAY, IT'S NOT YOUR PROBLEM. I BUILT THE POD, I'LL MAKE THE RUN. I JUST NEED ONE OF YOU TO FLY ME OUT THERE.
NOW WHO'S IT GONNA BE?

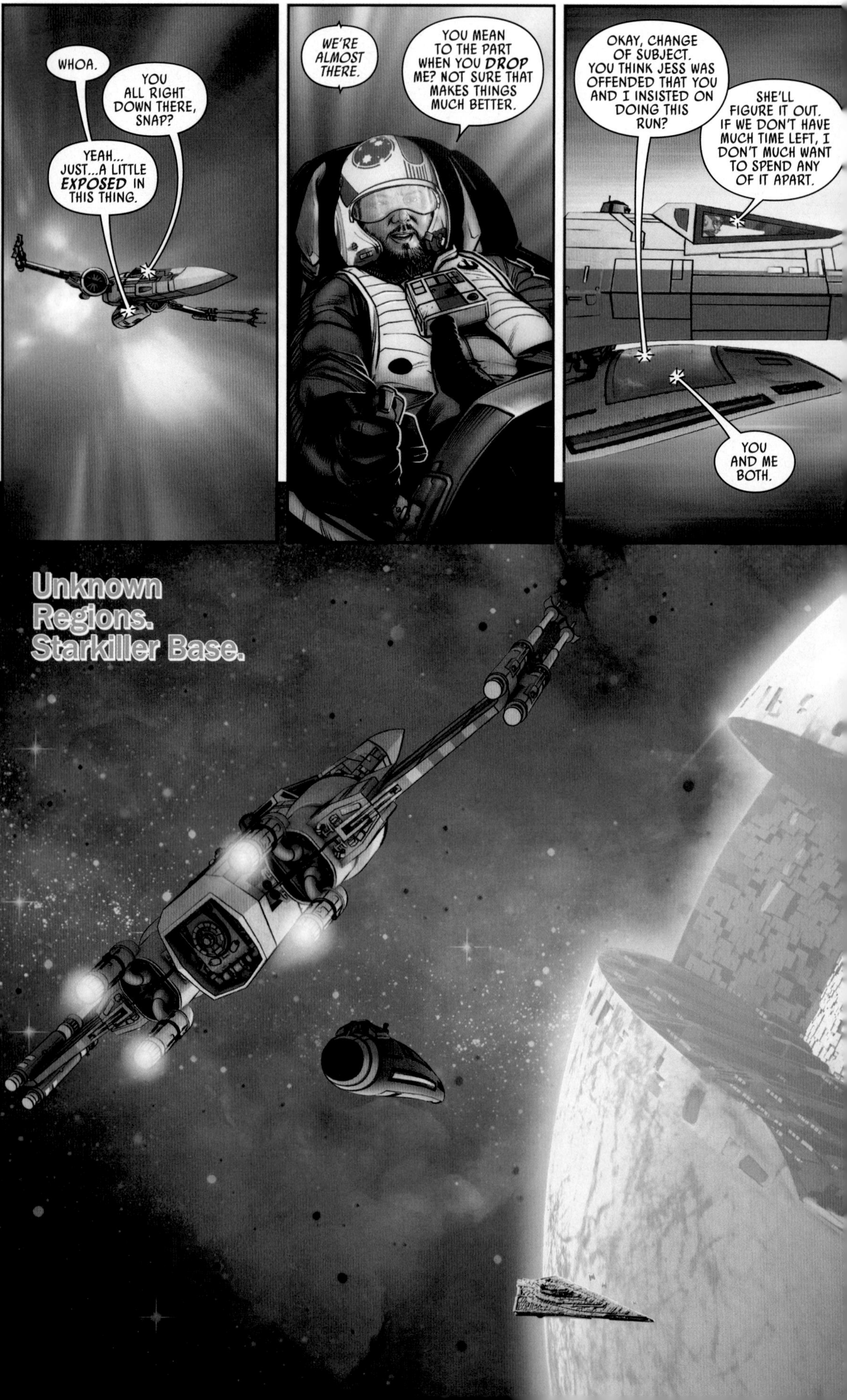
WHOA.
YOU ALL RIGHT DOWN THERE, SNAP?
YEAH... JUST...A LITTLE EXPOSED IN THIS THING.
WE'RE ALMOST THERE.
YOU MEAN TO THE PART WHEN YOU DROP ME? NOT SURE THAT MAKES THINGS MUCH BETTER.
OKAY, CHANGE OF SUBJECT. YOU THINK JESS WAS OFFENDED THAT YOU AND I INSISTED ON DOING THIS RUN?
SHE'LL FIGURE IT OUT. IF WE DON'T HAVE MUCH TIME LEFT, I DON'T MUCH WANT TO SPEND ANY OF IT APART.
YOU AND ME BOTH.
Unknown Regions. Starkiller Base.

OKAY. WE'RE HERE. DETACHING IN FIVE. GOOD LUCK, LOVE.

DON'T WORRY. REMEMBER, JESS SAID THIS'D BE EASY.

RECON POD AWAY. SEE YOU ON THE OTHER SIDE.

BEFORE YOU KNOW IT. AND KARÉ...

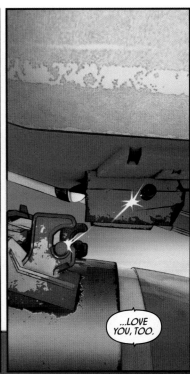

...LOVE YOU, TOO.

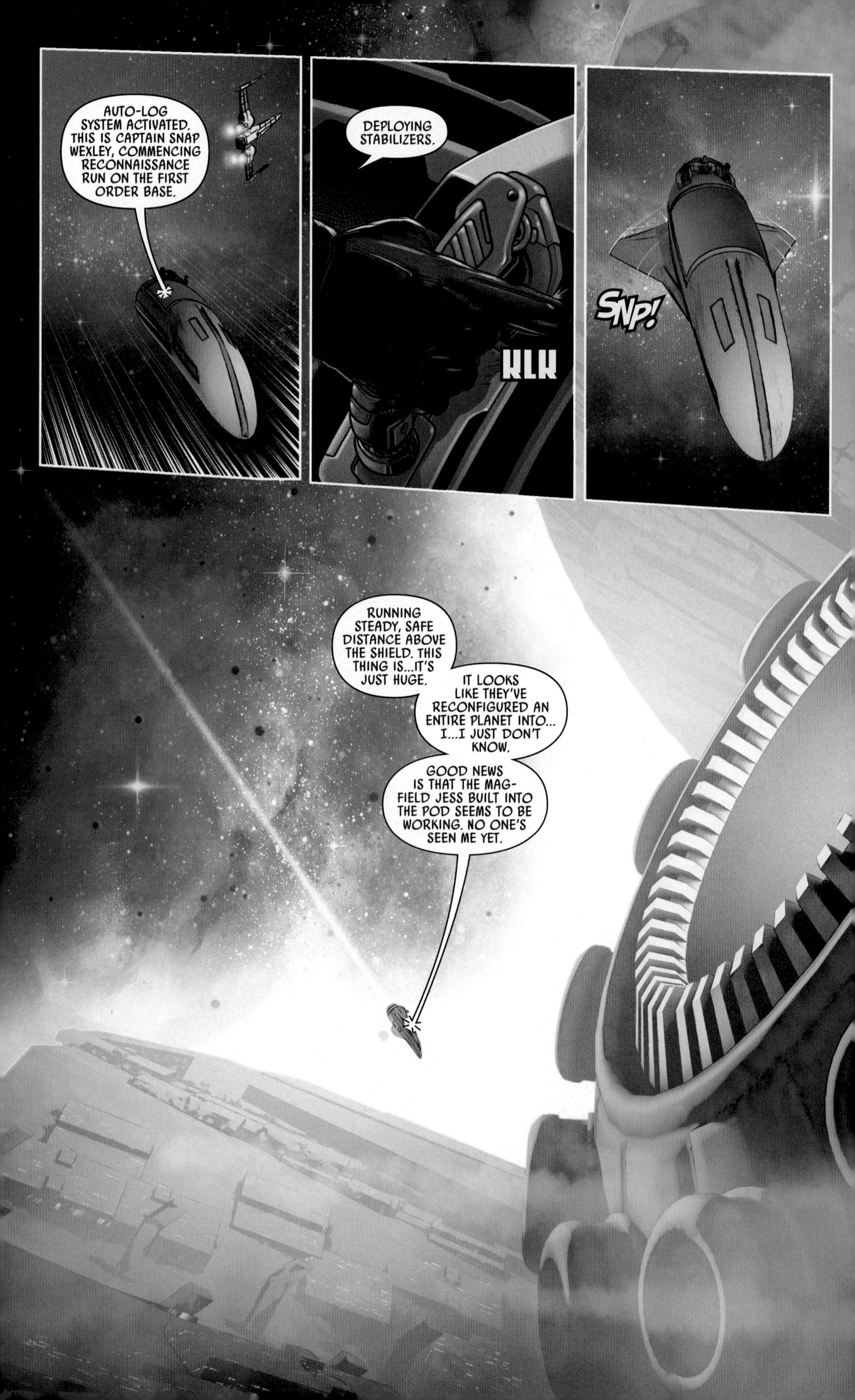
AUTO-LOG SYSTEM ACTIVATED. THIS IS CAPTAIN SNAP WEXLEY, COMMENCING RECONNAISSANCE RUN ON THE FIRST ORDER BASE.
DEPLOYING STABILIZERS.
KLK
SNP!
RUNNING STEADY, SAFE DISTANCE ABOVE THE SHIELD. THIS THING IS...IT'S JUST HUGE.
IT LOOKS LIKE THEY'VE RECONFIGURED AN ENTIRE PLANET INTO... I...I JUST DON'T KNOW.
GOOD NEWS IS THAT THE MAG-FIELD JESS BUILT INTO THE POD SEEMS TO BE WORKING. NO ONE'S SEEN ME YET.

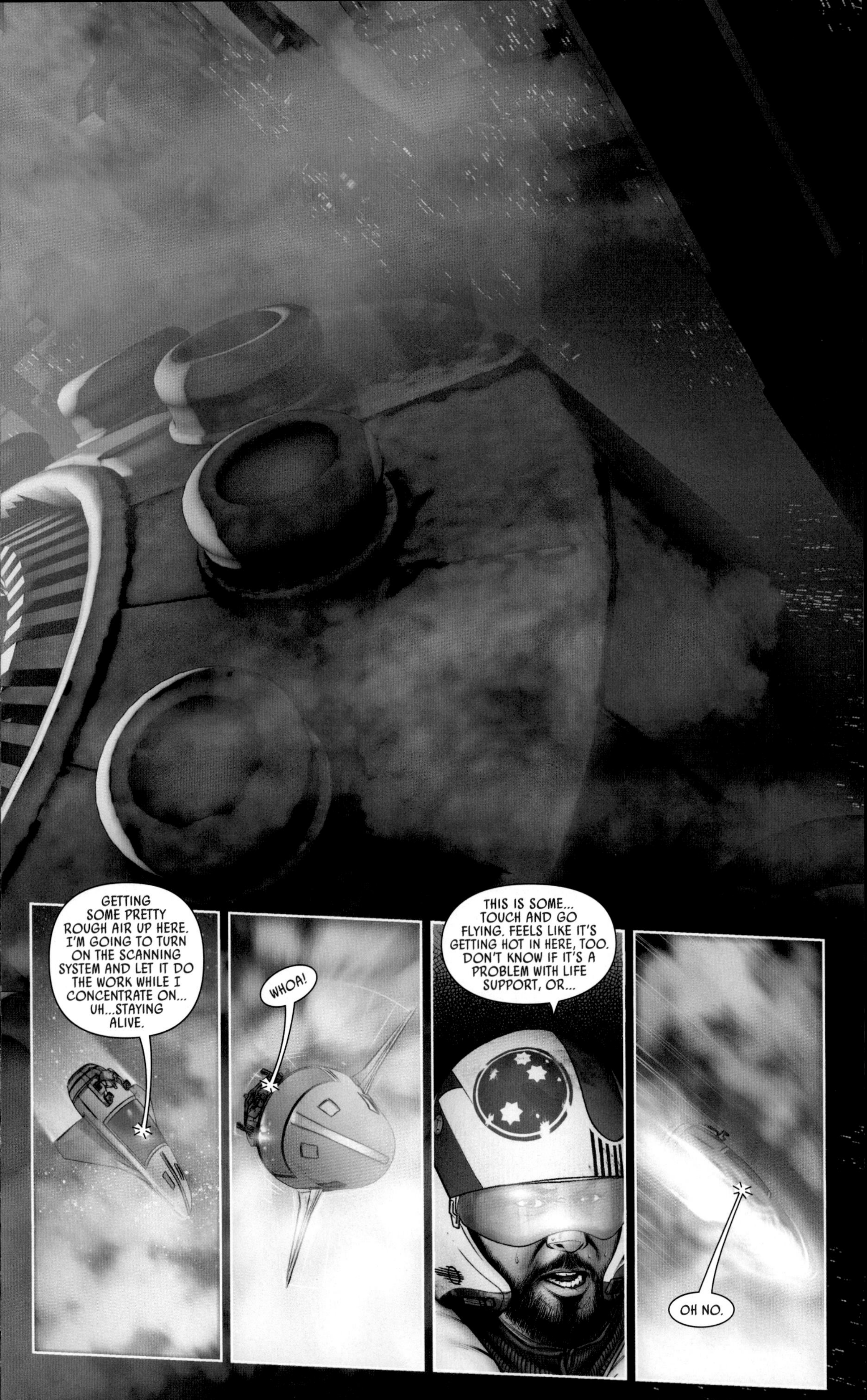

GETTING SOME PRETTY ROUGH AIR UP HERE. I'M GOING TO TURN ON THE SCANNING SYSTEM AND LET IT DO THE WORK WHILE I CONCENTRATE ON... UH...STAYING ALIVE.
WHOA!
THIS IS SOME... TOUCH AND GO FLYING. FEELS LIKE IT'S GETTING HOT IN HERE, TOO. DON'T KNOW IF IT'S A PROBLEM WITH LIFE SUPPORT, OR...
OH NO.

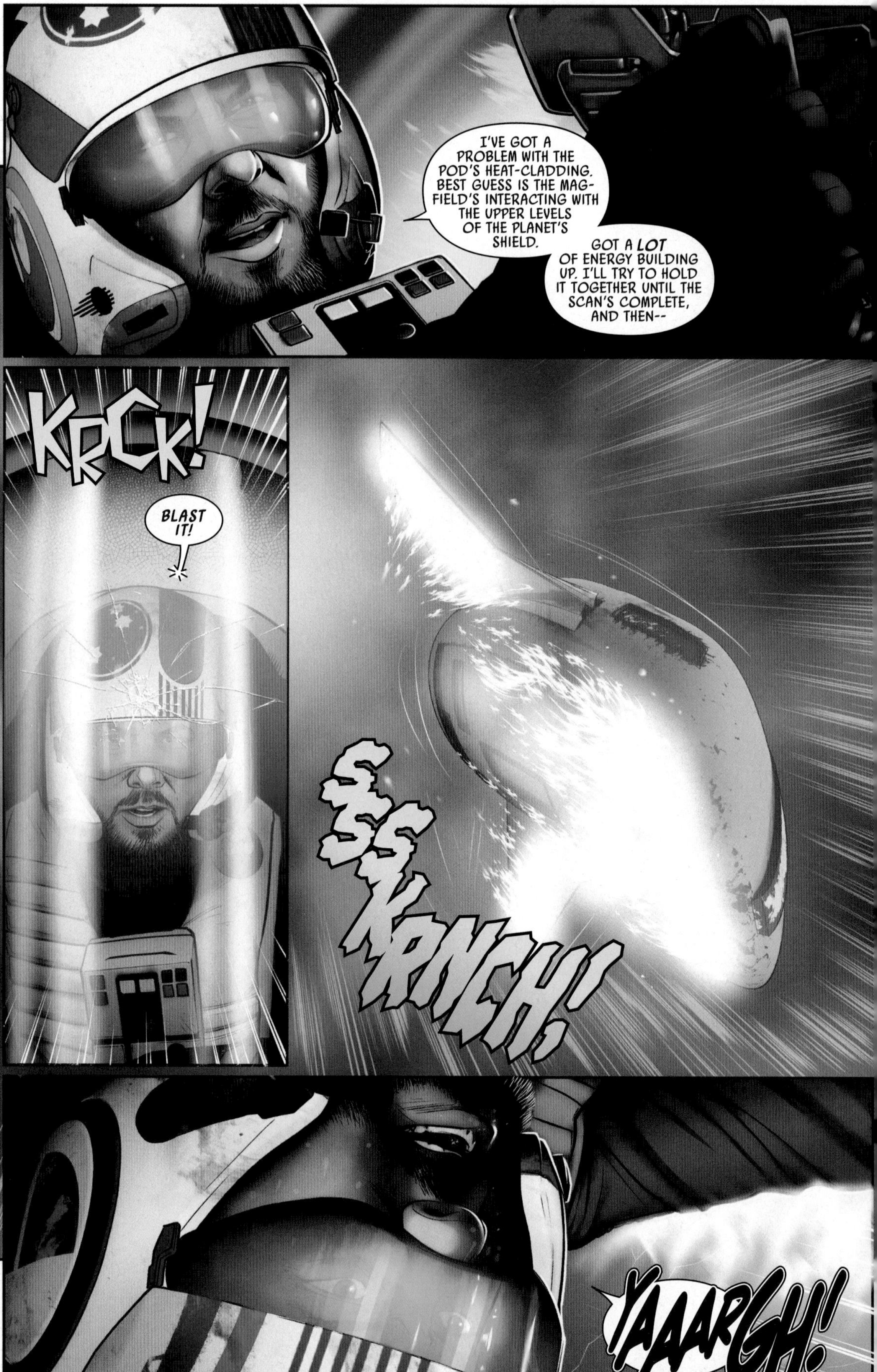
I'VE GOT A PROBLEM WITH THE POD'S HEAT-CLADDING. BEST GUESS IS THE MAG-FIELD'S INTERACTING WITH THE UPPER LEVELS OF THE PLANET'S SHIELD.
GOT A *LOT* OF ENERGY BUILDING UP. I'LL TRY TO HOLD IT TOGETHER UNTIL THE SCAN'S COMPLETE, AND THEN--
KRCK!
BLAST IT!
SSSKRNCH!
YAAARGH!

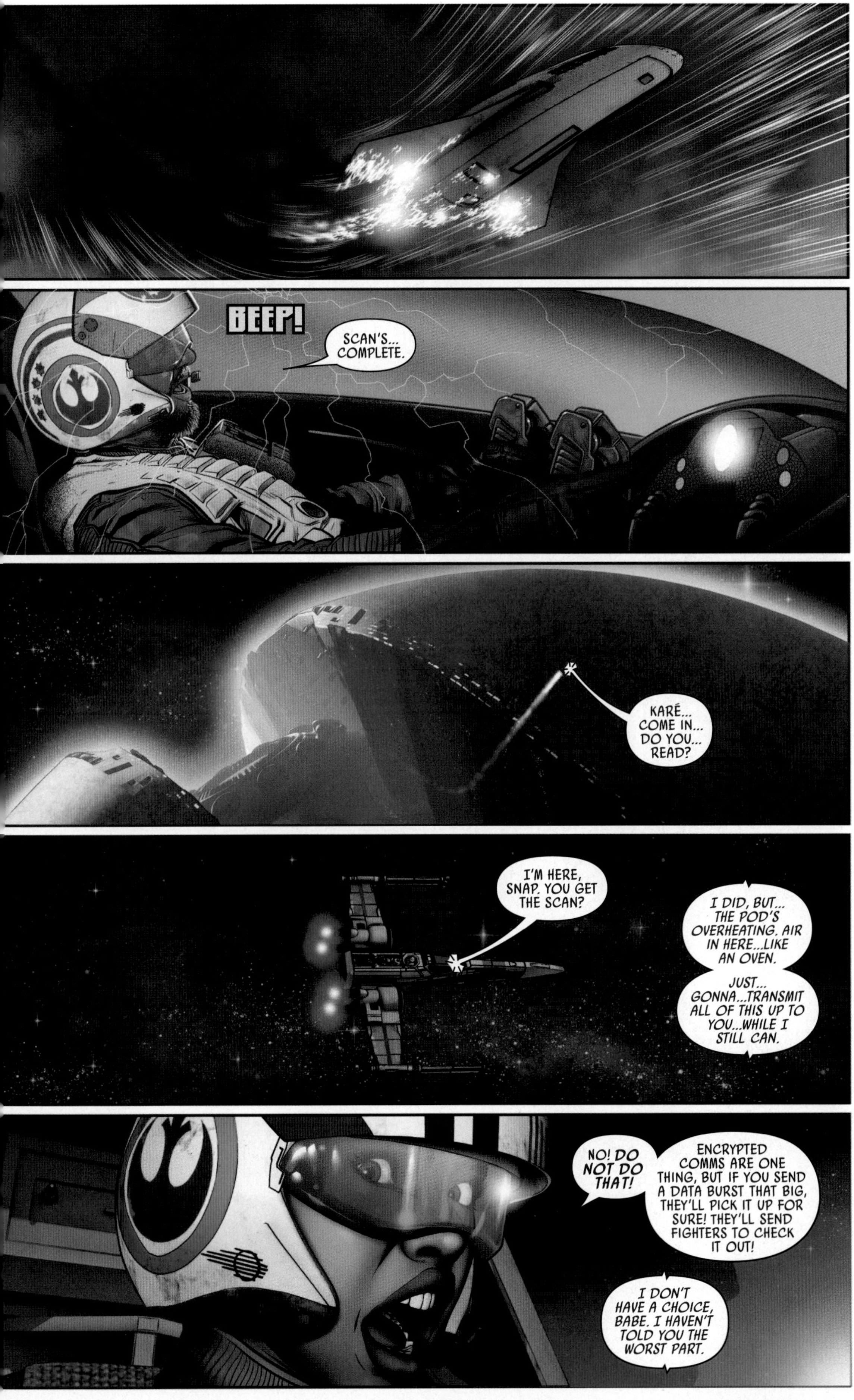
BEEP!
SCAN'S... COMPLETE.
KARÉ... COME IN... DO YOU... READ?
I'M HERE, SNAP. YOU GET THE SCAN?
I DID, BUT... THE POD'S OVERHEATING. AIR IN HERE...LIKE AN OVEN.
JUST... GONNA...TRANSMIT ALL OF THIS UP TO YOU...WHILE I STILL CAN.
NO! DO NOT DO THAT!
ENCRYPTED COMMS ARE ONE THING, BUT IF YOU SEND A DATA BURST THAT BIG, THEY'LL PICK IT UP FOR SURE! THEY'LL SEND FIGHTERS TO CHECK IT OUT!
I DON'T HAVE A CHOICE, BABE. I HAVEN'T TOLD YOU THE WORST PART.

THE... DOCKING ASSEMBLY. MUST HAVE...BURNED OFF...IN THE HEAT.

EVEN IF... I COULD GET TO YOU...NO WAY TO SLOW ME DOWN. NO WAY TO...GET ME... HOME.

NO. NO. DO **NOT** TRANSMIT THAT DATA. YOU GET YOURSELF **UP** HERE.

KARÉ...I'M FLARING LIKE...A COMET. EVEN IF I'M NOT... ON THEIR SCANNERS... THEY'RE BOUND TO JUST...**SEE** ME.

THEY HAVEN'T SEEN YOU **YET**. WHAT WAS IT LEIA SAID EVERY **HEIST** NEEDS? **LUCK**. AND YOU HAVEN'T RUN OUT YET.

THERE'S... NO TIME. SENDING... DATA.

SNAP WEXLEY, WE HAVE NOT BEEN MARRIED LONG ENOUGH FOR YOU TO MAKE ME A WIDOW, AND IF YOU HIT THAT TRANSMIT BUTTON I SWEAR I WILL **DIVORCE** YOU!

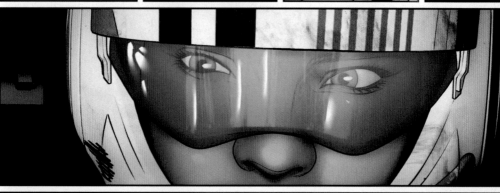

OKAY. I'M...I'M COMING.

DAMN RIGHT YOU ARE.

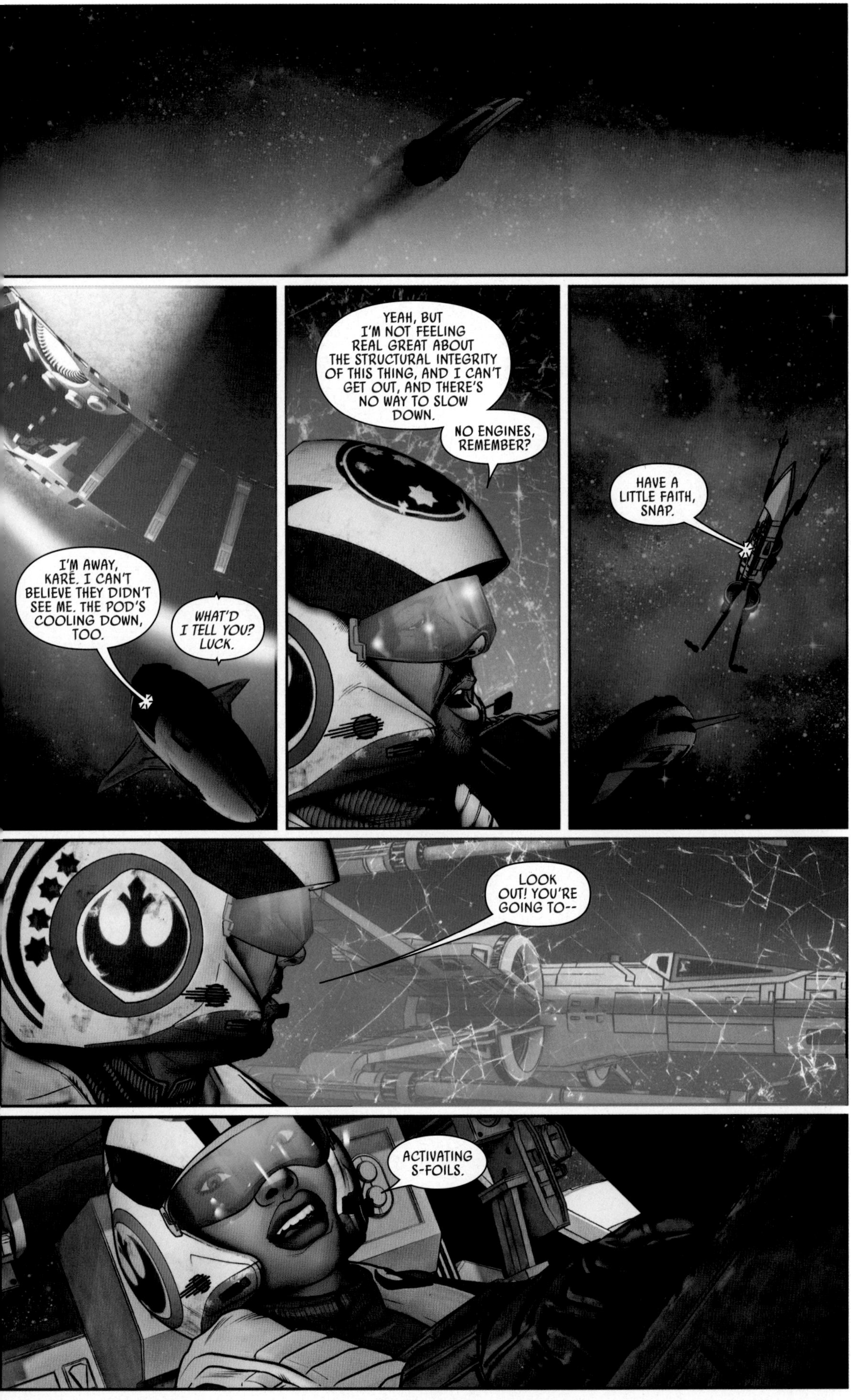
I'M AWAY, KARÉ. I CAN'T BELIEVE THEY DIDN'T SEE ME. THE POD'S COOLING DOWN, TOO.
WHAT'D I TELL YOU? LUCK.
YEAH, BUT I'M NOT FEELING REAL GREAT ABOUT THE STRUCTURAL INTEGRITY OF THIS THING, AND I CAN'T GET OUT, AND THERE'S NO WAY TO SLOW DOWN.
NO ENGINES, REMEMBER?
HAVE A LITTLE FAITH, SNAP.
LOOK OUT! YOU'RE GOING TO--
ACTIVATING S-FOILS.

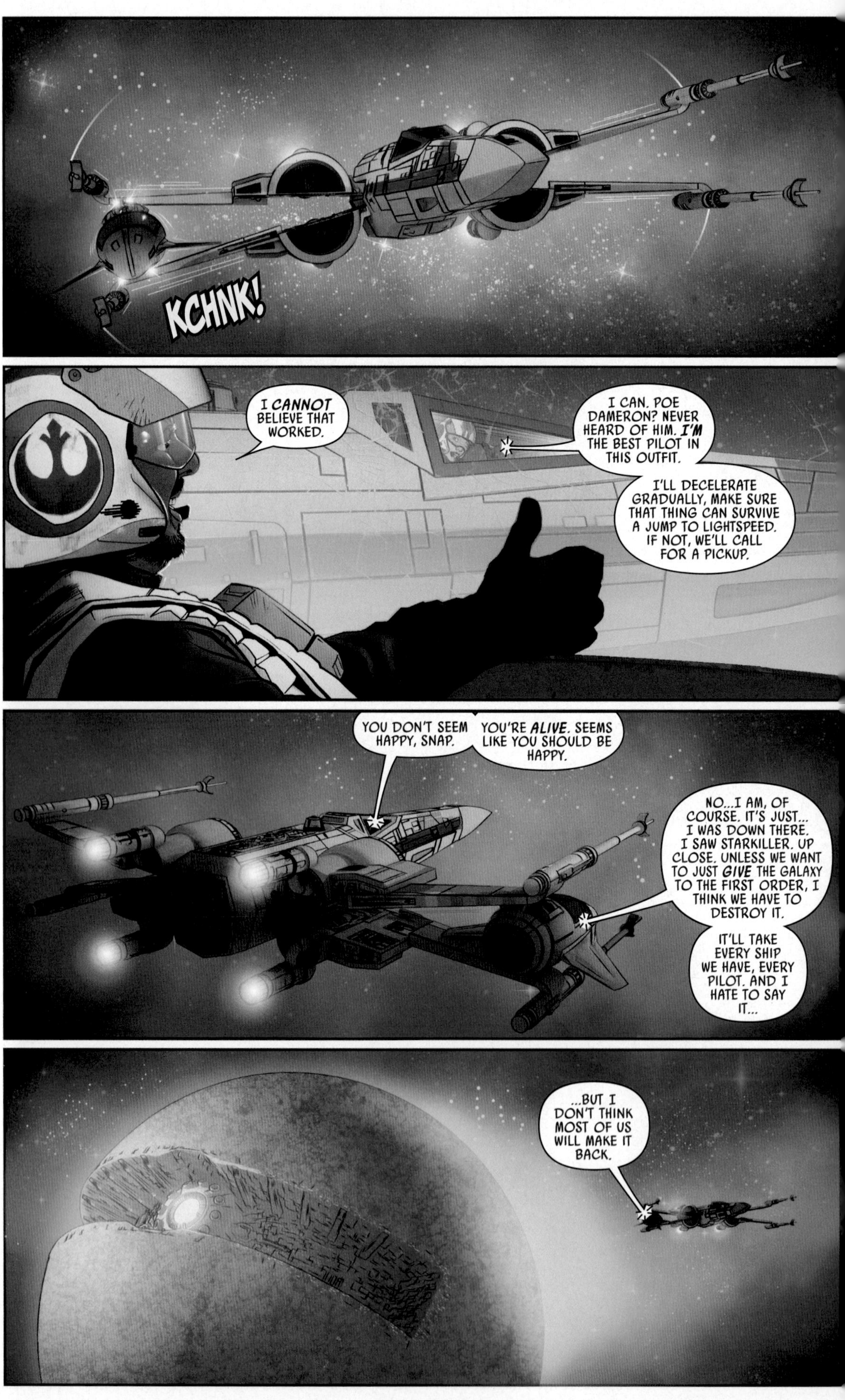
KCHNK!
I CANNOT BELIEVE THAT WORKED.
I CAN. POE DAMERON? NEVER HEARD OF HIM. I'M THE BEST PILOT IN THIS OUTFIT.
I'LL DECELERATE GRADUALLY, MAKE SURE THAT THING CAN SURVIVE A JUMP TO LIGHTSPEED. IF NOT, WE'LL CALL FOR A PICKUP.
YOU DON'T SEEM HAPPY, SNAP.
YOU'RE ALIVE. SEEMS LIKE YOU SHOULD BE HAPPY.
NO...I AM, OF COURSE. IT'S JUST... I WAS DOWN THERE. I SAW STARKILLER. UP CLOSE. UNLESS WE WANT TO JUST GIVE THE GALAXY TO THE FIRST ORDER, I THINK WE HAVE TO DESTROY IT.
IT'LL TAKE EVERY SHIP WE HAVE, EVERY PILOT. AND I HATE TO SAY IT...
...BUT I DON'T THINK MOST OF US WILL MAKE IT BACK.

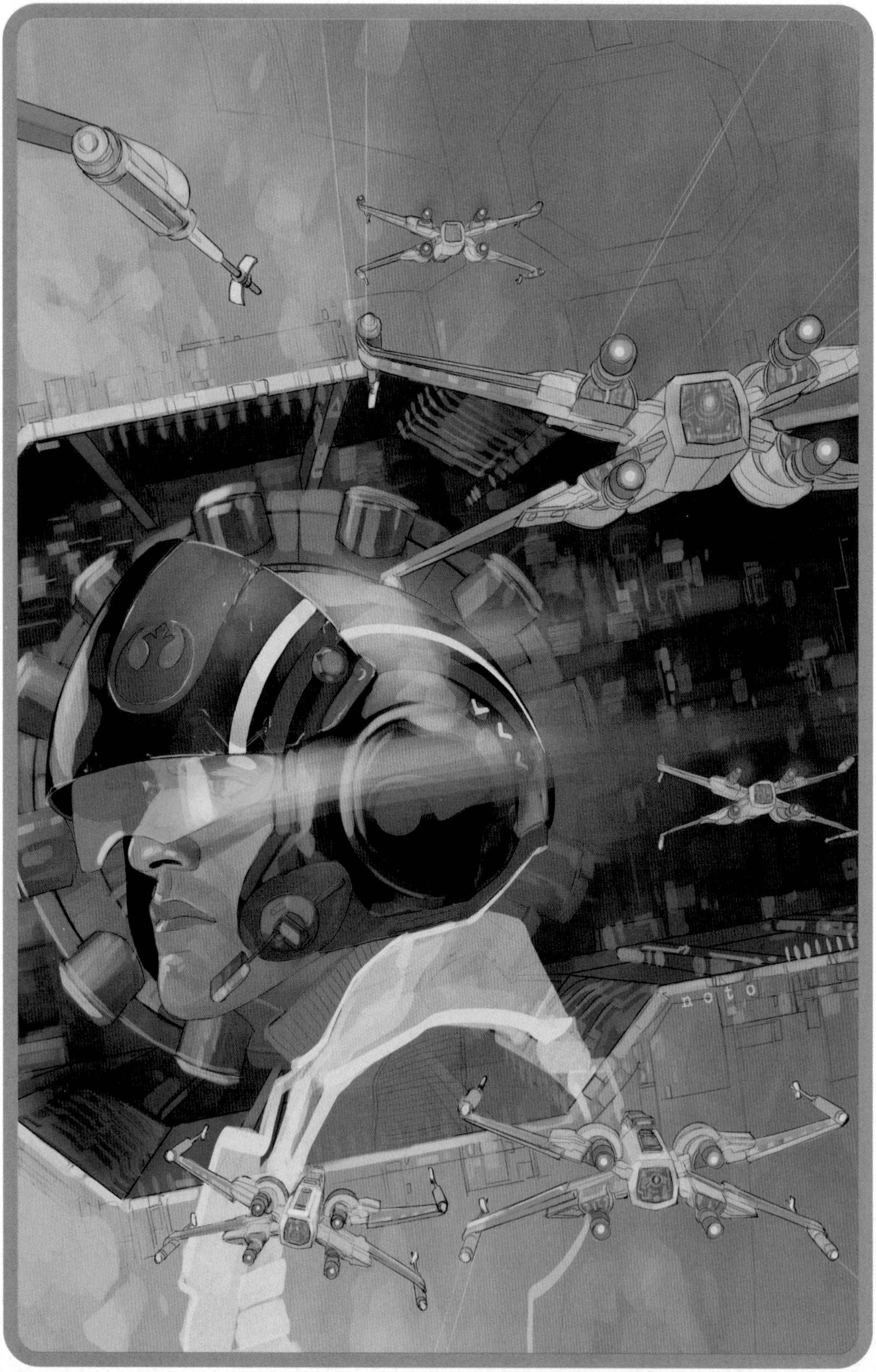
noto

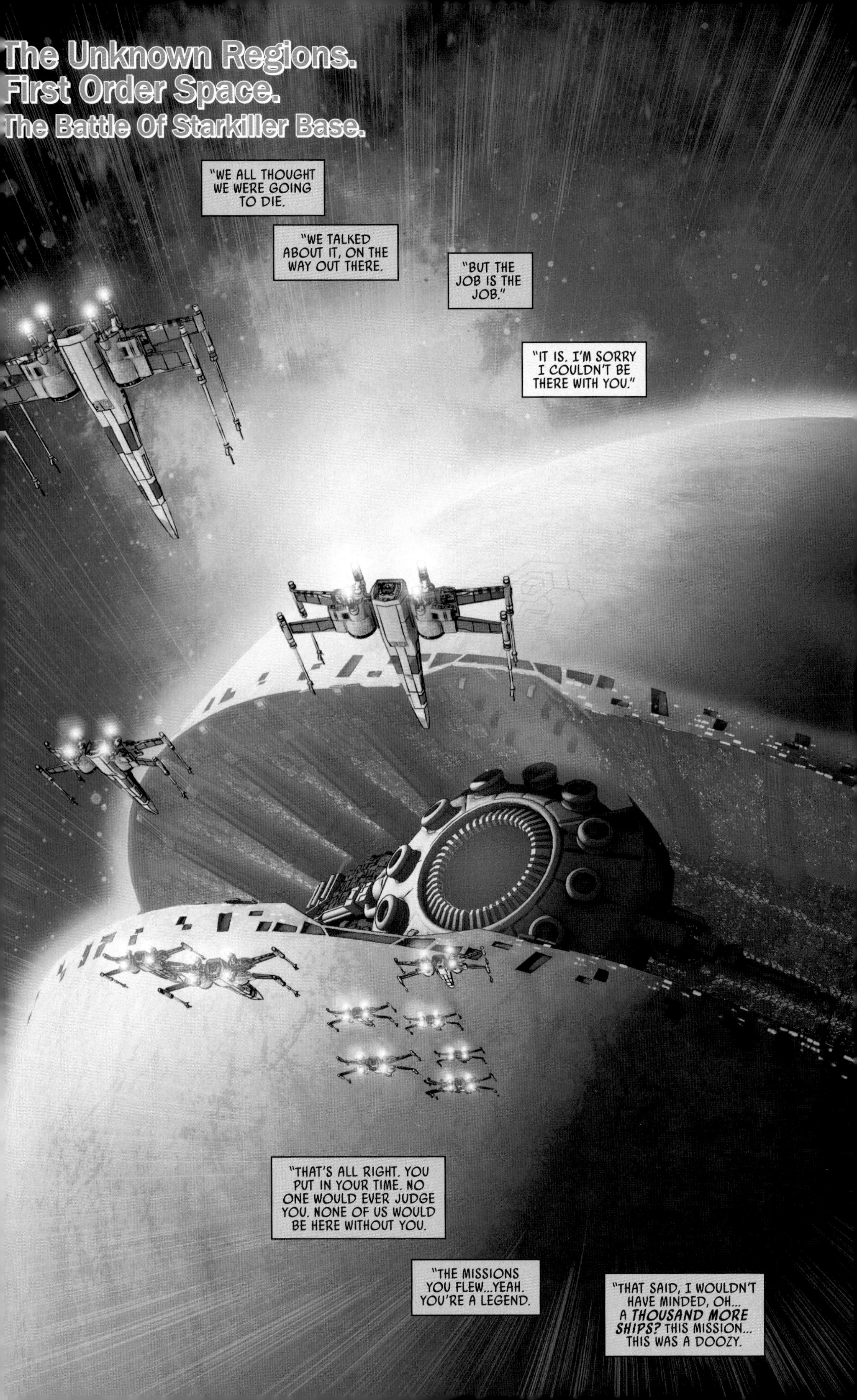
The Unknown Regions.
First Order Space.
The Battle Of Starkiller Base.
"WE ALL THOUGHT WE WERE GOING TO DIE.
"WE TALKED ABOUT IT, ON THE WAY OUT THERE.
"BUT THE JOB IS THE JOB."
"IT IS. I'M SORRY I COULDN'T BE THERE WITH YOU."
"THAT'S ALL RIGHT. YOU PUT IN YOUR TIME. NO ONE WOULD EVER JUDGE YOU. NONE OF US WOULD BE HERE WITHOUT YOU.
"THE MISSIONS YOU FLEW...YEAH. YOU'RE A LEGEND.
"THAT SAID, I WOULDN'T HAVE MINDED, OH... A *THOUSAND MORE SHIPS?* THIS MISSION... THIS WAS A DOOZY.

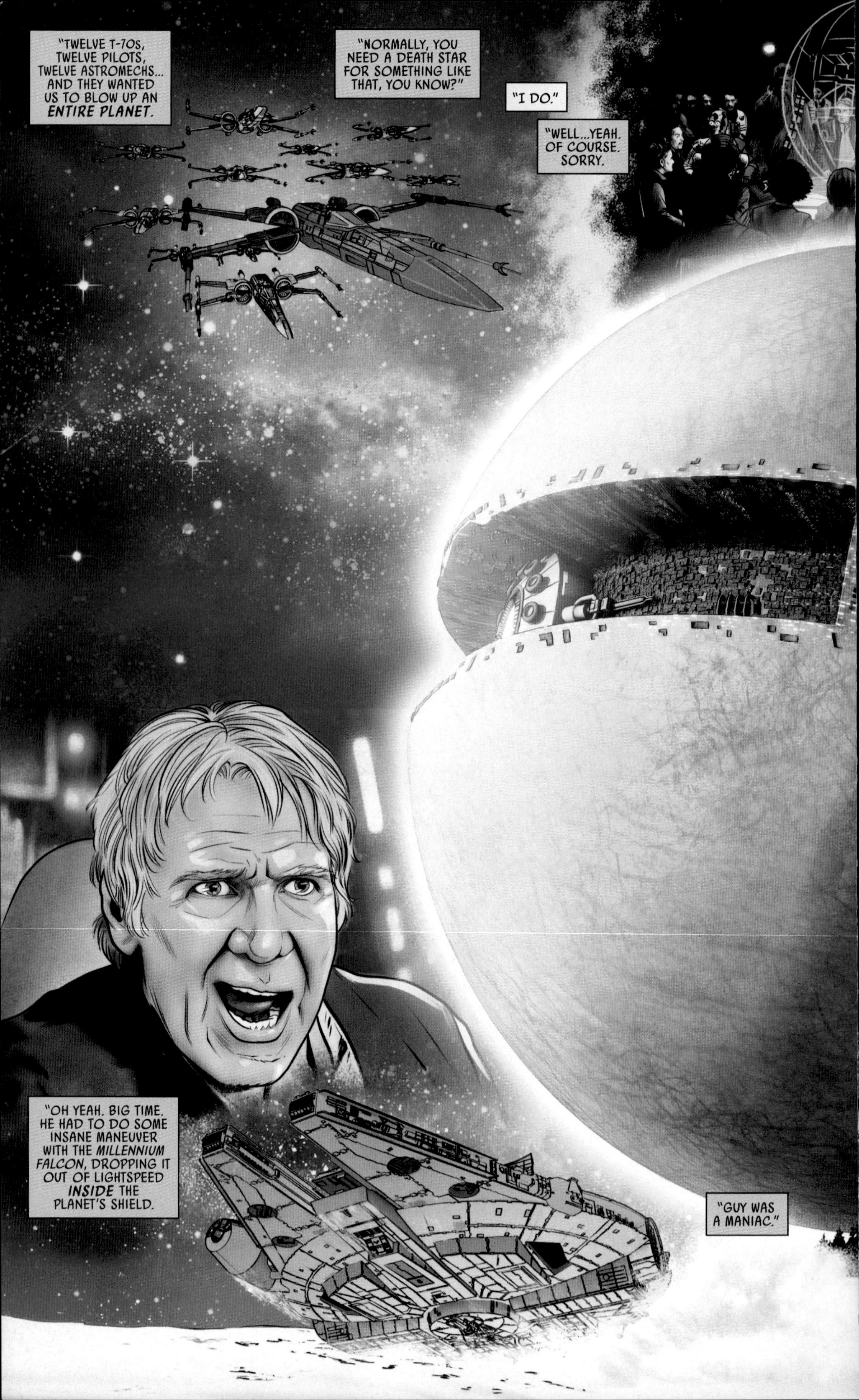
"TWELVE T-70s, TWELVE PILOTS, TWELVE ASTROMECHS... AND THEY WANTED US TO BLOW UP AN ENTIRE PLANET.
"NORMALLY, YOU NEED A DEATH STAR FOR SOMETHING LIKE THAT, YOU KNOW?"
"I DO."
"WELL...YEAH. OF COURSE. SORRY.
"OH YEAH. BIG TIME. HE HAD TO DO SOME INSANE MANEUVER WITH THE MILLENNIUM FALCON, DROPPING IT OUT OF LIGHTSPEED INSIDE THE PLANET'S SHIELD.
"GUY WAS A MANIAC."

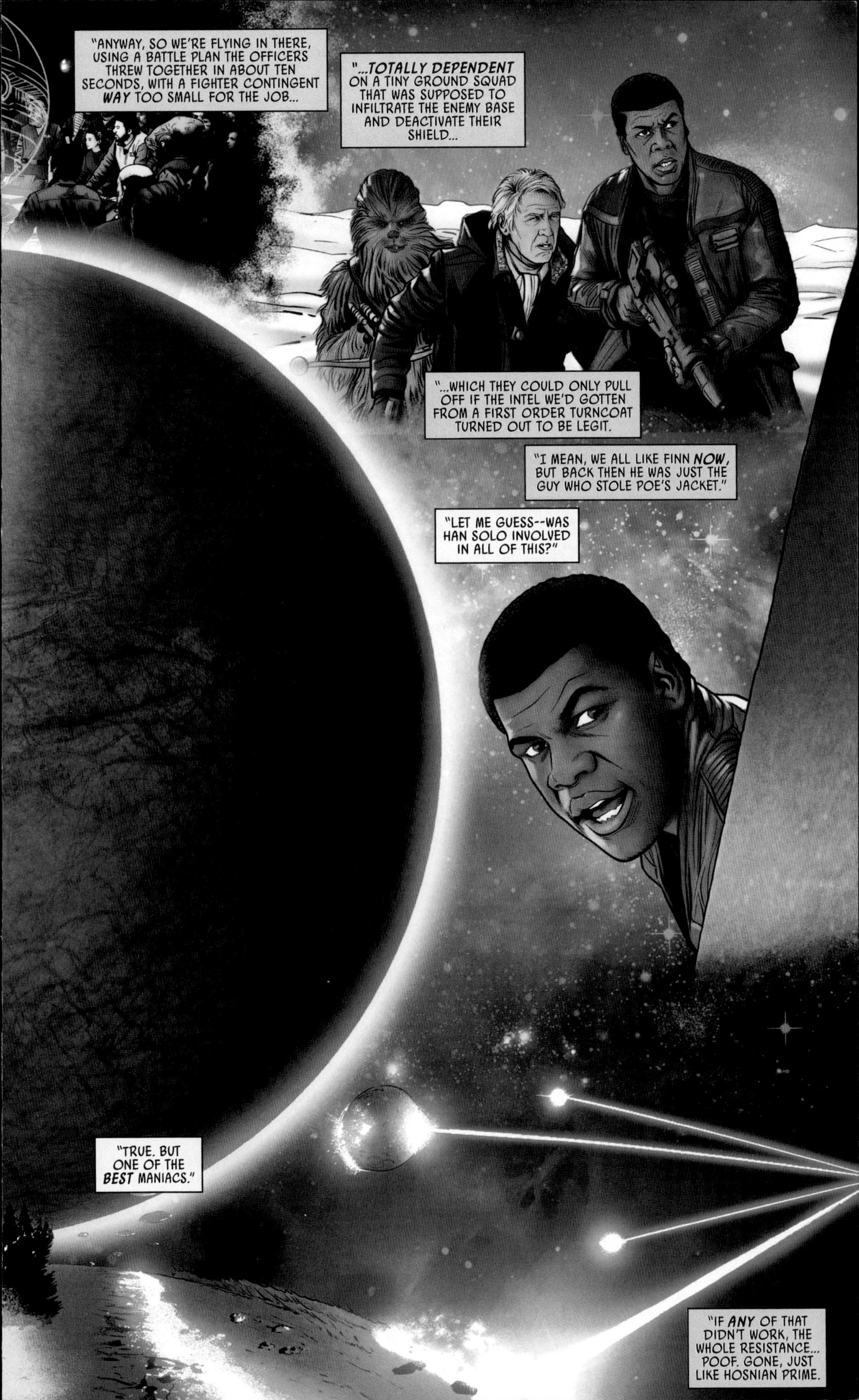
"ANYWAY, SO WE'RE FLYING IN THERE, USING A BATTLE PLAN THE OFFICERS THREW TOGETHER IN ABOUT TEN SECONDS, WITH A FIGHTER CONTINGENT *WAY* TOO SMALL FOR THE JOB...
"...*TOTALLY DEPENDENT* ON A TINY GROUND SQUAD THAT WAS SUPPOSED TO INFILTRATE THE ENEMY BASE AND DEACTIVATE THEIR SHIELD...
"...WHICH THEY COULD ONLY PULL OFF IF THE INTEL WE'D GOTTEN FROM A FIRST ORDER TURNCOAT TURNED OUT TO BE LEGIT.
"I MEAN, WE ALL LIKE FINN *NOW*, BUT BACK THEN HE WAS JUST THE GUY WHO STOLE POE'S JACKET."
"LET ME GUESS--WAS HAN SOLO INVOLVED IN ALL OF THIS?"
"TRUE. BUT ONE OF THE *BEST* MANIACS."
"IF *ANY* OF THAT DIDN'T WORK, THE WHOLE RESISTANCE... POOF. GONE, JUST LIKE HOSNIAN PRIME.

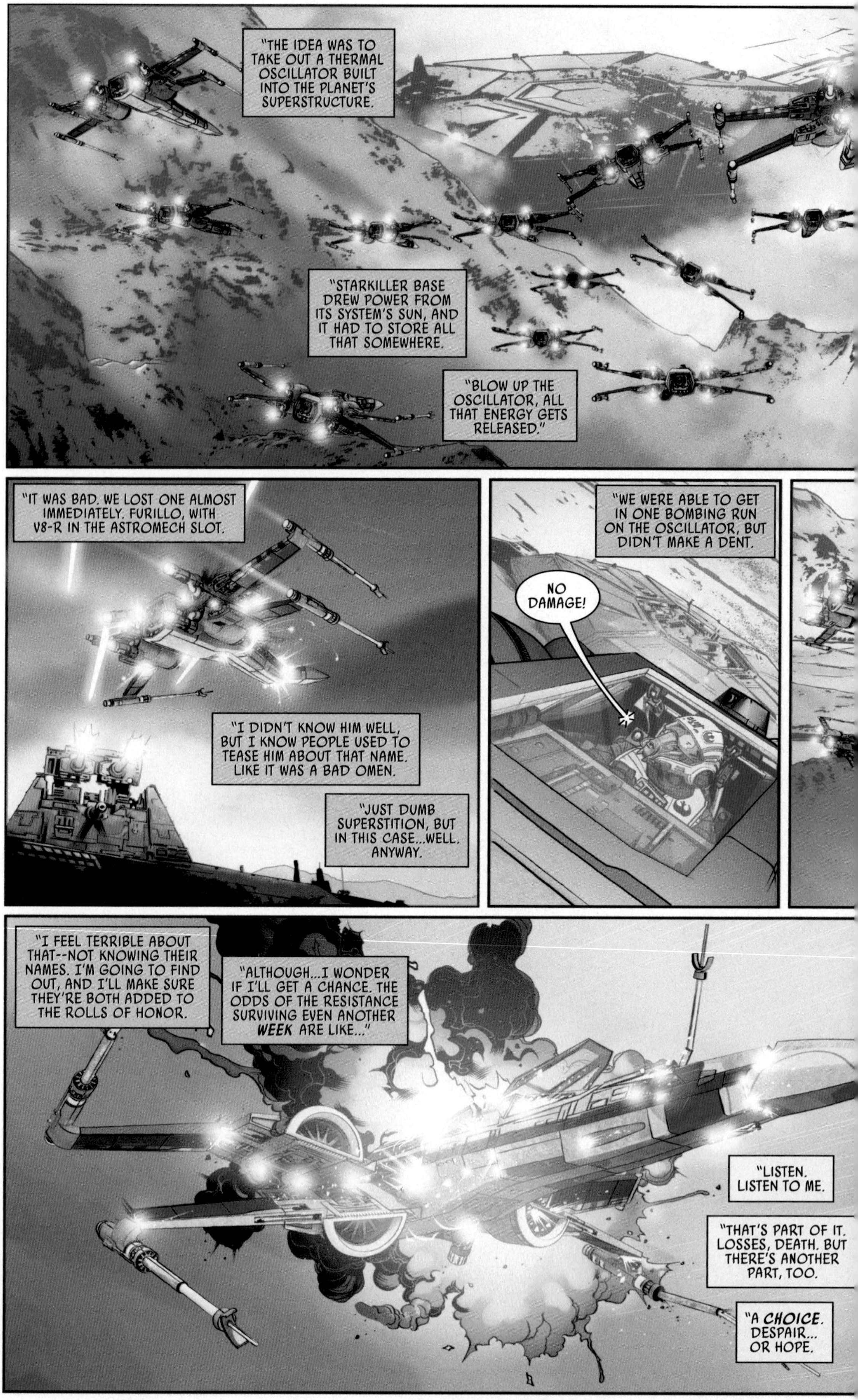
"THE IDEA WAS TO TAKE OUT A THERMAL OSCILLATOR BUILT INTO THE PLANET'S SUPERSTRUCTURE.
"STARKILLER BASE DREW POWER FROM ITS SYSTEM'S SUN, AND IT HAD TO STORE ALL THAT SOMEWHERE.
"BLOW UP THE OSCILLATOR, ALL THAT ENERGY GETS RELEASED."
"IT WAS BAD. WE LOST ONE ALMOST IMMEDIATELY. FURILLO, WITH V8-R IN THE ASTROMECH SLOT.
"I DIDN'T KNOW HIM WELL, BUT I KNOW PEOPLE USED TO TEASE HIM ABOUT THAT NAME. LIKE IT WAS A BAD OMEN.
"JUST DUMB SUPERSTITION, BUT IN THIS CASE...WELL. ANYWAY.
"WE WERE ABLE TO GET IN ONE BOMBING RUN ON THE OSCILLATOR, BUT DIDN'T MAKE A DENT.
NO DAMAGE!
"I FEEL TERRIBLE ABOUT THAT--NOT KNOWING THEIR NAMES. I'M GOING TO FIND OUT, AND I'LL MAKE SURE THEY'RE BOTH ADDED TO THE ROLLS OF HONOR.
"ALTHOUGH...I WONDER IF I'LL GET A CHANCE. THE ODDS OF THE RESISTANCE SURVIVING EVEN ANOTHER *WEEK* ARE LIKE..."
"LISTEN. LISTEN TO ME.
"THAT'S PART OF IT. LOSSES, DEATH. BUT THERE'S ANOTHER PART, TOO.
"A ***CHOICE***. DESPAIR... OR HOPE.

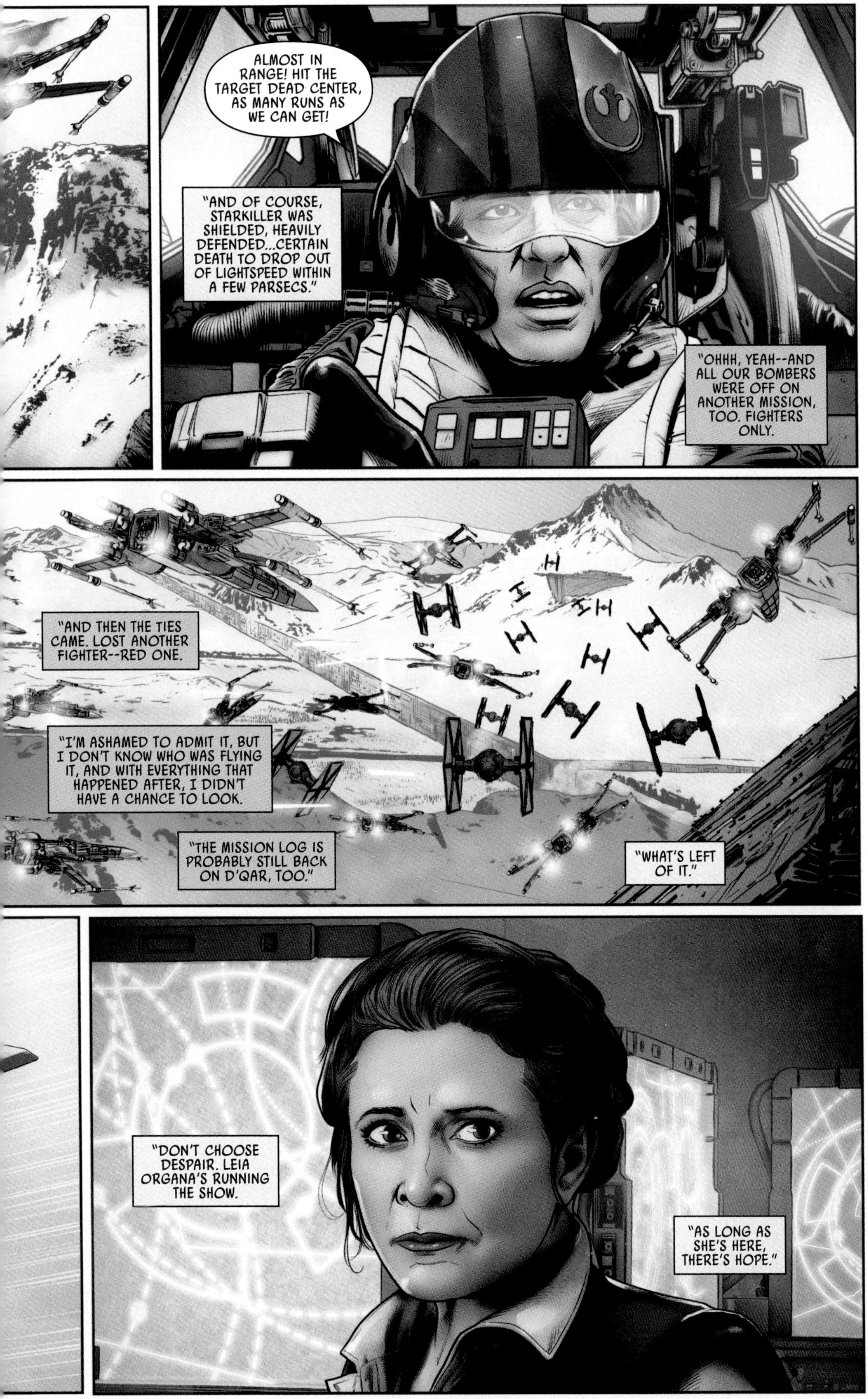
ALMOST IN RANGE! HIT THE TARGET DEAD CENTER, AS MANY RUNS AS WE CAN GET!
"AND OF COURSE, STARKILLER WAS SHIELDED, HEAVILY DEFENDED...CERTAIN DEATH TO DROP OUT OF LIGHTSPEED WITHIN A FEW PARSECS."
"OHHH, YEAH--AND ALL OUR BOMBERS WERE OFF ON ANOTHER MISSION, TOO. FIGHTERS ONLY.
"AND THEN THE TIES CAME. LOST ANOTHER FIGHTER--RED ONE.
"I'M ASHAMED TO ADMIT IT, BUT I DON'T KNOW WHO WAS FLYING IT, AND WITH EVERYTHING THAT HAPPENED AFTER, I DIDN'T HAVE A CHANCE TO LOOK.
"THE MISSION LOG IS PROBABLY STILL BACK ON D'QAR, TOO."
"WHAT'S LEFT OF IT."
"DON'T CHOOSE DESPAIR. LEIA ORGANA'S RUNNING THE SHOW.
"AS LONG AS SHE'S HERE, THERE'S HOPE."

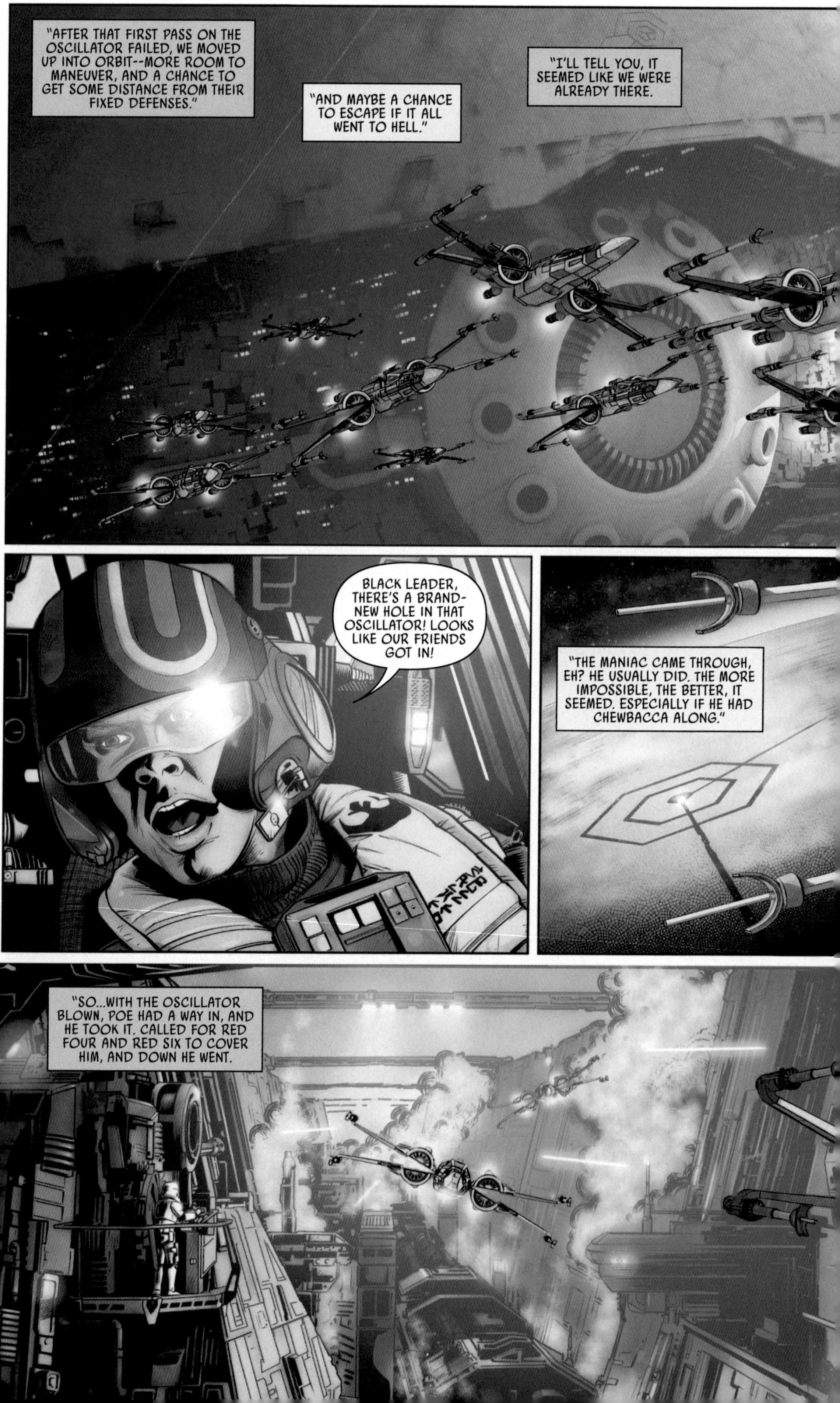
"AFTER THAT FIRST PASS ON THE OSCILLATOR FAILED, WE MOVED UP INTO ORBIT--MORE ROOM TO MANEUVER, AND A CHANCE TO GET SOME DISTANCE FROM THEIR FIXED DEFENSES."
"AND MAYBE A CHANCE TO ESCAPE IF IT ALL WENT TO HELL."
"I'LL TELL YOU, IT SEEMED LIKE WE WERE ALREADY THERE.
BLACK LEADER, THERE'S A BRAND-NEW HOLE IN THAT OSCILLATOR! LOOKS LIKE OUR FRIENDS GOT IN!
"THE MANIAC CAME THROUGH, EH? HE USUALLY DID. THE MORE IMPOSSIBLE, THE BETTER, IT SEEMED. ESPECIALLY IF HE HAD CHEWBACCA ALONG."
"SO...WITH THE OSCILLATOR BLOWN, POE HAD A WAY IN, AND HE TOOK IT. CALLED FOR RED FOUR AND RED SIX TO COVER HIM, AND DOWN HE WENT.

"BUT THEN, FINALLY... A LITTLE LUCK."

"YEAH, BUT NOT JUST THEM--FINN, TOO, AND REY."

"SURE. PLENTY OF HEROES TO GO AROUND."

"REY'S REALLY SOMETHING, BY THE WAY. I'VE SEEN SOME THINGS IN MY TIME, AND SHE'S...YEAH, SOMETHING'S GOING TO HAPPEN THERE."

"LET'S HOPE SO, RIGHT? WE COULD *USE* A LITTLE SOMETHING, AFTER CRAIT.

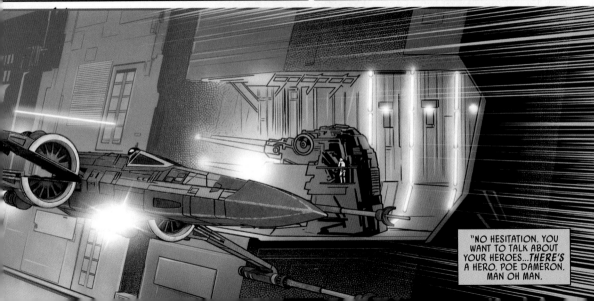

"NO HESITATION. YOU WANT TO TALK ABOUT YOUR HEROES...*THERE'S* A HERO. POE DAMERON. MAN OH MAN.

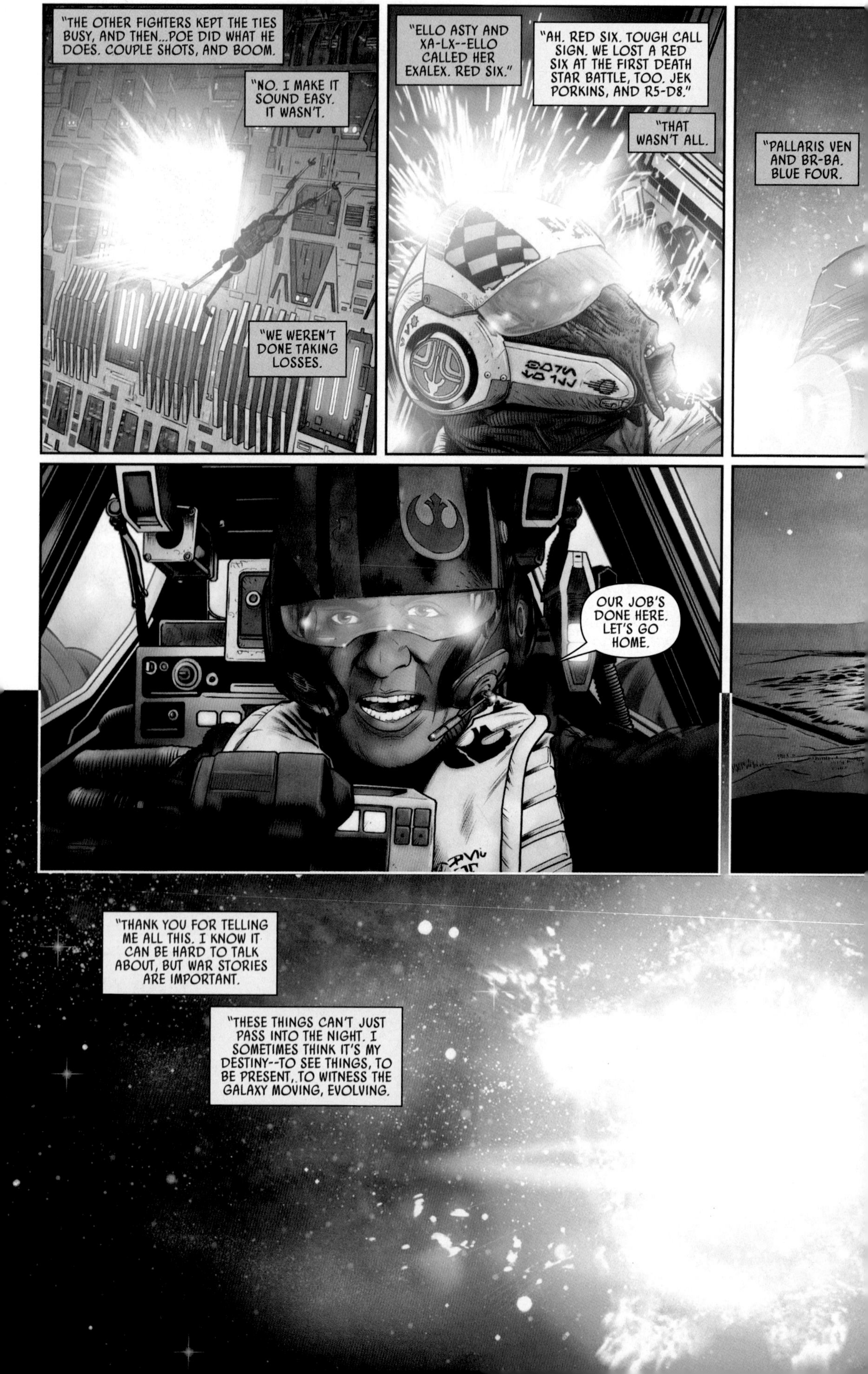
"THE OTHER FIGHTERS KEPT THE TIES BUSY, AND THEN...POE DID WHAT HE DOES. COUPLE SHOTS, AND BOOM.
"NO. I MAKE IT SOUND EASY. IT WASN'T.
"WE WEREN'T DONE TAKING LOSSES.
"ELLO ASTY AND XA-LX--ELLO CALLED HER EXALEX. RED SIX."
"AH. RED SIX. TOUGH CALL SIGN. WE LOST A RED SIX AT THE FIRST DEATH STAR BATTLE, TOO. JEK PORKINS, AND R5-D8."
"THAT WASN'T ALL.
"PALLARIS VEN AND BR-BA. BLUE FOUR.
OUR JOB'S DONE HERE. LET'S GO HOME.
"THANK YOU FOR TELLING ME ALL THIS. I KNOW IT CAN BE HARD TO TALK ABOUT, BUT WAR STORIES ARE IMPORTANT.
"THESE THINGS CAN'T JUST PASS INTO THE NIGHT. I SOMETIMES THINK IT'S MY DESTINY--TO SEE THINGS, TO BE PRESENT, TO WITNESS THE GALAXY MOVING, EVOLVING.

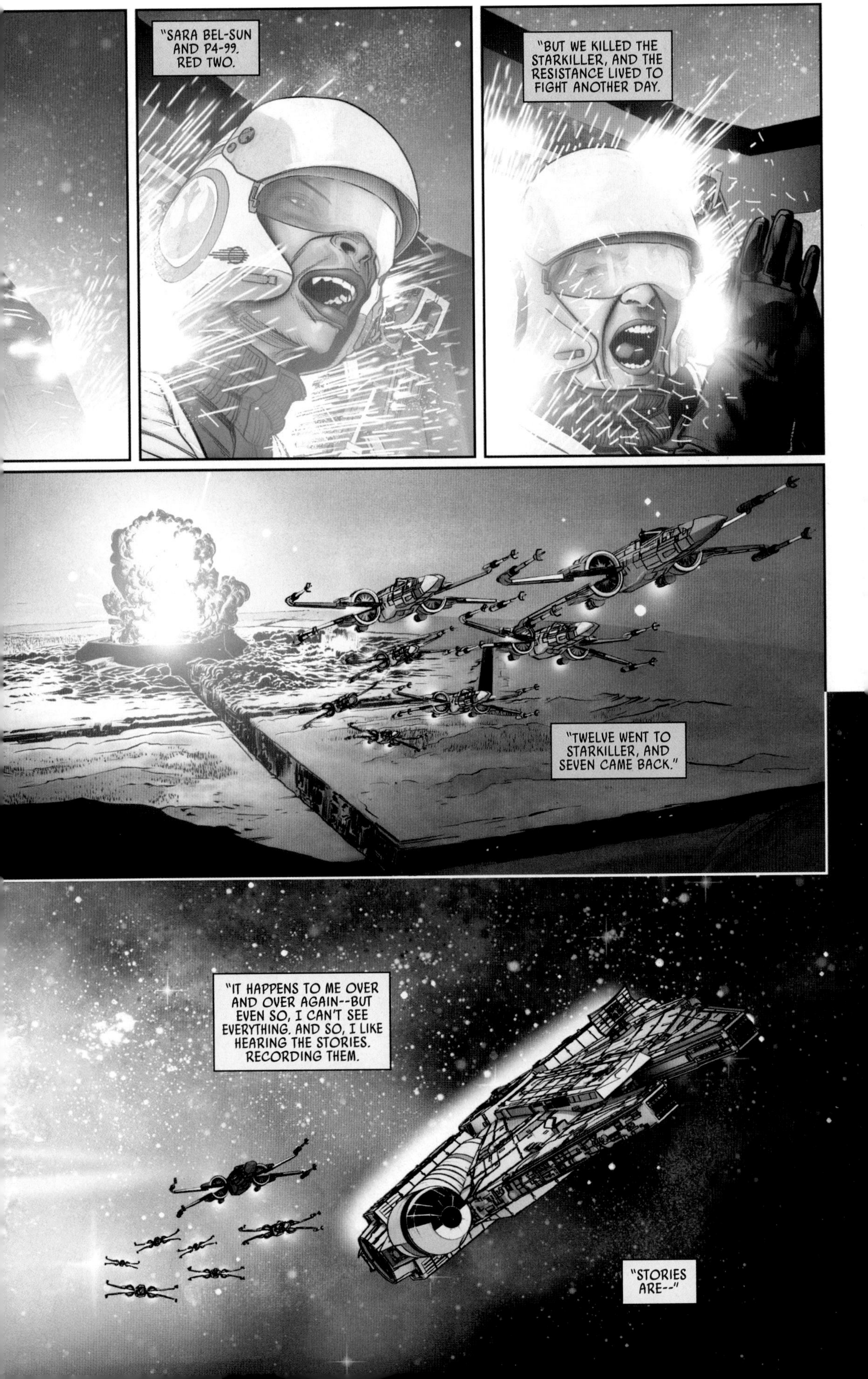
"SARA BEL-SUN AND P4-99. RED TWO.
"BUT WE KILLED THE STARKILLER, AND THE RESISTANCE LIVED TO FIGHT ANOTHER DAY.
"TWELVE WENT TO STARKILLER, AND SEVEN CAME BACK."
"IT HAPPENS TO ME OVER AND OVER AGAIN--BUT EVEN SO, I CAN'T SEE EVERYTHING. AND SO, I LIKE HEARING THE STORIES. RECORDING THEM.
"STORIES ARE--"

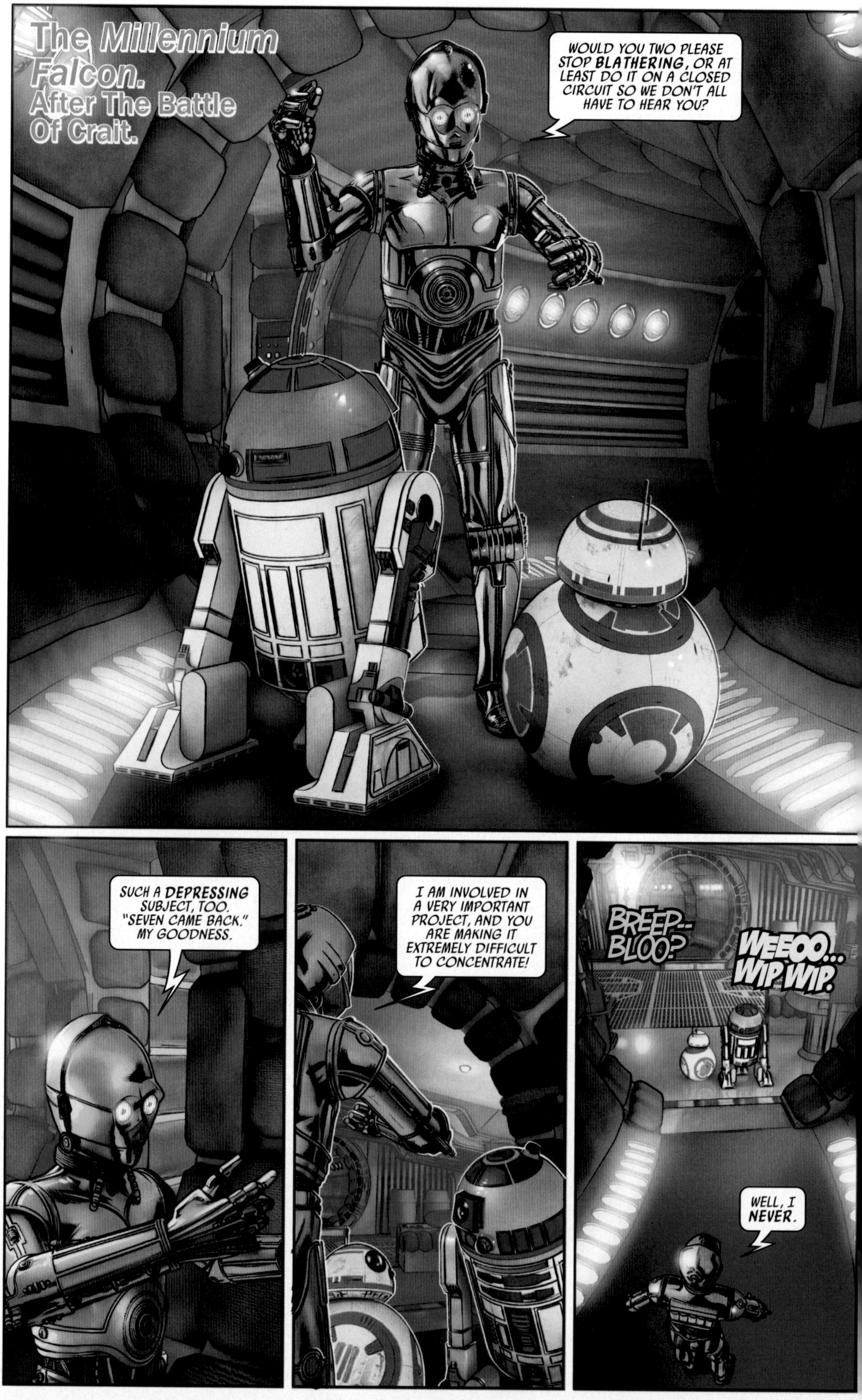
The Millennium Falcon. After The Battle Of Crait.
WOULD YOU TWO PLEASE STOP BLATHERING, OR AT LEAST DO IT ON A CLOSED CIRCUIT SO WE DON'T ALL HAVE TO HEAR YOU?
SUCH A DEPRESSING SUBJECT, TOO. "SEVEN CAME BACK." MY GOODNESS.
I AM INVOLVED IN A VERY IMPORTANT PROJECT, AND YOU ARE MAKING IT EXTREMELY DIFFICULT TO CONCENTRATE!
BREEP-BLOO?
WEEOO... WIP WIP.
WELL, I NEVER.

DON'T WORRY, MISS REY-- I DEALT WITH THOSE SILLY DROIDS. THEY WON'T BOTHER US ANY FURTHER.

NOW...WHERE WERE WE?

THIS PASSAGE HERE, THREEPIO.

AH, YES. I MUST SAY, THESE OLD JEDI TEXTS ARE EXTREMELY ANCIENT. THE LANGUAGES USED ARE...UNUSUAL, TO SAY THE LEAST.

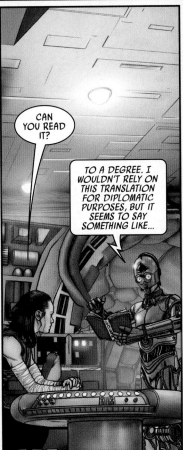

CAN YOU READ IT?

TO A DEGREE. I WOULDN'T RELY ON THIS TRANSLATION FOR DIPLOMATIC PURPOSES, BUT IT SEEMS TO SAY SOMETHING LIKE...

"THE FORCE IS THE LIGHT, THE FORCE IS THE DARK. JEDI CHOOSE THE LIGHT, FOR ALL IT REVEALS."

AH.

YOU KNOW, I LIKE THAT.

SEEMS LIKE A LOVELY PLACE TO BEGIN.

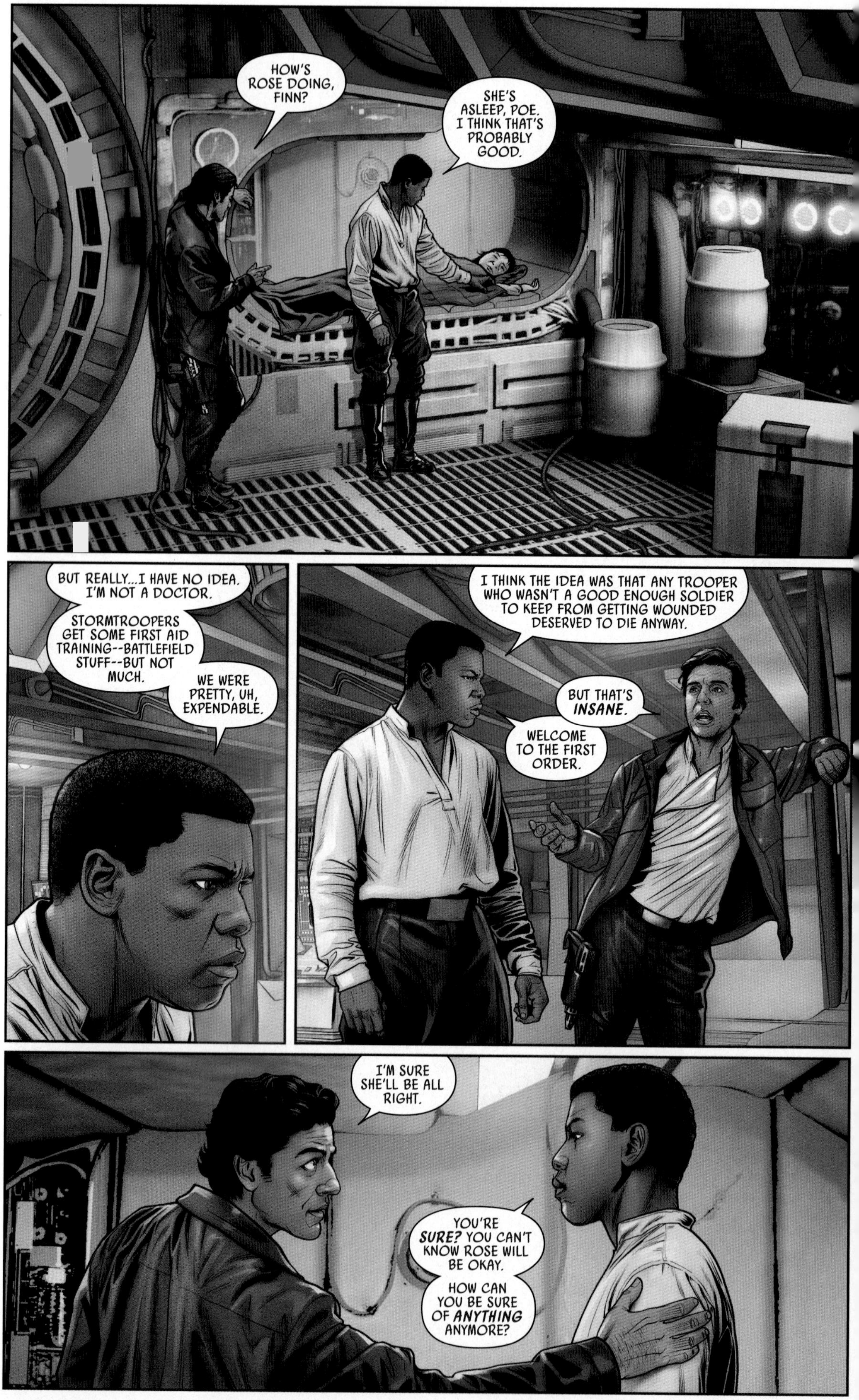

HOW'S ROSE DOING, FINN?
SHE'S ASLEEP, POE. I THINK THAT'S PROBABLY GOOD.
BUT REALLY...I HAVE NO IDEA. I'M NOT A DOCTOR.
STORMTROOPERS GET SOME FIRST AID TRAINING--BATTLEFIELD STUFF--BUT NOT MUCH.
WE WERE PRETTY, UH, EXPENDABLE.
I THINK THE IDEA WAS THAT ANY TROOPER WHO WASN'T A GOOD ENOUGH SOLDIER TO KEEP FROM GETTING WOUNDED DESERVED TO DIE ANYWAY.
BUT THAT'S INSANE.
WELCOME TO THE FIRST ORDER.
I'M SURE SHE'LL BE ALL RIGHT.
YOU'RE SURE? YOU CAN'T KNOW ROSE WILL BE OKAY.
HOW CAN YOU BE SURE OF ANYTHING ANYMORE?

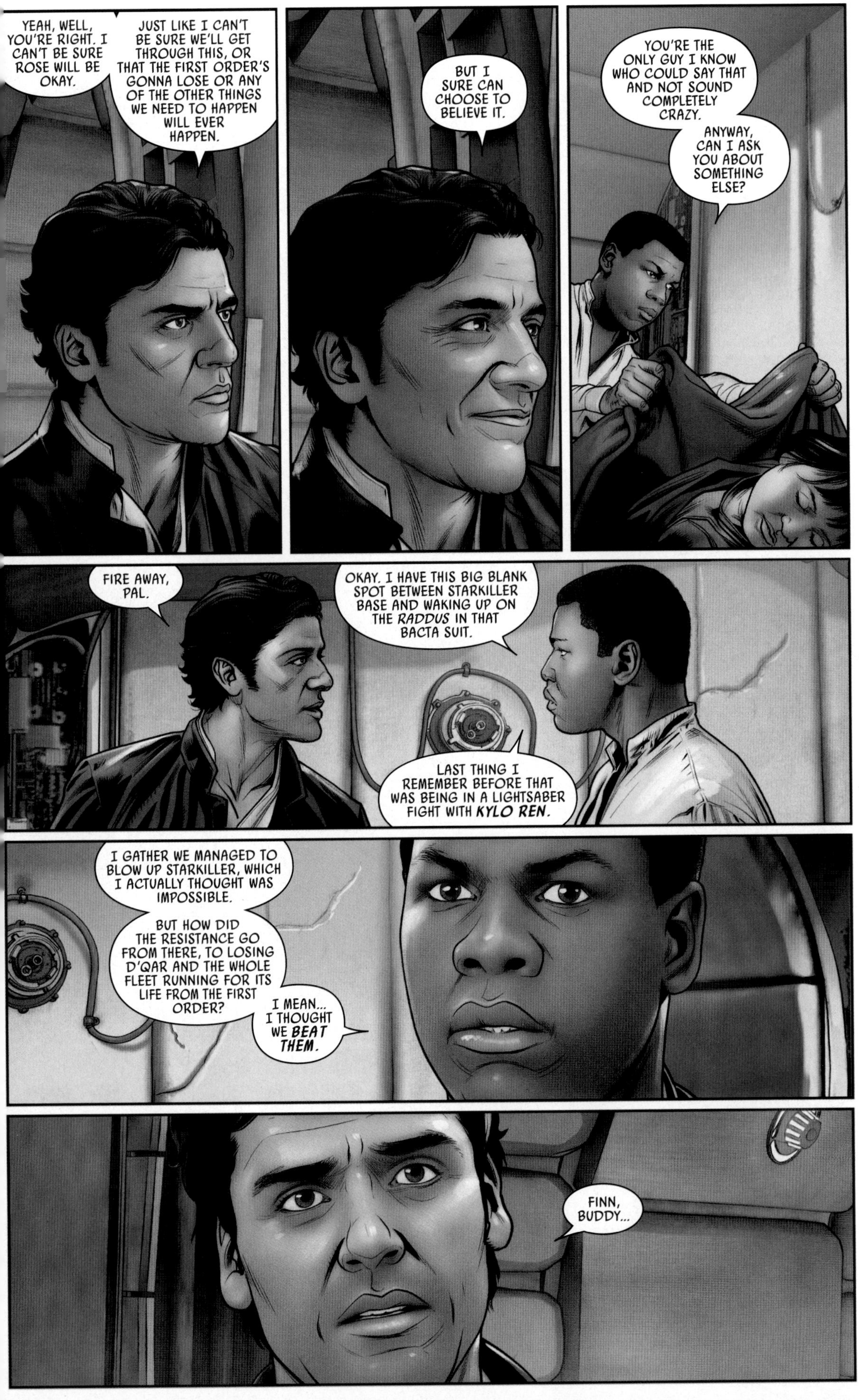
YEAH, WELL, YOU'RE RIGHT. I CAN'T BE SURE ROSE WILL BE OKAY.
JUST LIKE I CAN'T BE SURE WE'LL GET THROUGH THIS, OR THAT THE FIRST ORDER'S GONNA LOSE OR ANY OF THE OTHER THINGS WE NEED TO HAPPEN WILL EVER HAPPEN.
BUT I SURE CAN CHOOSE TO BELIEVE IT.
YOU'RE THE ONLY GUY I KNOW WHO COULD SAY THAT AND NOT SOUND COMPLETELY CRAZY.
ANYWAY, CAN I ASK YOU ABOUT SOMETHING ELSE?
FIRE AWAY, PAL.
OKAY. I HAVE THIS BIG BLANK SPOT BETWEEN STARKILLER BASE AND WAKING UP ON THE *RADDUS* IN THAT BACTA SUIT.
LAST THING I REMEMBER BEFORE THAT WAS BEING IN A LIGHTSABER FIGHT WITH ***KYLO REN.***
I GATHER WE MANAGED TO BLOW UP STARKILLER, WHICH I ACTUALLY THOUGHT WAS IMPOSSIBLE.
BUT HOW DID THE RESISTANCE GO FROM THERE, TO LOSING D'QAR AND THE WHOLE FLEET RUNNING FOR ITS LIFE FROM THE FIRST ORDER?
I MEAN... I THOUGHT WE ***BEAT THEM.***
FINN, BUDDY...

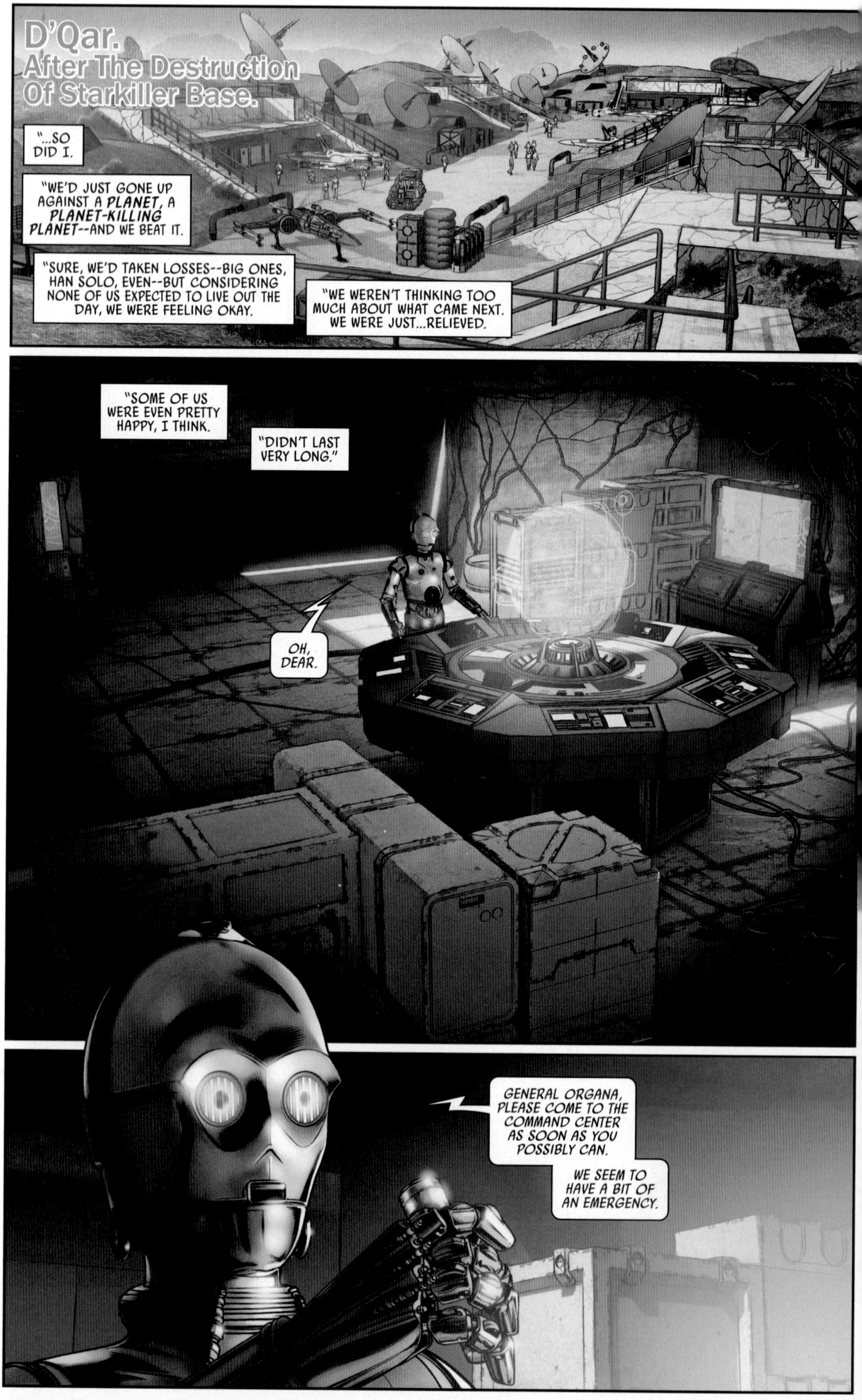
D'Qar.
After The Destruction Of Starkiller Base.
"...SO DID I.
"WE'D JUST GONE UP AGAINST A *PLANET*, A *PLANET-KILLING PLANET*--AND WE BEAT IT.
"SURE, WE'D TAKEN LOSSES--BIG ONES, HAN SOLO, EVEN--BUT CONSIDERING NONE OF US EXPECTED TO LIVE OUT THE DAY, WE WERE FEELING OKAY.
"WE WEREN'T THINKING TOO MUCH ABOUT WHAT CAME NEXT. WE WERE JUST...RELIEVED.
"SOME OF US WERE EVEN PRETTY HAPPY, I THINK.
"DIDN'T LAST VERY LONG."
OH, DEAR.
GENERAL ORGANA, PLEASE COME TO THE COMMAND CENTER AS SOON AS YOU POSSIBLY CAN.
WE SEEM TO HAVE A BIT OF AN EMERGENCY.

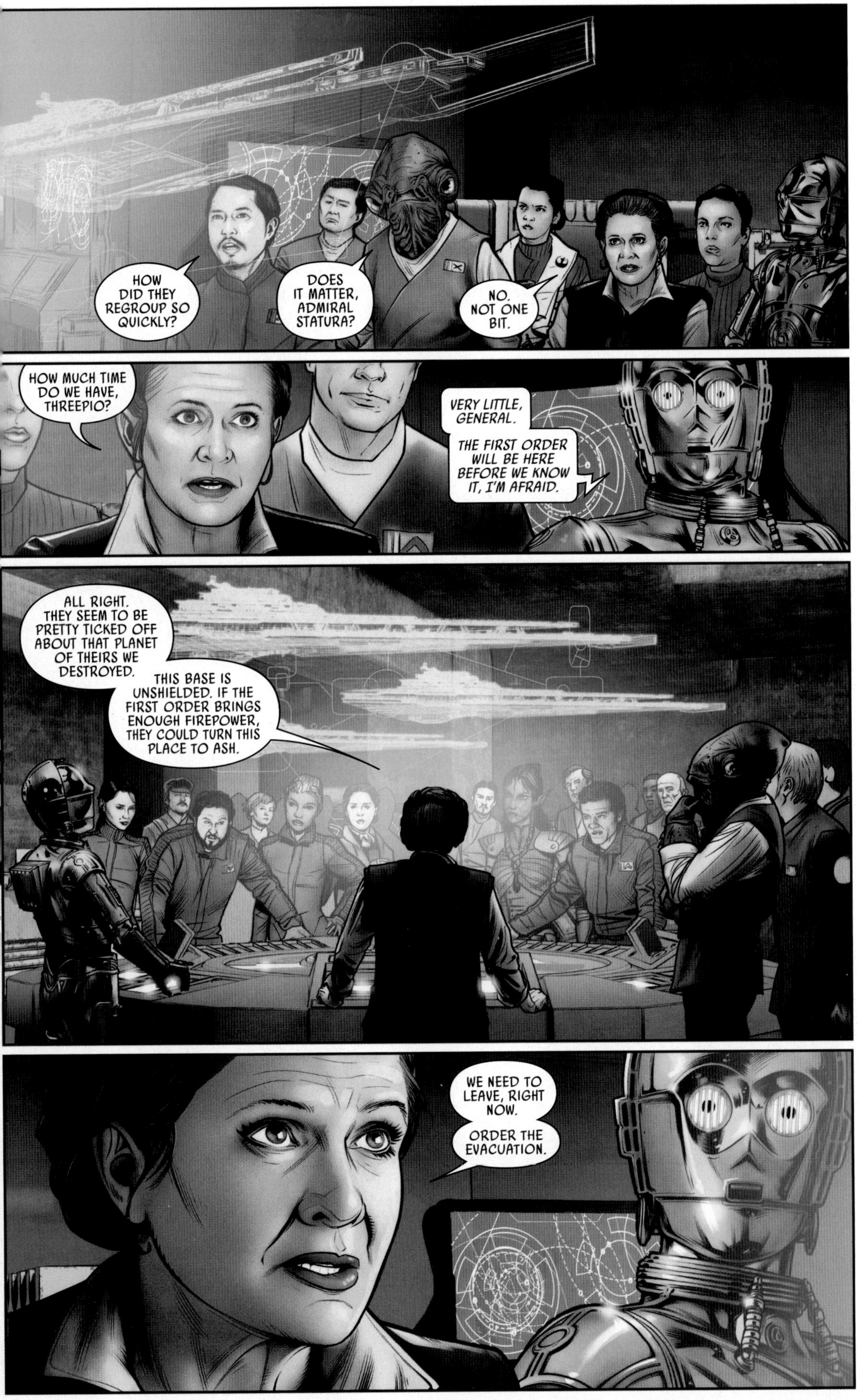
HOW DID THEY REGROUP SO QUICKLY?
DOES IT MATTER, ADMIRAL STATURA?
NO. NOT ONE BIT.
HOW MUCH TIME DO WE HAVE, THREEPIO?
VERY LITTLE, GENERAL.
THE FIRST ORDER WILL BE HERE BEFORE WE KNOW IT, I'M AFRAID.
ALL RIGHT. THEY SEEM TO BE PRETTY TICKED OFF ABOUT THAT PLANET OF THEIRS WE DESTROYED.
THIS BASE IS UNSHIELDED. IF THE FIRST ORDER BRINGS ENOUGH FIREPOWER, THEY COULD TURN THIS PLACE TO ASH.
WE NEED TO LEAVE, RIGHT NOW.
ORDER THE EVACUATION.

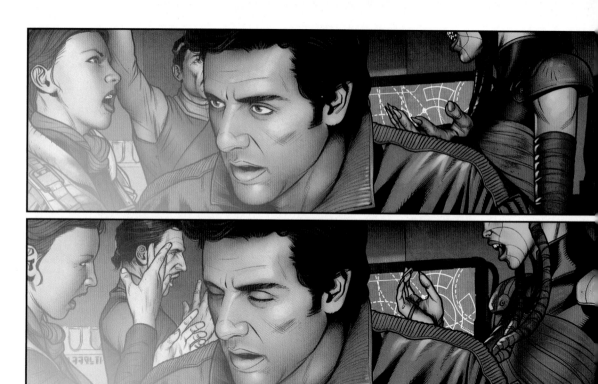

IT WON'T WORK.

THERE'S NOT ENOUGH TIME TO GET EVERYONE AWAY BEFORE THE FIRST ORDER GETS HERE.

BUT I HAVE AN IDEA.

IT'S PRETTY SIMPLE.

I'M LISTENING.

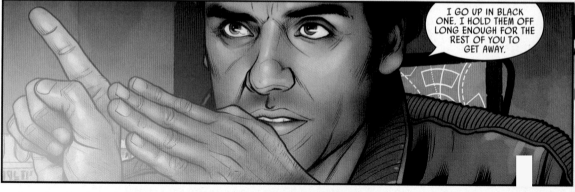

I GO UP IN BLACK ONE. I HOLD THEM OFF LONG ENOUGH FOR THE REST OF YOU TO GET AWAY.

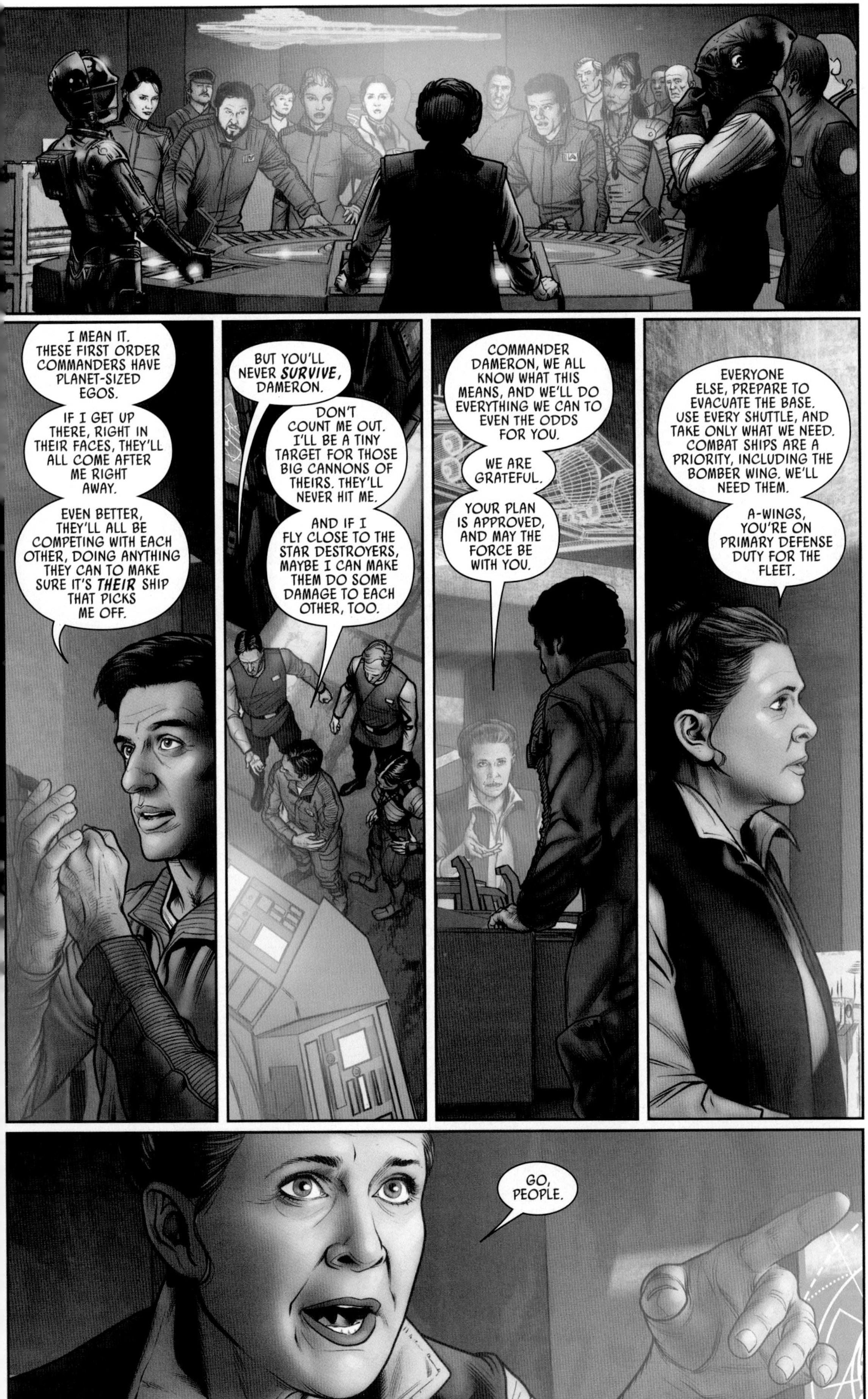
I MEAN IT. THESE FIRST ORDER COMMANDERS HAVE PLANET-SIZED EGOS.
IF I GET UP THERE, RIGHT IN THEIR FACES, THEY'LL ALL COME AFTER ME RIGHT AWAY.
EVEN BETTER, THEY'LL ALL BE COMPETING WITH EACH OTHER, DOING ANYTHING THEY CAN TO MAKE SURE IT'S ***THEIR*** SHIP THAT PICKS ME OFF.
BUT YOU'LL NEVER ***SURVIVE***, DAMERON.
DON'T COUNT ME OUT. I'LL BE A TINY TARGET FOR THOSE BIG CANNONS OF THEIRS. THEY'LL NEVER HIT ME.
AND IF I FLY CLOSE TO THE STAR DESTROYERS, MAYBE I CAN MAKE THEM DO SOME DAMAGE TO EACH OTHER, TOO.
COMMANDER DAMERON, WE ALL KNOW WHAT THIS MEANS, AND WE'LL DO EVERYTHING WE CAN TO EVEN THE ODDS FOR YOU.
WE ARE GRATEFUL.
YOUR PLAN IS APPROVED, AND MAY THE FORCE BE WITH YOU.
EVERYONE ELSE, PREPARE TO EVACUATE THE BASE. USE EVERY SHUTTLE, AND TAKE ONLY WHAT WE NEED. COMBAT SHIPS ARE A PRIORITY, INCLUDING THE BOMBER WING. WE'LL NEED THEM.
A-WINGS, YOU'RE ON PRIMARY DEFENSE DUTY FOR THE FLEET.
GO, PEOPLE.

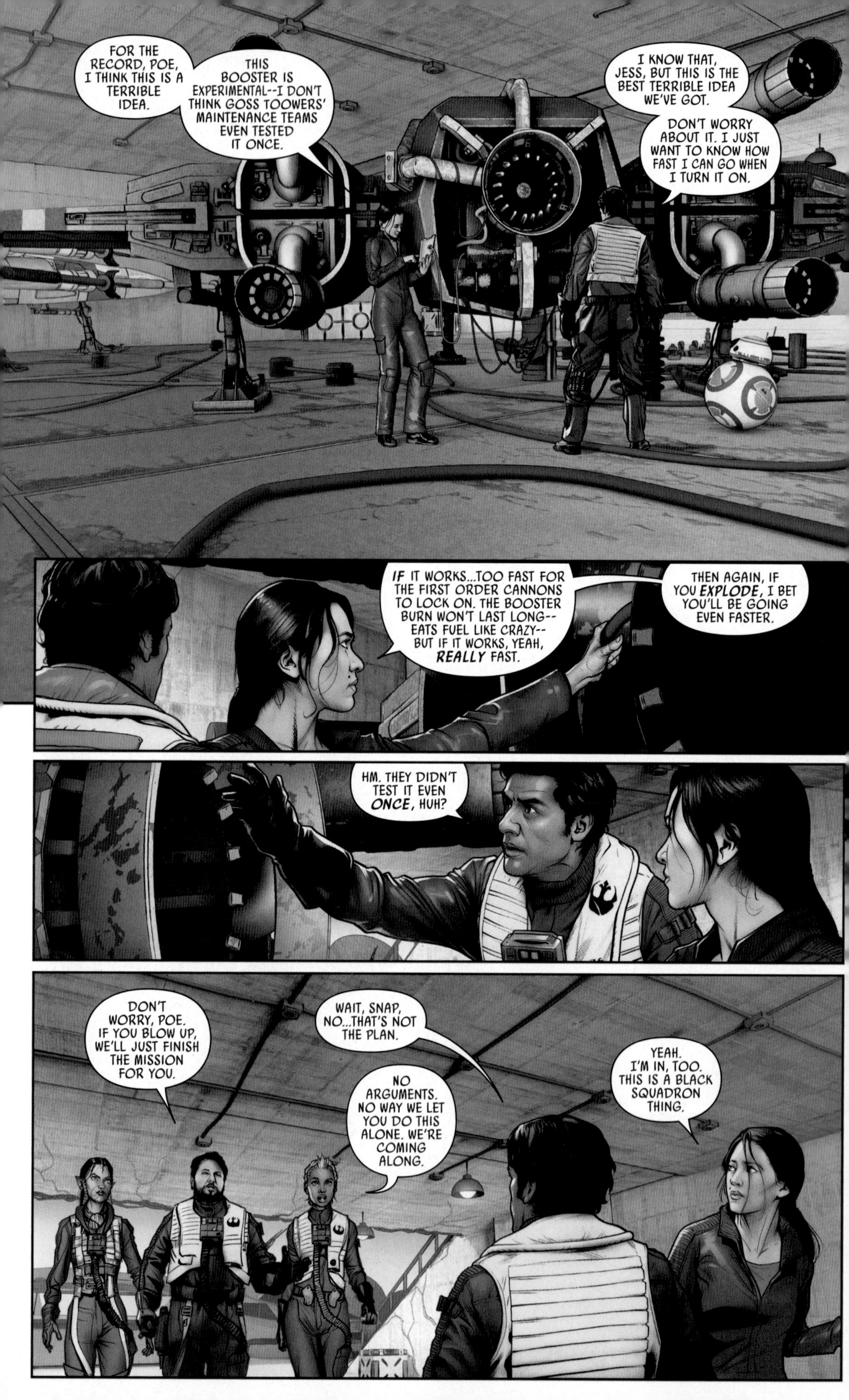
FOR THE RECORD, POE, I THINK THIS IS A TERRIBLE IDEA.
THIS BOOSTER IS EXPERIMENTAL--I DON'T THINK GOSS TOOWERS' MAINTENANCE TEAMS EVEN TESTED IT ONCE.
I KNOW THAT, JESS, BUT THIS IS THE BEST TERRIBLE IDEA WE'VE GOT.
DON'T WORRY ABOUT IT. I JUST WANT TO KNOW HOW FAST I CAN GO WHEN I TURN IT ON.
IF IT WORKS...TOO FAST FOR THE FIRST ORDER CANNONS TO LOCK ON. THE BOOSTER BURN WON'T LAST LONG-- EATS FUEL LIKE CRAZY-- BUT IF IT WORKS, YEAH, REALLY FAST.
THEN AGAIN, IF YOU EXPLODE, I BET YOU'LL BE GOING EVEN FASTER.
HM. THEY DIDN'T TEST IT EVEN ONCE, HUH?
DON'T WORRY, POE. IF YOU BLOW UP, WE'LL JUST FINISH THE MISSION FOR YOU.
WAIT, SNAP, NO...THAT'S NOT THE PLAN.
NO ARGUMENTS. NO WAY WE LET YOU DO THIS ALONE. WE'RE COMING ALONG.
YEAH. I'M IN, TOO. THIS IS A BLACK SQUADRON THING.

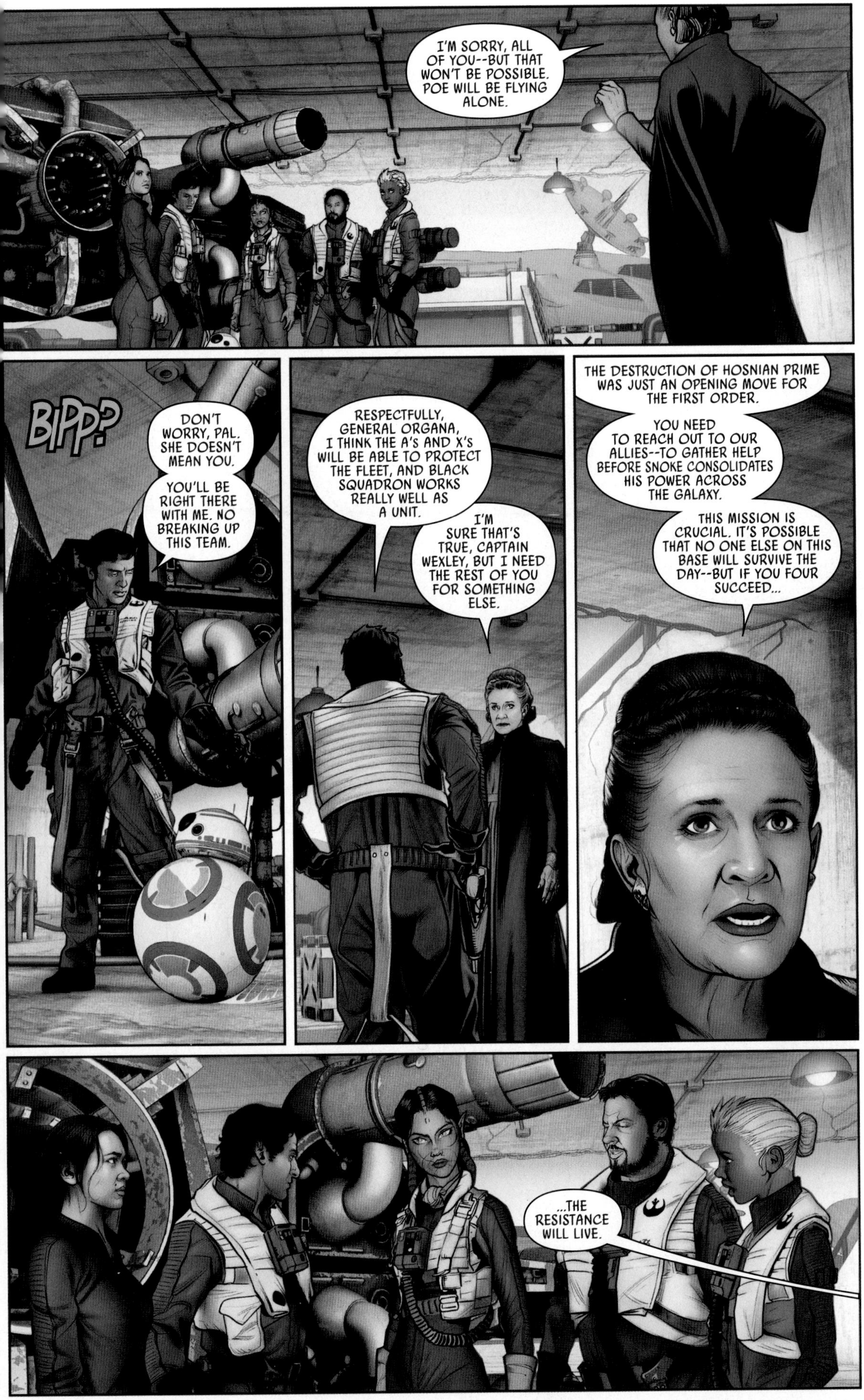
I'M SORRY, ALL OF YOU--BUT THAT WON'T BE POSSIBLE. POE WILL BE FLYING ALONE.
BIPP?
DON'T WORRY, PAL. SHE DOESN'T MEAN YOU.
YOU'LL BE RIGHT THERE WITH ME. NO BREAKING UP THIS TEAM.
RESPECTFULLY, GENERAL ORGANA, I THINK THE A'S AND X'S WILL BE ABLE TO PROTECT THE FLEET, AND BLACK SQUADRON WORKS REALLY WELL AS A UNIT.
I'M SURE THAT'S TRUE, CAPTAIN WEXLEY, BUT I NEED THE REST OF YOU FOR SOMETHING ELSE.
THE DESTRUCTION OF HOSNIAN PRIME WAS JUST AN OPENING MOVE FOR THE FIRST ORDER.
YOU NEED TO REACH OUT TO OUR ALLIES--TO GATHER HELP BEFORE SNOKE CONSOLIDATES HIS POWER ACROSS THE GALAXY.
THIS MISSION IS CRUCIAL. IT'S POSSIBLE THAT NO ONE ELSE ON THIS BASE WILL SURVIVE THE DAY--BUT IF YOU FOUR SUCCEED...
...THE RESISTANCE WILL LIVE.

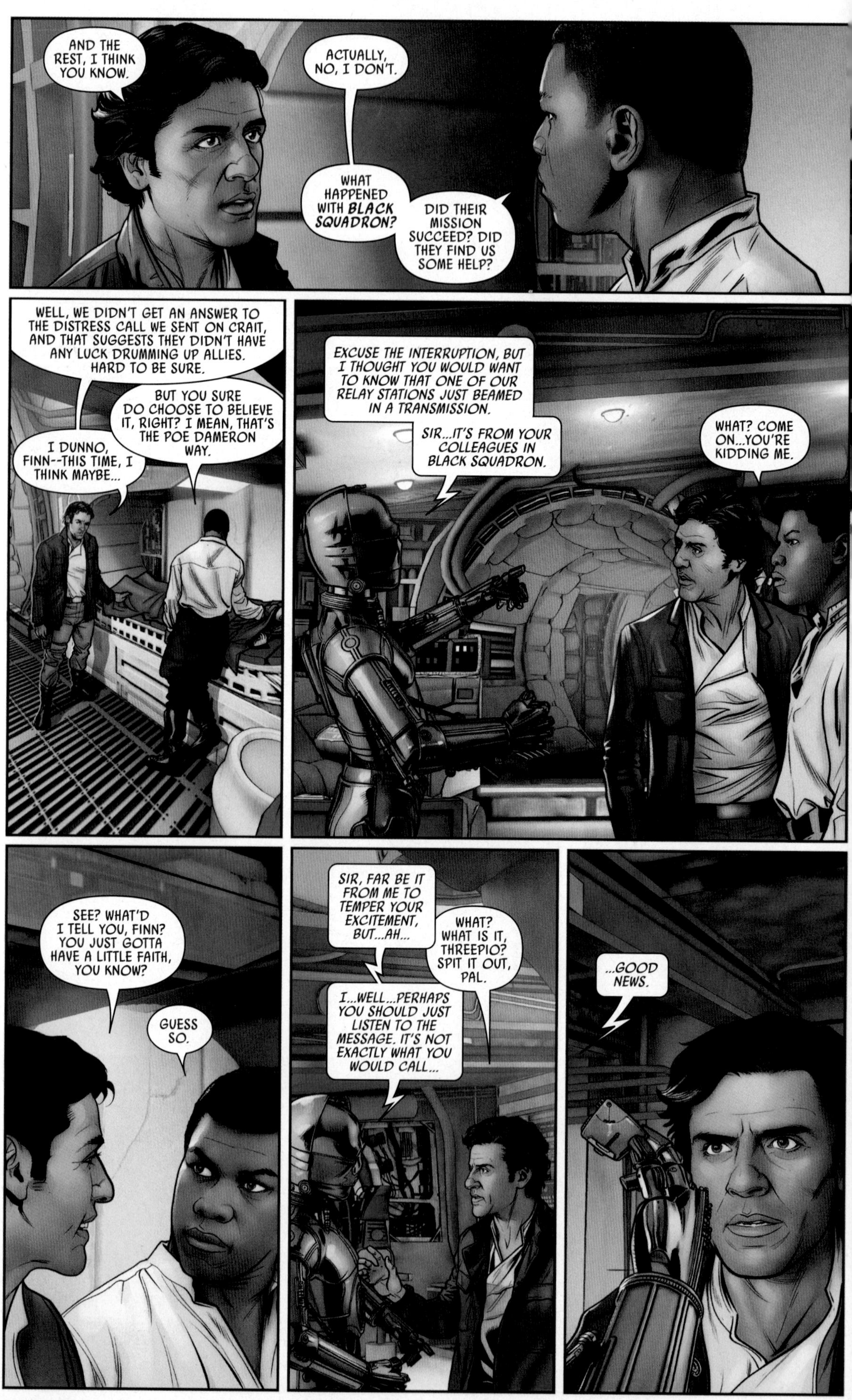
AND THE REST, I THINK YOU KNOW.
ACTUALLY, NO, I DON'T.
WHAT HAPPENED WITH BLACK SQUADRON?
DID THEIR MISSION SUCCEED? DID THEY FIND US SOME HELP?
WELL, WE DIDN'T GET AN ANSWER TO THE DISTRESS CALL WE SENT ON CRAIT, AND THAT SUGGESTS THEY DIDN'T HAVE ANY LUCK DRUMMING UP ALLIES. HARD TO BE SURE.
I DUNNO, FINN--THIS TIME, I THINK MAYBE...
BUT YOU SURE DO CHOOSE TO BELIEVE IT, RIGHT? I MEAN, THAT'S THE POE DAMERON WAY.
EXCUSE THE INTERRUPTION, BUT I THOUGHT YOU WOULD WANT TO KNOW THAT ONE OF OUR RELAY STATIONS JUST BEAMED IN A TRANSMISSION.
SIR...IT'S FROM YOUR COLLEAGUES IN BLACK SQUADRON.
WHAT? COME ON...YOU'RE KIDDING ME.
SEE? WHAT'D I TELL YOU, FINN? YOU JUST GOTTA HAVE A LITTLE FAITH, YOU KNOW?
GUESS SO.
SIR, FAR BE IT FROM ME TO TEMPER YOUR EXCITEMENT, BUT...AH...
WHAT? WHAT IS IT, THREEPIO? SPIT IT OUT, PAL.
I...WELL...PERHAPS YOU SHOULD JUST LISTEN TO THE MESSAGE. IT'S NOT EXACTLY WHAT YOU WOULD CALL...
...GOOD NEWS.

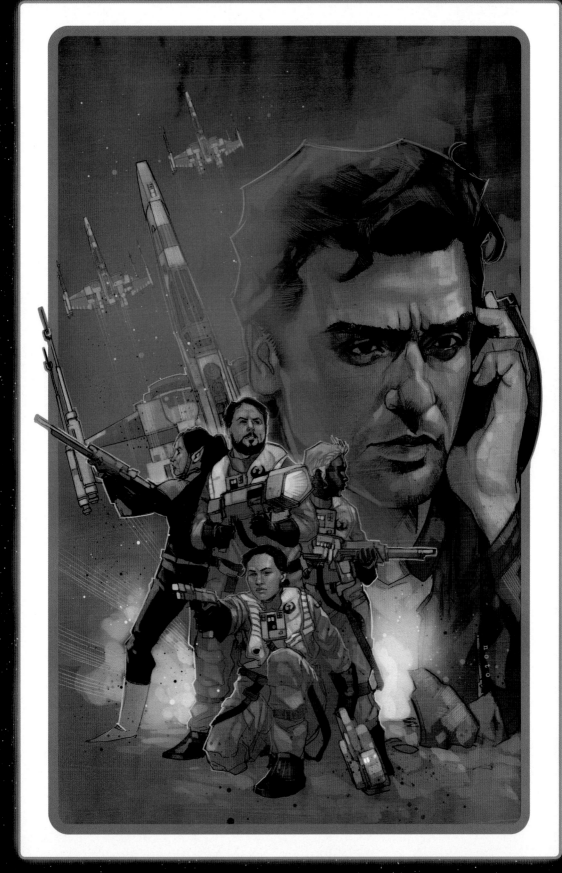

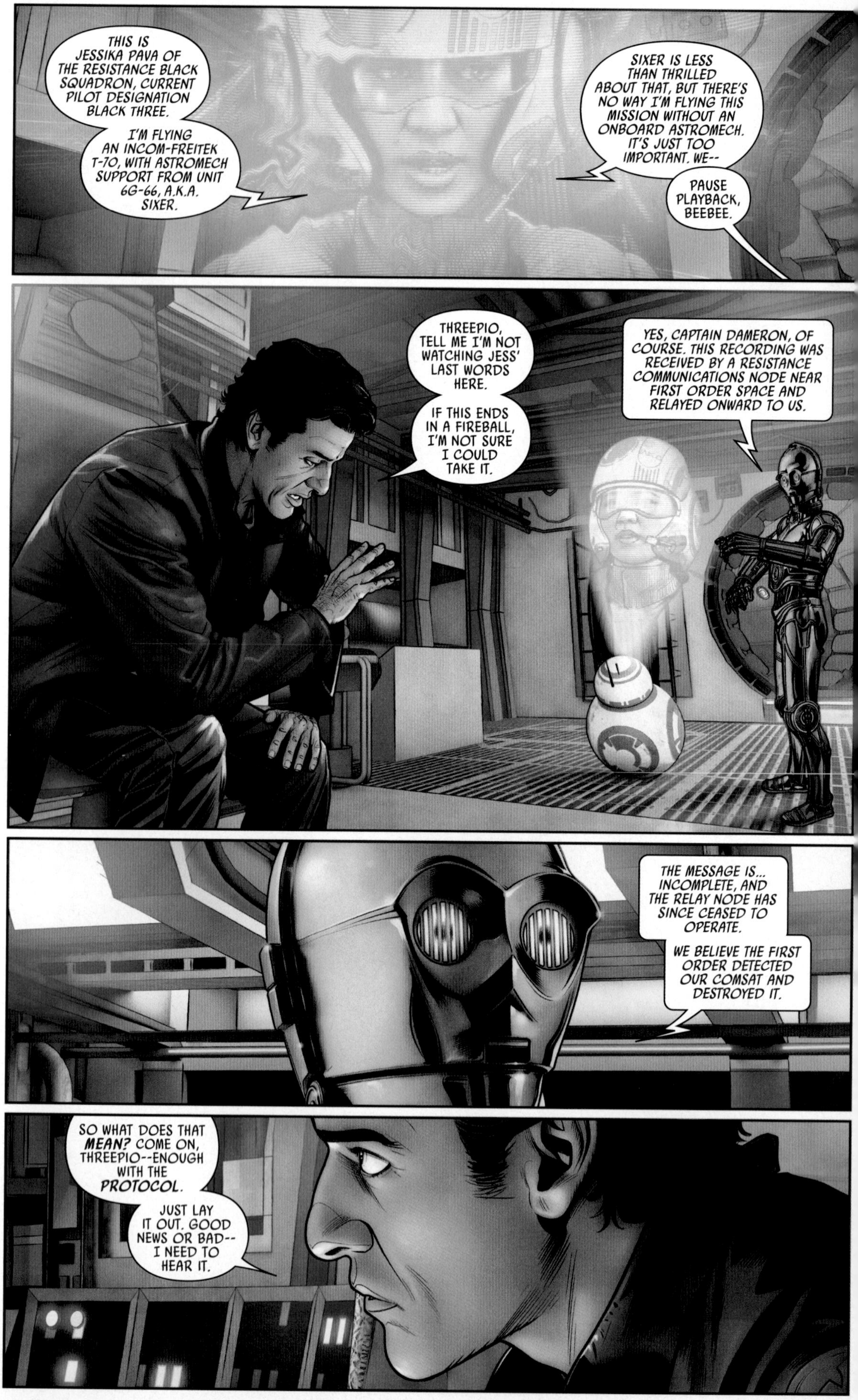
THIS IS JESSIKA PAVA OF THE RESISTANCE BLACK SQUADRON, CURRENT PILOT DESIGNATION BLACK THREE.
I'M FLYING AN INCOM-FREITEK T-70, WITH ASTROMECH SUPPORT FROM UNIT 6G-66, A.K.A. SIXER.
SIXER IS LESS THAN THRILLED ABOUT THAT, BUT THERE'S NO WAY I'M FLYING THIS MISSION WITHOUT AN ONBOARD ASTROMECH. IT'S JUST TOO IMPORTANT. WE--
PAUSE PLAYBACK, BEEBEE.
THREEPIO, TELL ME I'M NOT WATCHING JESS' LAST WORDS HERE.
IF THIS ENDS IN A FIREBALL, I'M NOT SURE I COULD TAKE IT.
YES, CAPTAIN DAMERON, OF COURSE. THIS RECORDING WAS RECEIVED BY A RESISTANCE COMMUNICATIONS NODE NEAR FIRST ORDER SPACE AND RELAYED ONWARD TO US.
THE MESSAGE IS... INCOMPLETE, AND THE RELAY NODE HAS SINCE CEASED TO OPERATE.
WE BELIEVE THE FIRST ORDER DETECTED OUR COMSAT AND DESTROYED IT.
SO WHAT DOES THAT **MEAN?** COME ON, THREEPIO--ENOUGH WITH THE **PROTOCOL**.
JUST LAY IT OUT. GOOD NEWS OR BAD-- I NEED TO HEAR IT.

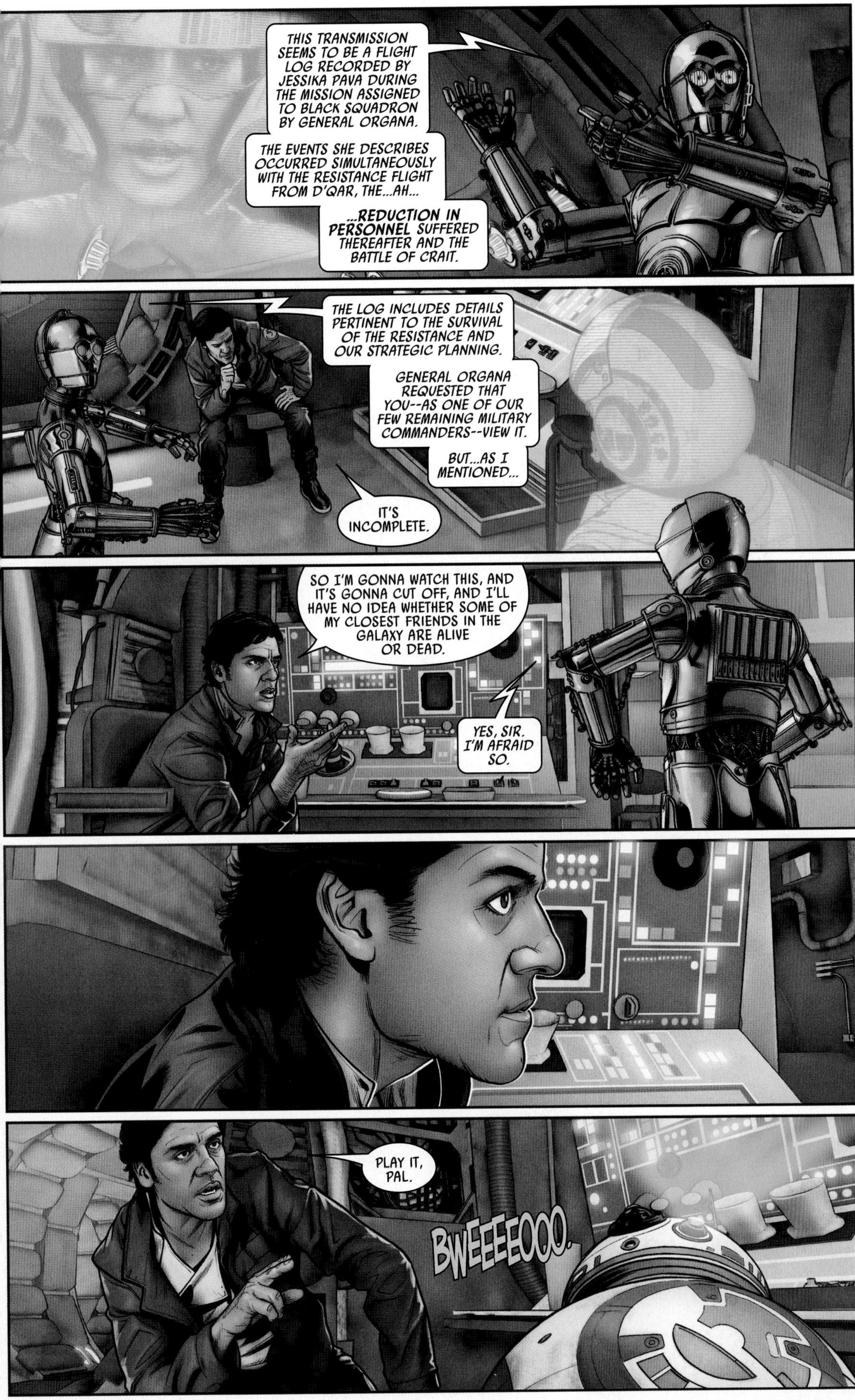
THIS TRANSMISSION SEEMS TO BE A FLIGHT LOG RECORDED BY JESSIKA PAVA DURING THE MISSION ASSIGNED TO BLACK SQUADRON BY GENERAL ORGANA.
THE EVENTS SHE DESCRIBES OCCURRED SIMULTANEOUSLY WITH THE RESISTANCE FLIGHT FROM D'QAR, THE...AH...
...REDUCTION IN PERSONNEL SUFFERED THEREAFTER AND THE BATTLE OF CRAIT.
THE LOG INCLUDES DETAILS PERTINENT TO THE SURVIVAL OF THE RESISTANCE AND OUR STRATEGIC PLANNING.
GENERAL ORGANA REQUESTED THAT YOU--AS ONE OF OUR FEW REMAINING MILITARY COMMANDERS--VIEW IT.
BUT...AS I MENTIONED...
IT'S INCOMPLETE.
SO I'M GONNA WATCH THIS, AND IT'S GONNA CUT OFF, AND I'LL HAVE NO IDEA WHETHER SOME OF MY CLOSEST FRIENDS IN THE GALAXY ARE ALIVE OR DEAD.
YES, SIR. I'M AFRAID SO.
PLAY IT, PAL.
BWEEEEOOO.

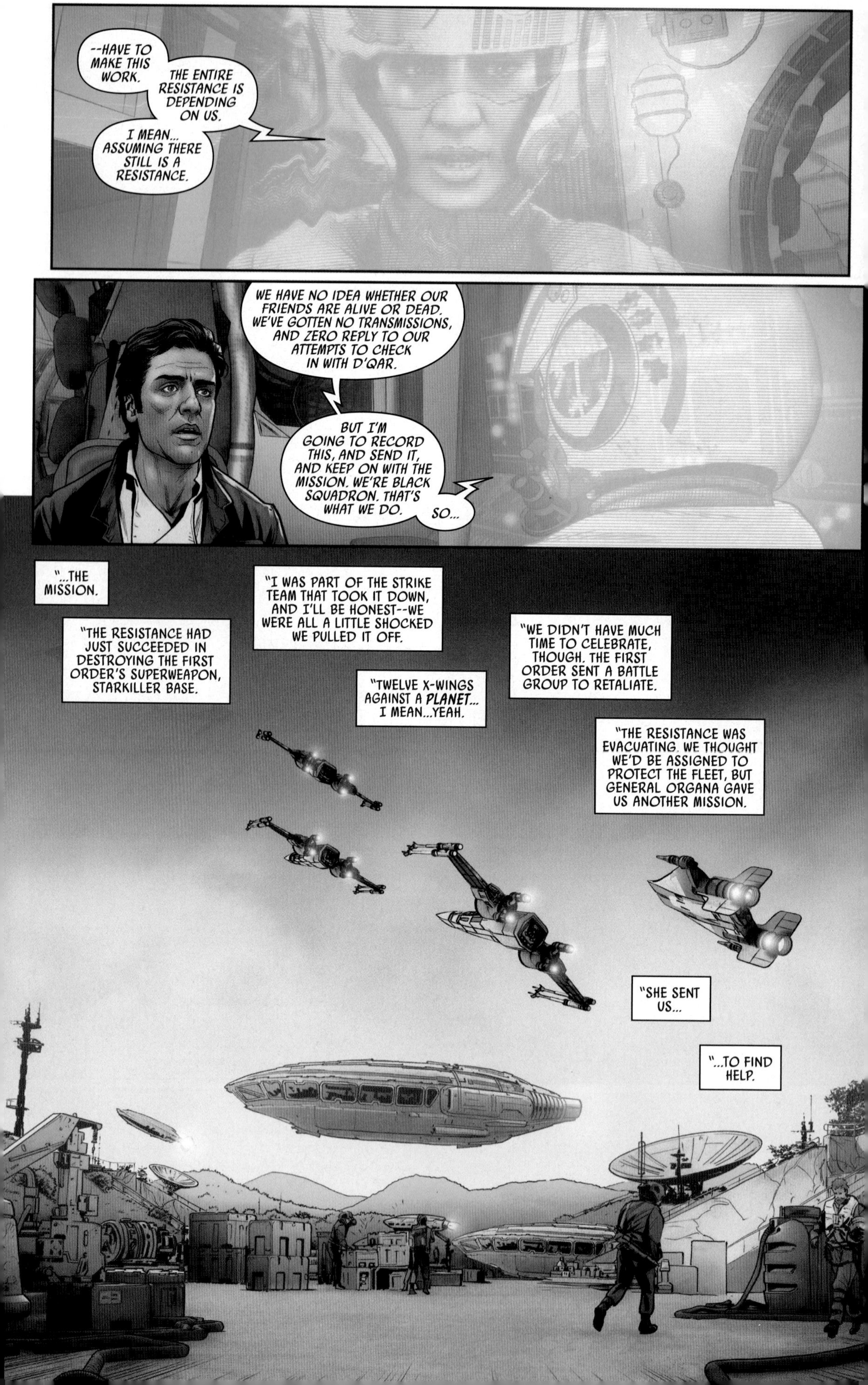
--HAVE TO MAKE THIS WORK.
THE ENTIRE RESISTANCE IS DEPENDING ON US.
I MEAN... ASSUMING THERE STILL IS A RESISTANCE.
WE HAVE NO IDEA WHETHER OUR FRIENDS ARE ALIVE OR DEAD. WE'VE GOTTEN NO TRANSMISSIONS, AND ZERO REPLY TO OUR ATTEMPTS TO CHECK IN WITH D'QAR.
BUT I'M GOING TO RECORD THIS, AND SEND IT, AND KEEP ON WITH THE MISSION. WE'RE BLACK SQUADRON. THAT'S WHAT WE DO.
SO...
"...THE MISSION.
"THE RESISTANCE HAD JUST SUCCEEDED IN DESTROYING THE FIRST ORDER'S SUPERWEAPON, STARKILLER BASE.
"I WAS PART OF THE STRIKE TEAM THAT TOOK IT DOWN, AND I'LL BE HONEST--WE WERE ALL A LITTLE SHOCKED WE PULLED IT OFF.
"TWELVE X-WINGS AGAINST A *PLANET*... I MEAN...YEAH.
"WE DIDN'T HAVE MUCH TIME TO CELEBRATE, THOUGH. THE FIRST ORDER SENT A BATTLE GROUP TO RETALIATE.
"THE RESISTANCE WAS EVACUATING. WE THOUGHT WE'D BE ASSIGNED TO PROTECT THE FLEET, BUT GENERAL ORGANA GAVE US ANOTHER MISSION.
"SHE SENT US...
"...TO FIND HELP.

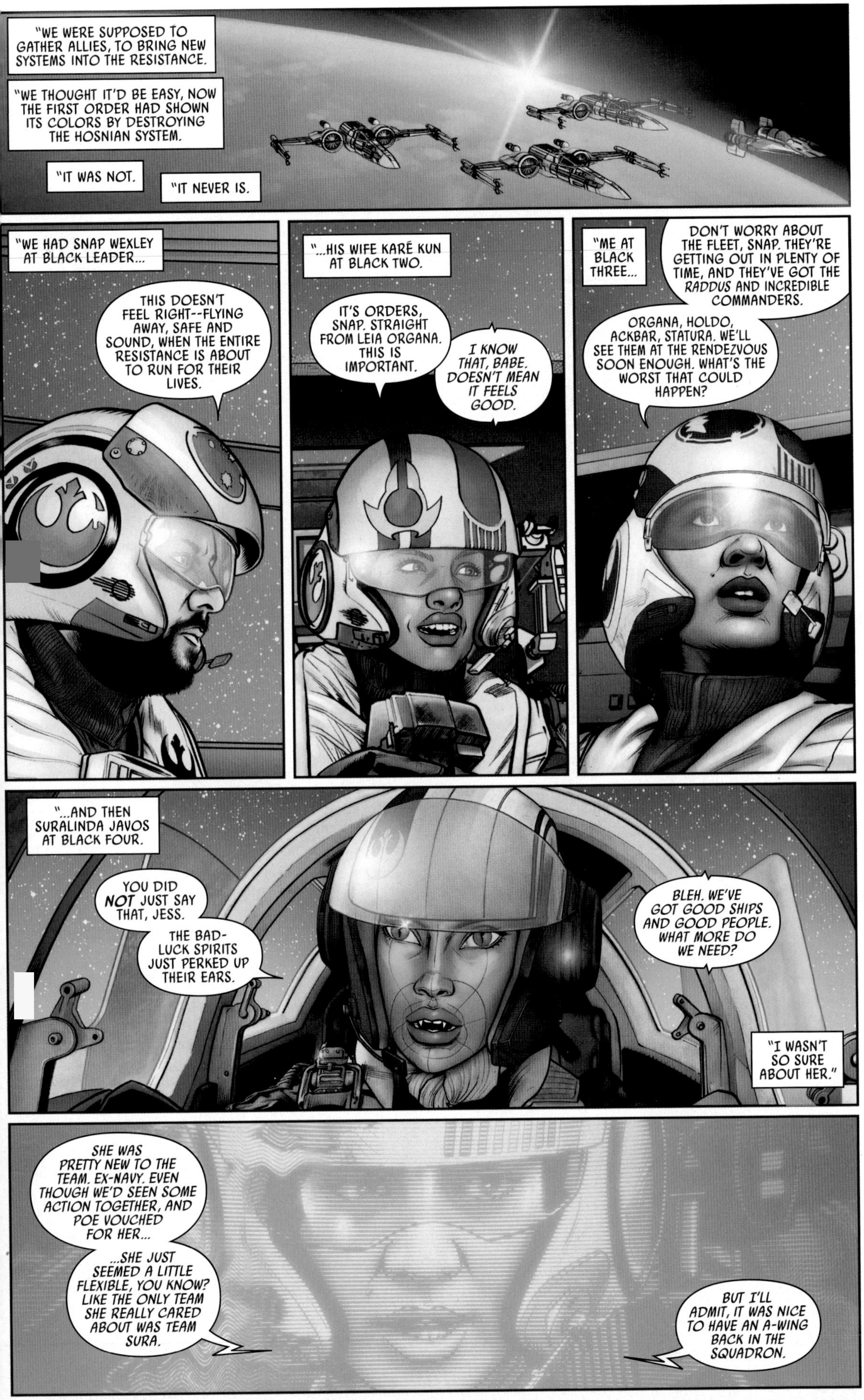

"WE WERE SUPPOSED TO GATHER ALLIES, TO BRING NEW SYSTEMS INTO THE RESISTANCE.
"WE THOUGHT IT'D BE EASY, NOW THE FIRST ORDER HAD SHOWN ITS COLORS BY DESTROYING THE HOSNIAN SYSTEM.
"IT WAS NOT.
"IT NEVER IS.
"WE HAD SNAP WEXLEY AT BLACK LEADER...
THIS DOESN'T FEEL RIGHT--FLYING AWAY, SAFE AND SOUND, WHEN THE ENTIRE RESISTANCE IS ABOUT TO RUN FOR THEIR LIVES.
"...HIS WIFE KARÉ KUN AT BLACK TWO.
IT'S ORDERS, SNAP. STRAIGHT FROM LEIA ORGANA. THIS IS IMPORTANT.
I KNOW THAT, BABE. DOESN'T MEAN IT FEELS GOOD.
"ME AT BLACK THREE...
DON'T WORRY ABOUT THE FLEET, SNAP. THEY'RE GETTING OUT IN PLENTY OF TIME, AND THEY'VE GOT THE RADDUS AND INCREDIBLE COMMANDERS.
ORGANA, HOLDO, ACKBAR, STATURA. WE'LL SEE THEM AT THE RENDEZVOUS SOON ENOUGH. WHAT'S THE WORST THAT COULD HAPPEN?
"...AND THEN SURALINDA JAVOS AT BLACK FOUR.
YOU DID NOT JUST SAY THAT, JESS.
THE BAD-LUCK SPIRITS JUST PERKED UP THEIR EARS.
BLEH. WE'VE GOT GOOD SHIPS AND GOOD PEOPLE. WHAT MORE DO WE NEED?
"I WASN'T SO SURE ABOUT HER."
SHE WAS PRETTY NEW TO THE TEAM. EX-NAVY. EVEN THOUGH WE'D SEEN SOME ACTION TOGETHER, AND POE VOUCHED FOR HER...
...SHE JUST SEEMED A LITTLE FLEXIBLE, YOU KNOW? LIKE THE ONLY TEAM SHE REALLY CARED ABOUT WAS TEAM SURA.
BUT I'LL ADMIT, IT WAS NICE TO HAVE AN A-WING BACK IN THE SQUADRON.

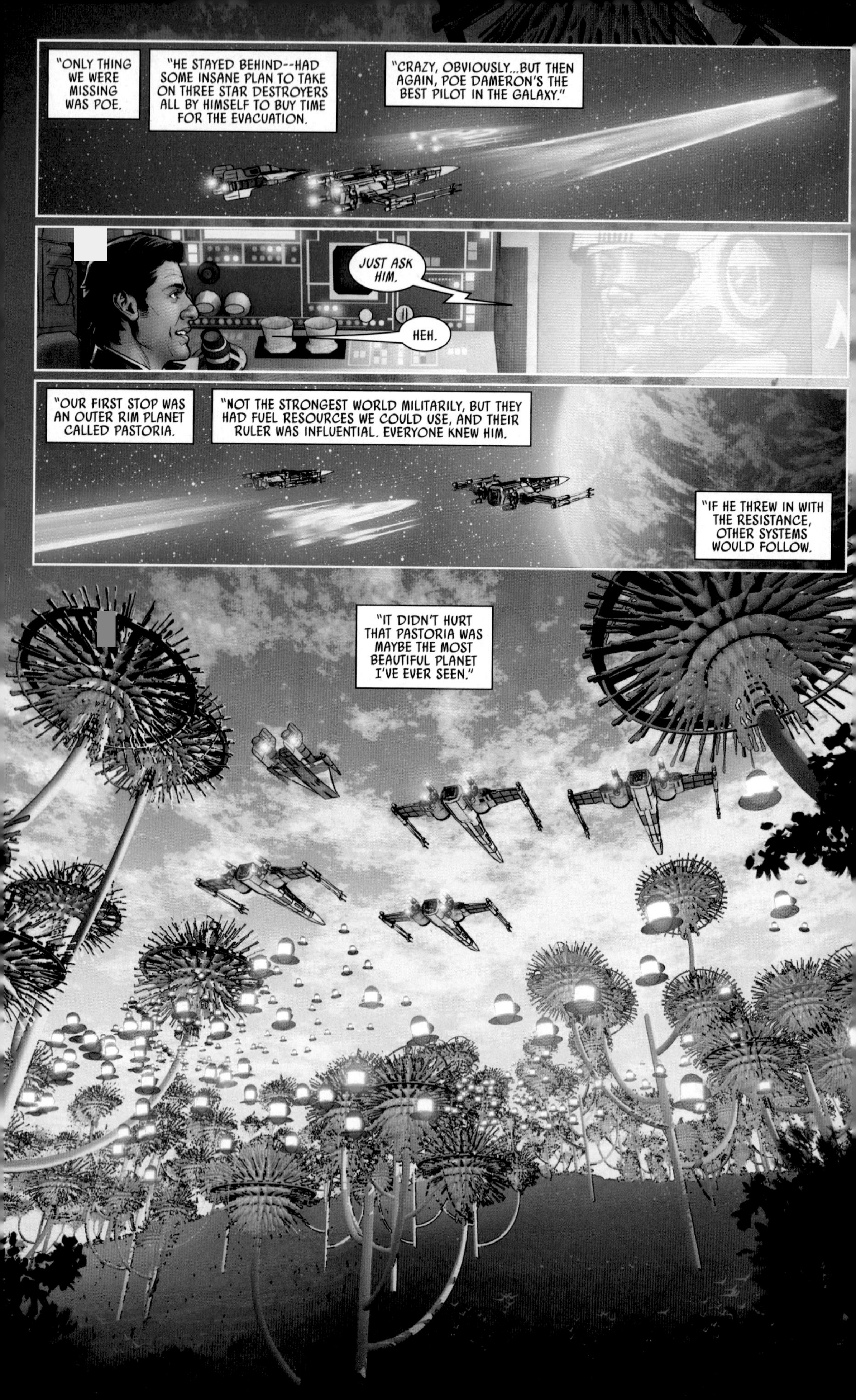
"ONLY THING WE WERE MISSING WAS POE.
"HE STAYED BEHIND--HAD SOME INSANE PLAN TO TAKE ON THREE STAR DESTROYERS ALL BY HIMSELF TO BUY TIME FOR THE EVACUATION.
"CRAZY, OBVIOUSLY...BUT THEN AGAIN, POE DAMERON'S THE BEST PILOT IN THE GALAXY."
JUST ASK HIM.
HEH.
"OUR FIRST STOP WAS AN OUTER RIM PLANET CALLED PASTORIA.
"NOT THE STRONGEST WORLD MILITARILY, BUT THEY HAD FUEL RESOURCES WE COULD USE, AND THEIR RULER WAS INFLUENTIAL. EVERYONE KNEW HIM.
"IF HE THREW IN WITH THE RESISTANCE, OTHER SYSTEMS WOULD FOLLOW.
"IT DIDN'T HURT THAT PASTORIA WAS MAYBE THE MOST BEAUTIFUL PLANET I'VE EVER SEEN."

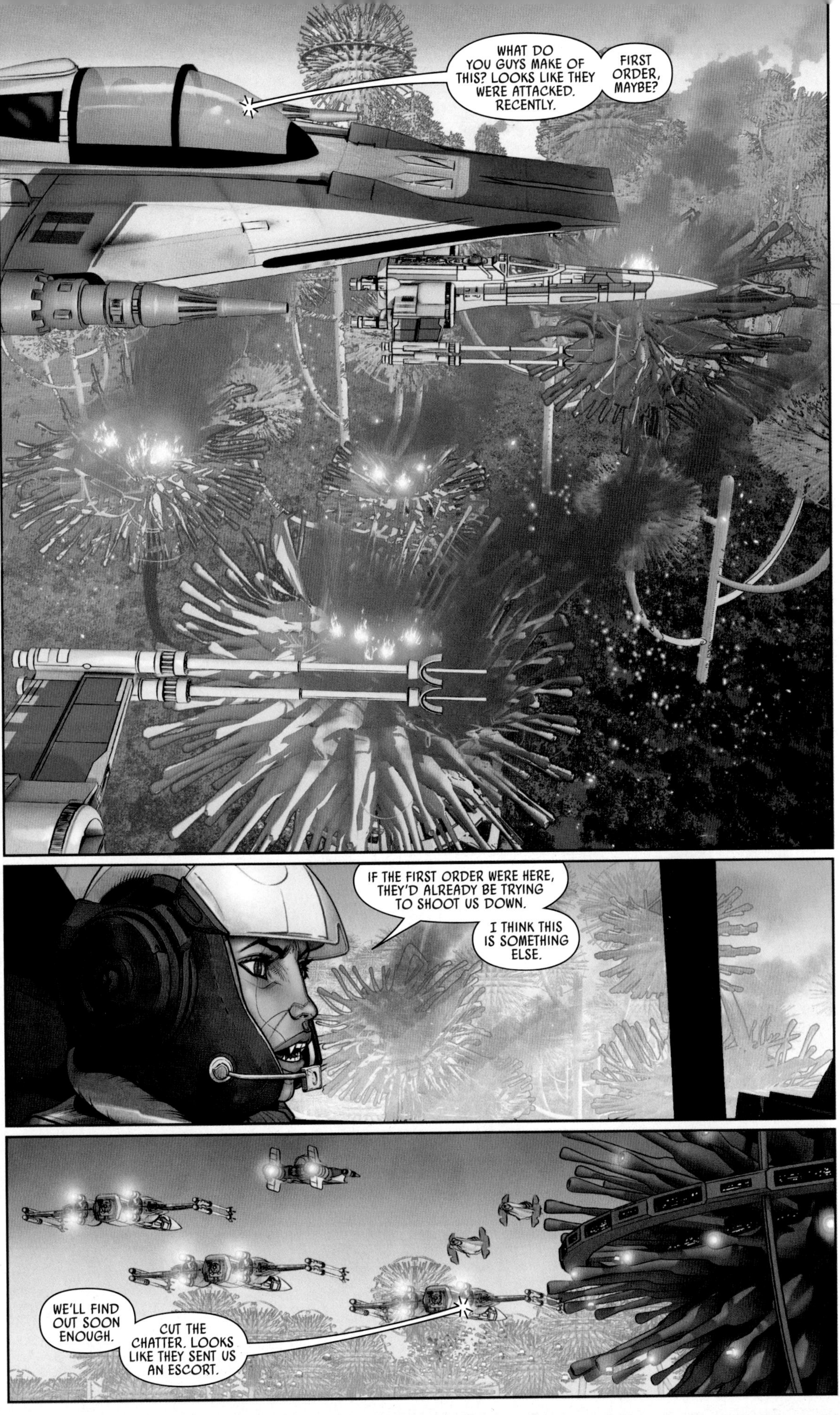
WHAT DO YOU GUYS MAKE OF THIS? LOOKS LIKE THEY WERE ATTACKED. RECENTLY.
FIRST ORDER, MAYBE?
IF THE FIRST ORDER WERE HERE, THEY'D ALREADY BE TRYING TO SHOOT US DOWN.
I THINK THIS IS SOMETHING ELSE.
WE'LL FIND OUT SOON ENOUGH.
CUT THE CHATTER. LOOKS LIKE THEY SENT US AN ESCORT.

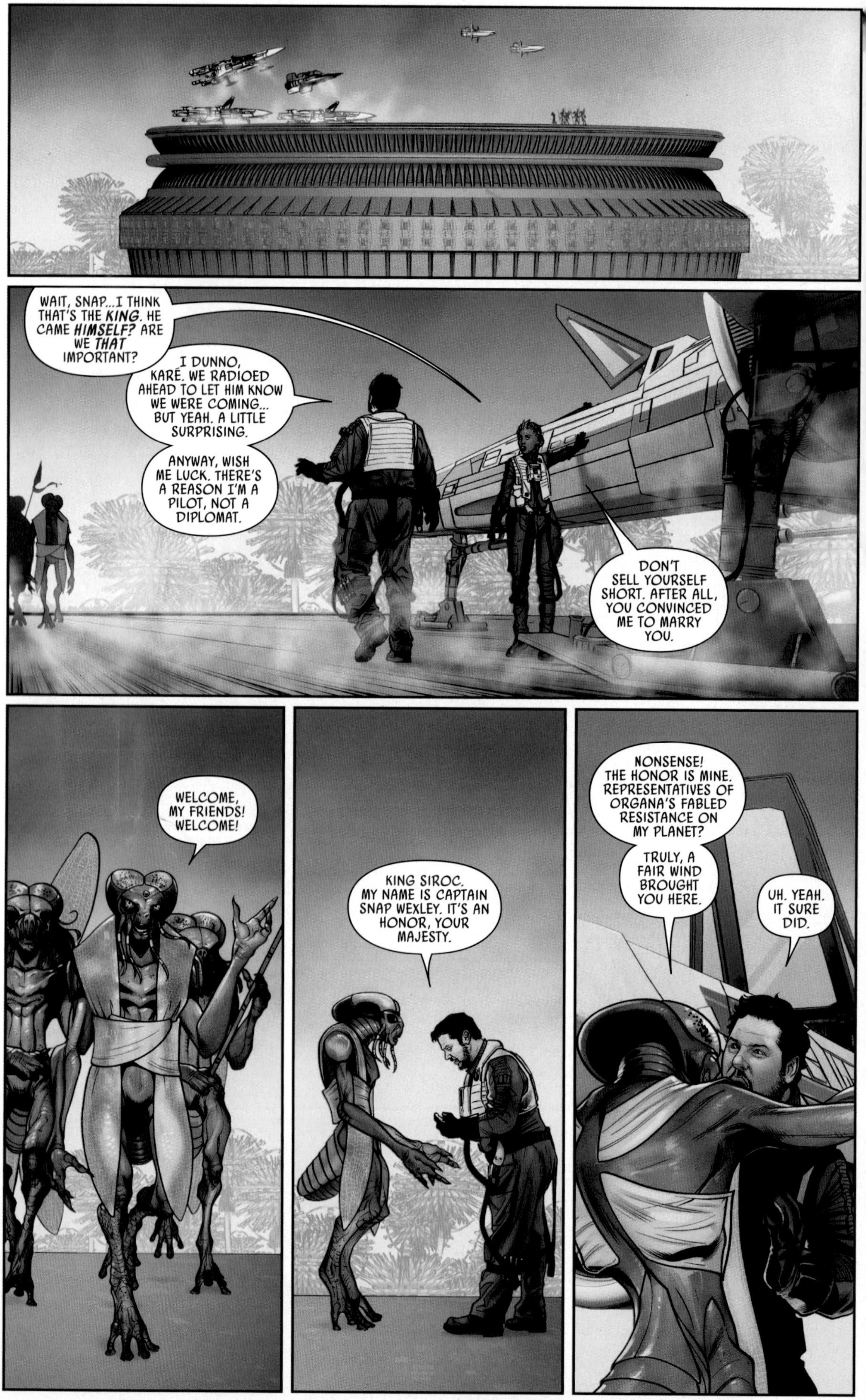
WAIT, SNAP...I THINK THAT'S THE KING. HE CAME HIMSELF? ARE WE THAT IMPORTANT?
I DUNNO, KARÉ. WE RADIOED AHEAD TO LET HIM KNOW WE WERE COMING... BUT YEAH. A LITTLE SURPRISING.
ANYWAY, WISH ME LUCK. THERE'S A REASON I'M A PILOT, NOT A DIPLOMAT.
DON'T SELL YOURSELF SHORT. AFTER ALL, YOU CONVINCED ME TO MARRY YOU.
WELCOME, MY FRIENDS! WELCOME!
KING SIROC. MY NAME IS CAPTAIN SNAP WEXLEY. IT'S AN HONOR, YOUR MAJESTY.
NONSENSE! THE HONOR IS MINE. REPRESENTATIVES OF ORGANA'S FABLED RESISTANCE ON MY PLANET?
TRULY, A FAIR WIND BROUGHT YOU HERE.
UH. YEAH. IT SURE DID.

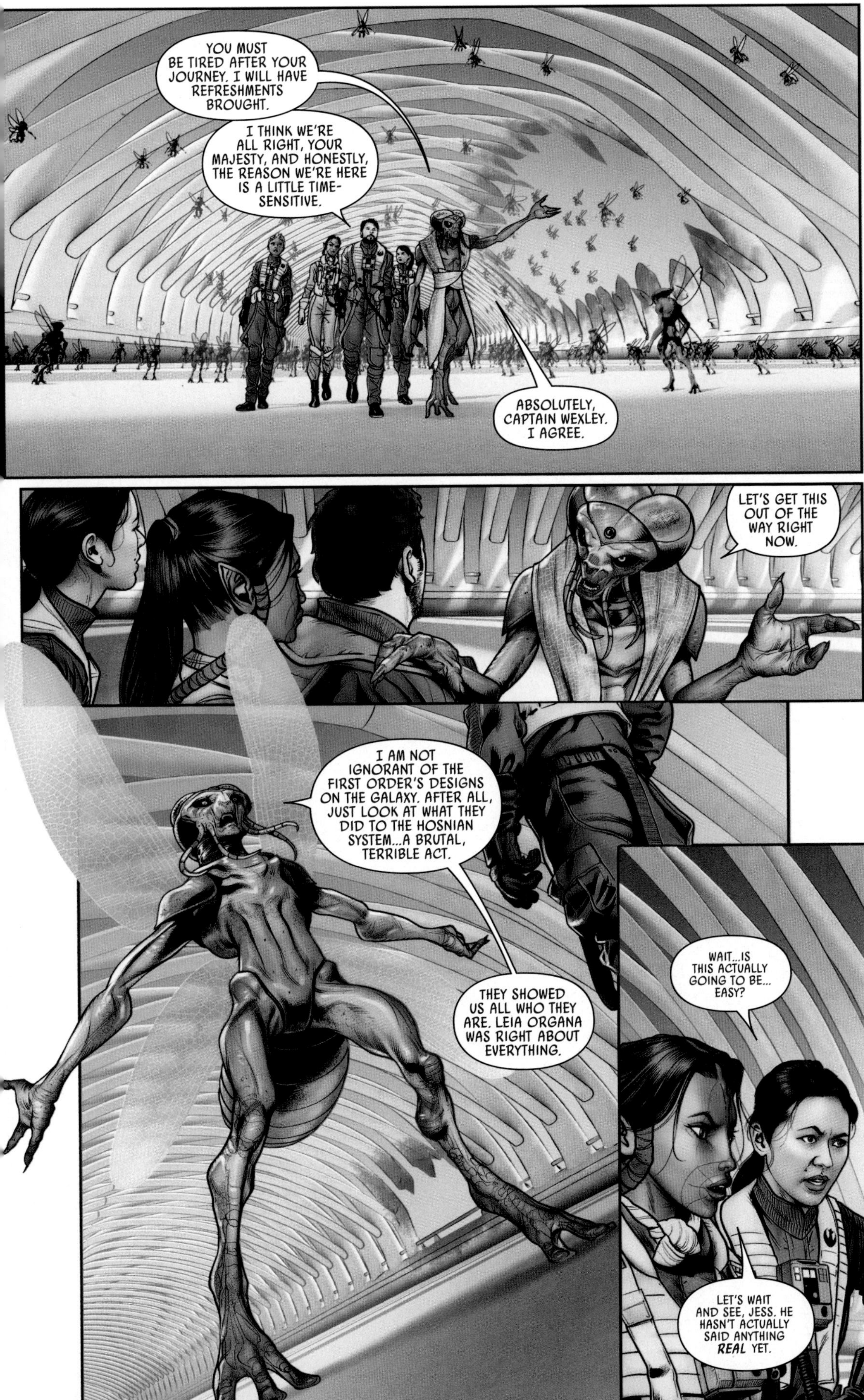
YOU MUST BE TIRED AFTER YOUR JOURNEY. I WILL HAVE REFRESHMENTS BROUGHT.
I THINK WE'RE ALL RIGHT, YOUR MAJESTY, AND HONESTLY, THE REASON WE'RE HERE IS A LITTLE TIME-SENSITIVE.
ABSOLUTELY, CAPTAIN WEXLEY. I AGREE.
LET'S GET THIS OUT OF THE WAY RIGHT NOW.
I AM NOT IGNORANT OF THE FIRST ORDER'S DESIGNS ON THE GALAXY. AFTER ALL, JUST LOOK AT WHAT THEY DID TO THE HOSNIAN SYSTEM...A BRUTAL, TERRIBLE ACT.
THEY SHOWED US ALL WHO THEY ARE. LEIA ORGANA WAS RIGHT ABOUT EVERYTHING.
WAIT...IS THIS ACTUALLY GOING TO BE... EASY?
LET'S WAIT AND SEE, JESS. HE HASN'T ACTUALLY SAID ANYTHING REAL YET.

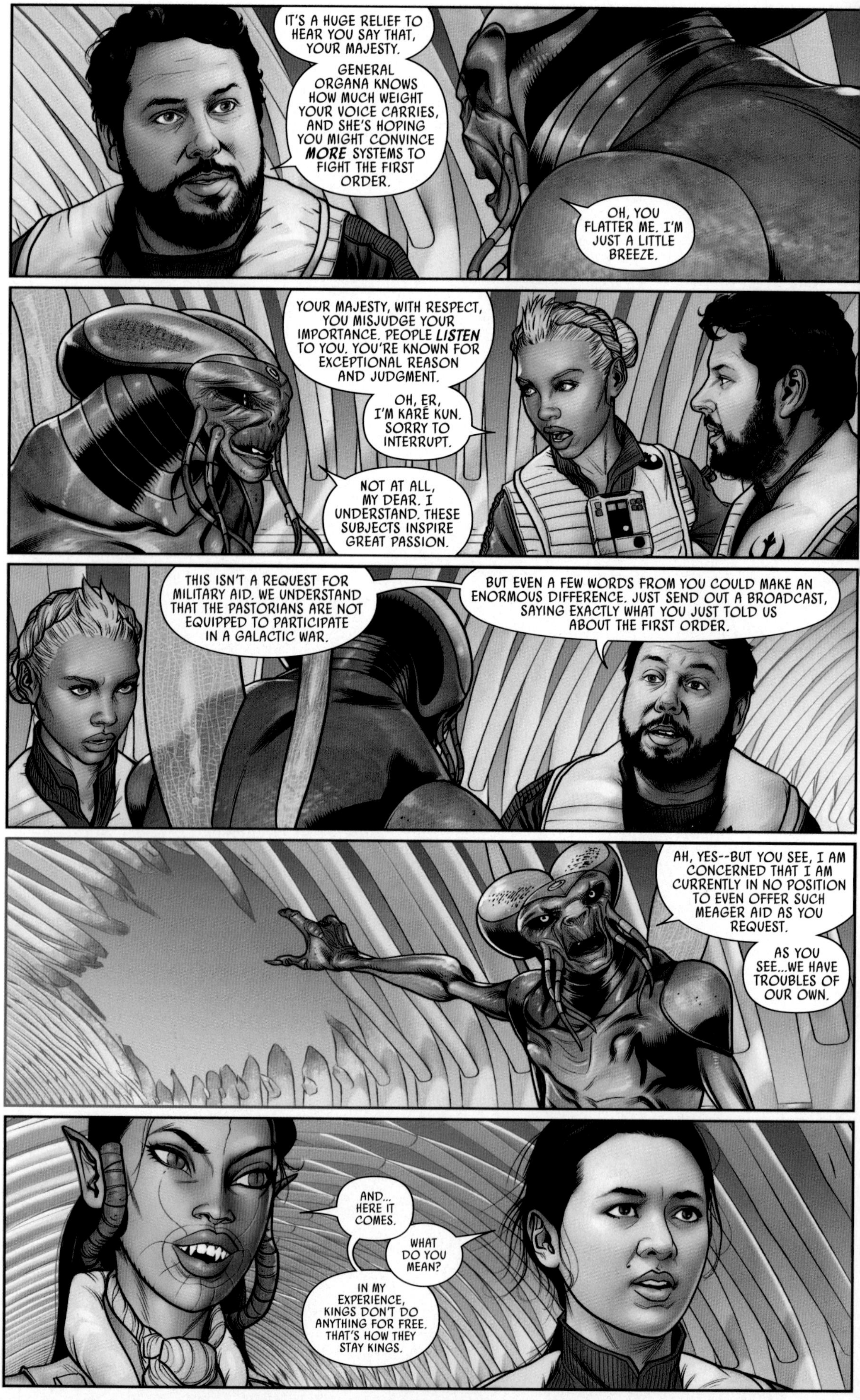
IT'S A HUGE RELIEF TO HEAR YOU SAY THAT, YOUR MAJESTY.
GENERAL ORGANA KNOWS HOW MUCH WEIGHT YOUR VOICE CARRIES, AND SHE'S HOPING YOU MIGHT CONVINCE MORE SYSTEMS TO FIGHT THE FIRST ORDER.
OH, YOU FLATTER ME. I'M JUST A LITTLE BREEZE.
YOUR MAJESTY, WITH RESPECT, YOU MISJUDGE YOUR IMPORTANCE. PEOPLE LISTEN TO YOU. YOU'RE KNOWN FOR EXCEPTIONAL REASON AND JUDGMENT.
OH, ER, I'M KARÉ KUN. SORRY TO INTERRUPT.
NOT AT ALL, MY DEAR. I UNDERSTAND. THESE SUBJECTS INSPIRE GREAT PASSION.
THIS ISN'T A REQUEST FOR MILITARY AID. WE UNDERSTAND THAT THE PASTORIANS ARE NOT EQUIPPED TO PARTICIPATE IN A GALACTIC WAR.
BUT EVEN A FEW WORDS FROM YOU COULD MAKE AN ENORMOUS DIFFERENCE. JUST SEND OUT A BROADCAST, SAYING EXACTLY WHAT YOU JUST TOLD US ABOUT THE FIRST ORDER.
AH, YES--BUT YOU SEE, I AM CONCERNED THAT I AM CURRENTLY IN NO POSITION TO EVEN OFFER SUCH MEAGER AID AS YOU REQUEST.
AS YOU SEE...WE HAVE TROUBLES OF OUR OWN.
AND... HERE IT COMES.
WHAT DO YOU MEAN?
IN MY EXPERIENCE, KINGS DON'T DO ANYTHING FOR FREE. THAT'S HOW THEY STAY KINGS.

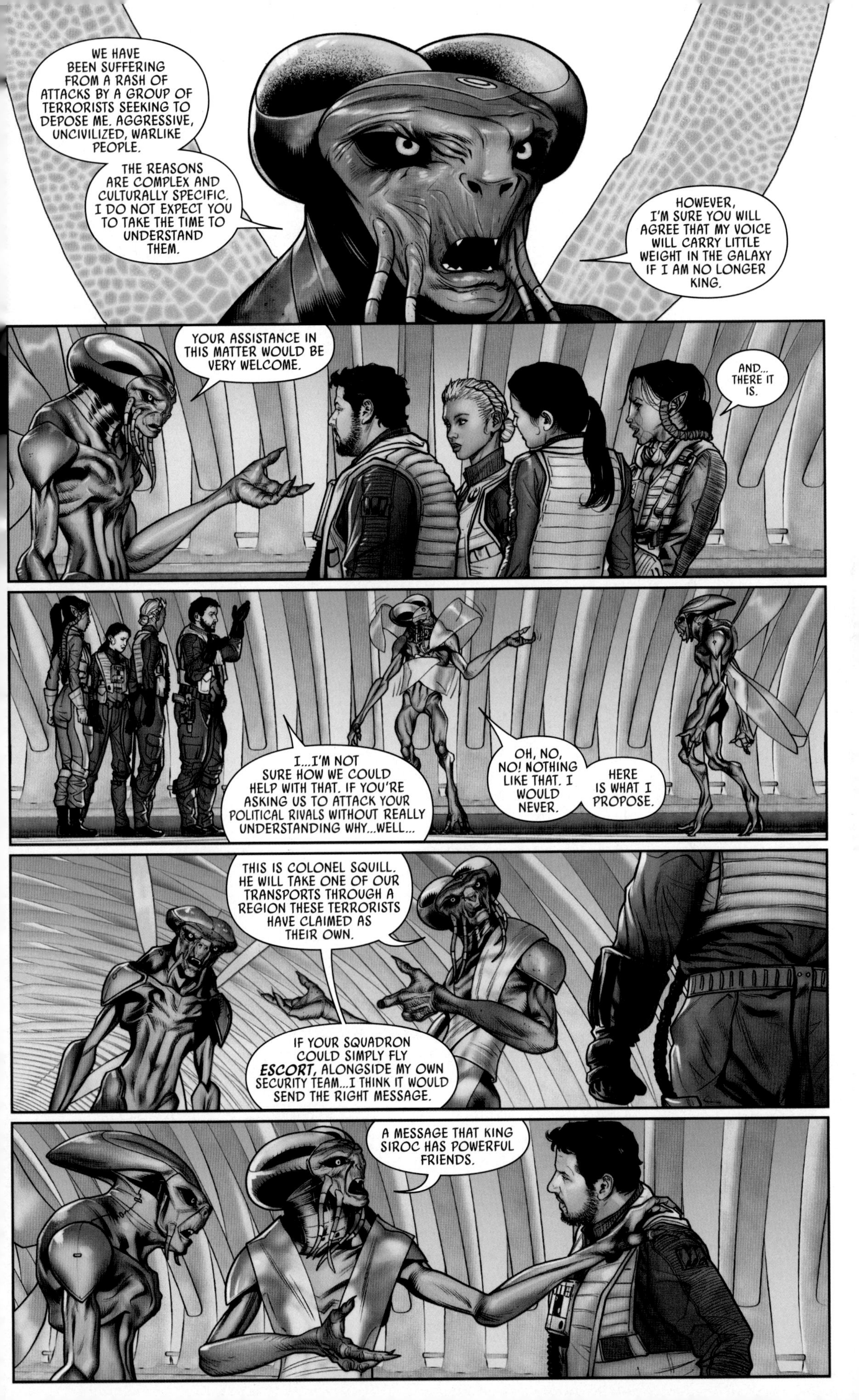
WE HAVE BEEN SUFFERING FROM A RASH OF ATTACKS BY A GROUP OF TERRORISTS SEEKING TO DEPOSE ME. AGGRESSIVE, UNCIVILIZED, WARLIKE PEOPLE.
THE REASONS ARE COMPLEX AND CULTURALLY SPECIFIC. I DO NOT EXPECT YOU TO TAKE THE TIME TO UNDERSTAND THEM.
HOWEVER, I'M SURE YOU WILL AGREE THAT MY VOICE WILL CARRY LITTLE WEIGHT IN THE GALAXY IF I AM NO LONGER KING.
YOUR ASSISTANCE IN THIS MATTER WOULD BE VERY WELCOME.
AND... THERE IT IS.
I...I'M NOT SURE HOW WE COULD HELP WITH THAT. IF YOU'RE ASKING US TO ATTACK YOUR POLITICAL RIVALS WITHOUT REALLY UNDERSTANDING WHY...WELL...
OH, NO, NO! NOTHING LIKE THAT. I WOULD NEVER.
HERE IS WHAT I PROPOSE.
THIS IS COLONEL SQUILL. HE WILL TAKE ONE OF OUR TRANSPORTS THROUGH A REGION THESE TERRORISTS HAVE CLAIMED AS THEIR OWN.
IF YOUR SQUADRON COULD SIMPLY FLY ESCORT, ALONGSIDE MY OWN SECURITY TEAM...I THINK IT WOULD SEND THE RIGHT MESSAGE.
A MESSAGE THAT KING SIROC HAS POWERFUL FRIENDS.

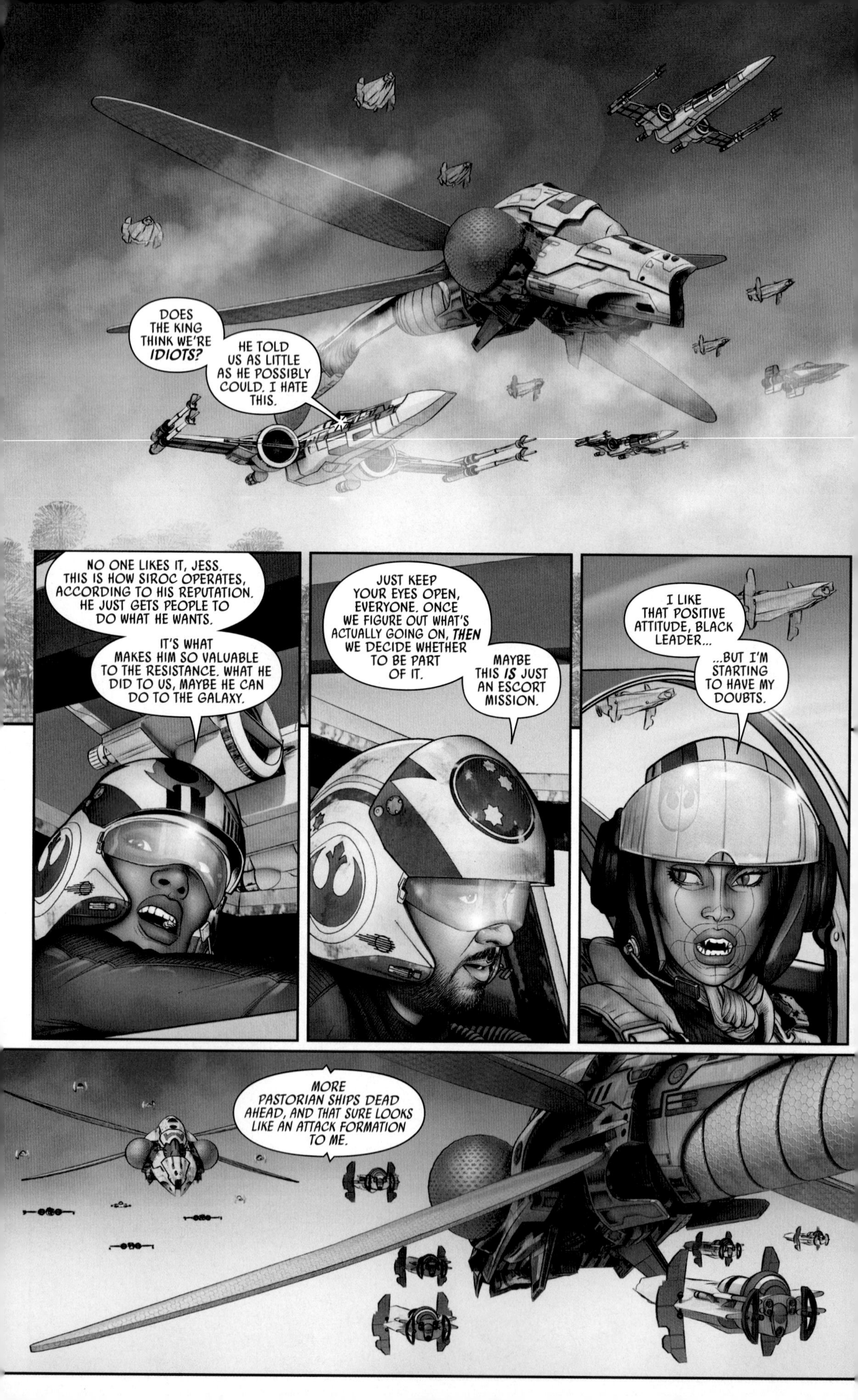
DOES THE KING THINK WE'RE IDIOTS?
HE TOLD US AS LITTLE AS HE POSSIBLY COULD. I HATE THIS.
NO ONE LIKES IT, JESS. THIS IS HOW SIROC OPERATES, ACCORDING TO HIS REPUTATION. HE JUST GETS PEOPLE TO DO WHAT HE WANTS.
IT'S WHAT MAKES HIM SO VALUABLE TO THE RESISTANCE. WHAT HE DID TO US, MAYBE HE CAN DO TO THE GALAXY.
JUST KEEP YOUR EYES OPEN, EVERYONE. ONCE WE FIGURE OUT WHAT'S ACTUALLY GOING ON, THEN WE DECIDE WHETHER TO BE PART OF IT.
MAYBE THIS IS JUST AN ESCORT MISSION.
I LIKE THAT POSITIVE ATTITUDE, BLACK LEADER...
...BUT I'M STARTING TO HAVE MY DOUBTS.
MORE PASTORIAN SHIPS DEAD AHEAD, AND THAT SURE LOOKS LIKE AN ATTACK FORMATION TO ME.

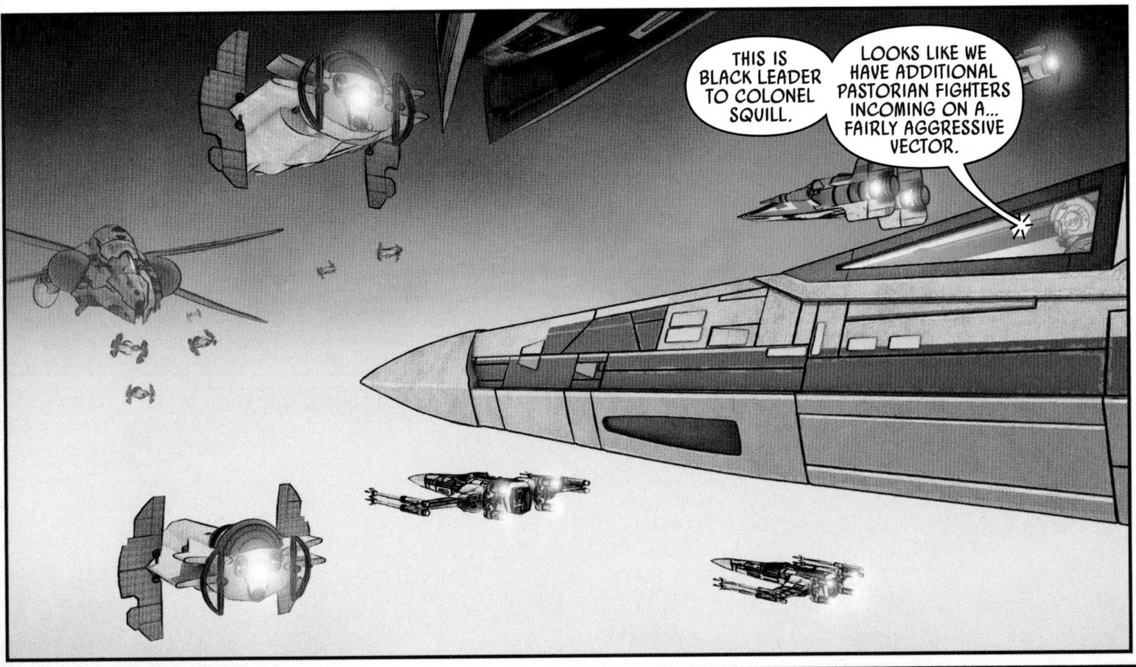
THIS IS BLACK LEADER TO COLONEL SQUILL.
LOOKS LIKE WE HAVE ADDITIONAL PASTORIAN FIGHTERS INCOMING ON A... FAIRLY AGGRESSIVE VECTOR.

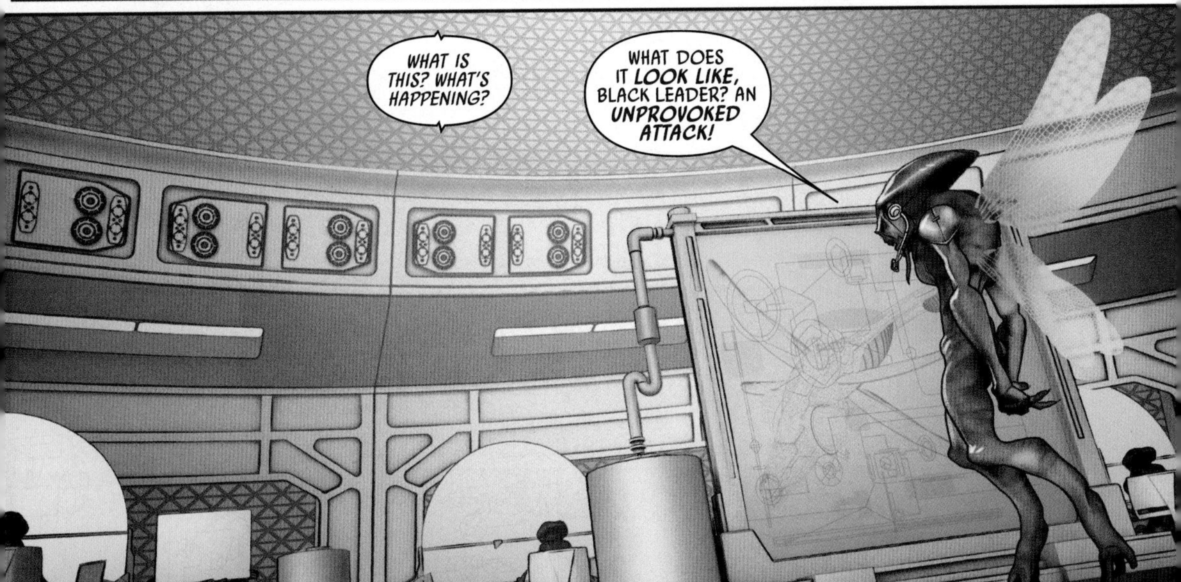
WHAT IS THIS? WHAT'S HAPPENING?
WHAT DOES IT LOOK LIKE, BLACK LEADER? AN UNPROVOKED ATTACK!

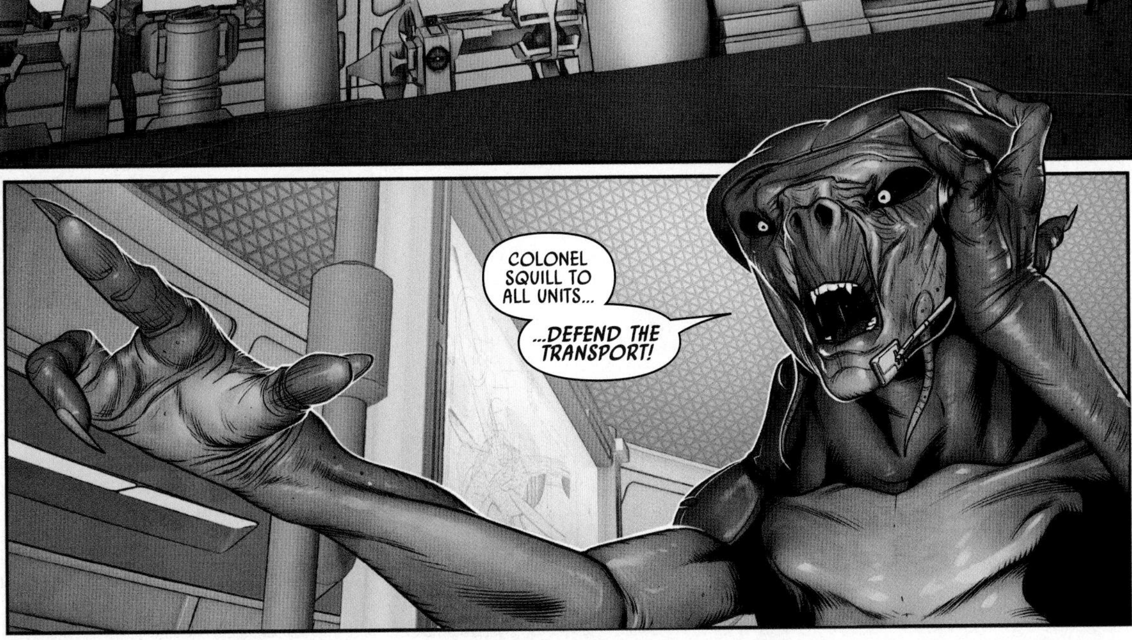
COLONEL SQUILL TO ALL UNITS...
...DEFEND THE TRANSPORT!

BLACK LEADER...WHAT ARE YOUR ORDERS?

HOLD POSITION, BLACK THREE. WE'RE JUST HERE TO FLY ESCORT.

WE DIDN'T AGREE TO GET INVOLVED IN ANY FIGHTS.

SNAP... THEY'RE DYING OUT THERE.

DO YOU THINK KING SIROC WILL BE ALL THAT EAGER TO JOIN THE RESISTANCE IF WE JUST SIT HERE AND WATCH HIS PEOPLE BURN?

BLAST IT.

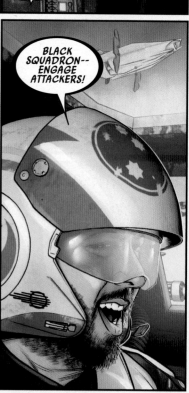

BLACK SQUADRON-- ENGAGE ATTACKERS!

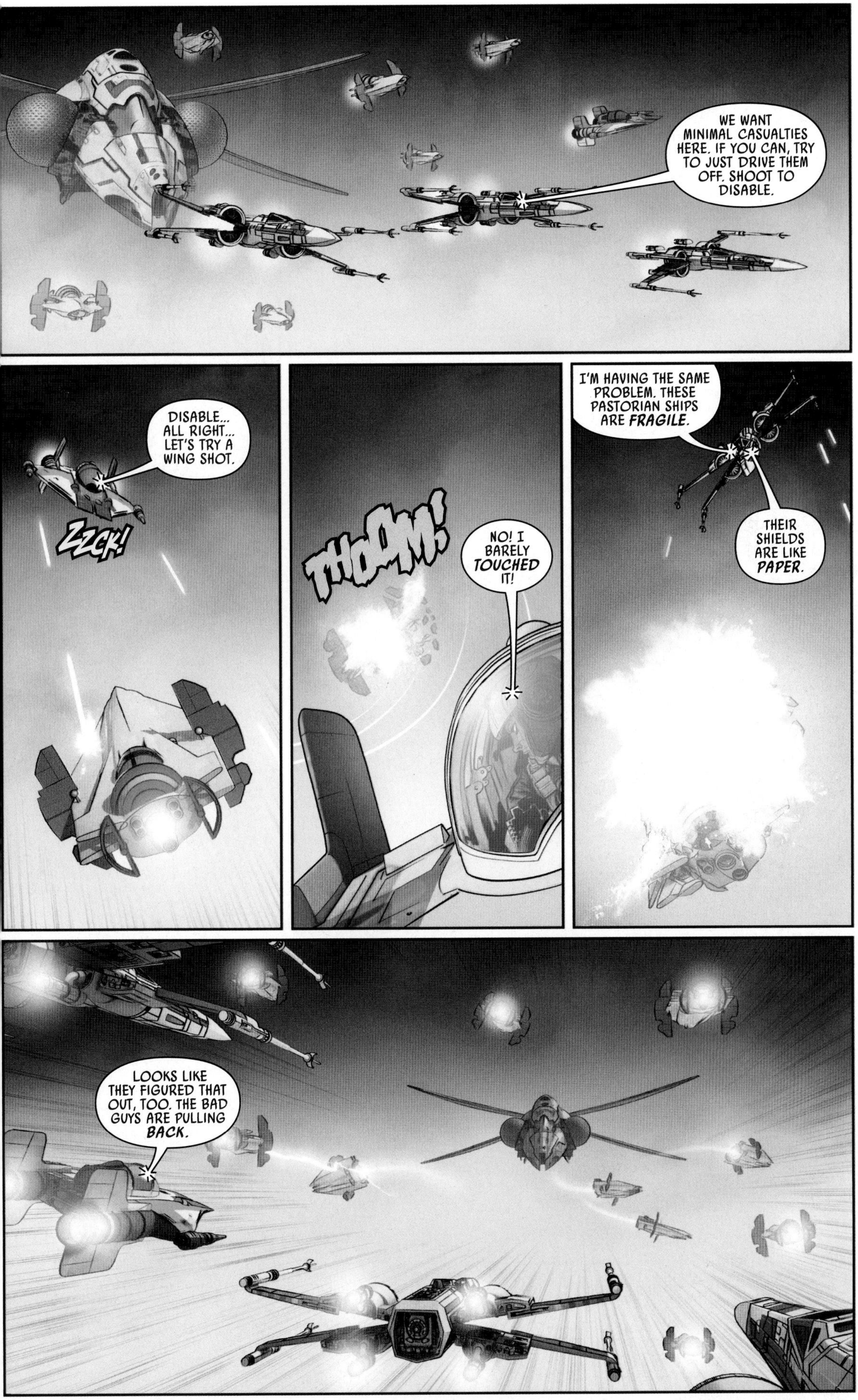
WE WANT MINIMAL CASUALTIES HERE. IF YOU CAN, TRY TO JUST DRIVE THEM OFF. SHOOT TO DISABLE.
DISABLE... ALL RIGHT... LET'S TRY A WING SHOT.
ZZCK!
THOOM!
NO! I BARELY TOUCHED IT!
I'M HAVING THE SAME PROBLEM. THESE PASTORIAN SHIPS ARE FRAGILE.
THEIR SHIELDS ARE LIKE PAPER.
LOOKS LIKE THEY FIGURED THAT OUT, TOO. THE BAD GUYS ARE PULLING BACK.

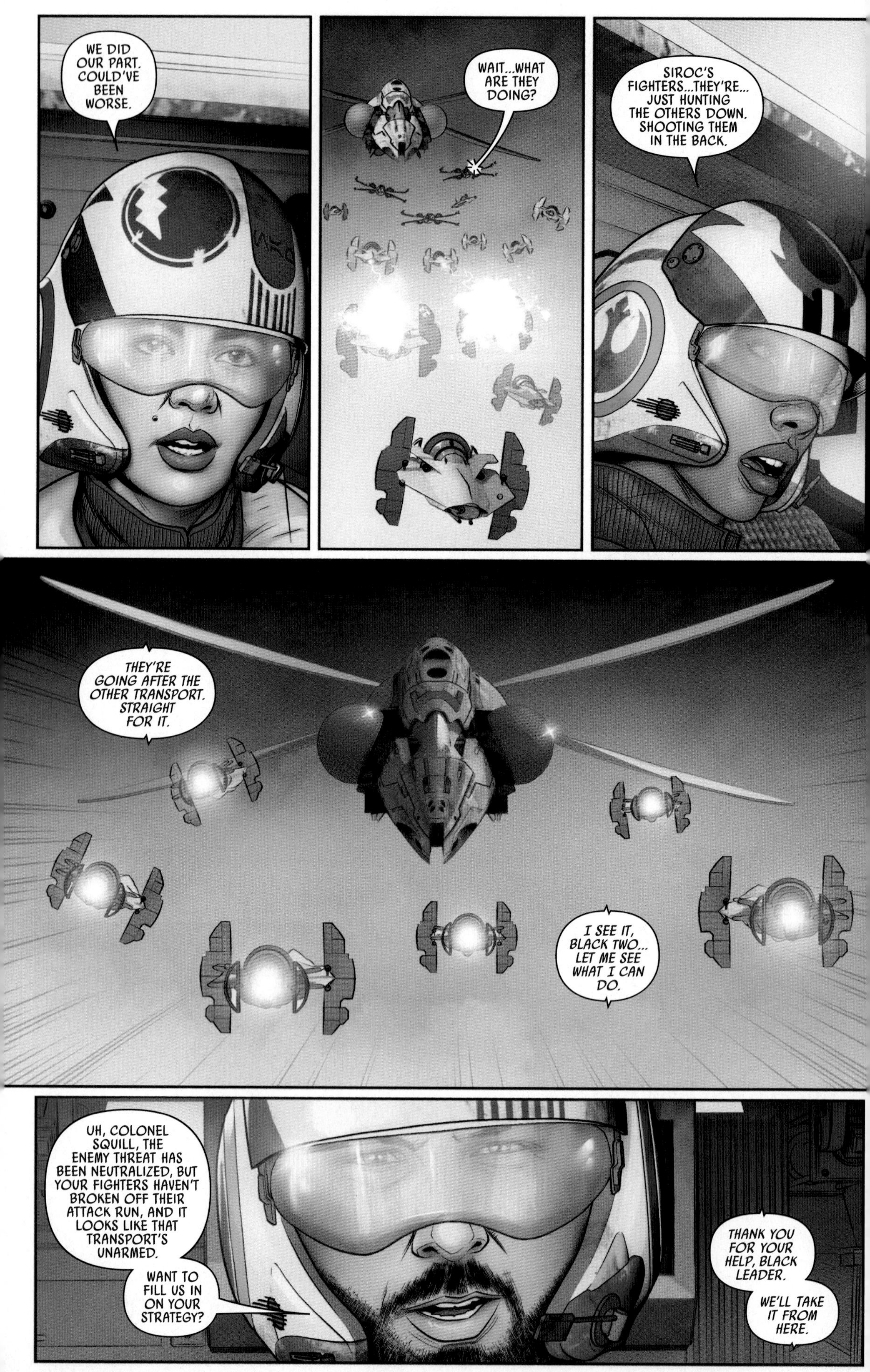
WE DID OUR PART. COULD'VE BEEN WORSE.
WAIT...WHAT ARE THEY DOING?
SIROC'S FIGHTERS...THEY'RE... JUST HUNTING THE OTHERS DOWN. SHOOTING THEM IN THE BACK.
THEY'RE GOING AFTER THE OTHER TRANSPORT. STRAIGHT FOR IT.
I SEE IT, BLACK TWO... LET ME SEE WHAT I CAN DO.
UH, COLONEL SQUILL, THE ENEMY THREAT HAS BEEN NEUTRALIZED, BUT YOUR FIGHTERS HAVEN'T BROKEN OFF THEIR ATTACK RUN, AND IT LOOKS LIKE THAT TRANSPORT'S UNARMED.
WANT TO FILL US IN ON YOUR STRATEGY?
THANK YOU FOR YOUR HELP, BLACK LEADER.
WE'LL TAKE IT FROM HERE.

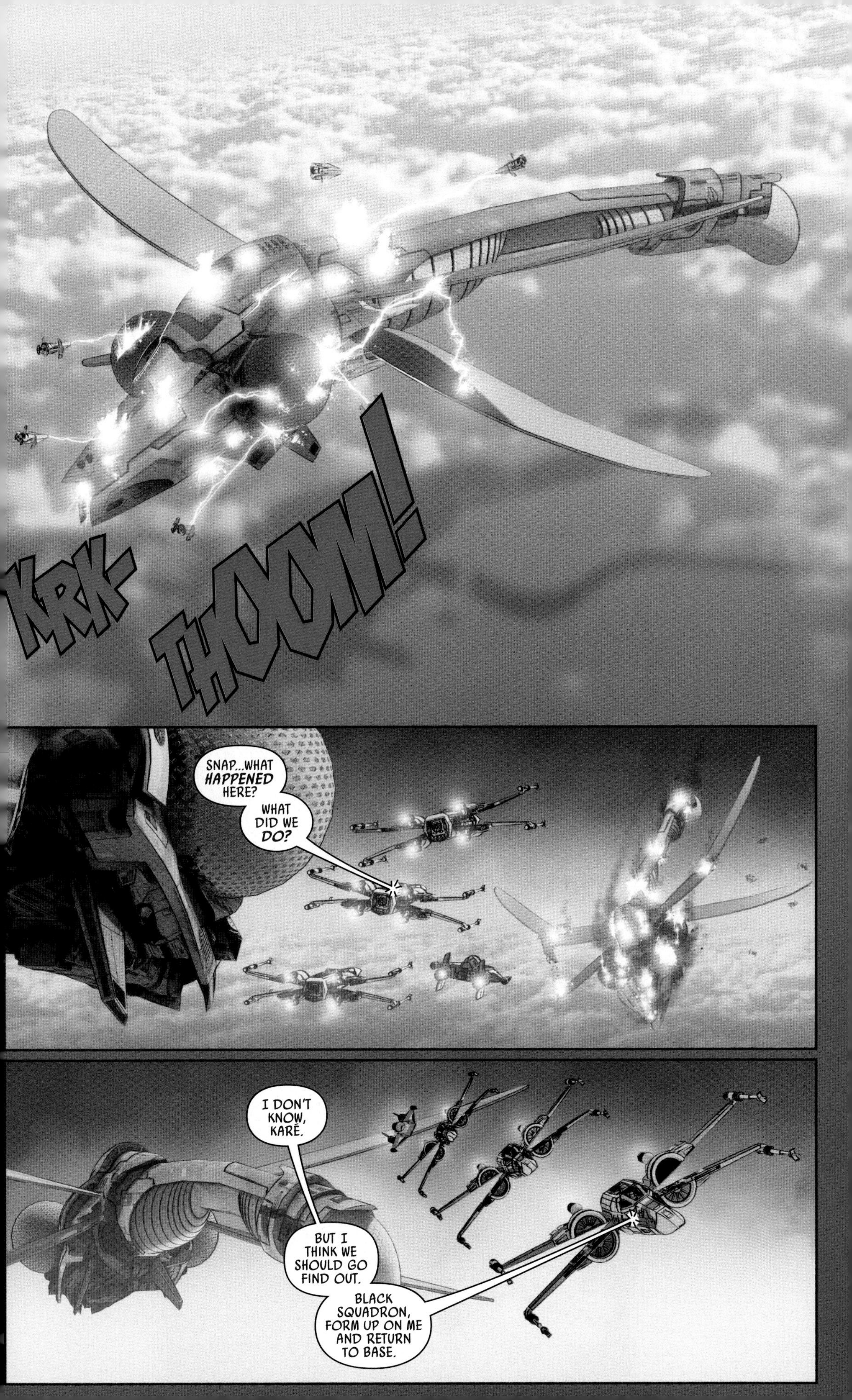

KRK-THOOM!
SNAP...WHAT HAPPENED HERE?
WHAT DID WE DO?
I DON'T KNOW, KARÉ.
BUT I THINK WE SHOULD GO FIND OUT.
BLACK SQUADRON, FORM UP ON ME AND RETURN TO BASE.

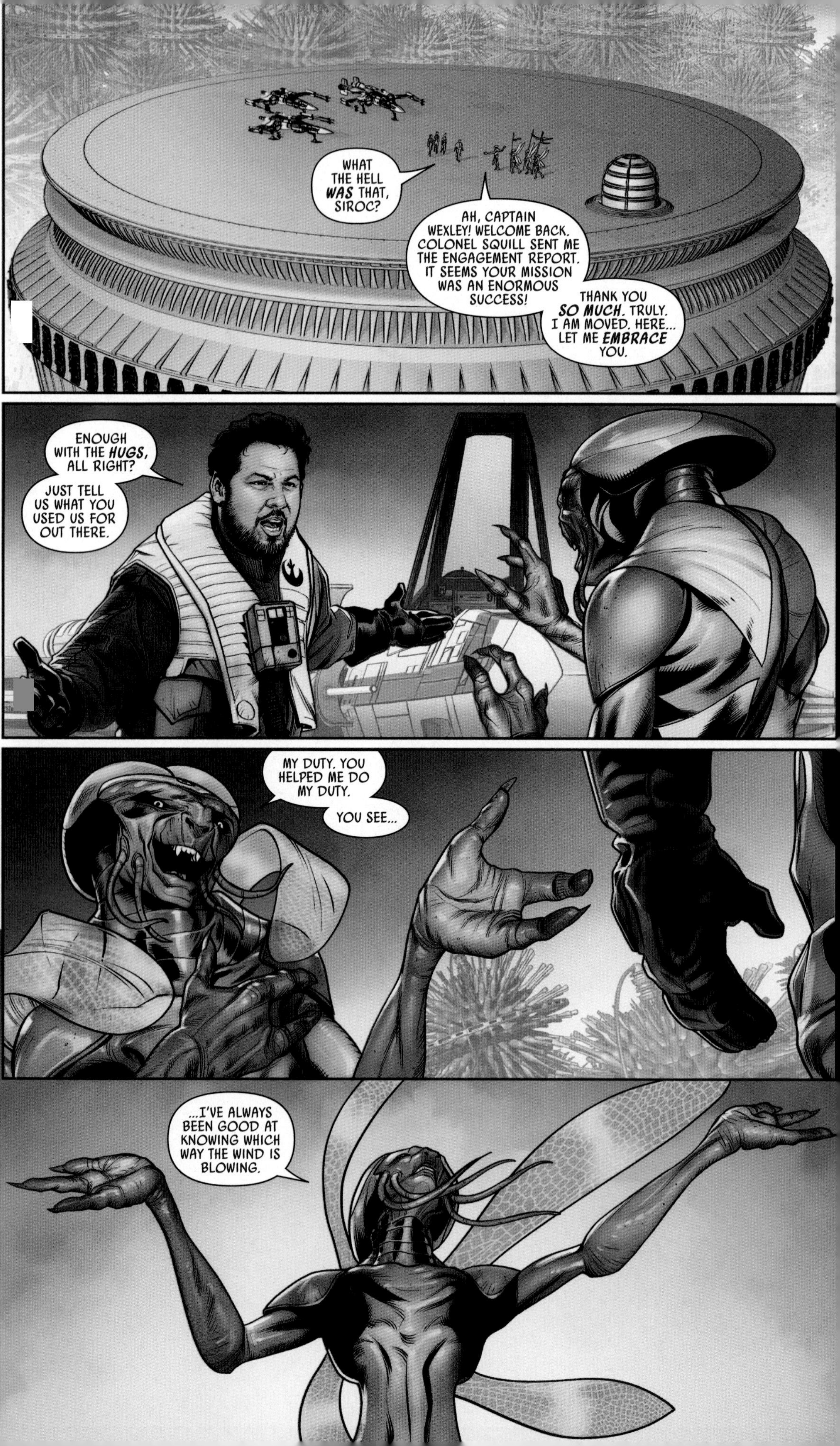
WHAT THE HELL *WAS* THAT, SIROC?
AH, CAPTAIN WEXLEY! WELCOME BACK. COLONEL SQUILL SENT ME THE ENGAGEMENT REPORT. IT SEEMS YOUR MISSION WAS AN ENORMOUS SUCCESS!
THANK YOU *SO MUCH.* TRULY. I AM MOVED. HERE... LET ME *EMBRACE* YOU.
ENOUGH WITH THE *HUGS,* ALL RIGHT?
JUST TELL US WHAT YOU USED US FOR OUT THERE.
MY DUTY. YOU HELPED ME DO MY DUTY.
YOU SEE...
...I'VE ALWAYS BEEN GOOD AT KNOWING WHICH WAY THE WIND IS BLOWING.

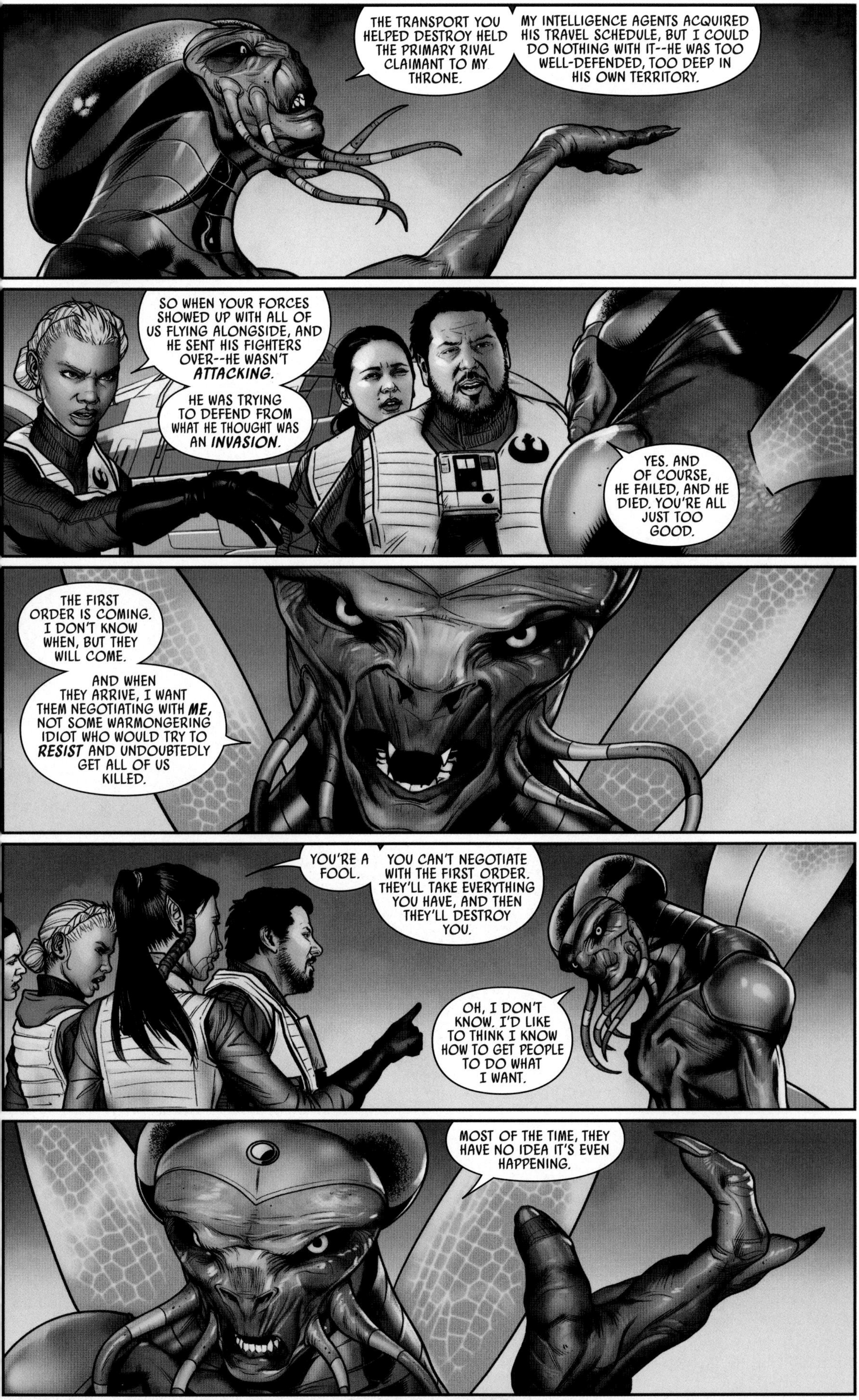
THE TRANSPORT YOU HELPED DESTROY HELD THE PRIMARY RIVAL CLAIMANT TO MY THRONE.
MY INTELLIGENCE AGENTS ACQUIRED HIS TRAVEL SCHEDULE, BUT I COULD DO NOTHING WITH IT--HE WAS TOO WELL-DEFENDED, TOO DEEP IN HIS OWN TERRITORY.
SO WHEN YOUR FORCES SHOWED UP WITH ALL OF US FLYING ALONGSIDE, AND HE SENT HIS FIGHTERS OVER--HE WASN'T ATTACKING.
HE WAS TRYING TO DEFEND FROM WHAT HE THOUGHT WAS AN INVASION.
YES. AND OF COURSE, HE FAILED, AND HE DIED. YOU'RE ALL JUST TOO GOOD.
THE FIRST ORDER IS COMING. I DON'T KNOW WHEN, BUT THEY WILL COME.
AND WHEN THEY ARRIVE, I WANT THEM NEGOTIATING WITH ME, NOT SOME WARMONGERING IDIOT WHO WOULD TRY TO RESIST AND UNDOUBTEDLY GET ALL OF US KILLED.
YOU'RE A FOOL.
YOU CAN'T NEGOTIATE WITH THE FIRST ORDER. THEY'LL TAKE EVERYTHING YOU HAVE, AND THEN THEY'LL DESTROY YOU.
OH, I DON'T KNOW. I'D LIKE TO THINK I KNOW HOW TO GET PEOPLE TO DO WHAT I WANT.
MOST OF THE TIME, THEY HAVE NO IDEA IT'S EVEN HAPPENING.

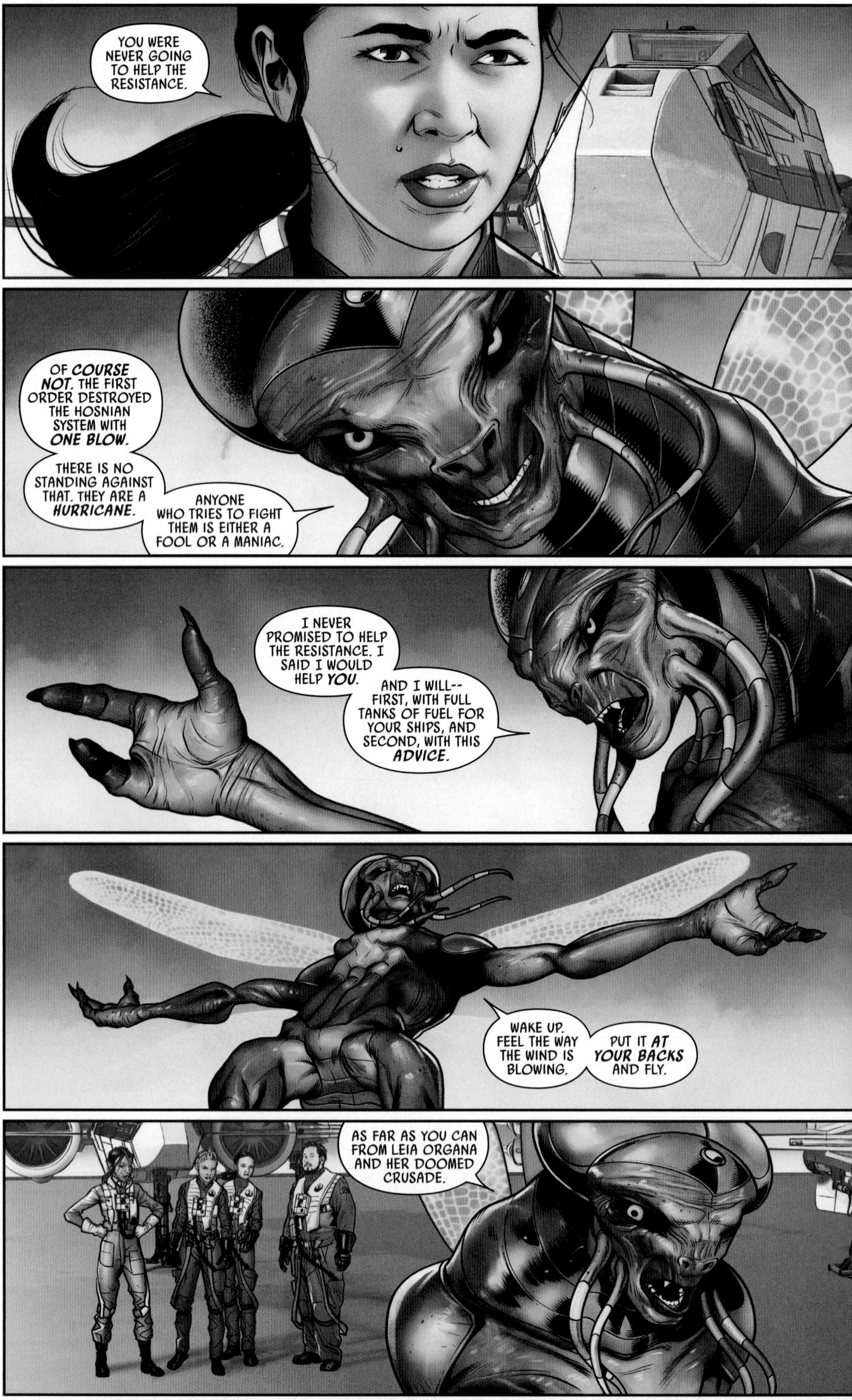
YOU WERE NEVER GOING TO HELP THE RESISTANCE.
OF COURSE NOT. THE FIRST ORDER DESTROYED THE HOSNIAN SYSTEM WITH ONE BLOW.
THERE IS NO STANDING AGAINST THAT. THEY ARE A HURRICANE.
ANYONE WHO TRIES TO FIGHT THEM IS EITHER A FOOL OR A MANIAC.
I NEVER PROMISED TO HELP THE RESISTANCE. I SAID I WOULD HELP YOU.
AND I WILL-- FIRST, WITH FULL TANKS OF FUEL FOR YOUR SHIPS, AND SECOND, WITH THIS ADVICE.
WAKE UP. FEEL THE WAY THE WIND IS BLOWING.
PUT IT AT YOUR BACKS AND FLY.
AS FAR AS YOU CAN FROM LEIA ORGANA AND HER DOOMED CRUSADE.

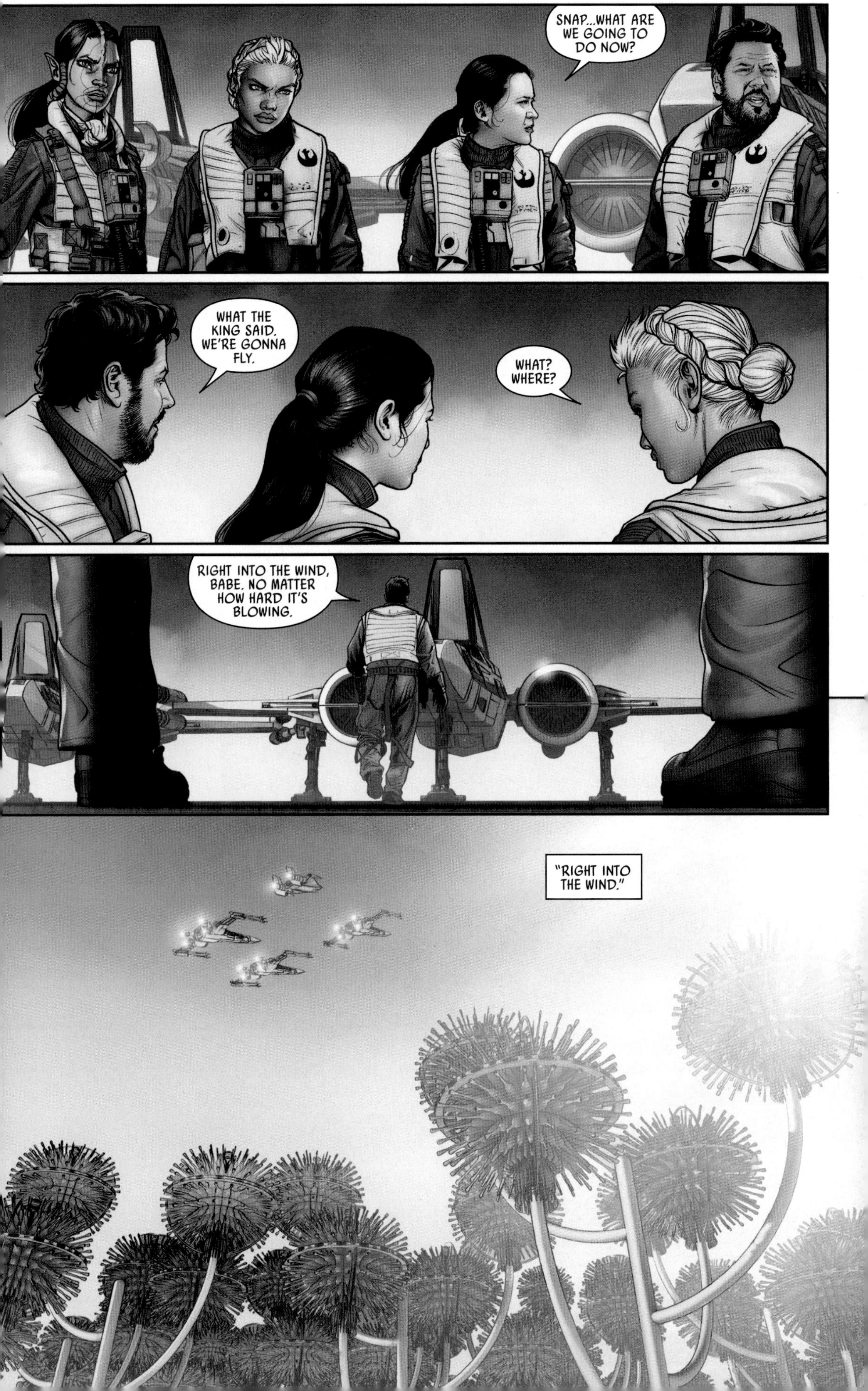
SNAP...WHAT ARE WE GOING TO DO NOW?
WHAT THE KING SAID. WE'RE GONNA FLY.
WHAT? WHERE?
RIGHT INTO THE WIND, BABE. NO MATTER HOW HARD IT'S BLOWING.
"RIGHT INTO THE WIND."

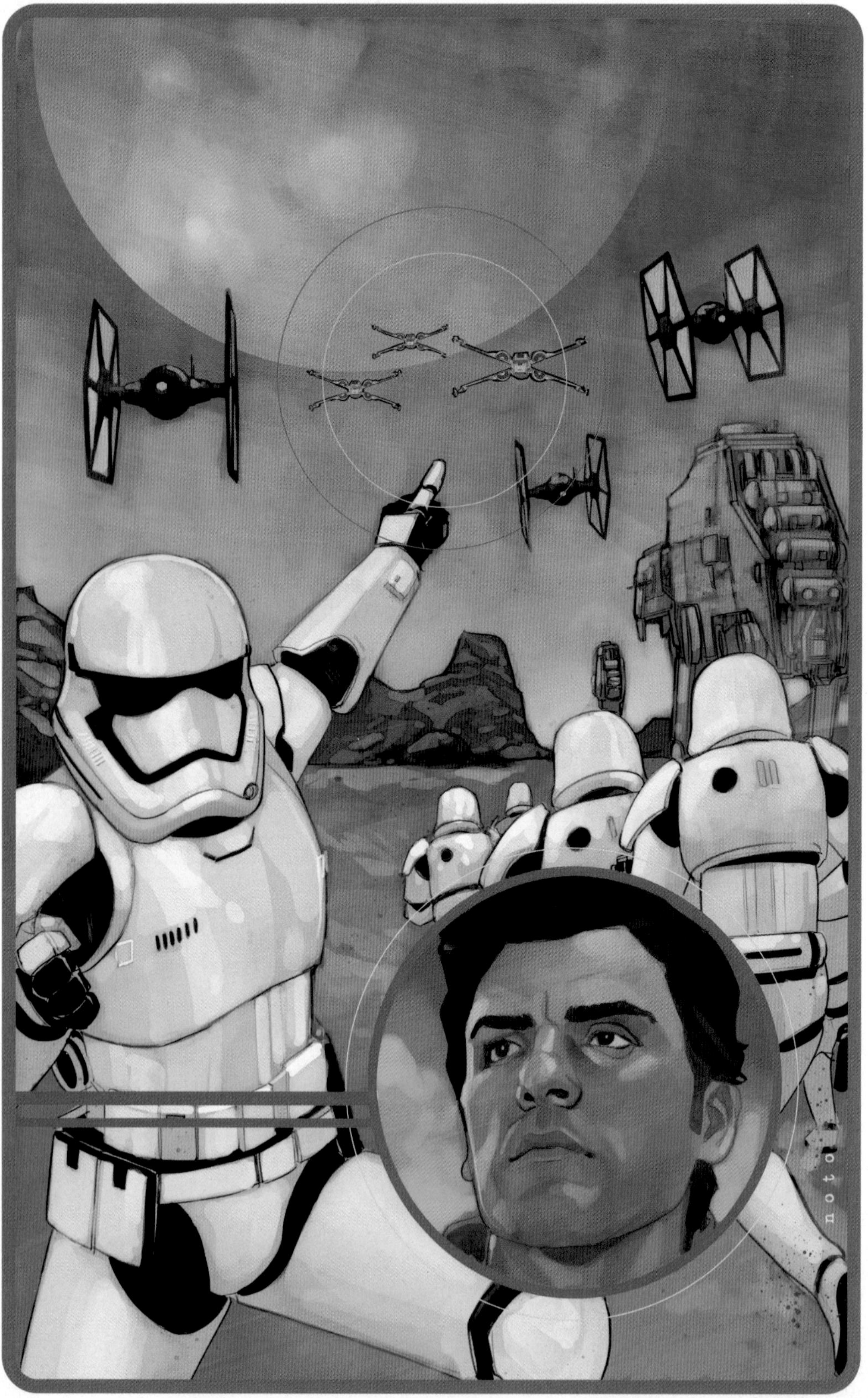

**Black Squadron.
During The Battle
Of Crait.**

"THIS IS JESS PAVA OF RESISTANCE BLACK SQUADRON, PILOT DESIGNATION BLACK THREE.

"IT'S THE FIRST CHANCE I'VE HAD TO UPDATE MY MISSION LOG SINCE THE DISASTER ON PASTORIA.

"THIS MIGHT BE MY LAST TRANSMISSION FOR A WHILE.

"I'M ABOUT TO DO SOMETHING THAT'S...WELL, IT'S JUST LIKE EVERYTHING BLACK SQUADRON DOES.

"INCREDIBLY BRAVE, INCREDIBLY IMPORTANT AND... INCREDIBLY STUPID.

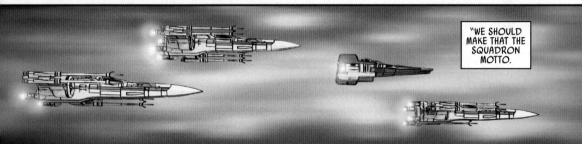

"WE SHOULD MAKE THAT THE SQUADRON MOTTO.

"WE LEFT PASTORIA AND HEADED TO THE NEXT STOP ON GENERAL ORGANA'S LIST OF POTENTIAL RESISTANCE ALLIES--A MID RIM WORLD CALLED IKKRUKK.

"I'LL BE HONEST, MORALE WAS PRETTY LOW. SNAP WEXLEY WAS COMMANDING THE MISSION, AND HE WAS DOING WHAT HE COULD TO HELP...

ALL RIGHT, PILOTS, YOU READY TO SAVE THE GALAXY?

EH.

EH.

COME ON, KARÉ! WHERE'S THE POSITIVITY? SURALINDA, *YOU'RE* FEELING GOOD, RIGHT?

"...BUT HE WASN'T GETTING VERY FAR."

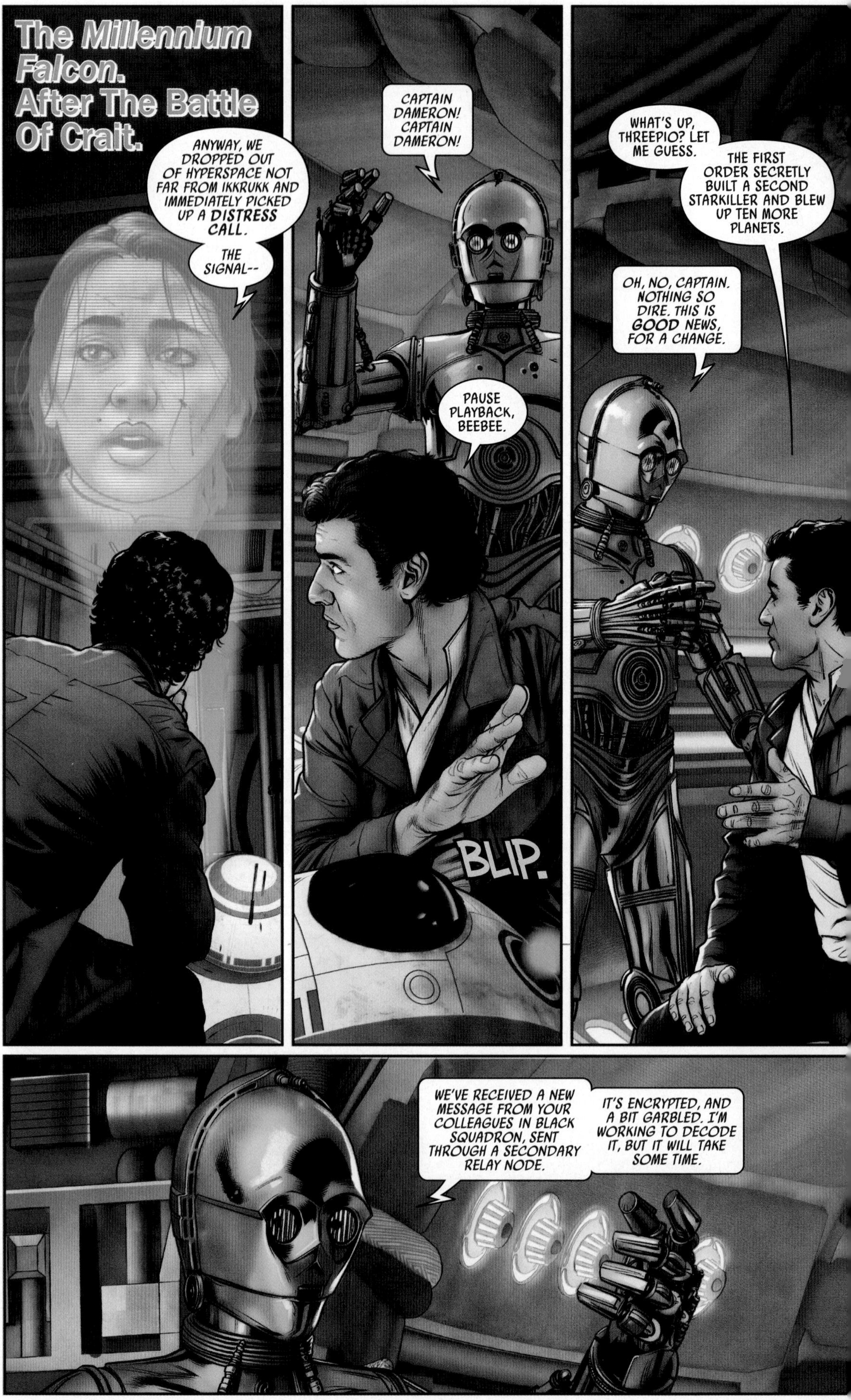

The Millennium Falcon. After The Battle Of Crait.
ANYWAY, WE DROPPED OUT OF HYPERSPACE NOT FAR FROM IKKRUKK AND IMMEDIATELY PICKED UP A DISTRESS CALL.
THE SIGNAL--
CAPTAIN DAMERON! CAPTAIN DAMERON!
PAUSE PLAYBACK, BEEBEE.
BLIP.
WHAT'S UP, THREEPIO? LET ME GUESS.
THE FIRST ORDER SECRETLY BUILT A SECOND STARKILLER AND BLEW UP TEN MORE PLANETS.
OH, NO, CAPTAIN. NOTHING SO DIRE. THIS IS GOOD NEWS, FOR A CHANGE.
WE'VE RECEIVED A NEW MESSAGE FROM YOUR COLLEAGUES IN BLACK SQUADRON, SENT THROUGH A SECONDARY RELAY NODE.
IT'S ENCRYPTED, AND A BIT GARBLED. I'M WORKING TO DECODE IT, BUT IT WILL TAKE SOME TIME.

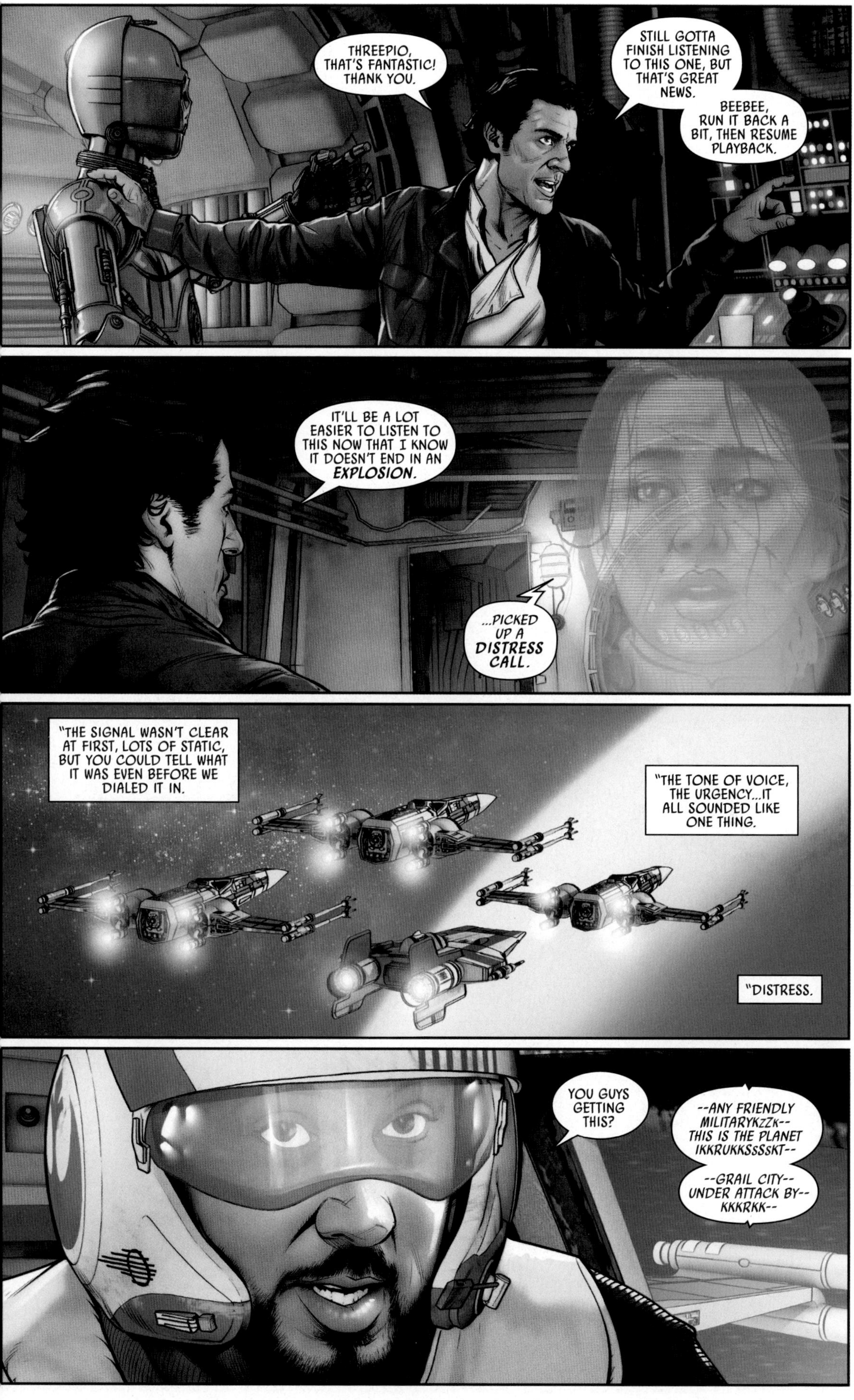
THREEPIO, THAT'S FANTASTIC! THANK YOU.
STILL GOTTA FINISH LISTENING TO THIS ONE, BUT THAT'S GREAT NEWS.
BEEBEE, RUN IT BACK A BIT, THEN RESUME PLAYBACK.
IT'LL BE A LOT EASIER TO LISTEN TO THIS NOW THAT I KNOW IT DOESN'T END IN AN EXPLOSION.
...PICKED UP A DISTRESS CALL.
"THE SIGNAL WASN'T CLEAR AT FIRST, LOTS OF STATIC, BUT YOU COULD TELL WHAT IT WAS EVEN BEFORE WE DIALED IT IN.
"THE TONE OF VOICE, THE URGENCY...IT ALL SOUNDED LIKE ONE THING.
"DISTRESS.
YOU GUYS GETTING THIS?
--ANY FRIENDLY MILITARYKzZK-- THIS IS THE PLANET IKKRUKKSSSSKT--
--GRAIL CITY-- UNDER ATTACK BY-- KKKRKK--

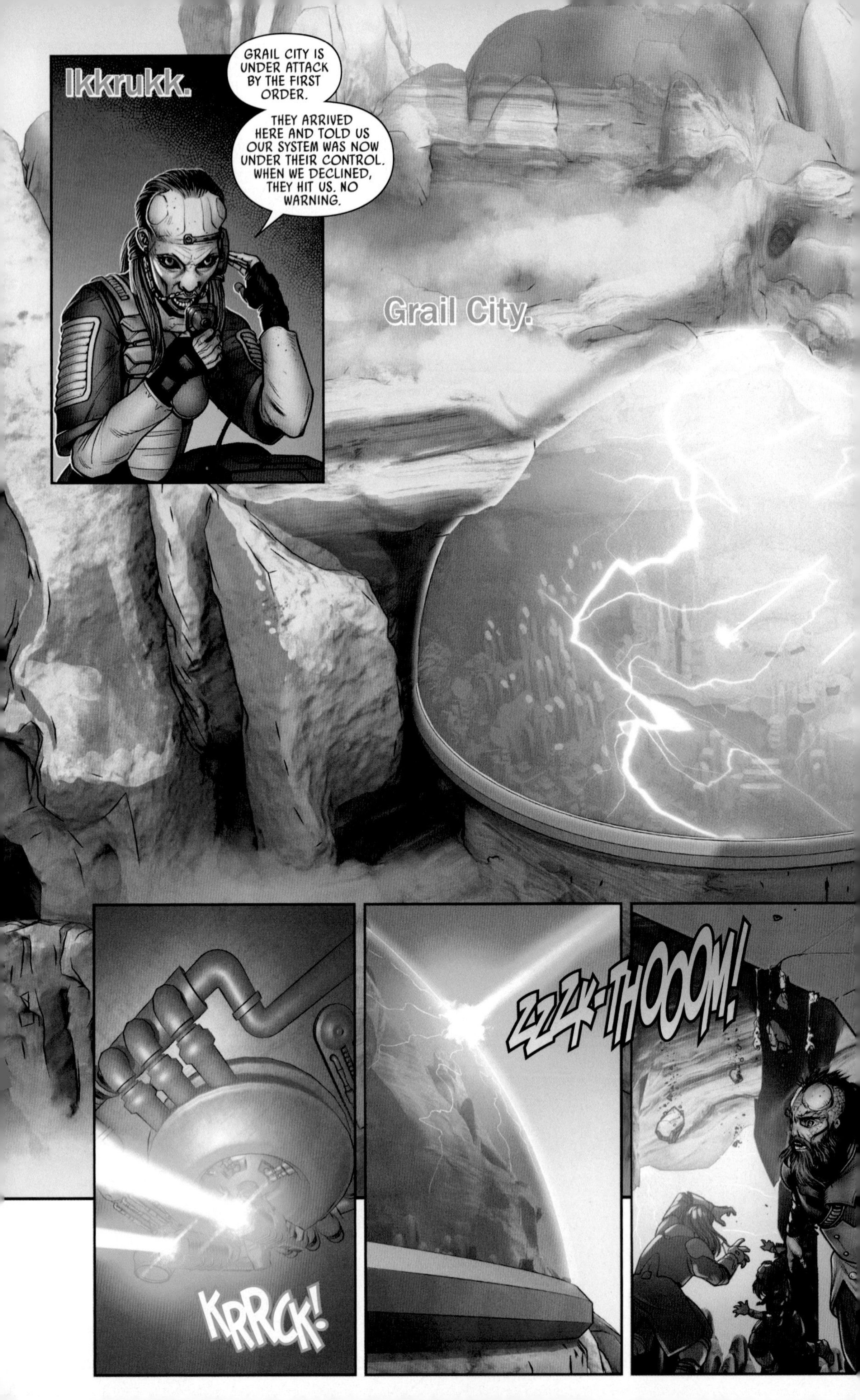
Ikkrukk.
GRAIL CITY IS UNDER ATTACK BY THE FIRST ORDER.
THEY ARRIVED HERE AND TOLD US OUR SYSTEM WAS NOW UNDER THEIR CONTROL. WHEN WE DECLINED, THEY HIT US. NO WARNING.
Grail City.
KRRCK!
ZZZK-THOOOM!

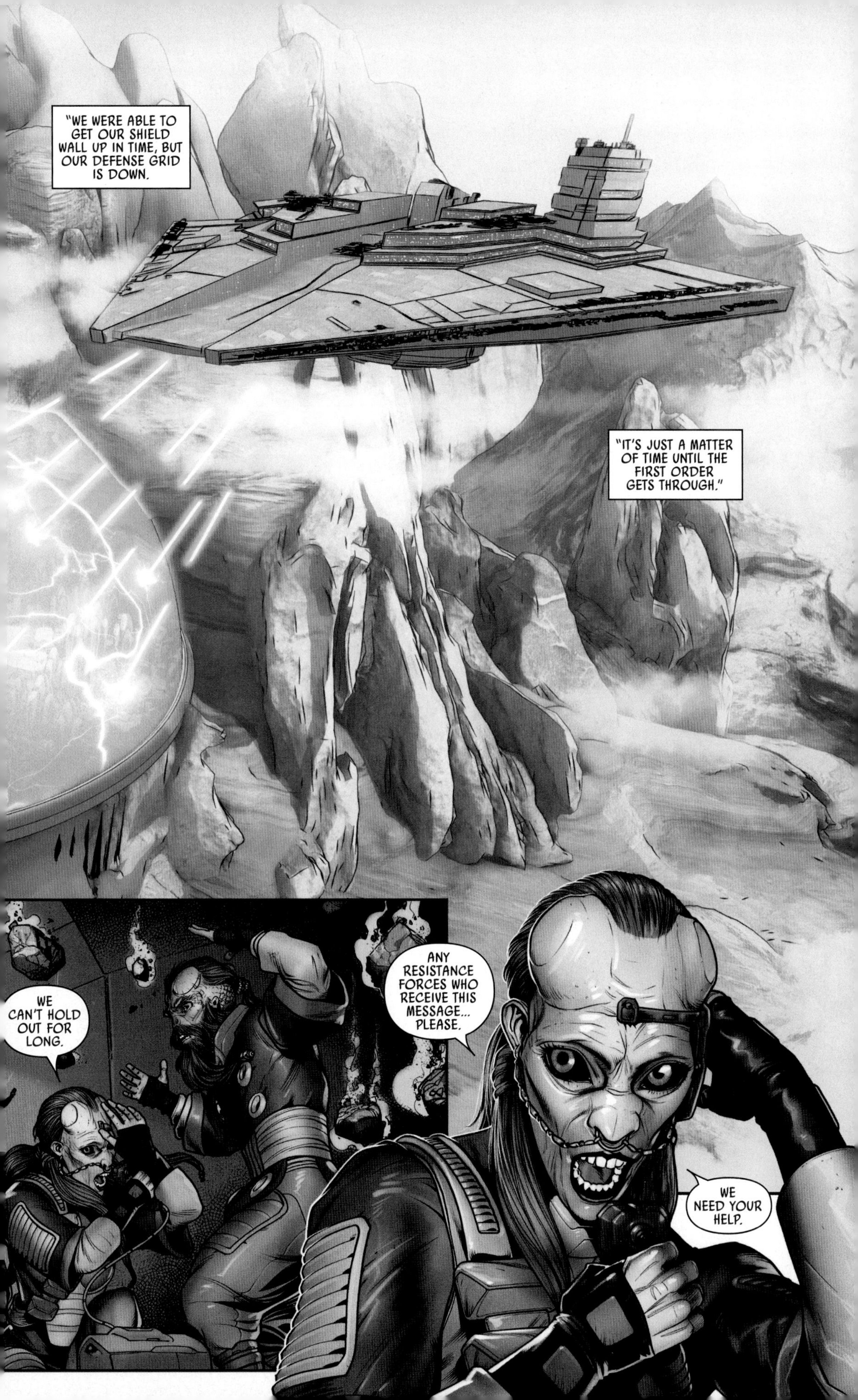
"WE WERE ABLE TO GET OUR SHIELD WALL UP IN TIME, BUT OUR DEFENSE GRID IS DOWN.
"IT'S JUST A MATTER OF TIME UNTIL THE FIRST ORDER GETS THROUGH."
WE CAN'T HOLD OUT FOR LONG.
ANY RESISTANCE FORCES WHO RECEIVE THIS MESSAGE... PLEASE.
WE NEED YOUR HELP.

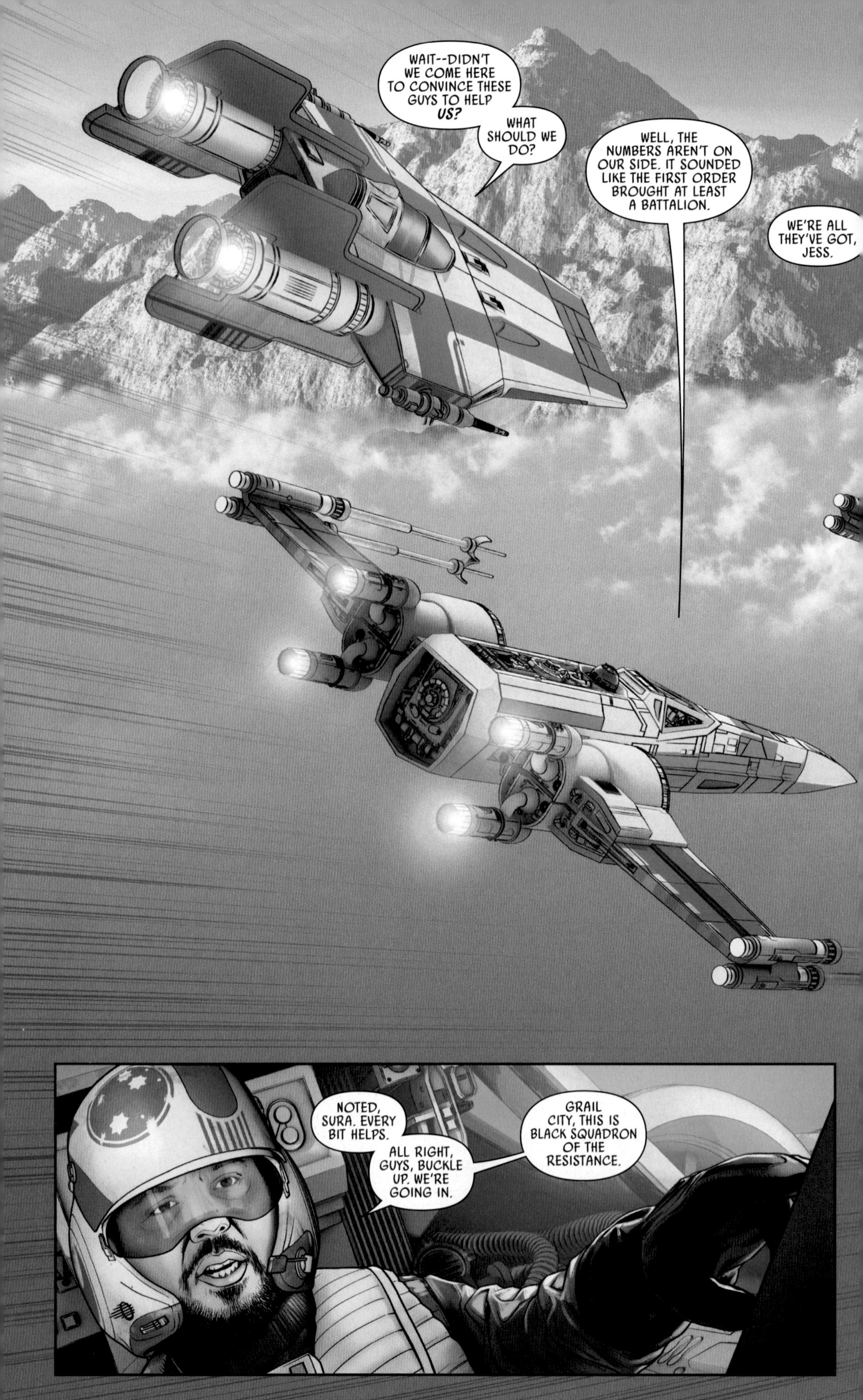

WAIT--DIDN'T WE COME HERE TO CONVINCE THESE GUYS TO HELP *US?*
WHAT SHOULD WE DO?
WELL, THE NUMBERS AREN'T ON OUR SIDE. IT SOUNDED LIKE THE FIRST ORDER BROUGHT AT LEAST A BATTALION.
WE'RE ALL THEY'VE GOT, JESS.
NOTED, SURA. EVERY BIT HELPS.
ALL RIGHT, GUYS, BUCKLE UP. WE'RE GOING IN.
GRAIL CITY, THIS IS BLACK SQUADRON OF THE RESISTANCE.

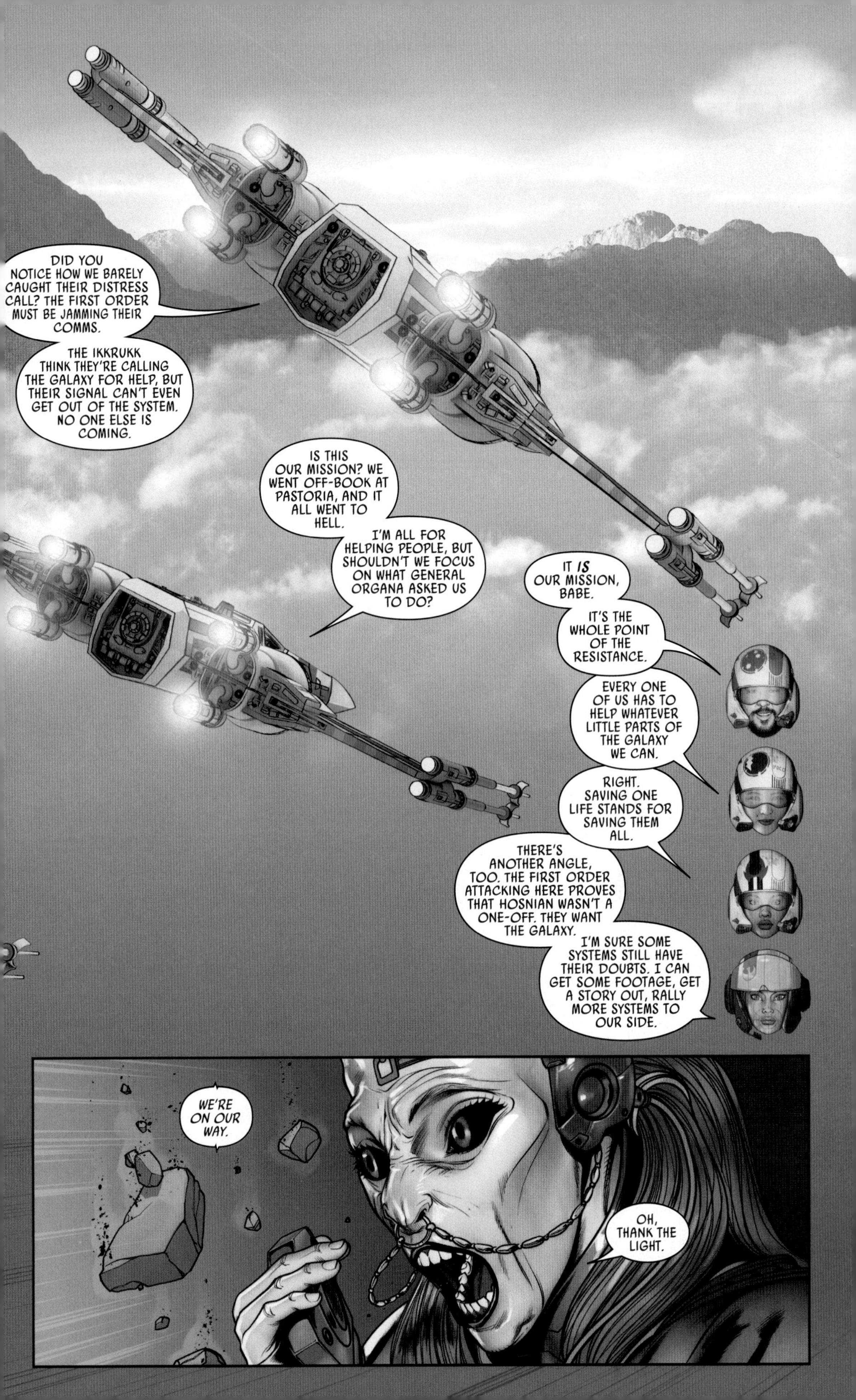
DID YOU NOTICE HOW WE BARELY CAUGHT THEIR DISTRESS CALL? THE FIRST ORDER MUST BE JAMMING THEIR COMMS.
THE IKKRUKK THINK THEY'RE CALLING THE GALAXY FOR HELP, BUT THEIR SIGNAL CAN'T EVEN GET OUT OF THE SYSTEM. NO ONE ELSE IS COMING.
IS THIS OUR MISSION? WE WENT OFF-BOOK AT PASTORIA, AND IT ALL WENT TO HELL.
I'M ALL FOR HELPING PEOPLE, BUT SHOULDN'T WE FOCUS ON WHAT GENERAL ORGANA ASKED US TO DO?
IT *IS* OUR MISSION, BABE.
IT'S THE WHOLE POINT OF THE RESISTANCE.
EVERY ONE OF US HAS TO HELP WHATEVER LITTLE PARTS OF THE GALAXY WE CAN.
RIGHT. SAVING ONE LIFE STANDS FOR SAVING THEM ALL.
THERE'S ANOTHER ANGLE, TOO. THE FIRST ORDER ATTACKING HERE PROVES THAT HOSNIAN WASN'T A ONE-OFF. THEY WANT THE GALAXY.
I'M SURE SOME SYSTEMS STILL HAVE THEIR DOUBTS. I CAN GET SOME FOOTAGE, GET A STORY OUT, RALLY MORE SYSTEMS TO OUR SIDE.
WE'RE ON OUR WAY.
OH, THANK THE LIGHT.

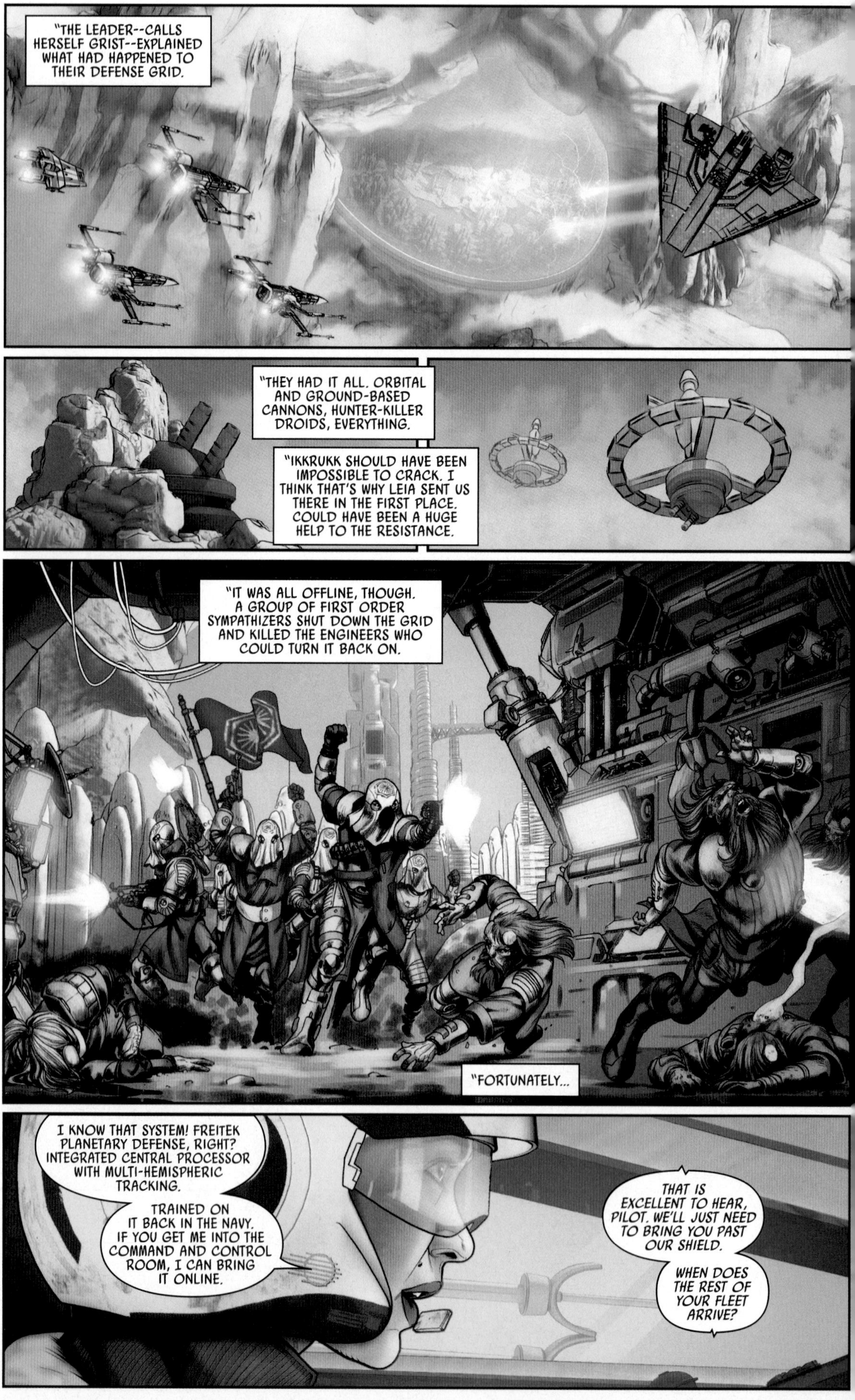
"THE LEADER--CALLS HERSELF GRIST--EXPLAINED WHAT HAD HAPPENED TO THEIR DEFENSE GRID.
"THEY HAD IT ALL. ORBITAL AND GROUND-BASED CANNONS, HUNTER-KILLER DROIDS, EVERYTHING.
"IKKRUKK SHOULD HAVE BEEN IMPOSSIBLE TO CRACK. I THINK THAT'S WHY LEIA SENT US THERE IN THE FIRST PLACE. COULD HAVE BEEN A HUGE HELP TO THE RESISTANCE.
"IT WAS ALL OFFLINE, THOUGH. A GROUP OF FIRST ORDER SYMPATHIZERS SHUT DOWN THE GRID AND KILLED THE ENGINEERS WHO COULD TURN IT BACK ON.
"FORTUNATELY...
I KNOW THAT SYSTEM! FREITEK PLANETARY DEFENSE, RIGHT? INTEGRATED CENTRAL PROCESSOR WITH MULTI-HEMISPHERIC TRACKING.
TRAINED ON IT BACK IN THE NAVY. IF YOU GET ME INTO THE COMMAND AND CONTROL ROOM, I CAN BRING IT ONLINE.
THAT IS EXCELLENT TO HEAR, PILOT. WE'LL JUST NEED TO BRING YOU PAST OUR SHIELD.
WHEN DOES THE REST OF YOUR FLEET ARRIVE?

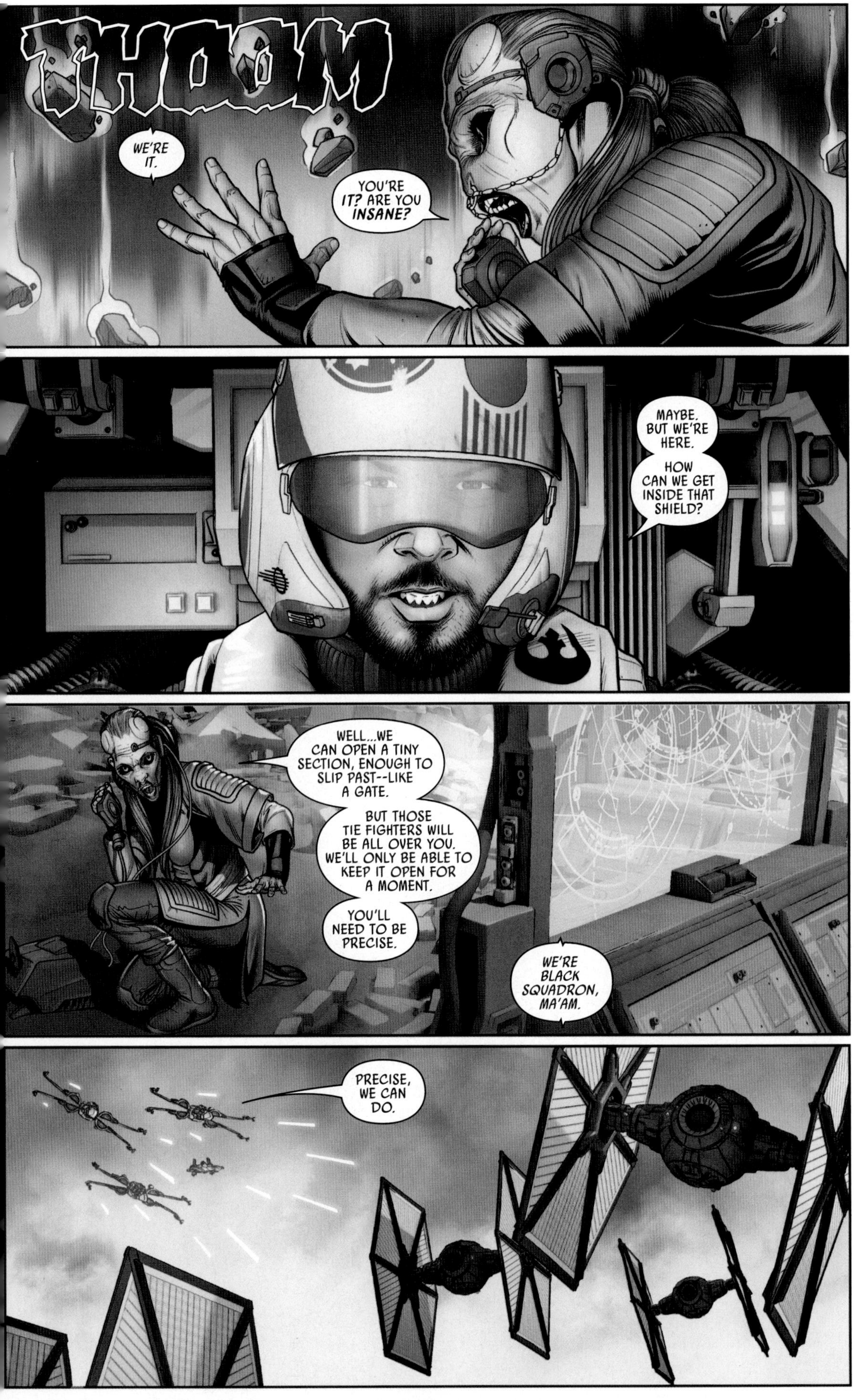
THOOM
WE'RE IT.
YOU'RE IT? ARE YOU INSANE?
MAYBE. BUT WE'RE HERE.
HOW CAN WE GET INSIDE THAT SHIELD?
WELL...WE CAN OPEN A TINY SECTION, ENOUGH TO SLIP PAST--LIKE A GATE.
BUT THOSE TIE FIGHTERS WILL BE ALL OVER YOU. WE'LL ONLY BE ABLE TO KEEP IT OPEN FOR A MOMENT.
YOU'LL NEED TO BE PRECISE.
WE'RE BLACK SQUADRON, MA'AM.
PRECISE, WE CAN DO.

First Order Heavy Cruiser Fortitude.

THE CITY'S SHIELDS ARE DOWN TO 54 PERCENT, COLONEL.

EXCELLENT. IT'S ONLY A MATTER OF TIME.

PICKING UP INCOMING FIGHTERS!

THAT'S *ALL* OF THEM? JUST FOUR? HNH.

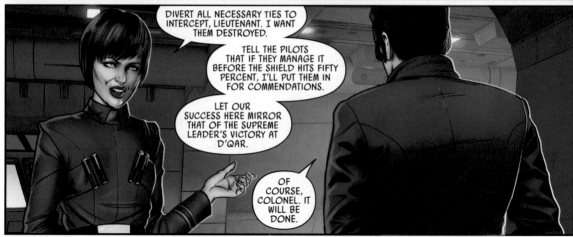

DIVERT ALL NECESSARY TIES TO INTERCEPT, LIEUTENANT. I WANT THEM DESTROYED.

TELL THE PILOTS THAT IF THEY MANAGE IT BEFORE THE SHIELD HITS FIFTY PERCENT, I'LL PUT THEM IN FOR COMMENDATIONS.

LET OUR SUCCESS HERE MIRROR THAT OF THE SUPREME LEADER'S VICTORY AT D'QAR.

OF COURSE, COLONEL. IT WILL BE DONE.

UH...I GUESS I'LL TAKE THE HUNDRED ON THE LEFT?

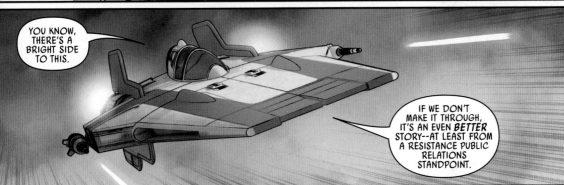

YOU KNOW, THERE'S A BRIGHT SIDE TO THIS.

IF WE DON'T MAKE IT THROUGH, IT'S AN EVEN *BETTER* STORY--AT LEAST FROM A RESISTANCE PUBLIC RELATIONS STANDPOINT.

FOUR BRAVE HEROES PERISH FIGHTING FIRST ORDER TYRANNY IN A BATTLE AGAINST IMPOSSIBLE ODDS...THAT'S BEAUTIFUL!

THIS IS BLACK LEADER. EVERYONE IGNORE EVERYTHING SURA JUST SAID.

THAT IS AN ORDER.

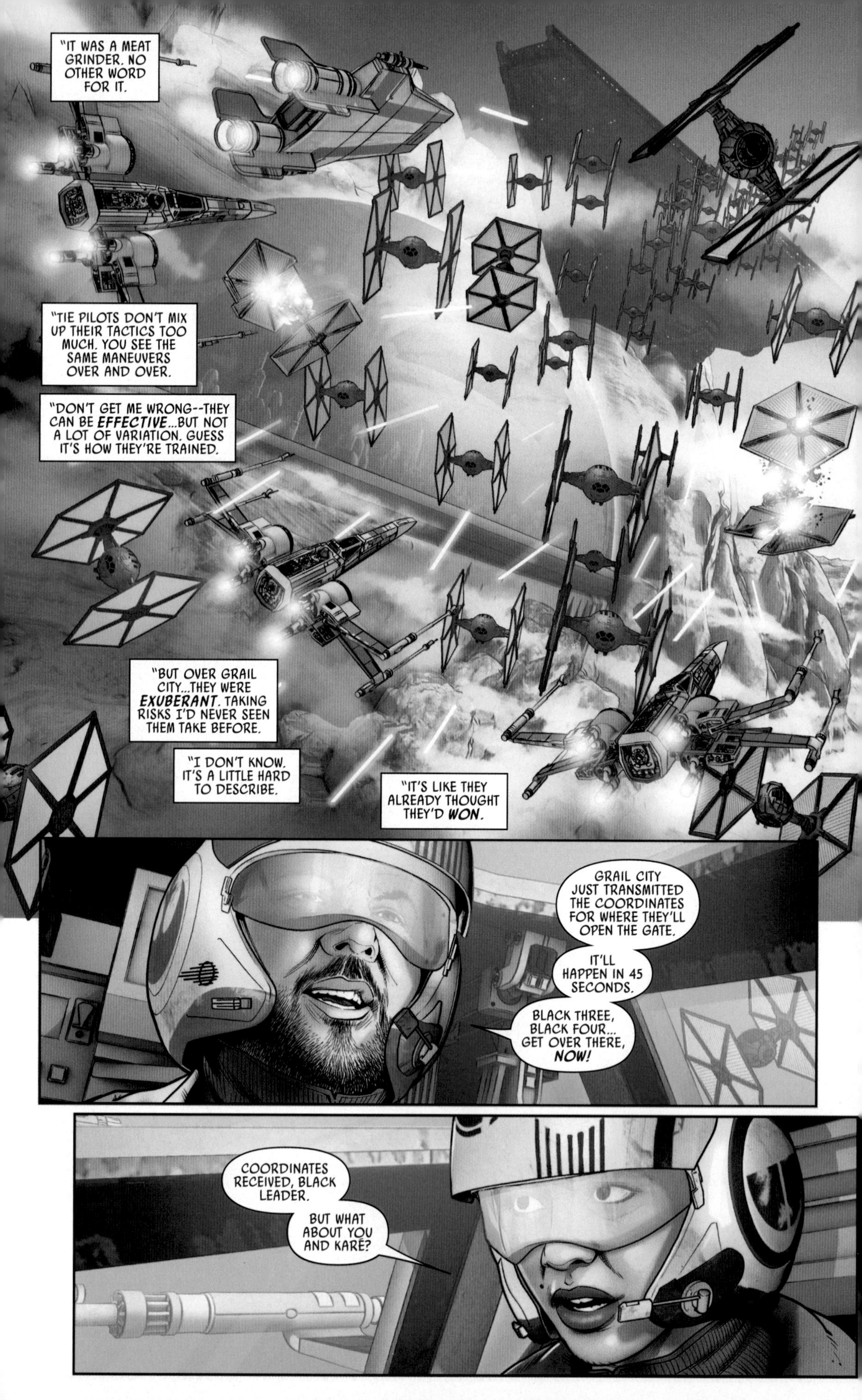
"IT WAS A MEAT GRINDER. NO OTHER WORD FOR IT.
"TIE PILOTS DON'T MIX UP THEIR TACTICS TOO MUCH. YOU SEE THE SAME MANEUVERS OVER AND OVER.
"DON'T GET ME WRONG--THEY CAN BE EFFECTIVE...BUT NOT A LOT OF VARIATION. GUESS IT'S HOW THEY'RE TRAINED.
"BUT OVER GRAIL CITY...THEY WERE EXUBERANT. TAKING RISKS I'D NEVER SEEN THEM TAKE BEFORE.
"I DON'T KNOW. IT'S A LITTLE HARD TO DESCRIBE.
"IT'S LIKE THEY ALREADY THOUGHT THEY'D WON.
GRAIL CITY JUST TRANSMITTED THE COORDINATES FOR WHERE THEY'LL OPEN THE GATE.
IT'LL HAPPEN IN 45 SECONDS.
BLACK THREE, BLACK FOUR... GET OVER THERE, NOW!
COORDINATES RECEIVED, BLACK LEADER.
BUT WHAT ABOUT YOU AND KARÉ?

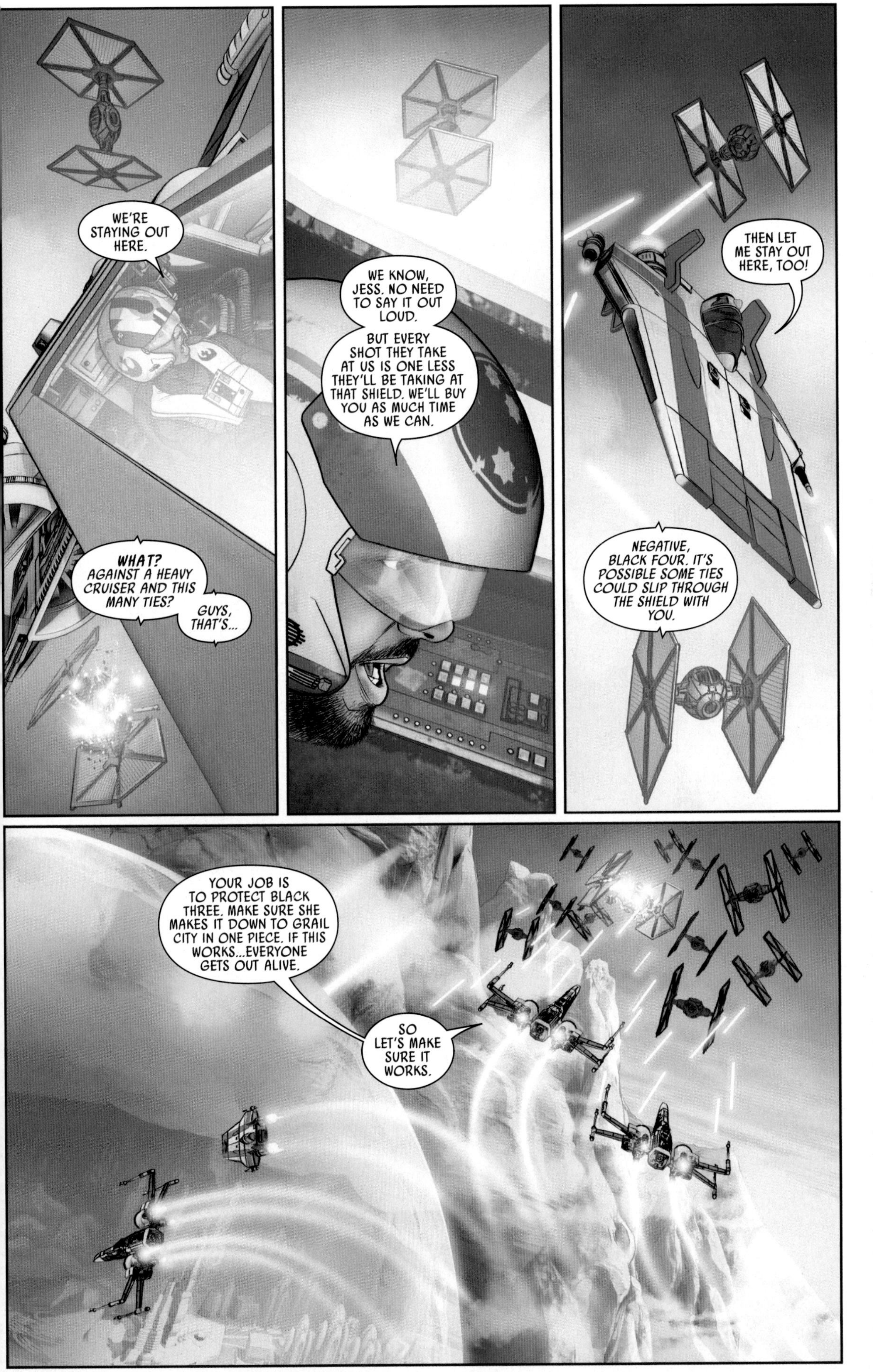
WE'RE STAYING OUT HERE.
WHAT? AGAINST A HEAVY CRUISER AND THIS MANY TIES?
GUYS, THAT'S...
WE KNOW, JESS. NO NEED TO SAY IT OUT LOUD.
BUT EVERY SHOT THEY TAKE AT US IS ONE LESS THEY'LL BE TAKING AT THAT SHIELD. WE'LL BUY YOU AS MUCH TIME AS WE CAN.
THEN LET ME STAY OUT HERE, TOO!
NEGATIVE, BLACK FOUR. IT'S POSSIBLE SOME TIES COULD SLIP THROUGH THE SHIELD WITH YOU.
YOUR JOB IS TO PROTECT BLACK THREE. MAKE SURE SHE MAKES IT DOWN TO GRAIL CITY IN ONE PIECE. IF THIS WORKS...EVERYONE GETS OUT ALIVE.
SO LET'S MAKE SURE IT WORKS.

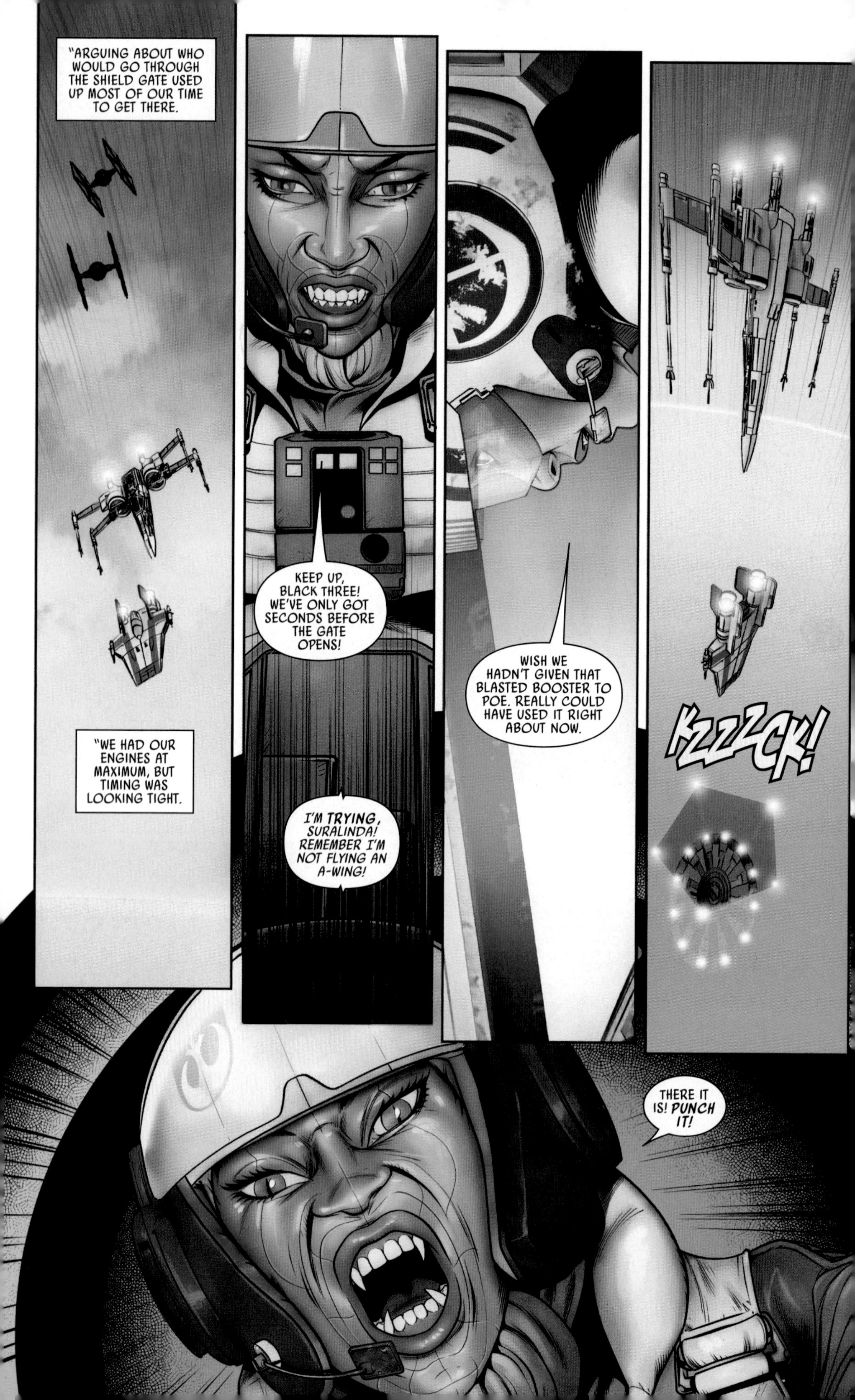
"ARGUING ABOUT WHO WOULD GO THROUGH THE SHIELD GATE USED UP MOST OF OUR TIME TO GET THERE.
"WE HAD OUR ENGINES AT MAXIMUM, BUT TIMING WAS LOOKING TIGHT.
KEEP UP, BLACK THREE! WE'VE ONLY GOT SECONDS BEFORE THE GATE OPENS!
I'M TRYING, SURALINDA! REMEMBER I'M NOT FLYING AN A-WING!
WISH WE HADN'T GIVEN THAT BLASTED BOOSTER TO POE. REALLY COULD HAVE USED IT RIGHT ABOUT NOW.
KZZZCK!
THERE IT IS! PUNCH IT!

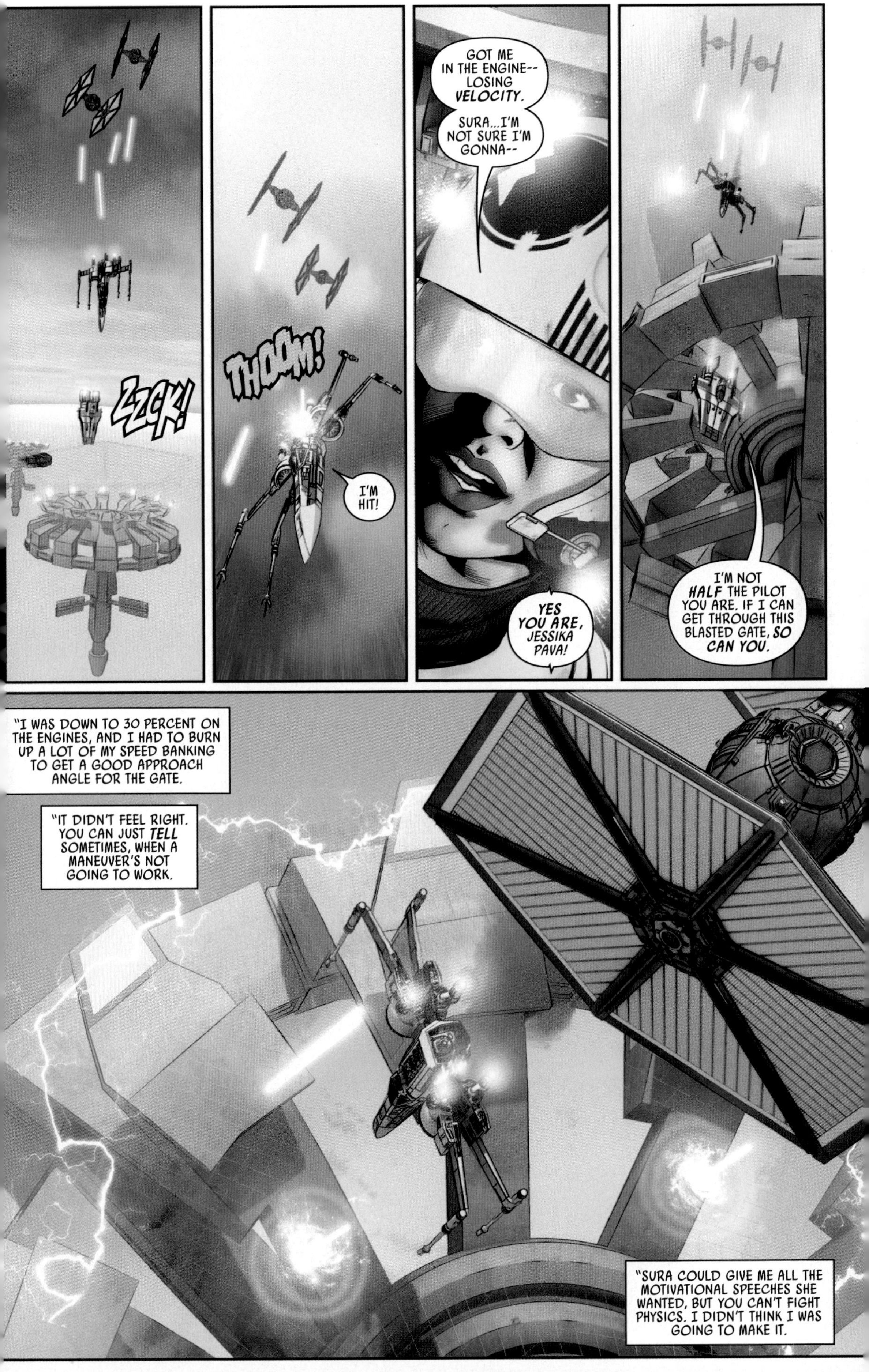
ZZCK!
THOOM!
I'M HIT!
GOT ME IN THE ENGINE-- LOSING VELOCITY.
SURA...I'M NOT SURE I'M GONNA--
YES YOU ARE, JESSIKA PAVA!
I'M NOT HALF THE PILOT YOU ARE. IF I CAN GET THROUGH THIS BLASTED GATE, SO CAN YOU.
"I WAS DOWN TO 30 PERCENT ON THE ENGINES, AND I HAD TO BURN UP A LOT OF MY SPEED BANKING TO GET A GOOD APPROACH ANGLE FOR THE GATE.
"IT DIDN'T FEEL RIGHT. YOU CAN JUST TELL SOMETIMES, WHEN A MANEUVER'S NOT GOING TO WORK.
"SURA COULD GIVE ME ALL THE MOTIVATIONAL SPEECHES SHE WANTED, BUT YOU CAN'T FIGHT PHYSICS. I DIDN'T THINK I WAS GOING TO MAKE IT.

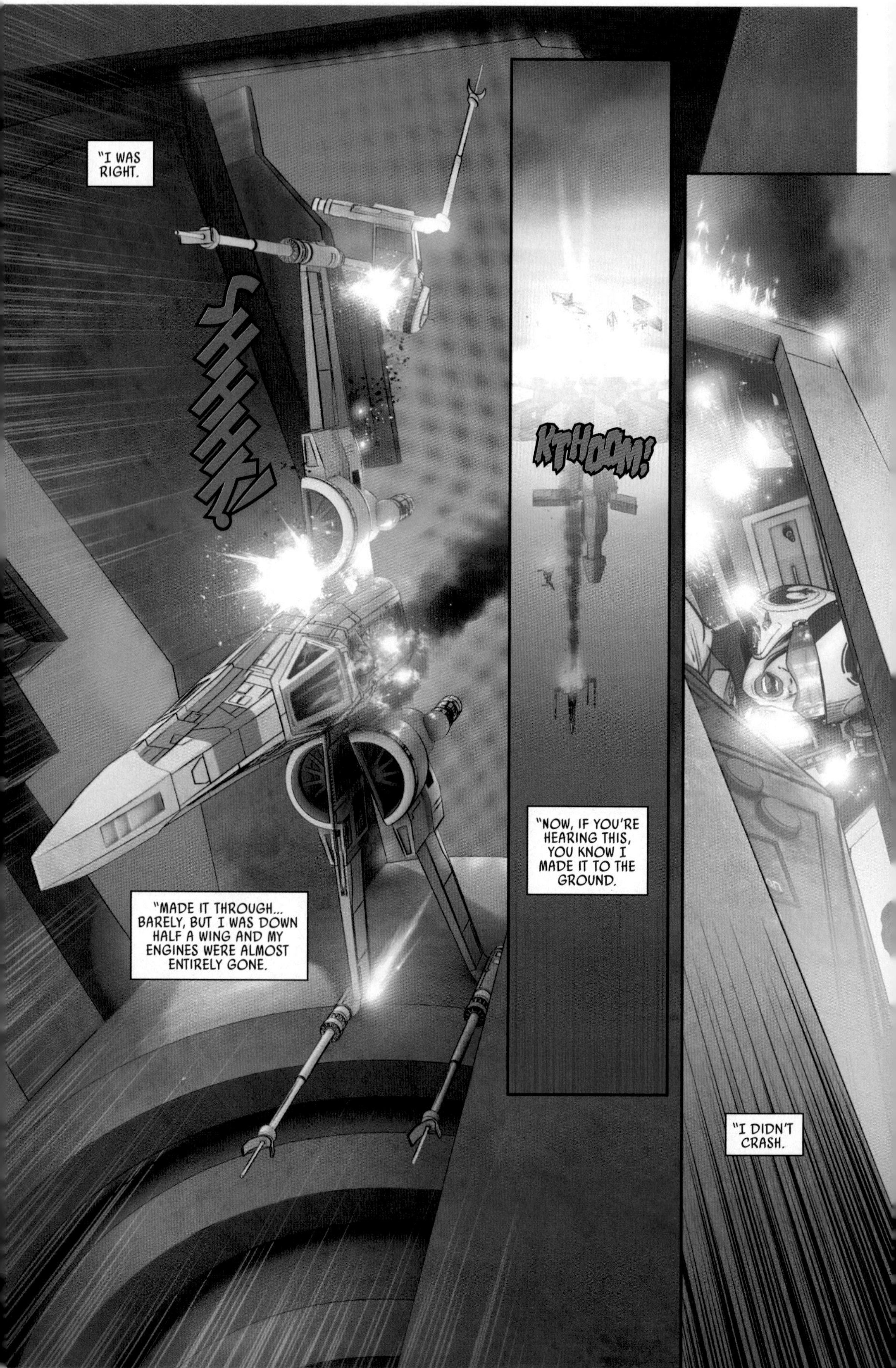
"I WAS RIGHT.
SHHHK!
"MADE IT THROUGH... BARELY, BUT I WAS DOWN HALF A WING AND MY ENGINES WERE ALMOST ENTIRELY GONE.
KTHOOM!
"NOW, IF YOU'RE HEARING THIS, YOU KNOW I MADE IT TO THE GROUND.
"I DIDN'T CRASH.

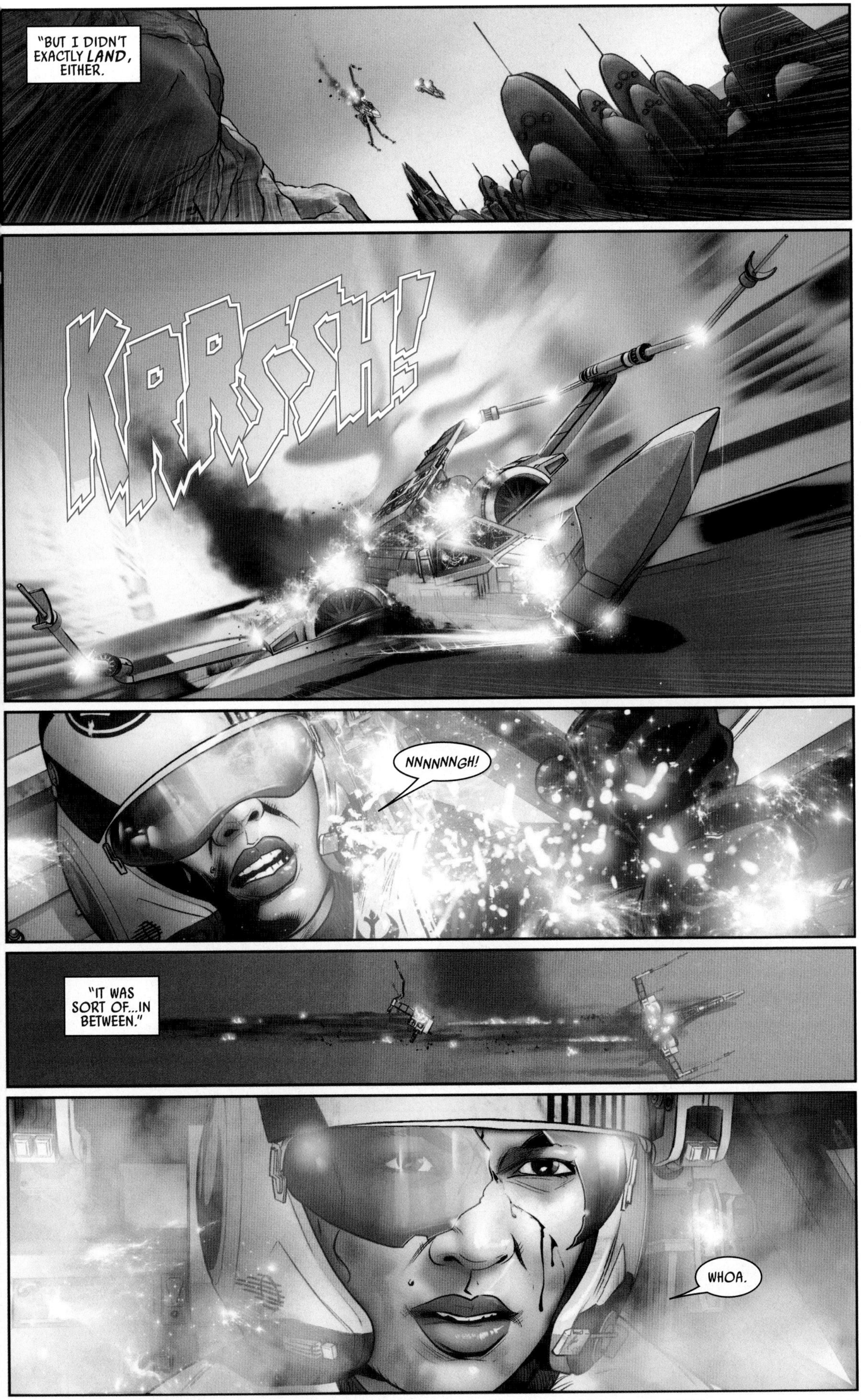
"BUT I DIDN'T EXACTLY LAND, EITHER.
KRRSSH!
NNNNNNGH!
"IT WAS SORT OF...IN BETWEEN."
WHOA.

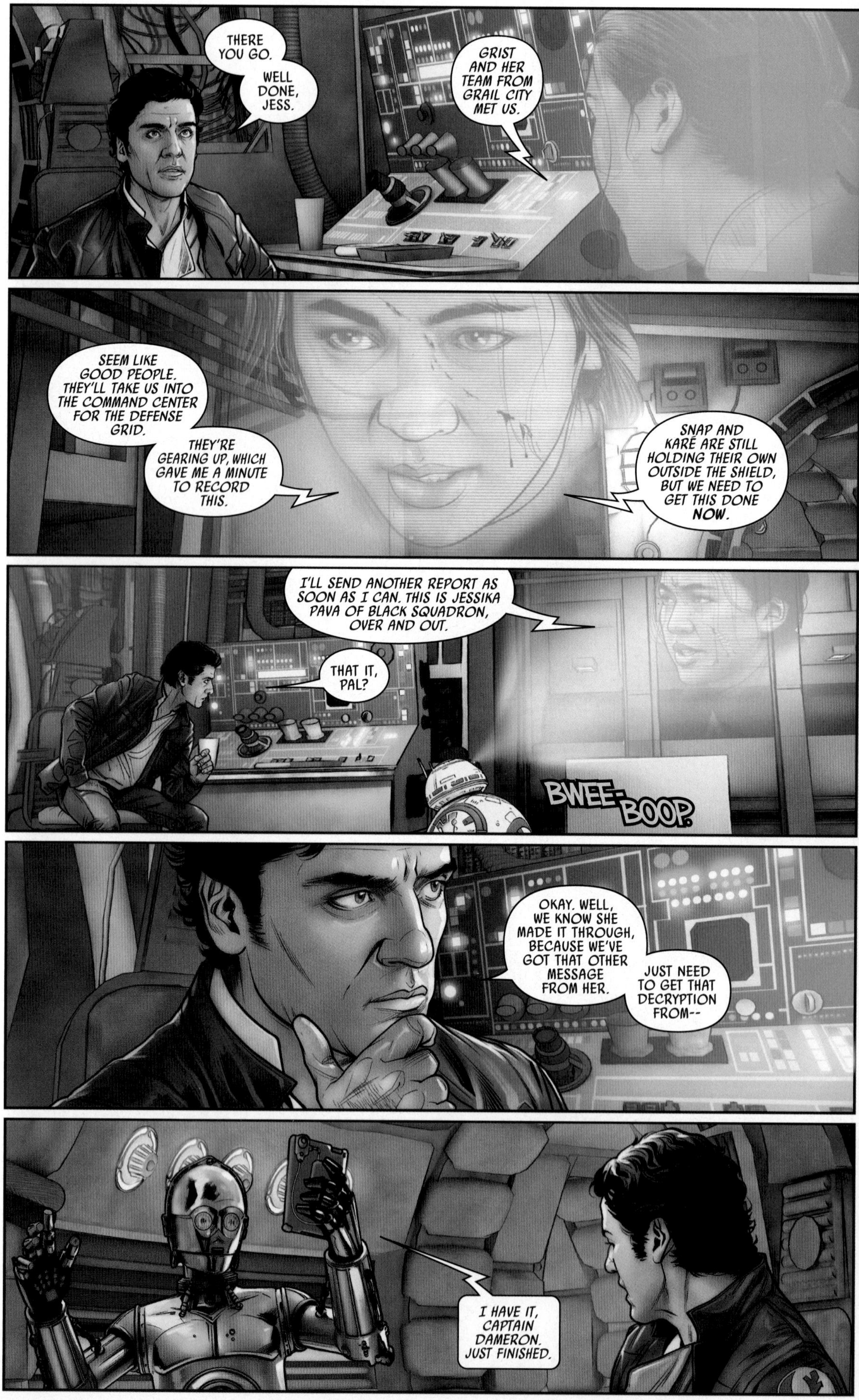
THERE YOU GO.
WELL DONE, JESS.
GRIST AND HER TEAM FROM GRAIL CITY MET US.
SEEM LIKE GOOD PEOPLE. THEY'LL TAKE US INTO THE COMMAND CENTER FOR THE DEFENSE GRID.
THEY'RE GEARING UP, WHICH GAVE ME A MINUTE TO RECORD THIS.
SNAP AND KARÉ ARE STILL HOLDING THEIR OWN OUTSIDE THE SHIELD, BUT WE NEED TO GET THIS DONE NOW.
I'LL SEND ANOTHER REPORT AS SOON AS I CAN. THIS IS JESSIKA PAVA OF BLACK SQUADRON, OVER AND OUT.
THAT IT, PAL?
BWEE-BOOP.
OKAY. WELL, WE KNOW SHE MADE IT THROUGH, BECAUSE WE'VE GOT THAT OTHER MESSAGE FROM HER.
JUST NEED TO GET THAT DECRYPTION FROM--
I HAVE IT, CAPTAIN DAMERON. JUST FINISHED.

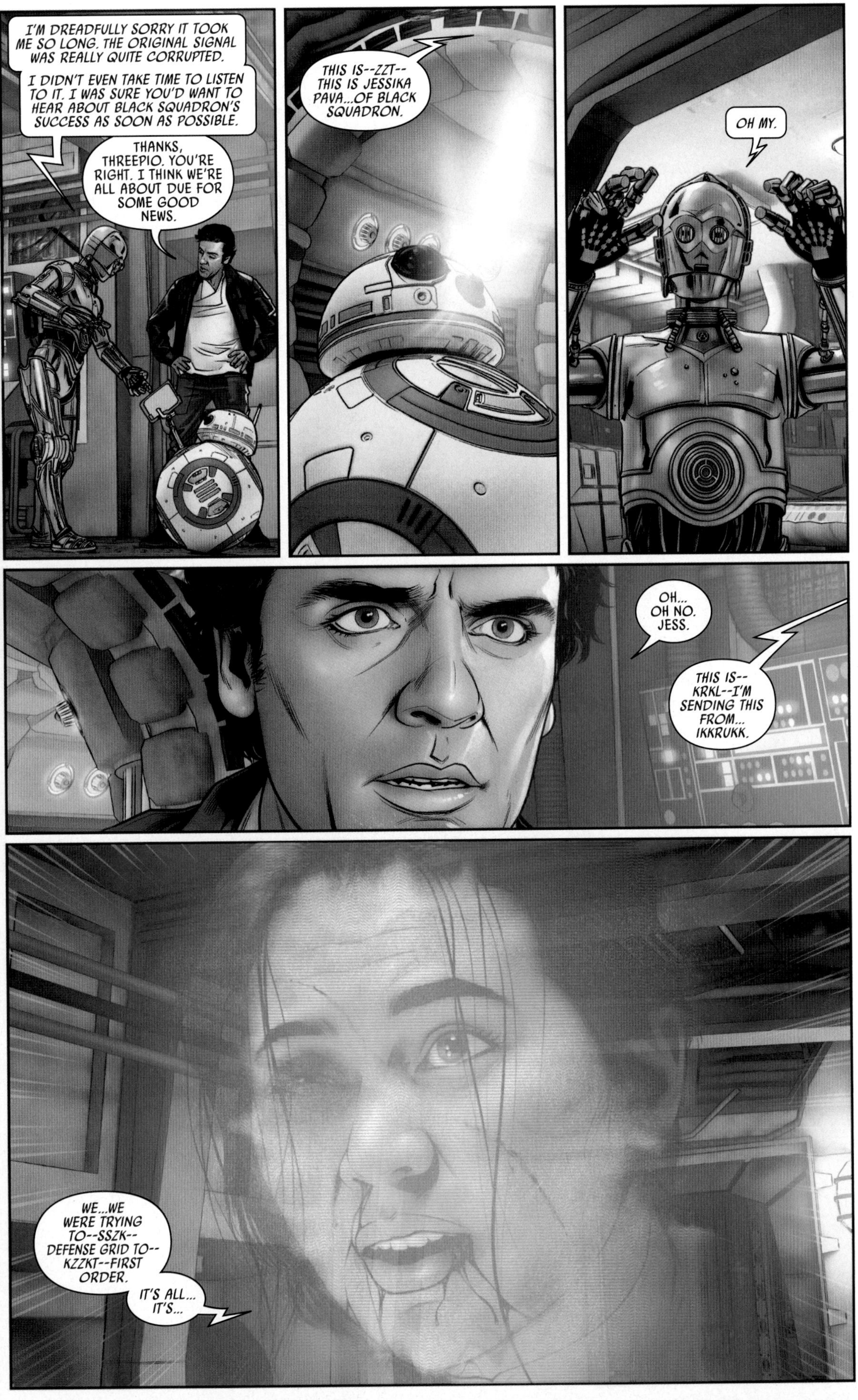
I'M DREADFULLY SORRY IT TOOK ME SO LONG. THE ORIGINAL SIGNAL WAS REALLY QUITE CORRUPTED.
I DIDN'T EVEN TAKE TIME TO LISTEN TO IT. I WAS SURE YOU'D WANT TO HEAR ABOUT BLACK SQUADRON'S SUCCESS AS SOON AS POSSIBLE.
THANKS, THREEPIO. YOU'RE RIGHT. I THINK WE'RE ALL ABOUT DUE FOR SOME GOOD NEWS.
THIS IS--ZZT--THIS IS JESSIKA PAVA...OF BLACK SQUADRON.
OH MY.
OH... OH NO. JESS.
THIS IS--KRKL--I'M SENDING THIS FROM... IKKRUKK.
WE...WE WERE TRYING TO--SSZK--DEFENSE GRID TO--KZZKT--FIRST ORDER.
IT'S ALL... IT'S...

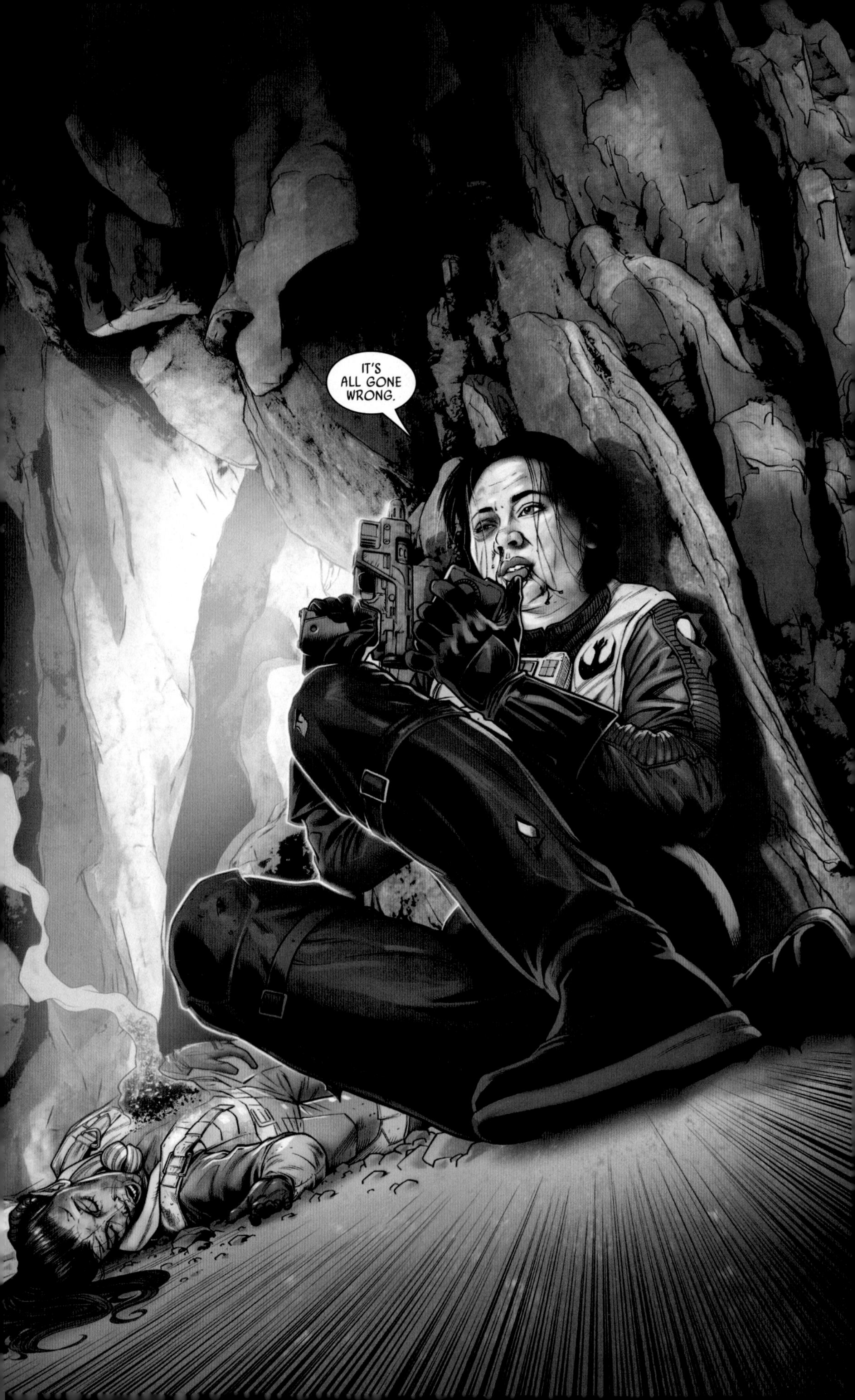
IT'S ALL GONE WRONG.

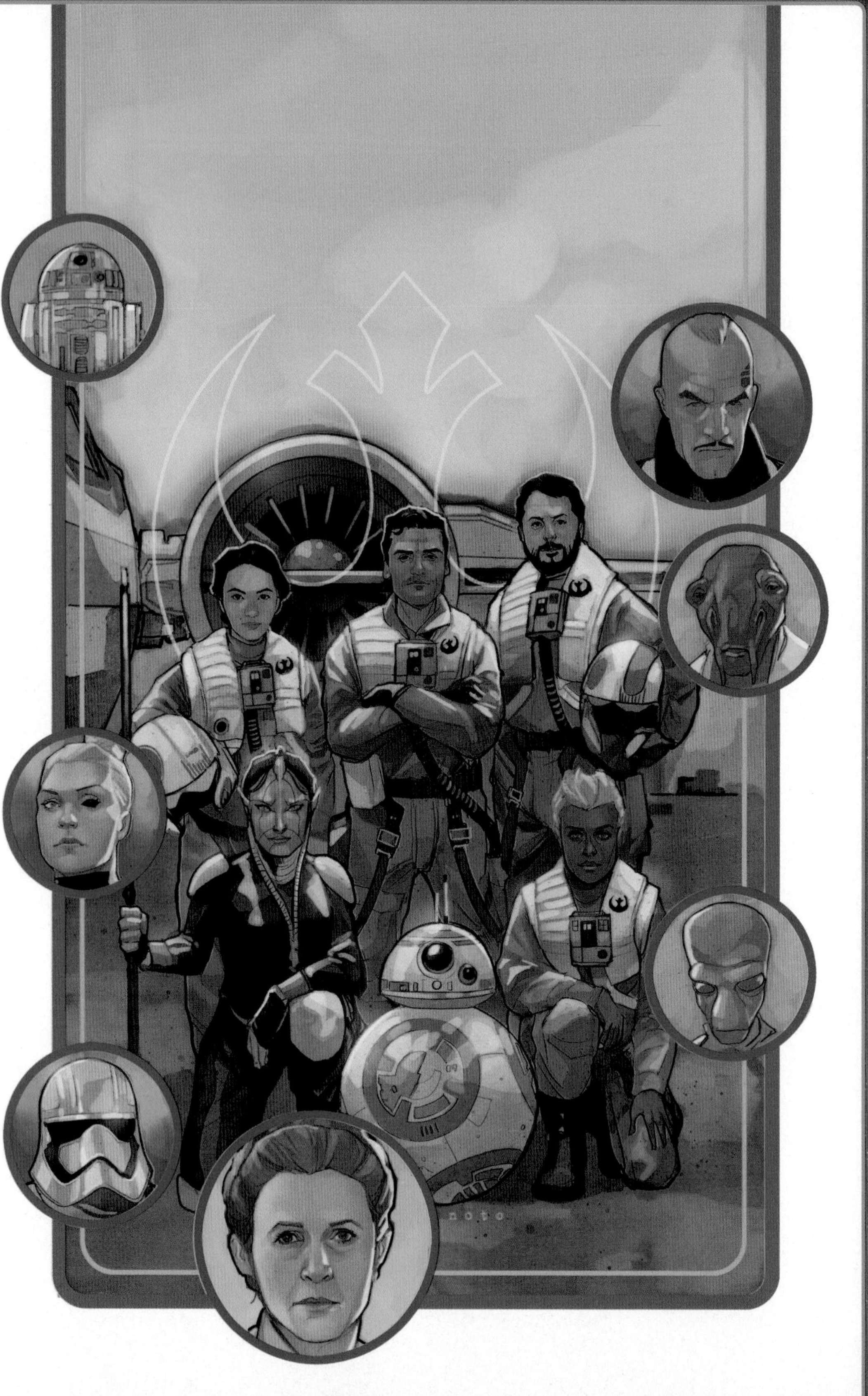
noto

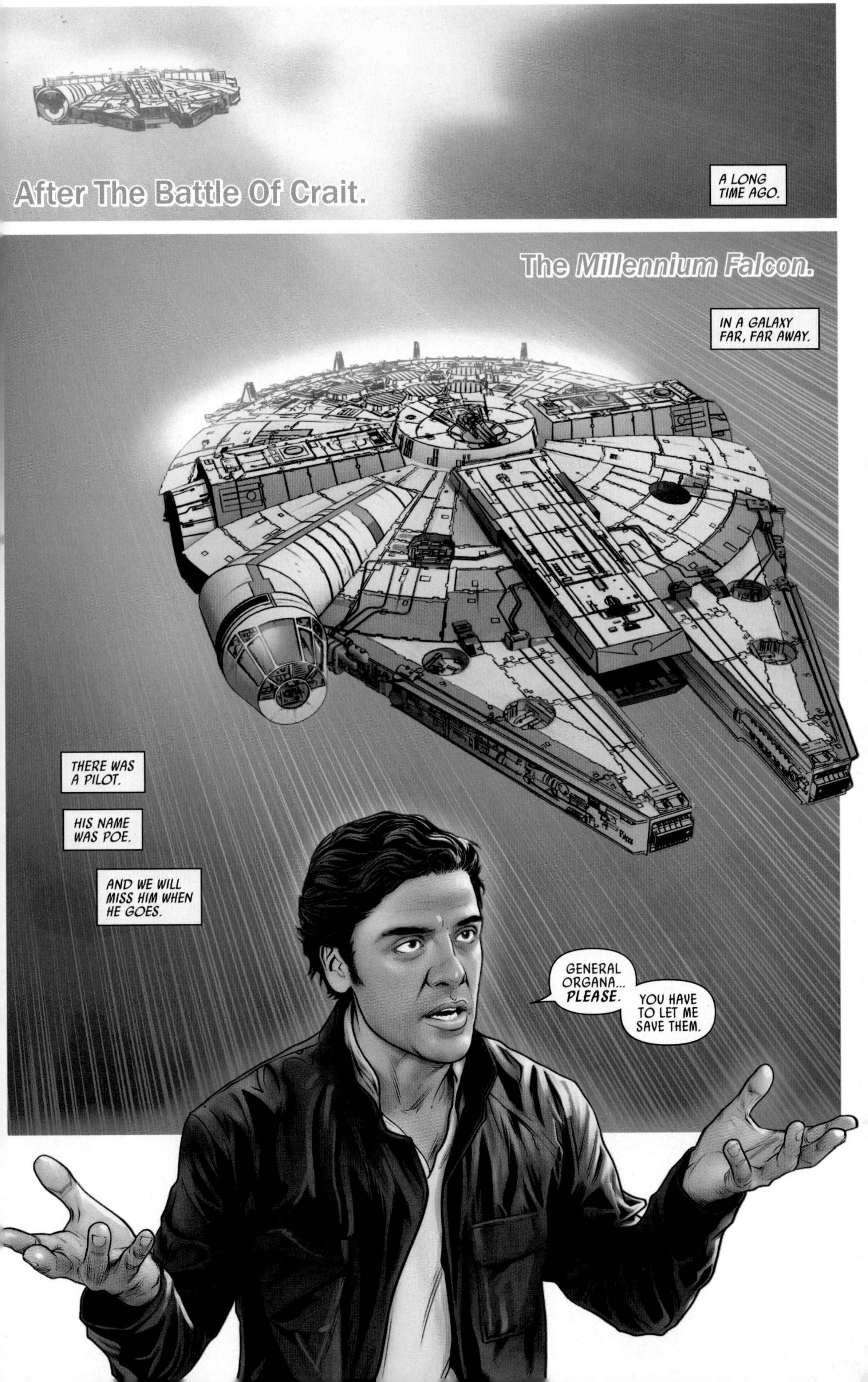
After The Battle Of Crait.
A LONG TIME AGO.
The Millennium Falcon.
IN A GALAXY FAR, FAR AWAY.
THERE WAS A PILOT.
HIS NAME WAS POE.
AND WE WILL MISS HIM WHEN HE GOES.
GENERAL ORGANA... PLEASE.
YOU HAVE TO LET ME SAVE THEM.

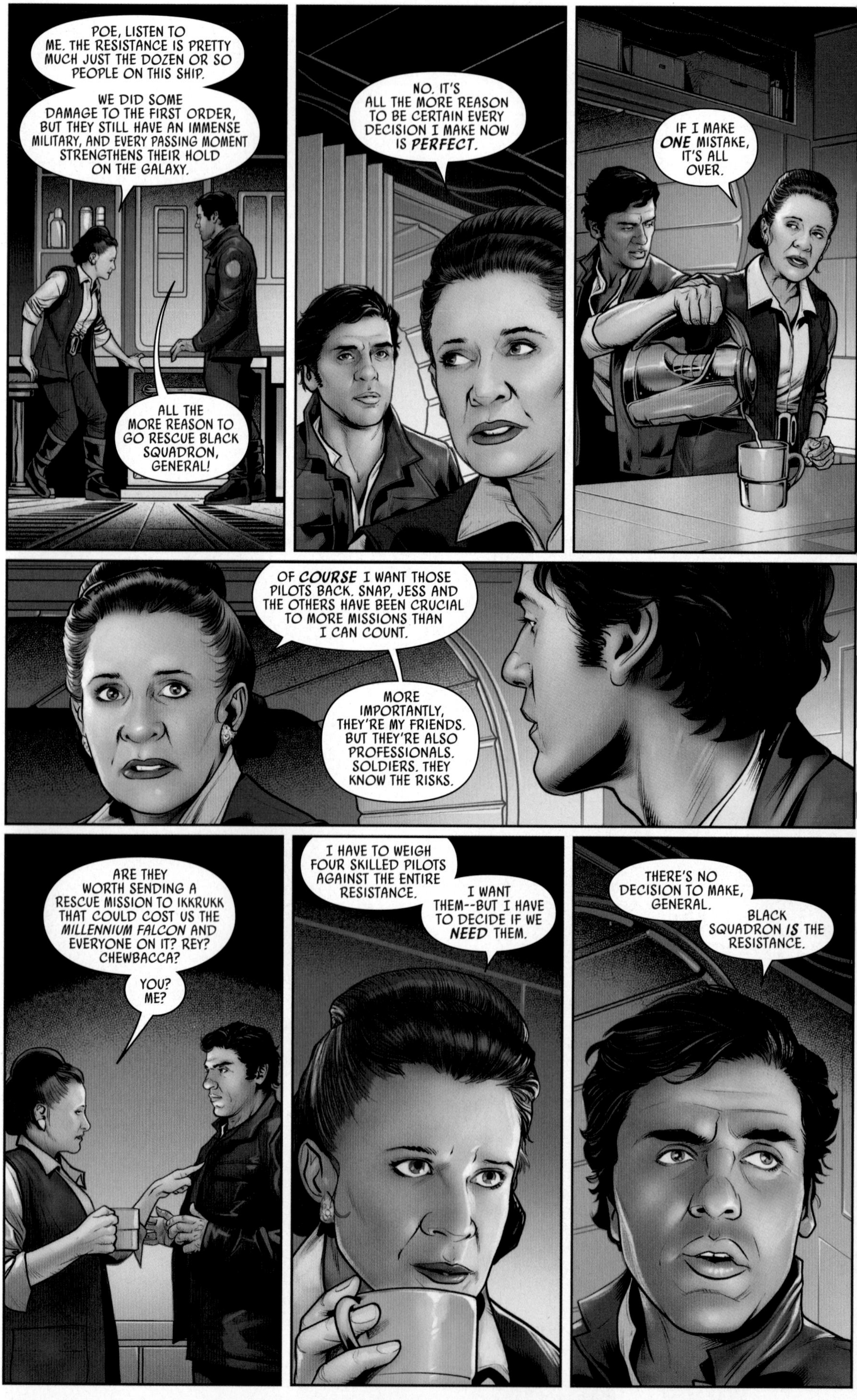

POE, LISTEN TO ME. THE RESISTANCE IS PRETTY MUCH JUST THE DOZEN OR SO PEOPLE ON THIS SHIP.
WE DID SOME DAMAGE TO THE FIRST ORDER, BUT THEY STILL HAVE AN IMMENSE MILITARY, AND EVERY PASSING MOMENT STRENGTHENS THEIR HOLD ON THE GALAXY.
ALL THE MORE REASON TO GO RESCUE BLACK SQUADRON, GENERAL!
NO. IT'S ALL THE MORE REASON TO BE CERTAIN EVERY DECISION I MAKE NOW IS *PERFECT.*
IF I MAKE *ONE* MISTAKE, IT'S ALL OVER.
OF *COURSE* I WANT THOSE PILOTS BACK. SNAP, JESS AND THE OTHERS HAVE BEEN CRUCIAL TO MORE MISSIONS THAN I CAN COUNT.
MORE IMPORTANTLY, THEY'RE MY FRIENDS. BUT THEY'RE ALSO PROFESSIONALS. SOLDIERS. THEY KNOW THE RISKS.
ARE THEY WORTH SENDING A RESCUE MISSION TO IKKRUKK THAT COULD COST US THE *MILLENNIUM FALCON* AND EVERYONE ON IT? REY? CHEWBACCA?
YOU? ME?
I HAVE TO WEIGH FOUR SKILLED PILOTS AGAINST THE ENTIRE RESISTANCE.
I WANT THEM--BUT I HAVE TO DECIDE IF WE *NEED* THEM.
THERE'S NO DECISION TO MAKE, GENERAL.
BLACK SQUADRON *IS* THE RESISTANCE.

I KNOW YOU NEED ME TO BE MORE THAN JUST A FIGHTER PILOT. YOU WANT ME TO **LEAD**, AND LEADERSHIP MEANS MAKING THE HARD CHOICES.

I GET IT.

BUT I **AM** A PILOT, AND THERE'S SOMETHING WE SAY TO EACH OTHER. ONE OF THE MOST IMPORTANT THINGS.

NO ONE GETS LEFT BEHIND.

YES, POE, YOU'RE A PILOT, AND I'M AN OLD WOMAN WHO HAS TO RALLY A GALAXY AGAINST IMPOSSIBLE ODDS.

FOR THE **THIRD** TIME.

GENERAL, **THIS IS HOW YOU DO IT**. YOU THINK THE FIRST ORDER WOULD GO RESCUE FOUR PILOTS? HELL NO.

AND THAT'S **EVERYTHING THE RESISTANCE STANDS FOR.**

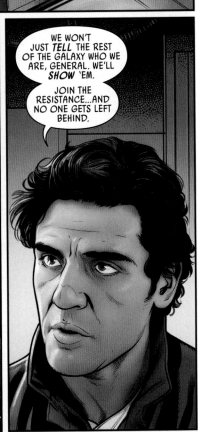

WE WON'T JUST **TELL** THE REST OF THE GALAXY WHO WE ARE, GENERAL. WE'LL **SHOW** 'EM.

JOIN THE RESISTANCE...AND NO ONE GETS LEFT BEHIND.

POE, POE, POE...

FINE. YOU HAVE MY AUTHORIZATION, BUT YOU CAN'T TAKE THE **FALCON**. FIND ANOTHER WAY.

MAY THE FORCE BE WITH YOU... **COMMANDER** DAMERON.

COMMANDER?

COMMANDER. BUT THIS TIME...DON'T BLOW IT.

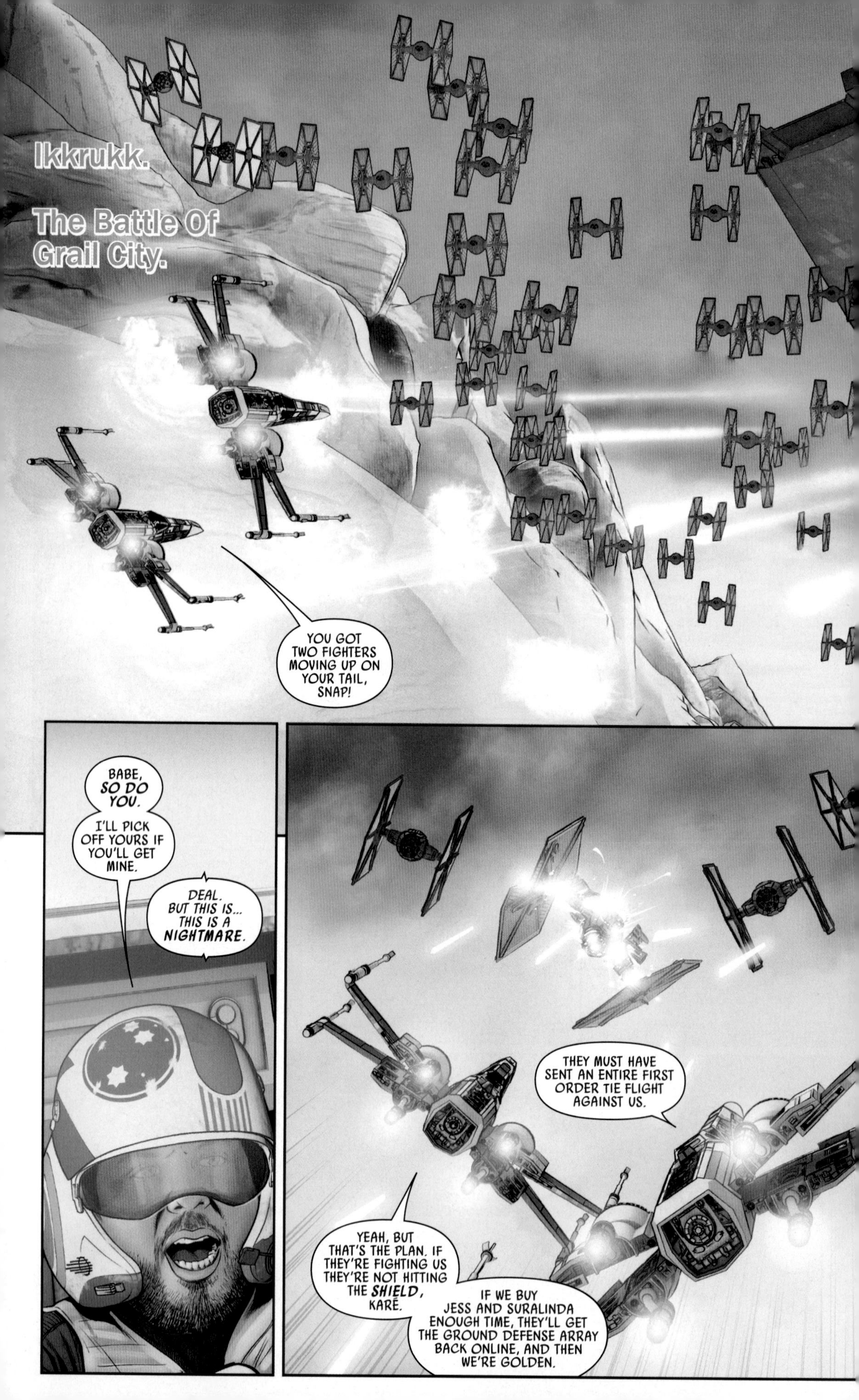
Ikkrukk.
The Battle Of Grail City.
YOU GOT TWO FIGHTERS MOVING UP ON YOUR TAIL, SNAP!
BABE, SO DO YOU.
I'LL PICK OFF YOURS IF YOU'LL GET MINE.
DEAL. BUT THIS IS... THIS IS A NIGHTMARE.
THEY MUST HAVE SENT AN ENTIRE FIRST ORDER TIE FLIGHT AGAINST US.
YEAH, BUT THAT'S THE PLAN. IF THEY'RE FIGHTING US THEY'RE NOT HITTING THE SHIELD, KARÉ.
IF WE BUY JESS AND SURALINDA ENOUGH TIME, THEY'LL GET THE GROUND DEFENSE ARRAY BACK ONLINE, AND THEN WE'RE GOLDEN.

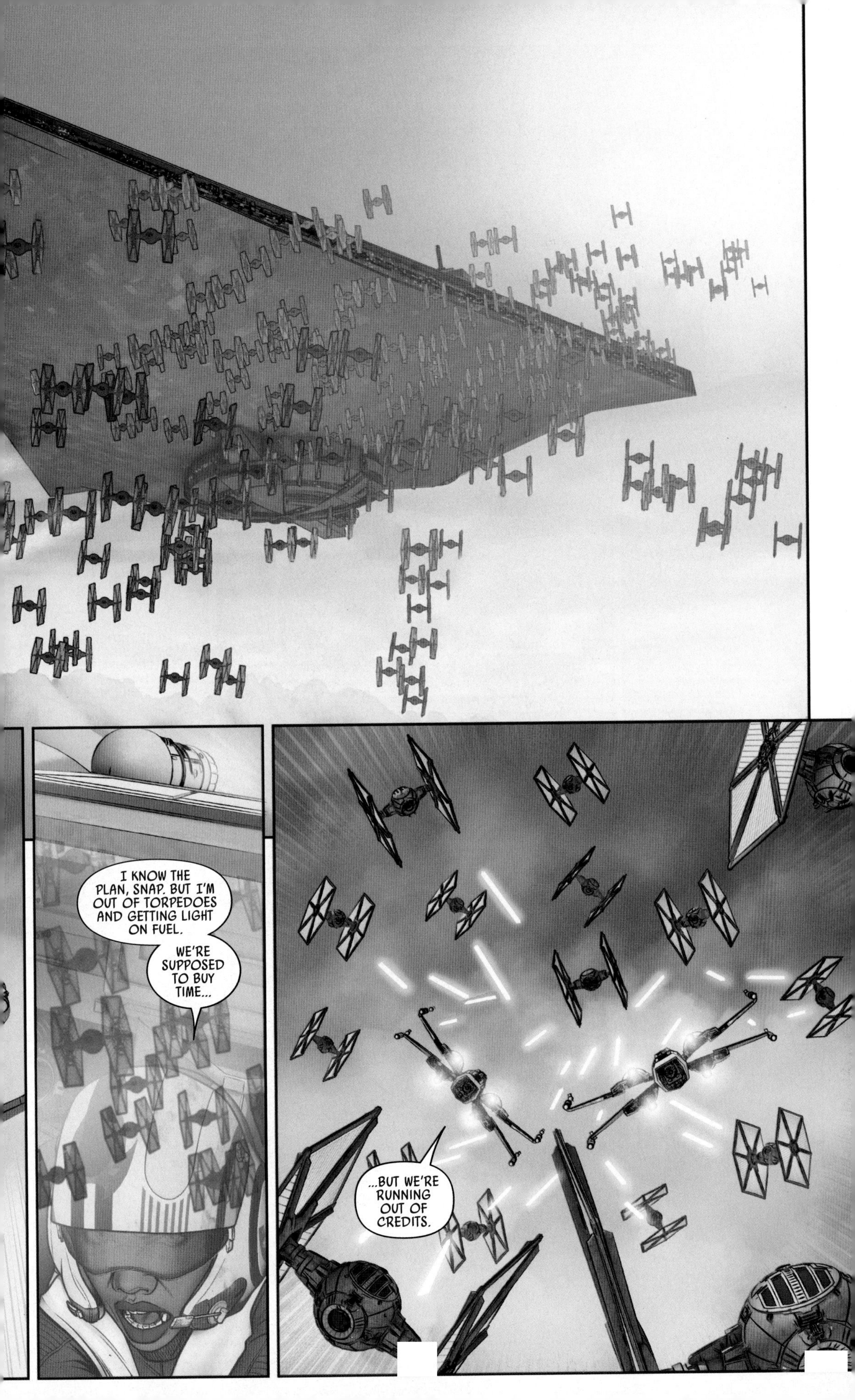
I KNOW THE PLAN, SNAP. BUT I'M OUT OF TORPEDOES AND GETTING LIGHT ON FUEL.
WE'RE SUPPOSED TO BUY TIME...
...BUT WE'RE RUNNING OUT OF CREDITS.

COME ON, SURALINDA...

...YOU NEED TO WAKE UP NOW.

PFFT

NNNNNGH!

I DON'T *WANT* TO WAKE UP, JESS. THOSE DELUDED IDIOTS SHOT A *HOLE* INTO ME.

I KNOW. BUT THEY'RE COMING BACK, AND--

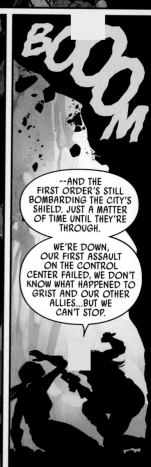

BOOOM

--AND THE FIRST ORDER'S STILL BOMBARDING THE CITY'S SHIELD. JUST A MATTER OF TIME UNTIL THEY'RE THROUGH.

WE'RE DOWN, OUR FIRST ASSAULT ON THE CONTROL CENTER FAILED, WE DON'T KNOW WHAT HAPPENED TO GRIST AND OUR OTHER ALLIES...BUT WE CAN'T STOP.

I... I DON'T KNOW.

WITH JUST THE TWO OF US... AND WE'RE NOT AT FULL STRENGTH...I *JUST DON'T KNOW* HOW WE CAN DO THIS.

I KNOW, SURA. EVERYTHING HURTS. I'M NOT SAYING IT WILL BE EASY.

BUT THERE'S SOMETHING YOU SHOULD THINK ABOUT.

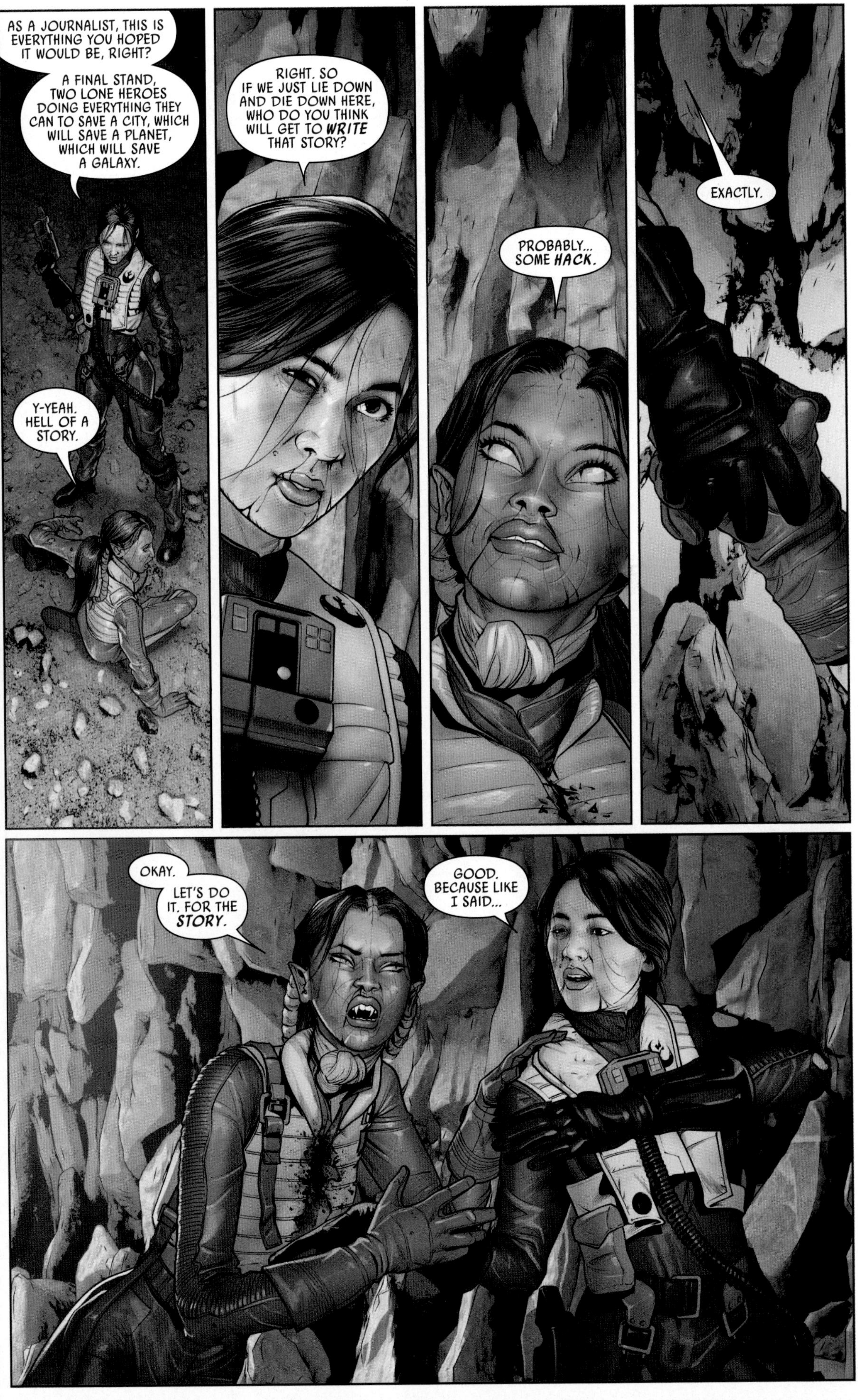
AS A JOURNALIST, THIS IS EVERYTHING YOU HOPED IT WOULD BE, RIGHT?
A FINAL STAND, TWO LONE HEROES DOING EVERYTHING THEY CAN TO SAVE A CITY, WHICH WILL SAVE A PLANET, WHICH WILL SAVE A GALAXY.
Y-YEAH. HELL OF A STORY.
RIGHT. SO IF WE JUST LIE DOWN AND DIE DOWN HERE, WHO DO YOU THINK WILL GET TO *WRITE* THAT STORY?
PROBABLY... SOME *HACK*.
EXACTLY.
OKAY. LET'S DO IT. FOR THE *STORY*.
GOOD. BECAUSE LIKE I SAID...

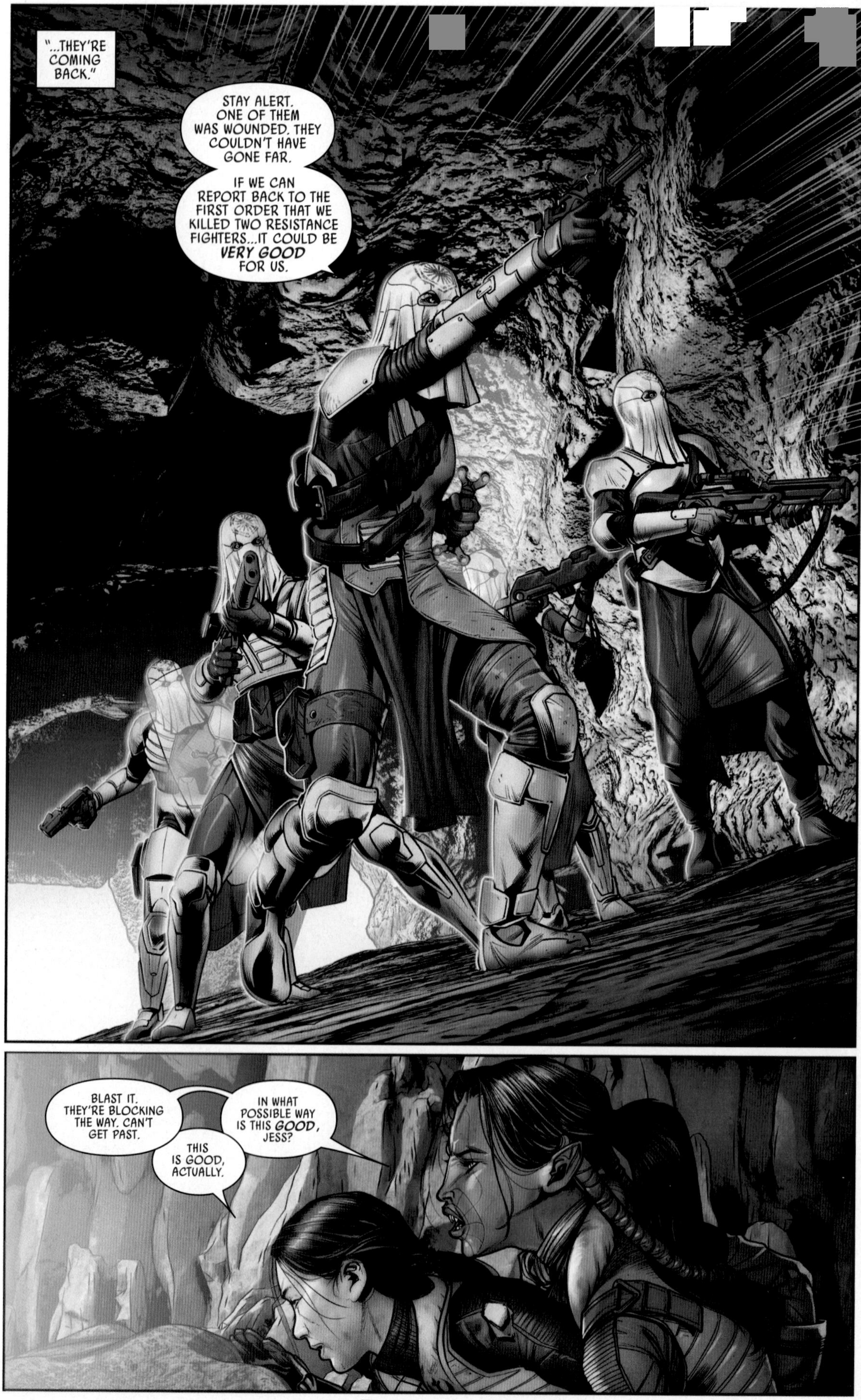
"...THEY'RE COMING BACK."
STAY ALERT. ONE OF THEM WAS WOUNDED. THEY COULDN'T HAVE GONE FAR.
IF WE CAN REPORT BACK TO THE FIRST ORDER THAT WE KILLED TWO RESISTANCE FIGHTERS...IT COULD BE *VERY GOOD* FOR US.
BLAST IT. THEY'RE BLOCKING THE WAY. CAN'T GET PAST.
THIS IS GOOD, ACTUALLY.
IN WHAT POSSIBLE WAY IS THIS *GOOD*, JESS?

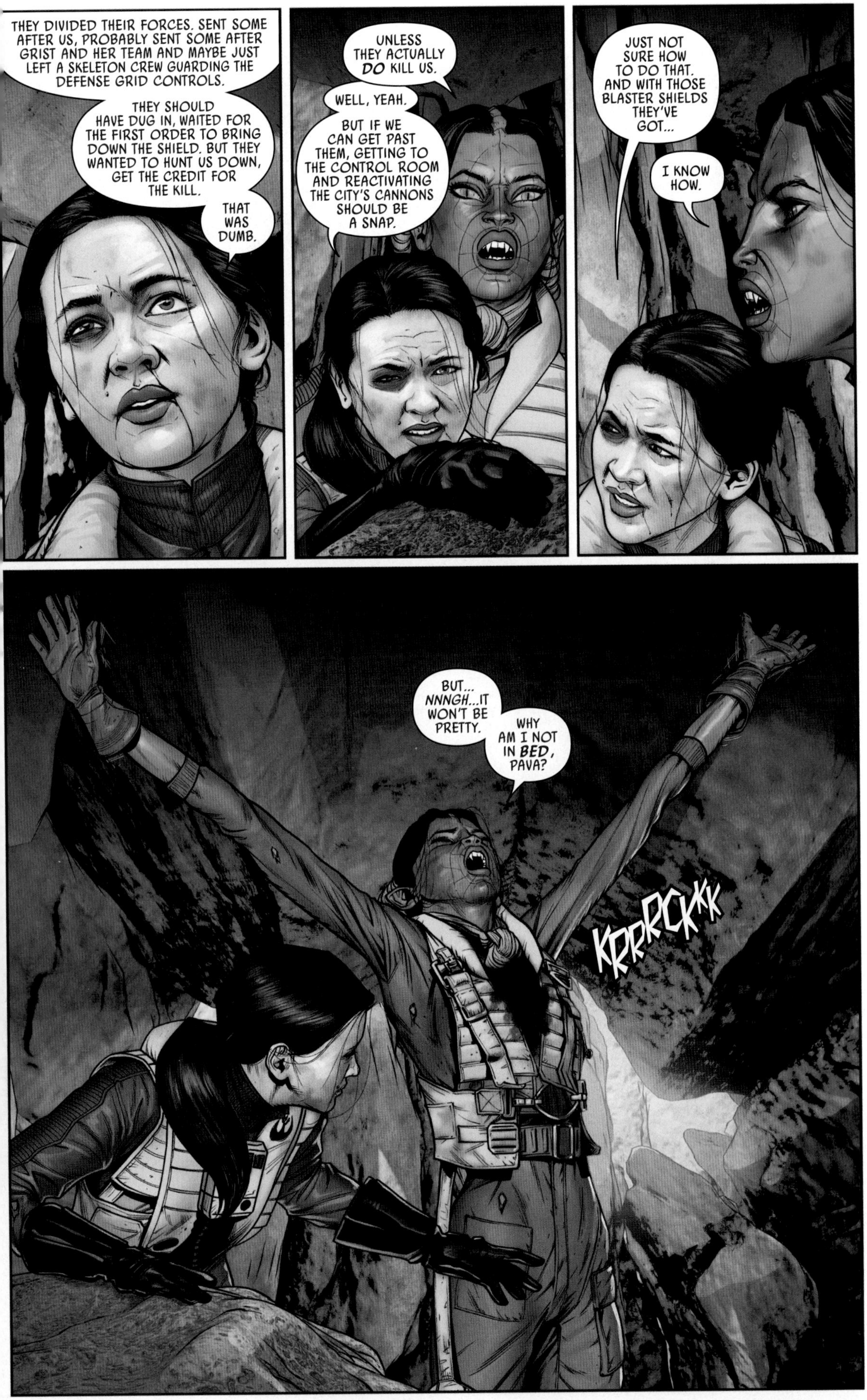
THEY DIVIDED THEIR FORCES. SENT SOME AFTER US, PROBABLY SENT SOME AFTER GRIST AND HER TEAM AND MAYBE JUST LEFT A SKELETON CREW GUARDING THE DEFENSE GRID CONTROLS.
THEY SHOULD HAVE DUG IN, WAITED FOR THE FIRST ORDER TO BRING DOWN THE SHIELD. BUT THEY WANTED TO HUNT US DOWN, GET THE CREDIT FOR THE KILL.
THAT WAS DUMB.
UNLESS THEY ACTUALLY DO KILL US.
WELL, YEAH.
BUT IF WE CAN GET PAST THEM, GETTING TO THE CONTROL ROOM AND REACTIVATING THE CITY'S CANNONS SHOULD BE A SNAP.
JUST NOT SURE HOW TO DO THAT. AND WITH THOSE BLASTER SHIELDS THEY'VE GOT...
I KNOW HOW.
BUT... NNNGH...IT WON'T BE PRETTY.
WHY AM I NOT IN BED, PAVA?
KRRRCKKK

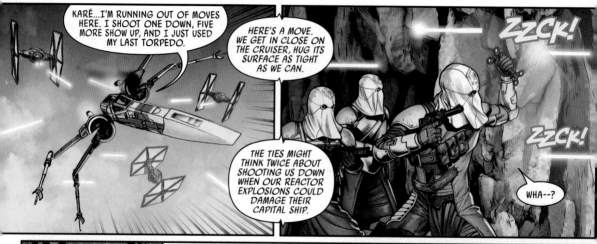

KARÉ...I'M RUNNING OUT OF MOVES HERE. I SHOOT ONE DOWN, FIVE MORE SHOW UP, AND I JUST USED MY LAST TORPEDO.

HERE'S A MOVE. WE GET IN CLOSE ON THE CRUISER, HUG ITS SURFACE AS TIGHT AS WE CAN.

ZZCK!

ZZCK!

THE TIES MIGHT THINK TWICE ABOUT SHOOTING US DOWN WHEN OUR REACTOR EXPLOSIONS COULD DAMAGE THEIR CAPITAL SHIP.

WHA--?

SKETCHY, KARÉ. EVEN IF IT WORKS, WE'LL BE SITTING DUCKS FOR THE CRUISER'S POINT-DEFENSE CANNONS--AND WITH NO TORPEDOES, WE CAN'T EVEN MAKE A DENT IN THEM.

ONE PROBLEM AT A TIME, DARLING.

THEY'RE HERE! SHOOT TO KILL!

KTHOOM!

KZZCK!

BLAST IT! WINGED ME!

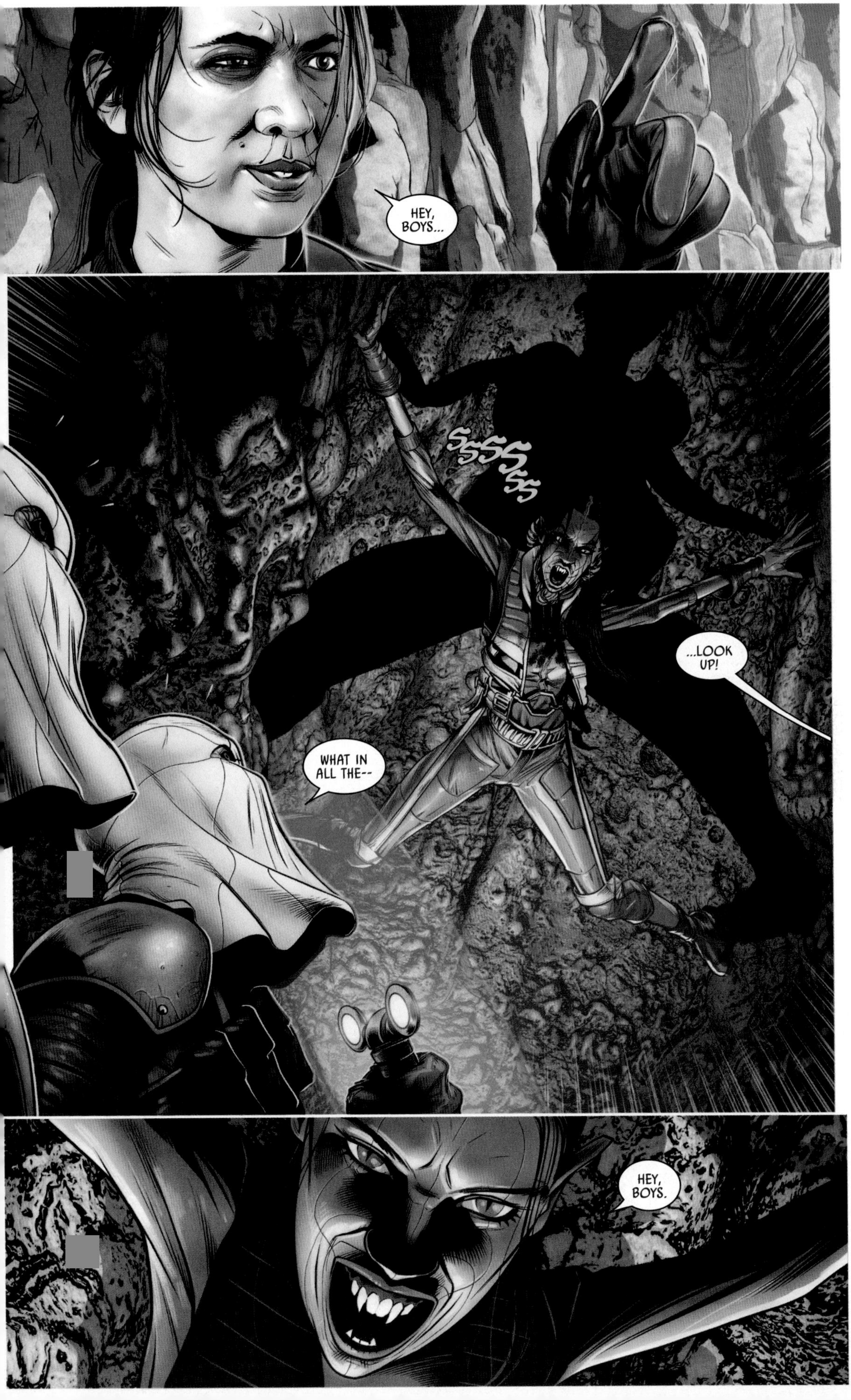
HEY, BOYS...
SSSSSS
...LOOK UP!
WHAT IN ALL THE--
HEY, BOYS.

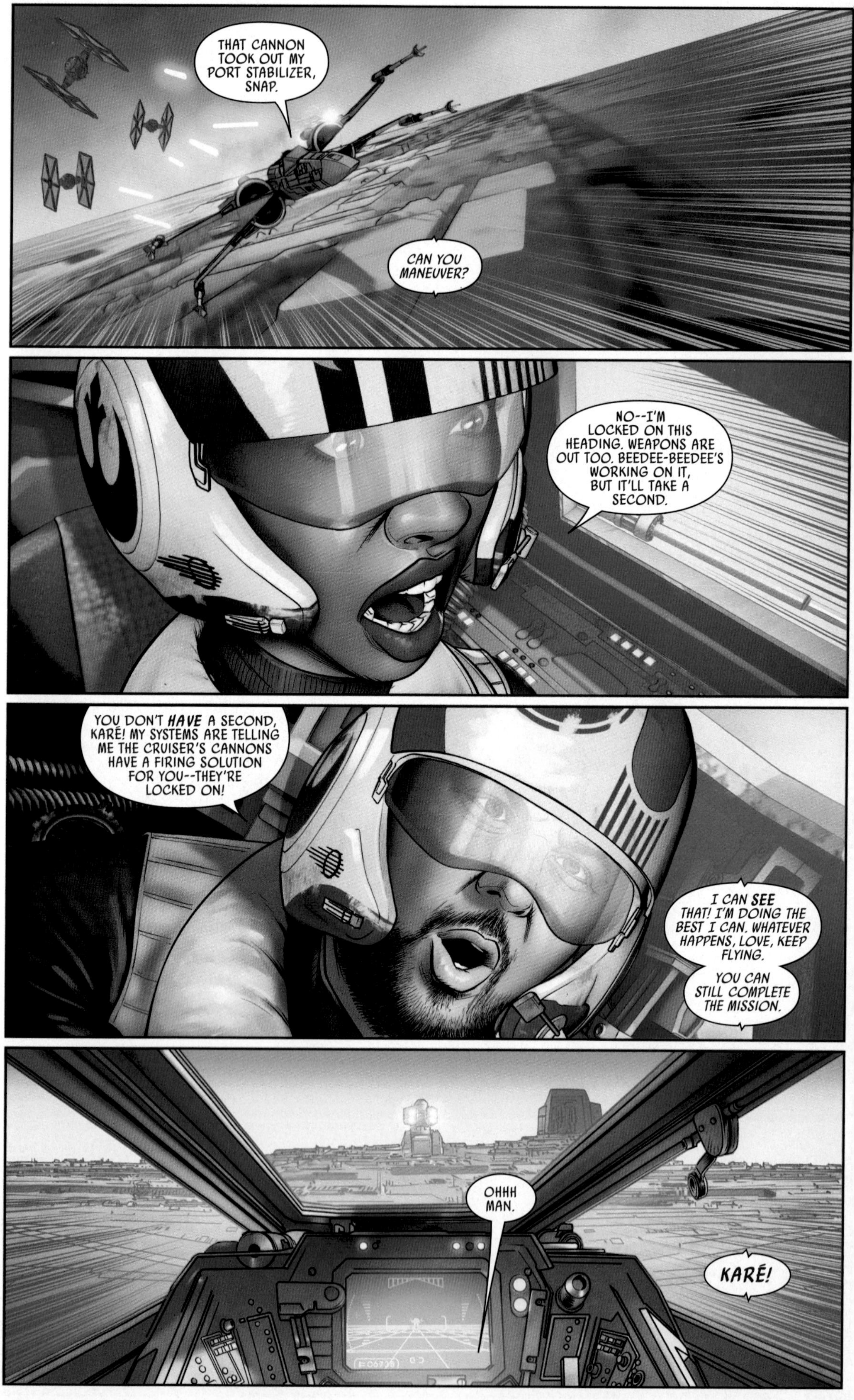
THAT CANNON TOOK OUT MY PORT STABILIZER, SNAP.
CAN YOU MANEUVER?
NO--I'M LOCKED ON THIS HEADING. WEAPONS ARE OUT TOO. BEEDEE-BEEDEE'S WORKING ON IT, BUT IT'LL TAKE A SECOND.
YOU DON'T HAVE A SECOND, KARÉ! MY SYSTEMS ARE TELLING ME THE CRUISER'S CANNONS HAVE A FIRING SOLUTION FOR YOU--THEY'RE LOCKED ON!
I CAN SEE THAT! I'M DOING THE BEST I CAN. WHATEVER HAPPENS, LOVE, KEEP FLYING.
YOU CAN STILL COMPLETE THE MISSION.
OHHH MAN.
KARÉ!

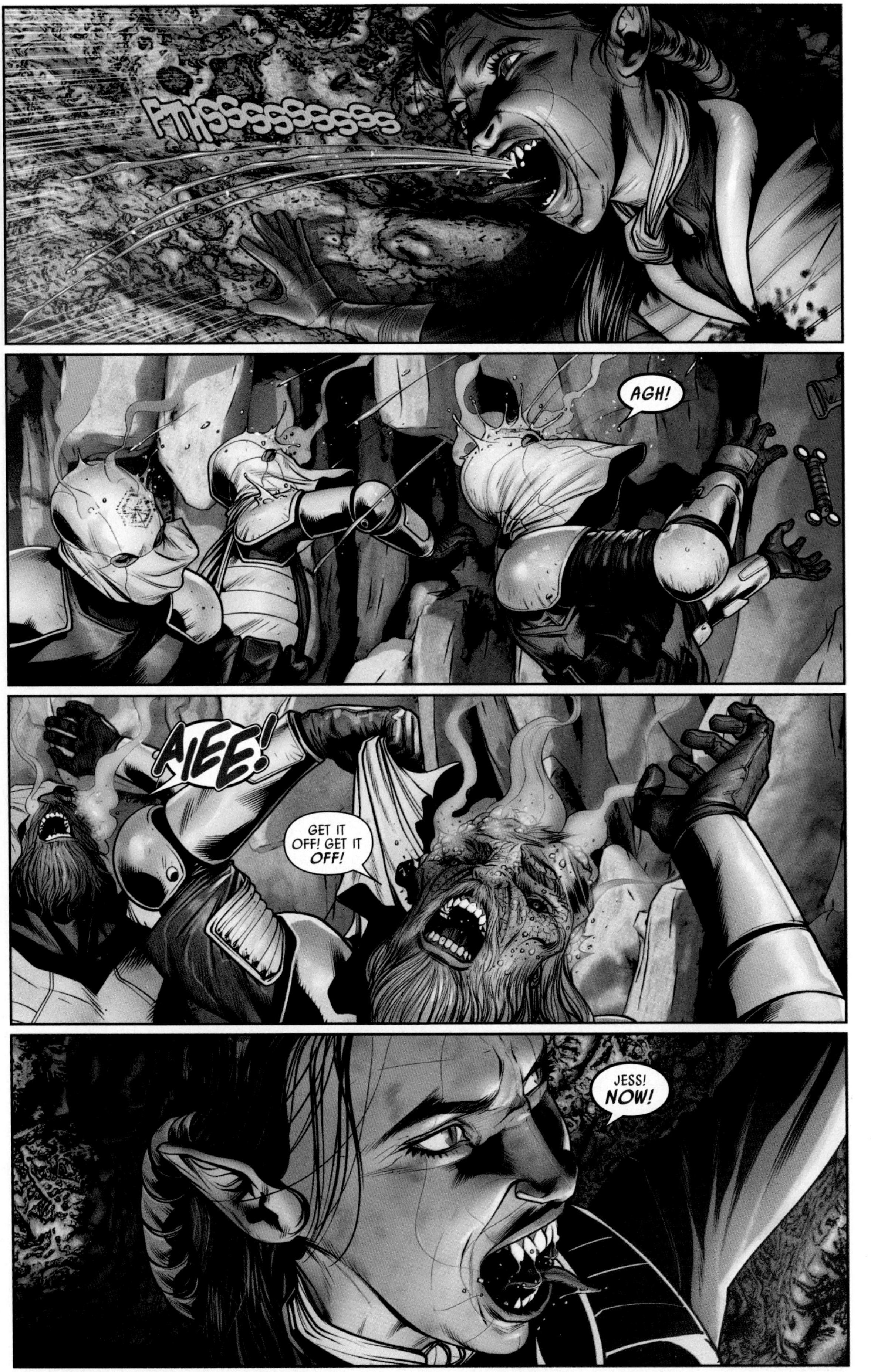
FTHSSSSSSSSSS
AGH!
AIEE!
GET IT OFF! GET IT OFF!
JESS! NOW!

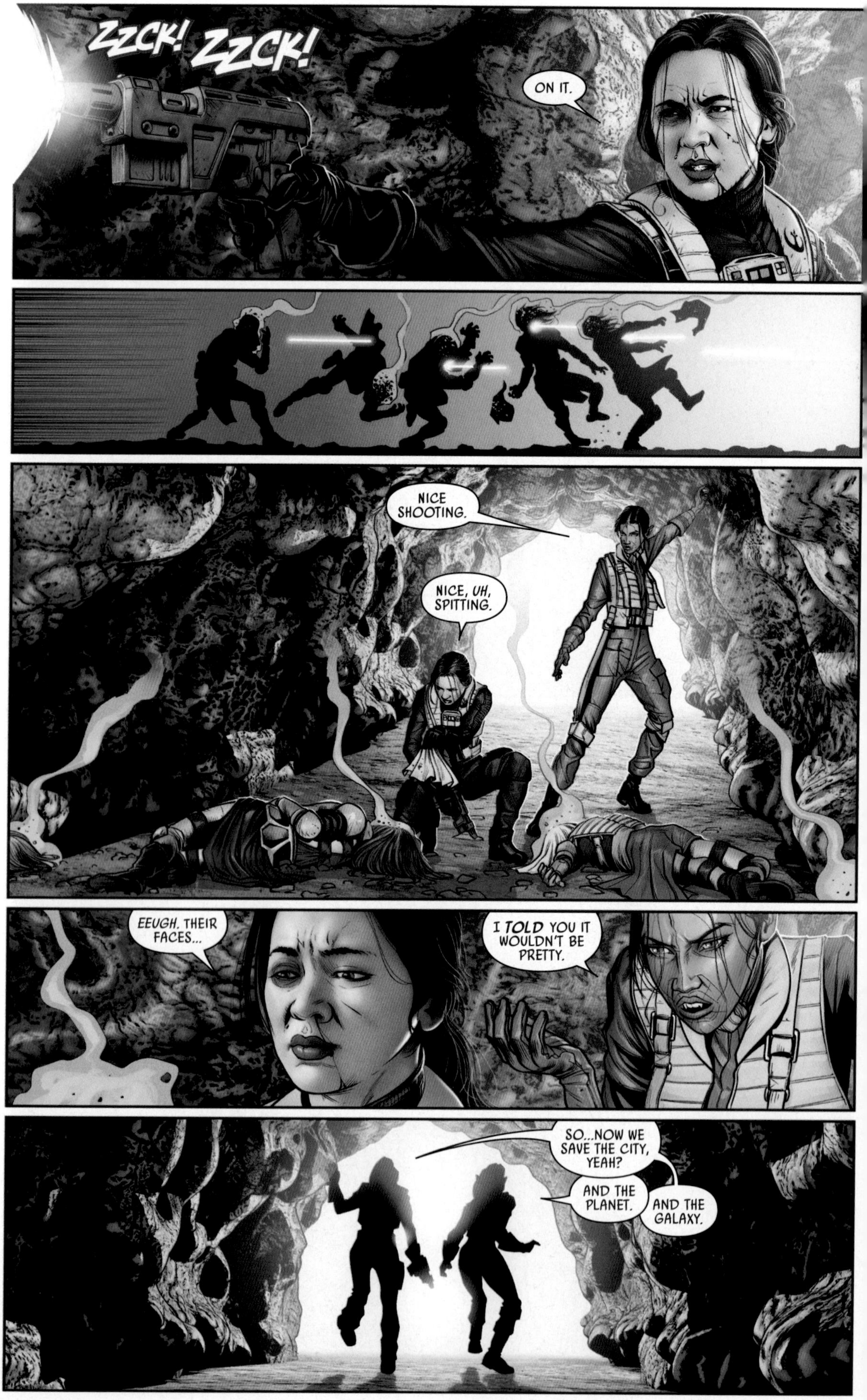
ZZCK! ZZCK!
ON IT.
NICE SHOOTING.
NICE, UH, SPITTING.
EEUGH. THEIR FACES...
I TOLD YOU IT WOULDN'T BE PRETTY.
SO...NOW WE SAVE THE CITY, YEAH?
AND THE PLANET.
AND THE GALAXY.

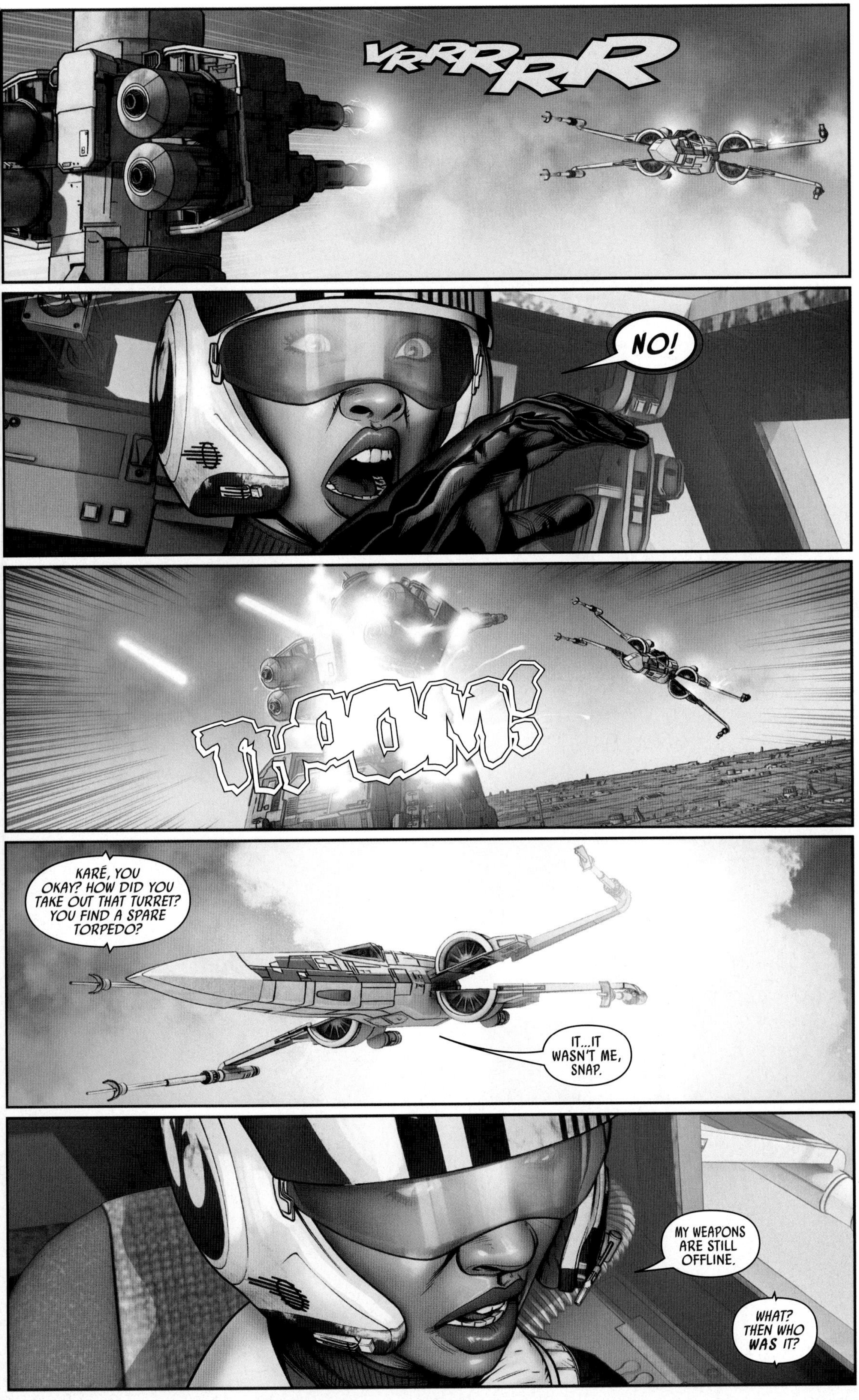
VRRRRRR
NO!
THOOM!
KARÉ, YOU OKAY? HOW DID YOU TAKE OUT THAT TURRET? YOU FIND A SPARE TORPEDO?
IT...IT WASN'T ME, SNAP.
MY WEAPONS ARE STILL OFFLINE.
WHAT? THEN WHO WAS IT?

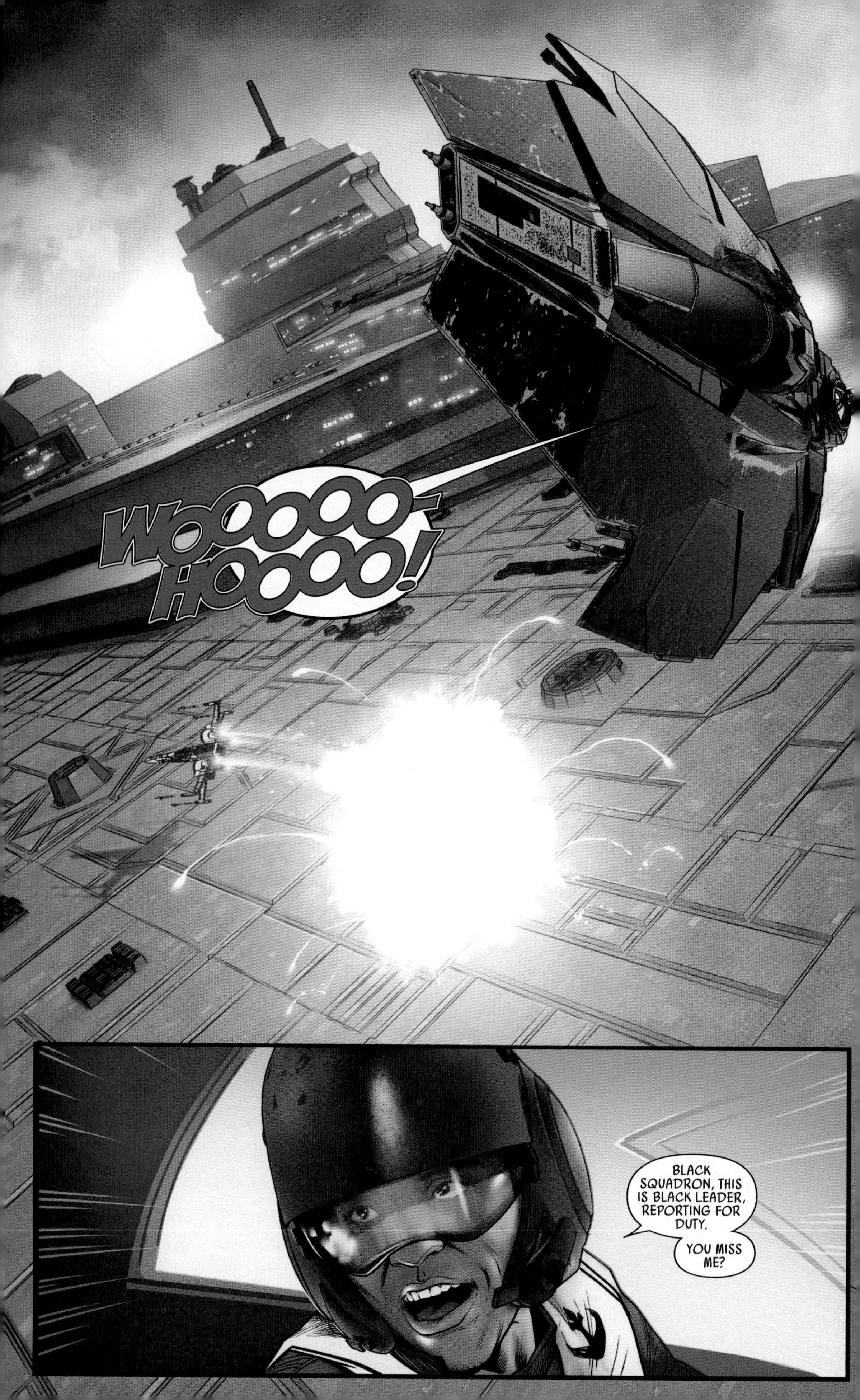
WOOOOO-HOOOO!
BLACK SQUADRON, THIS IS BLACK LEADER, REPORTING FOR DUTY.
YOU MISS ME?

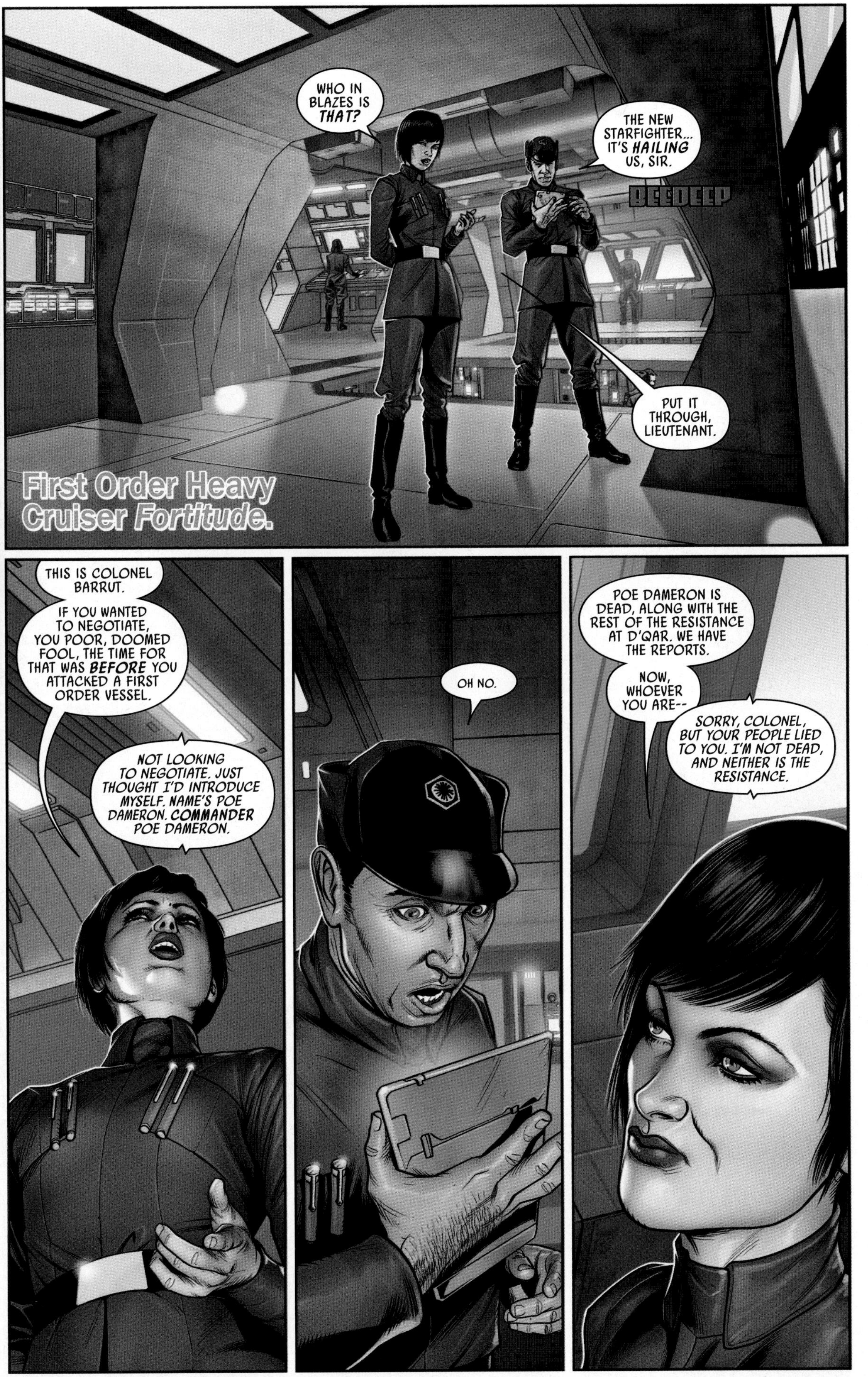
First Order Heavy Cruiser Fortitude.
WHO IN BLAZES IS THAT?
THE NEW STARFIGHTER... IT'S HAILING US, SIR.
BEEDEEP
PUT IT THROUGH, LIEUTENANT.
THIS IS COLONEL BARRUT.
IF YOU WANTED TO NEGOTIATE, YOU POOR, DOOMED FOOL, THE TIME FOR THAT WAS BEFORE YOU ATTACKED A FIRST ORDER VESSEL.
NOT LOOKING TO NEGOTIATE. JUST THOUGHT I'D INTRODUCE MYSELF. NAME'S POE DAMERON. COMMANDER POE DAMERON.
OH NO.
POE DAMERON IS DEAD, ALONG WITH THE REST OF THE RESISTANCE AT D'QAR. WE HAVE THE REPORTS.
NOW, WHOEVER YOU ARE--
SORRY, COLONEL, BUT YOUR PEOPLE LIED TO YOU. I'M NOT DEAD, AND NEITHER IS THE RESISTANCE.

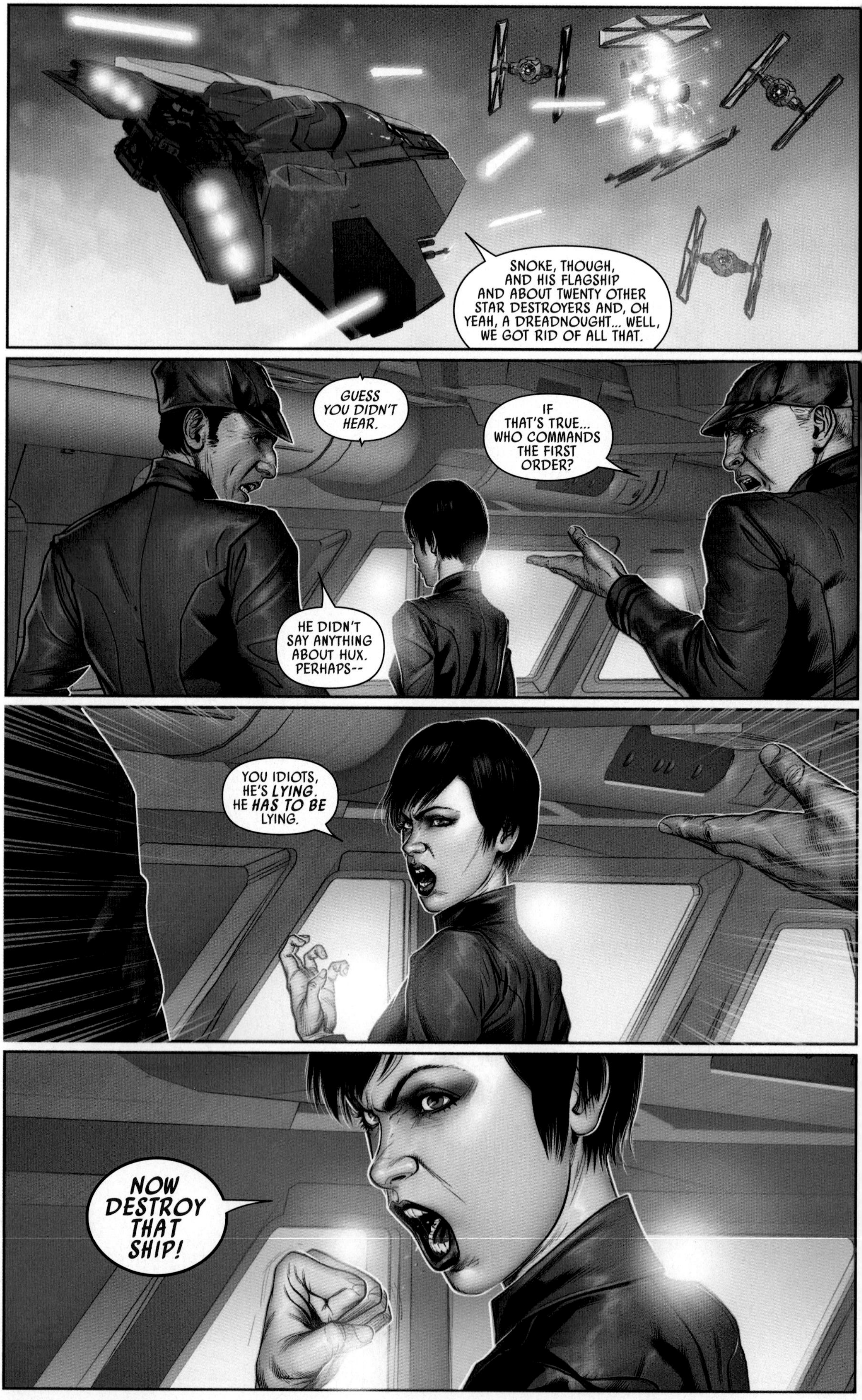
SNOKE, THOUGH, AND HIS FLAGSHIP AND ABOUT TWENTY OTHER STAR DESTROYERS AND, OH YEAH, A DREADNOUGHT... WELL, WE GOT RID OF ALL THAT.
GUESS YOU DIDN'T HEAR.
IF THAT'S TRUE... WHO COMMANDS THE FIRST ORDER?
HE DIDN'T SAY ANYTHING ABOUT HUX. PERHAPS--
YOU IDIOTS, HE'S LYING. HE HAS TO BE LYING.
NOW DESTROY THAT SHIP!

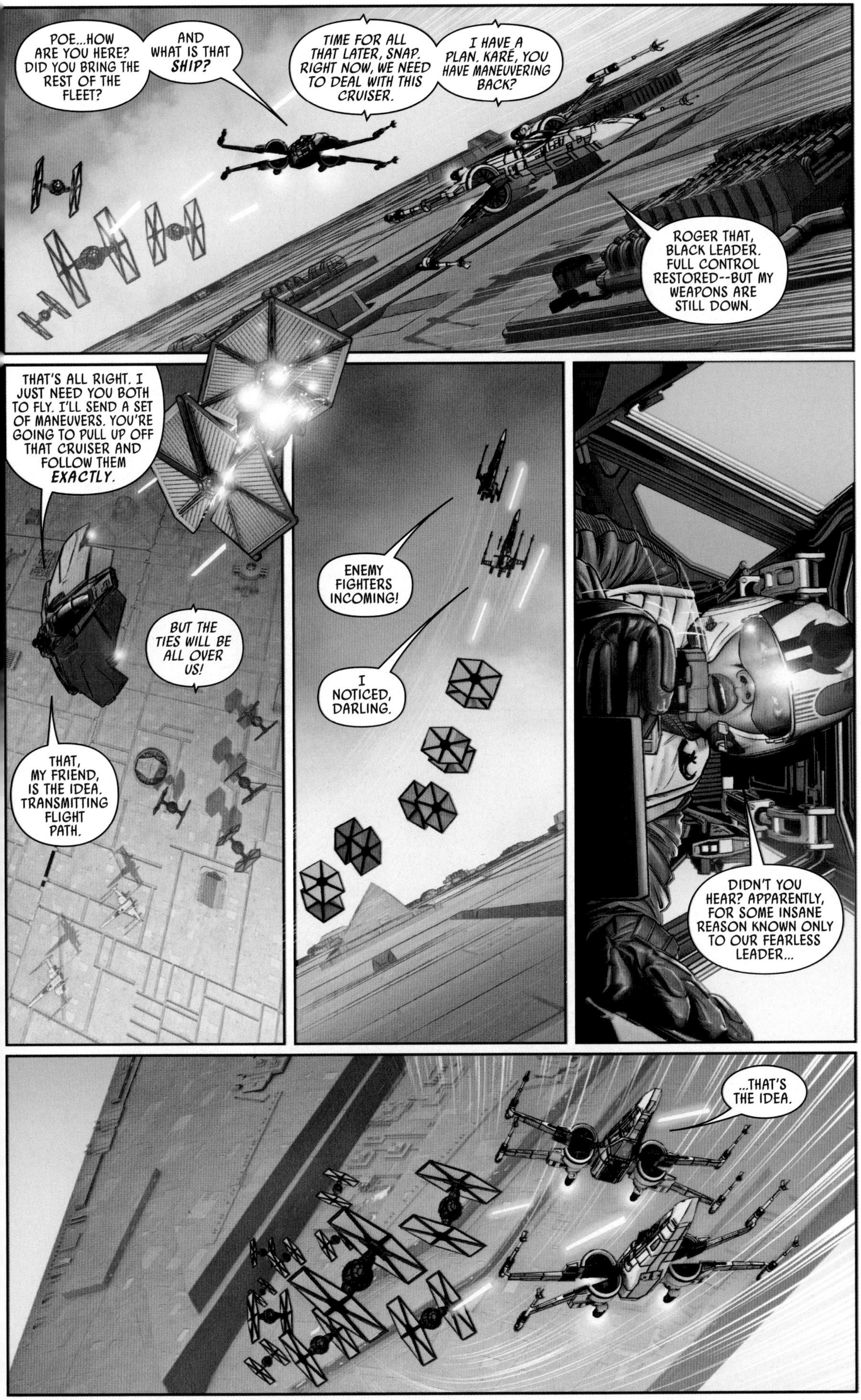
POE...HOW ARE YOU HERE? DID YOU BRING THE REST OF THE FLEET?
AND WHAT IS THAT SHIP?
TIME FOR ALL THAT LATER, SNAP. RIGHT NOW, WE NEED TO DEAL WITH THIS CRUISER.
I HAVE A PLAN. KARÉ, YOU HAVE MANEUVERING BACK?
ROGER THAT, BLACK LEADER. FULL CONTROL RESTORED--BUT MY WEAPONS ARE STILL DOWN.
THAT'S ALL RIGHT. I JUST NEED YOU BOTH TO FLY. I'LL SEND A SET OF MANEUVERS. YOU'RE GOING TO PULL UP OFF THAT CRUISER AND FOLLOW THEM EXACTLY.
BUT THE TIES WILL BE ALL OVER US!
THAT, MY FRIEND, IS THE IDEA. TRANSMITTING FLIGHT PATH.
ENEMY FIGHTERS INCOMING!
I NOTICED, DARLING.
DIDN'T YOU HEAR? APPARENTLY, FOR SOME INSANE REASON KNOWN ONLY TO OUR FEARLESS LEADER...
...THAT'S THE IDEA.

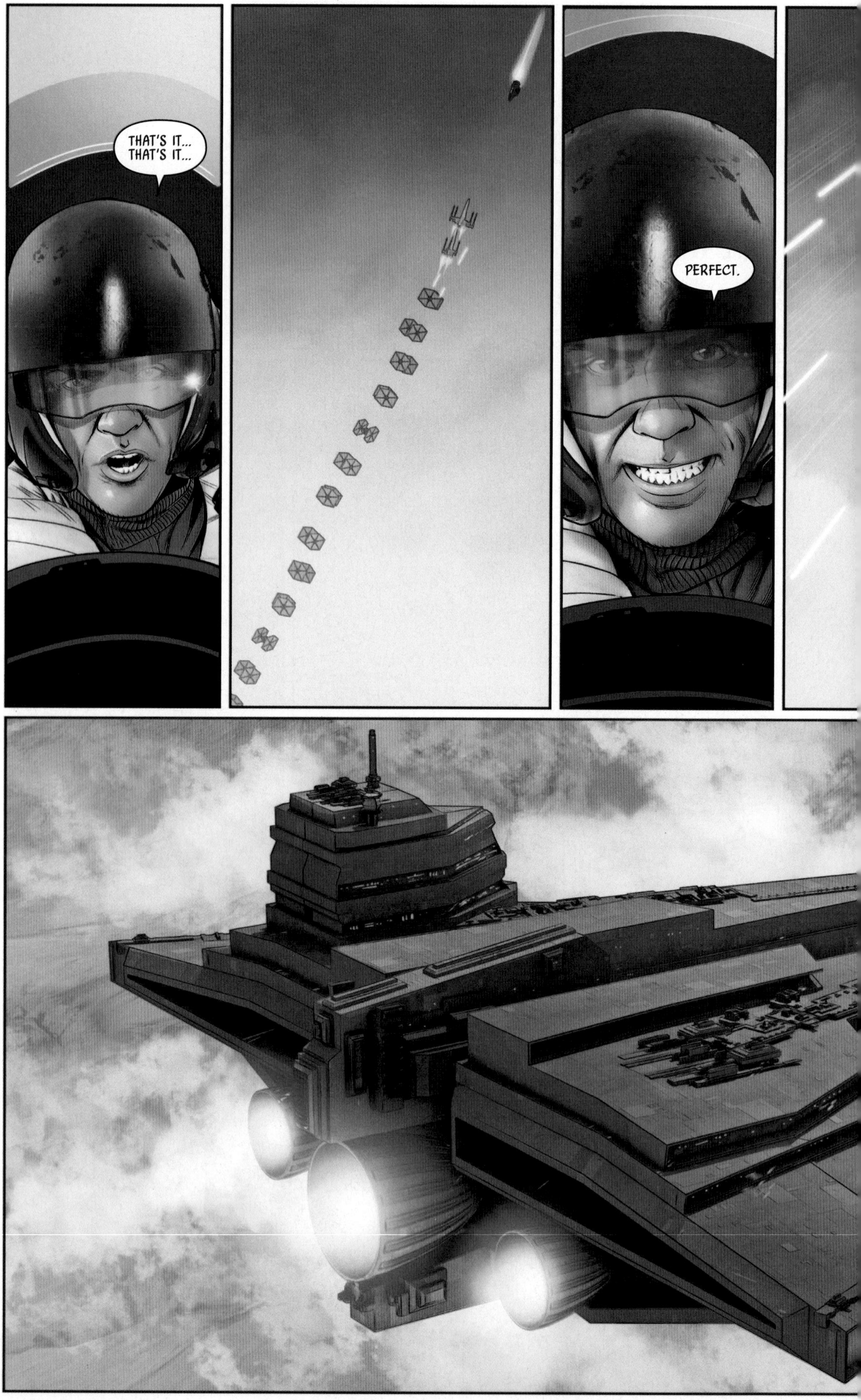
THAT'S IT... THAT'S IT...
PERFECT.

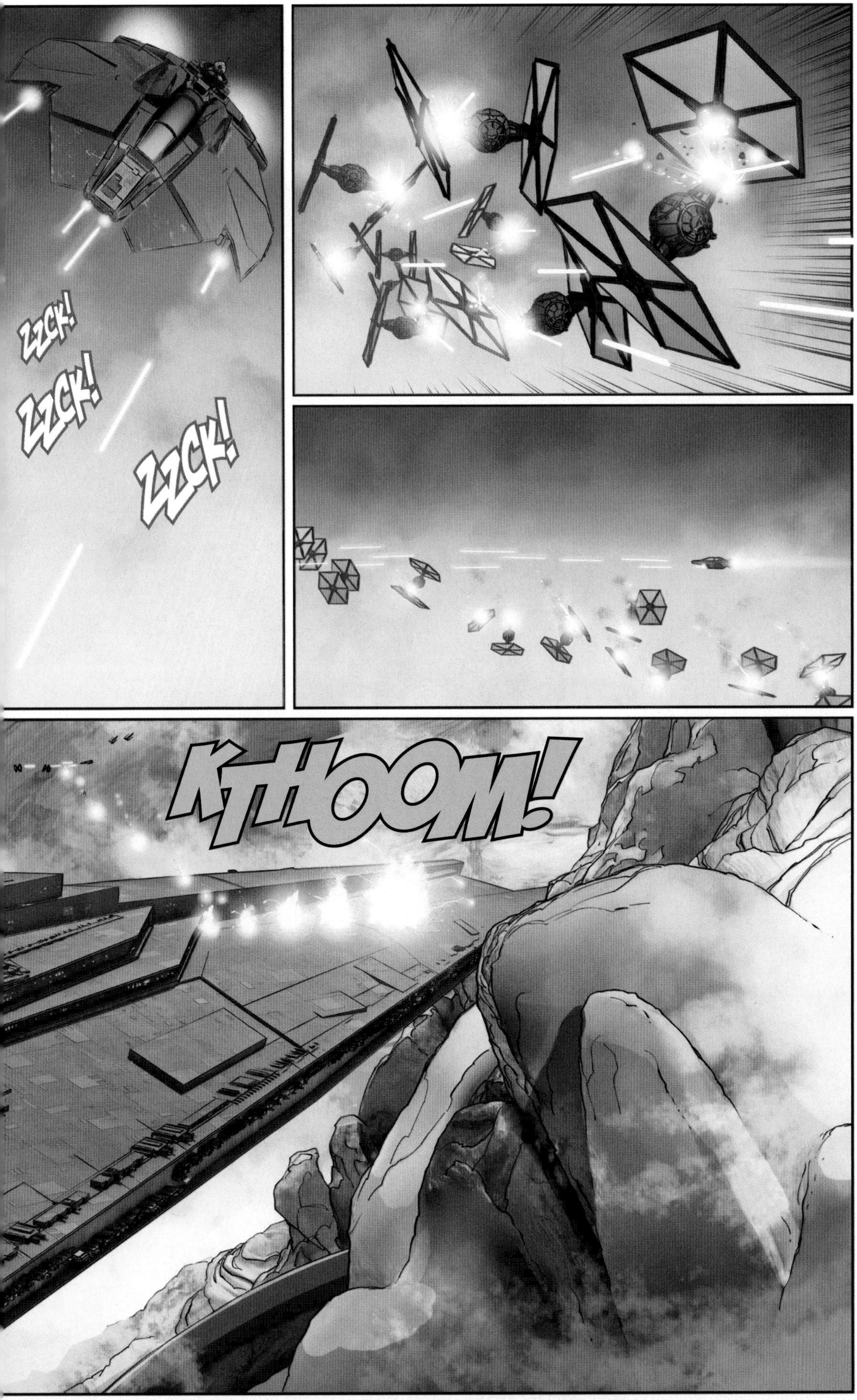
ZZCK!
ZZCK!
ZZCK!
KTHOOM!

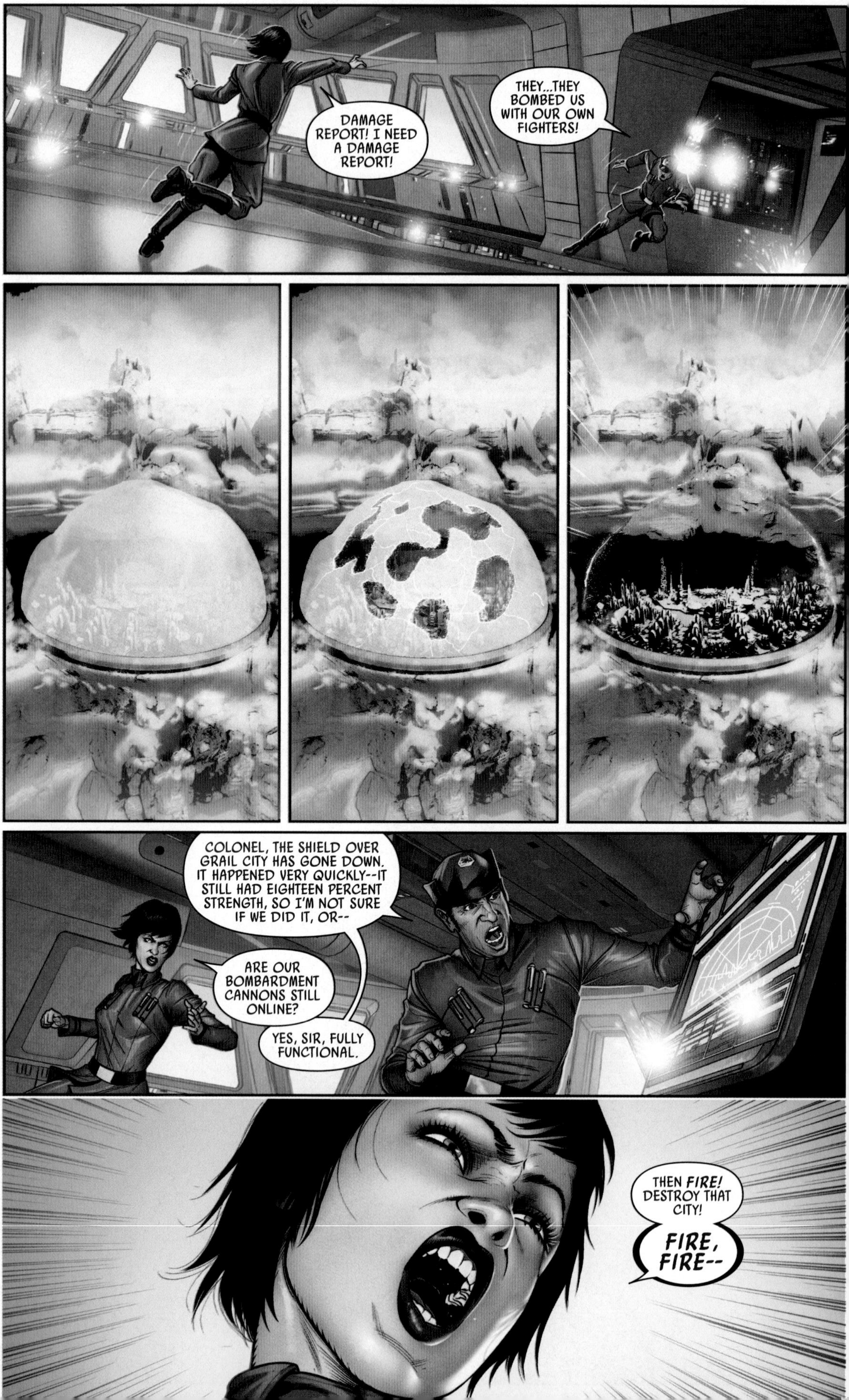
DAMAGE REPORT! I NEED A DAMAGE REPORT!
THEY...THEY BOMBED US WITH OUR OWN FIGHTERS!
COLONEL, THE SHIELD OVER GRAIL CITY HAS GONE DOWN. IT HAPPENED VERY QUICKLY--IT STILL HAD EIGHTEEN PERCENT STRENGTH, SO I'M NOT SURE IF WE DID IT, OR--
ARE OUR BOMBARDMENT CANNONS STILL ONLINE?
YES, SIR, FULLY FUNCTIONAL.
THEN *FIRE!* DESTROY THAT CITY!
FIRE, FIRE--

FIRE.
KLK
SHRRRLLCK!
KRCK!
KRCK!
KRCK!
KRCK!

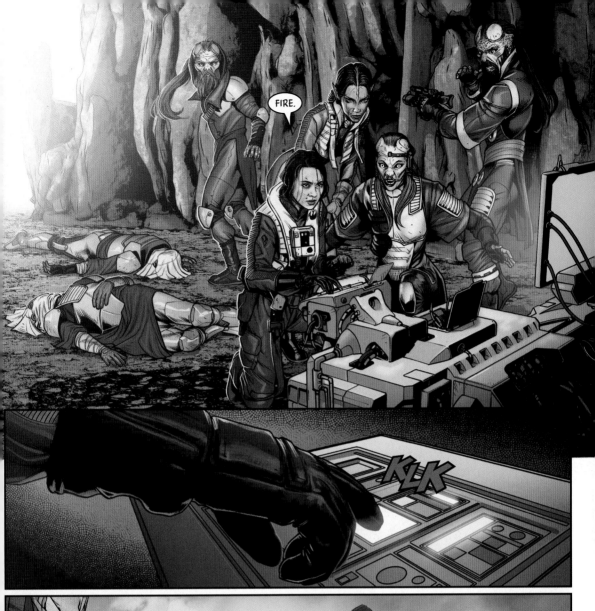

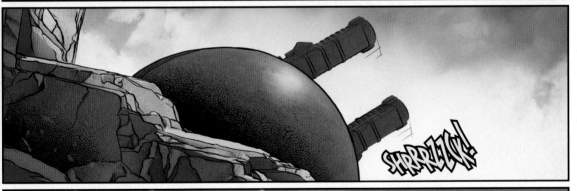

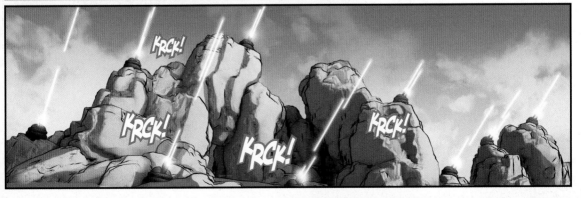

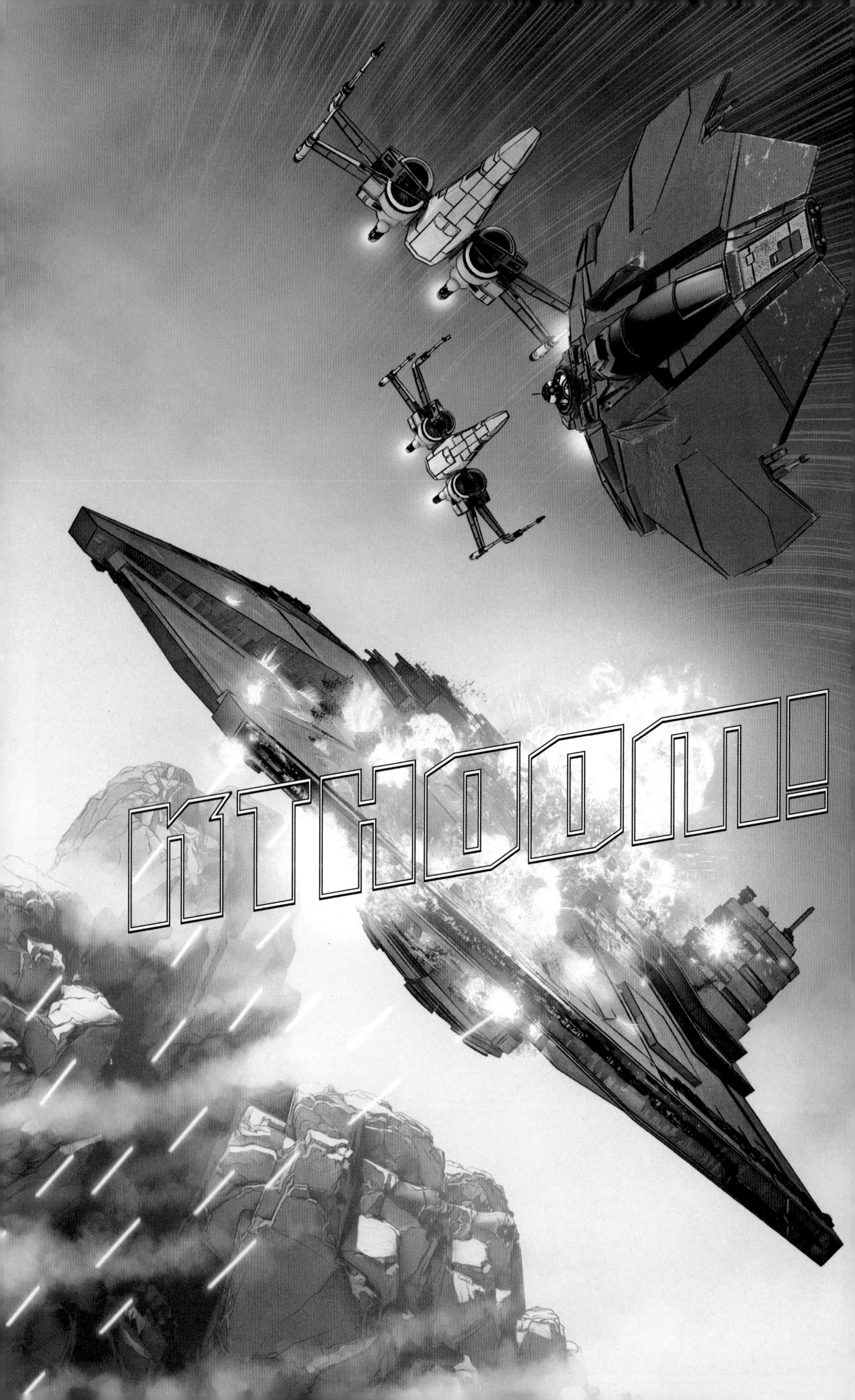
KTHOOM!

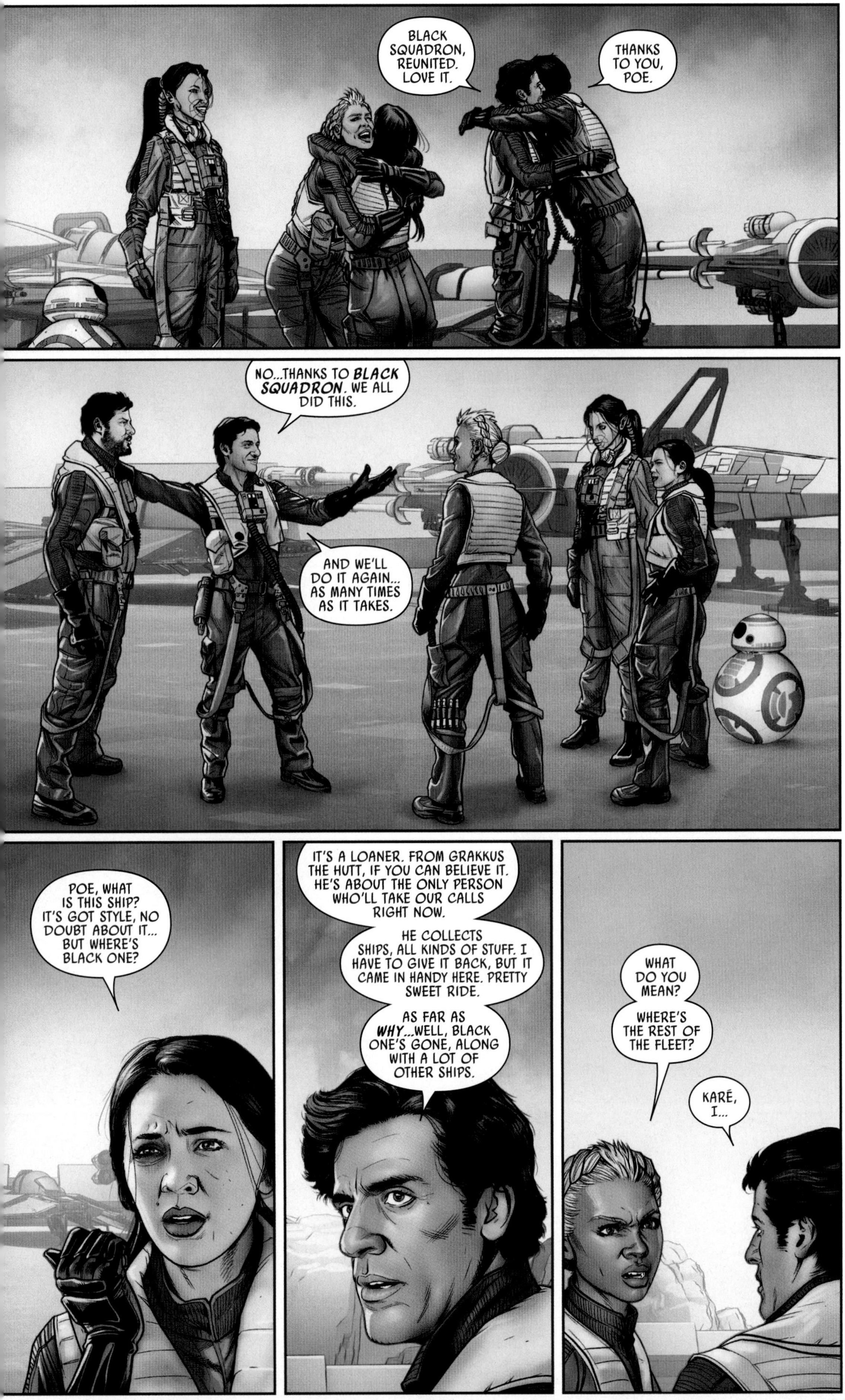
BLACK SQUADRON, REUNITED. LOVE IT.
THANKS TO YOU, POE.
NO...THANKS TO BLACK SQUADRON. WE ALL DID THIS.
AND WE'LL DO IT AGAIN... AS MANY TIMES AS IT TAKES.
POE, WHAT IS THIS SHIP? IT'S GOT STYLE, NO DOUBT ABOUT IT... BUT WHERE'S BLACK ONE?
IT'S A LOANER. FROM GRAKKUS THE HUTT, IF YOU CAN BELIEVE IT. HE'S ABOUT THE ONLY PERSON WHO'LL TAKE OUR CALLS RIGHT NOW.
HE COLLECTS SHIPS, ALL KINDS OF STUFF. I HAVE TO GIVE IT BACK, BUT IT CAME IN HANDY HERE. PRETTY SWEET RIDE.
AS FAR AS WHY...WELL, BLACK ONE'S GONE, ALONG WITH A LOT OF OTHER SHIPS.
WHAT DO YOU MEAN?
WHERE'S THE REST OF THE FLEET?
KARÉ, I...

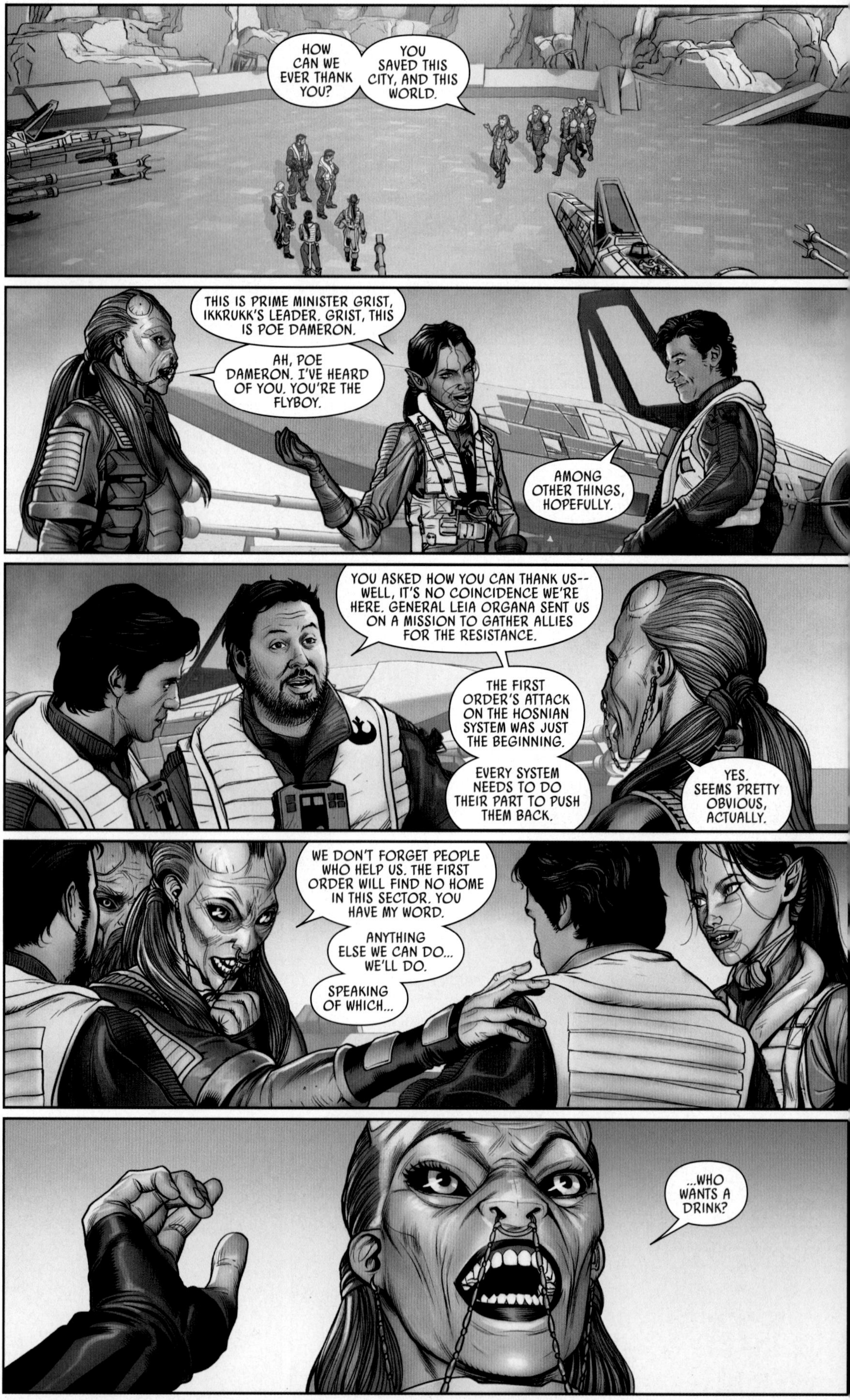
HOW CAN WE EVER THANK YOU?
YOU SAVED THIS CITY, AND THIS WORLD.
THIS IS PRIME MINISTER GRIST, IKKRUKK'S LEADER. GRIST, THIS IS POE DAMERON.
AH, POE DAMERON. I'VE HEARD OF YOU. YOU'RE THE FLYBOY.
AMONG OTHER THINGS, HOPEFULLY.
YOU ASKED HOW YOU CAN THANK US-- WELL, IT'S NO COINCIDENCE WE'RE HERE. GENERAL LEIA ORGANA SENT US ON A MISSION TO GATHER ALLIES FOR THE RESISTANCE.
THE FIRST ORDER'S ATTACK ON THE HOSNIAN SYSTEM WAS JUST THE BEGINNING.
EVERY SYSTEM NEEDS TO DO THEIR PART TO PUSH THEM BACK.
YES. SEEMS PRETTY OBVIOUS, ACTUALLY.
WE DON'T FORGET PEOPLE WHO HELP US. THE FIRST ORDER WILL FIND NO HOME IN THIS SECTOR. YOU HAVE MY WORD.
ANYTHING ELSE WE CAN DO... WE'LL DO.
SPEAKING OF WHICH...
...WHO WANTS A DRINK?

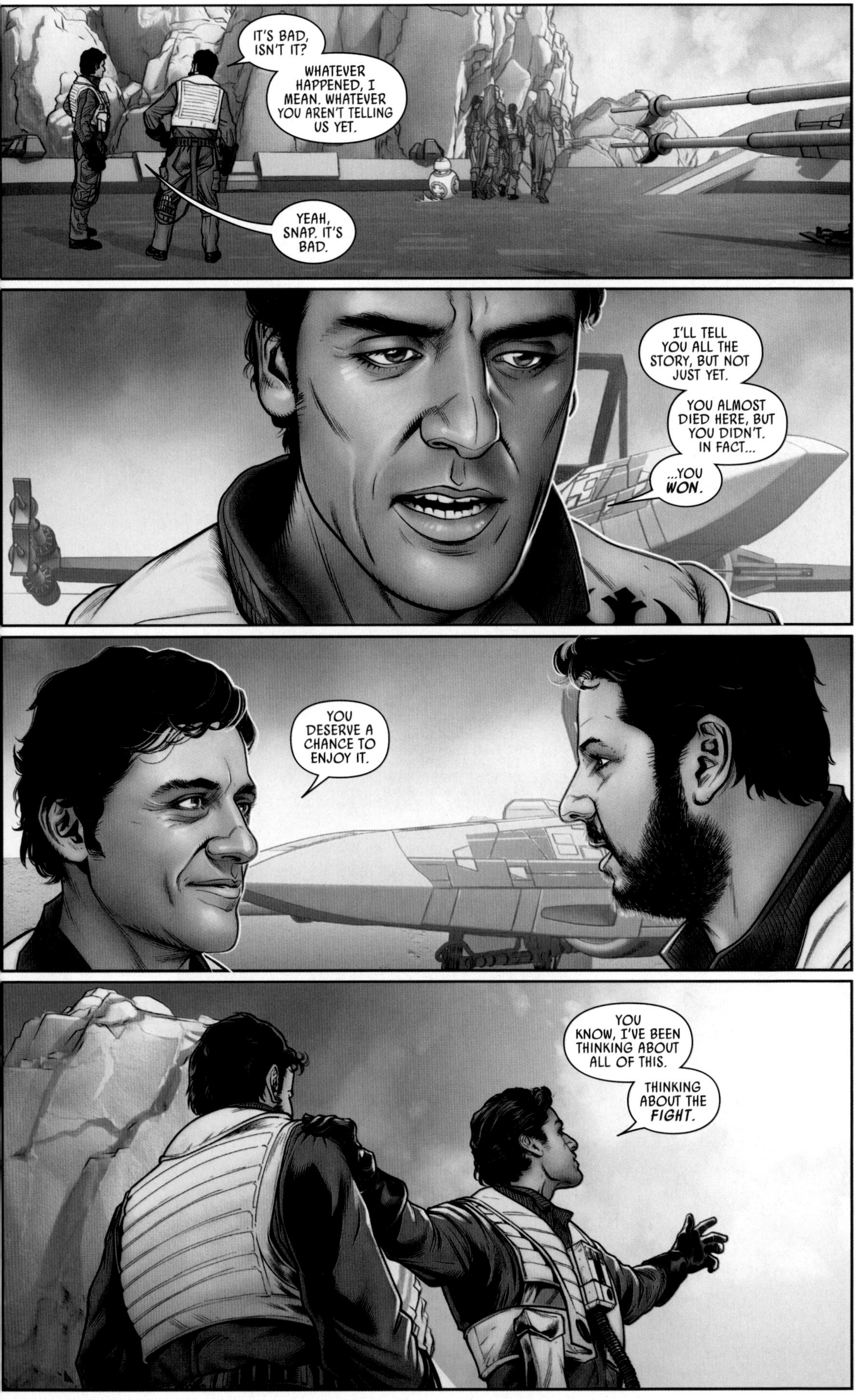
IT'S BAD, ISN'T IT?
WHATEVER HAPPENED, I MEAN. WHATEVER YOU AREN'T TELLING US YET.
YEAH, SNAP. IT'S BAD.
I'LL TELL YOU ALL THE STORY, BUT NOT JUST YET.
YOU ALMOST DIED HERE, BUT YOU DIDN'T. IN FACT...
...YOU WON.
YOU DESERVE A CHANCE TO ENJOY IT.
YOU KNOW, I'VE BEEN THINKING ABOUT ALL OF THIS.
THINKING ABOUT THE FIGHT.

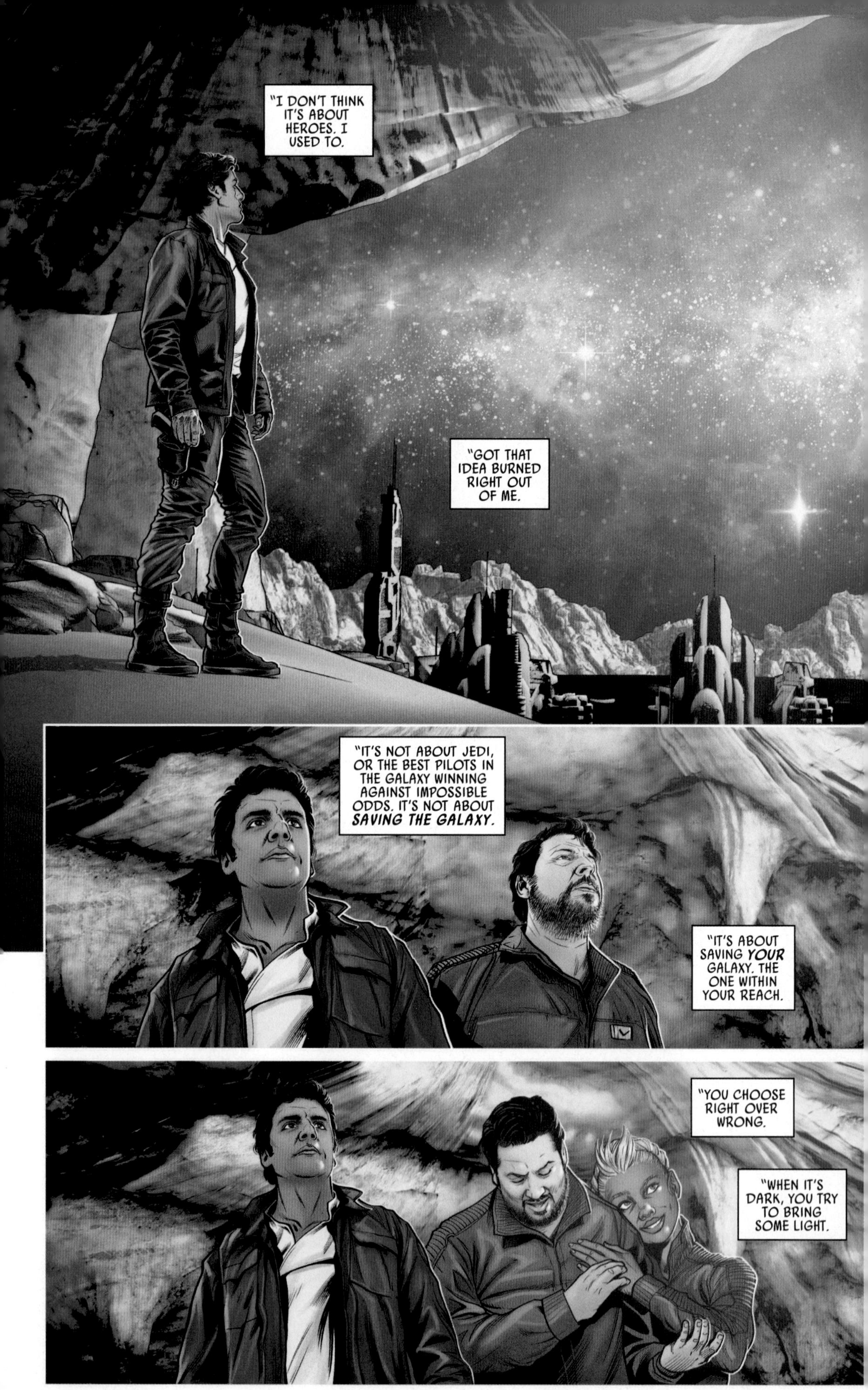
"I DON'T THINK IT'S ABOUT HEROES. I USED TO.
"GOT THAT IDEA BURNED RIGHT OUT OF ME.
"IT'S NOT ABOUT JEDI, OR THE BEST PILOTS IN THE GALAXY WINNING AGAINST IMPOSSIBLE ODDS. IT'S NOT ABOUT *SAVING THE GALAXY.*
"IT'S ABOUT SAVING *YOUR* GALAXY. THE ONE WITHIN YOUR REACH.
"YOU CHOOSE RIGHT OVER WRONG.
"WHEN IT'S DARK, YOU TRY TO BRING SOME LIGHT.

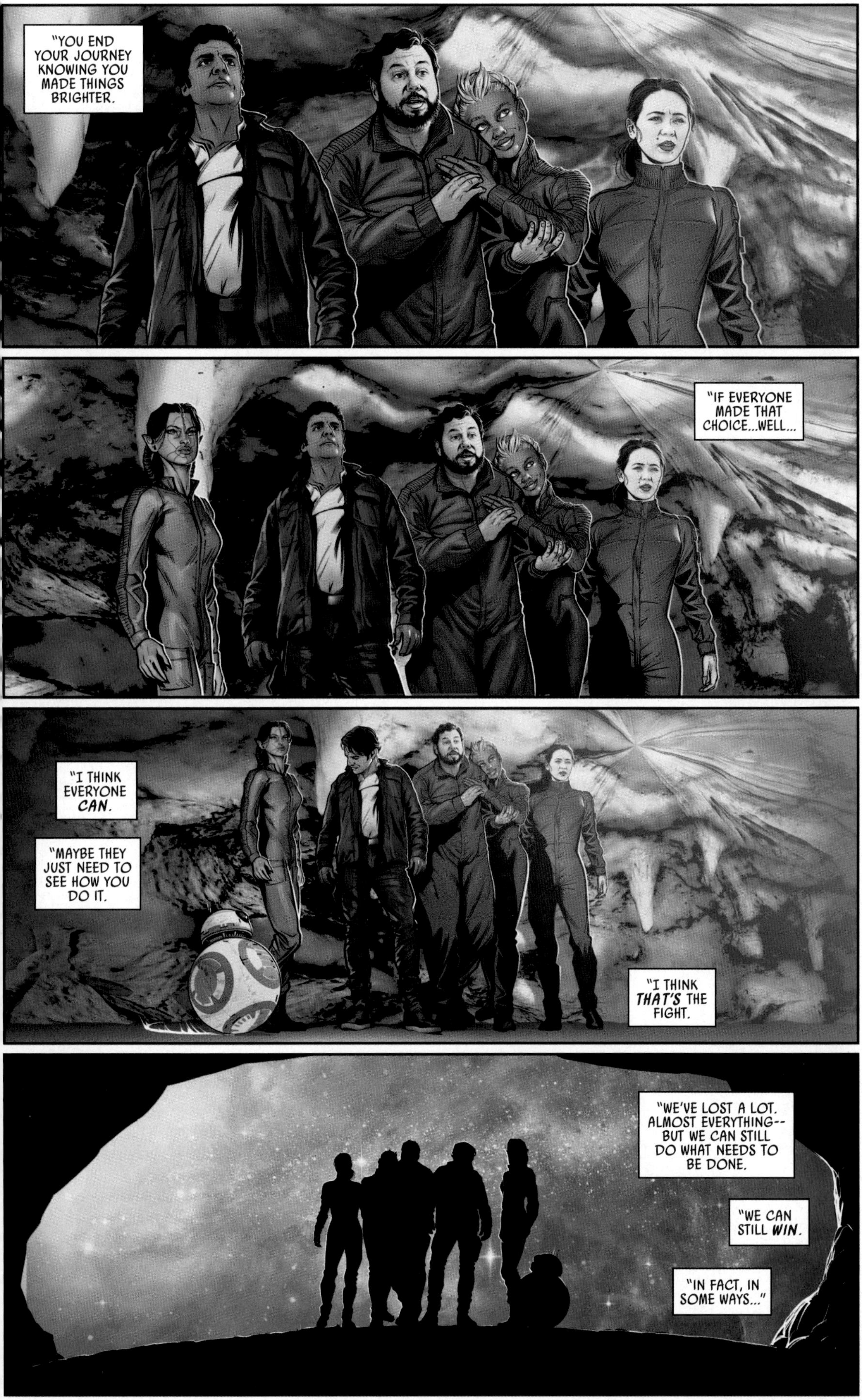
"YOU END YOUR JOURNEY KNOWING YOU MADE THINGS BRIGHTER.
"IF EVERYONE MADE THAT CHOICE...WELL...
"I THINK EVERYONE CAN.
"MAYBE THEY JUST NEED TO SEE HOW YOU DO IT.
"I THINK THAT'S THE FIGHT.
"WE'VE LOST A LOT. ALMOST EVERYTHING-- BUT WE CAN STILL DO WHAT NEEDS TO BE DONE.
"WE CAN STILL WIN.
"IN FACT, IN SOME WAYS..."

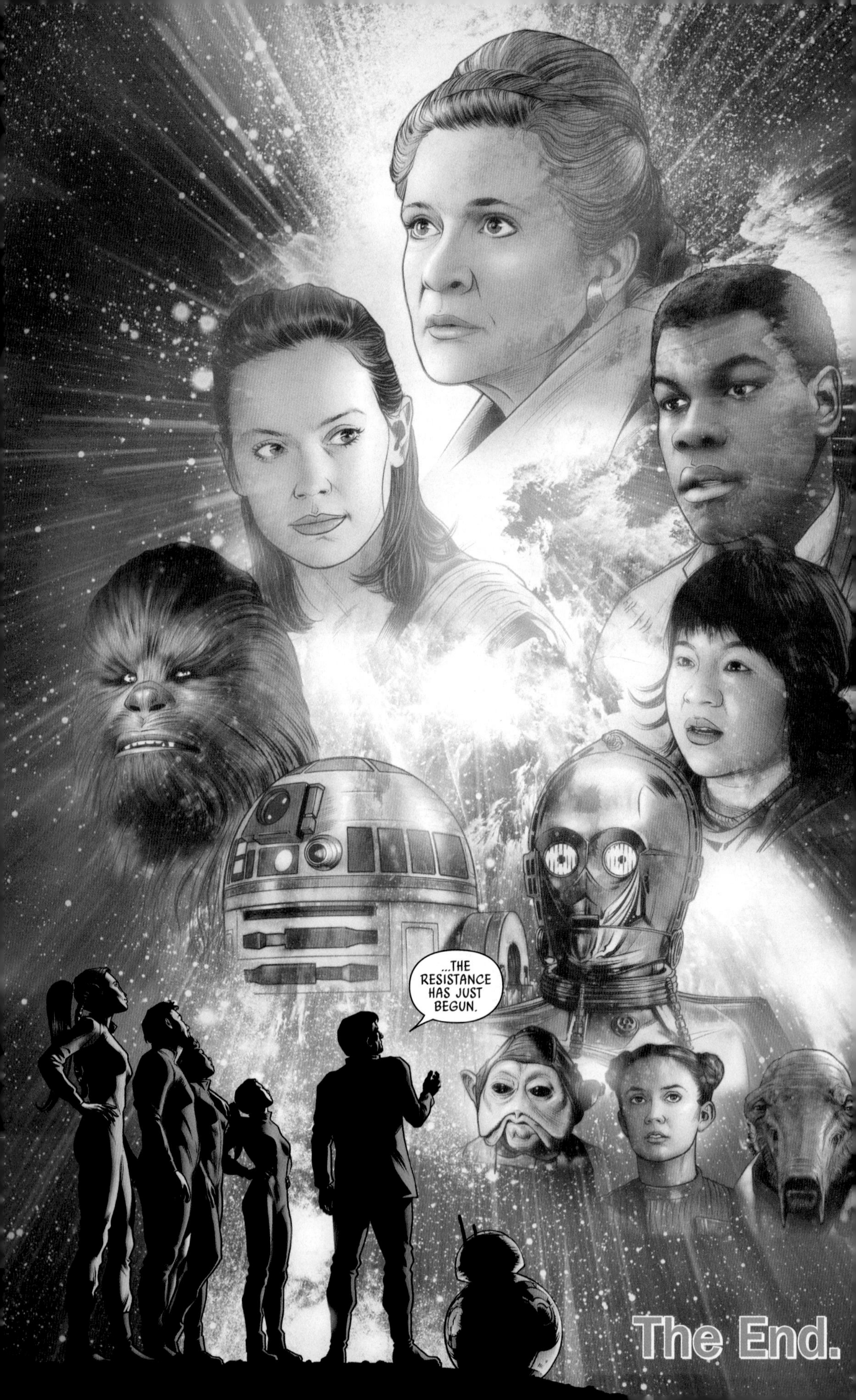
...THE RESISTANCE HAS JUST BEGUN.
The End.

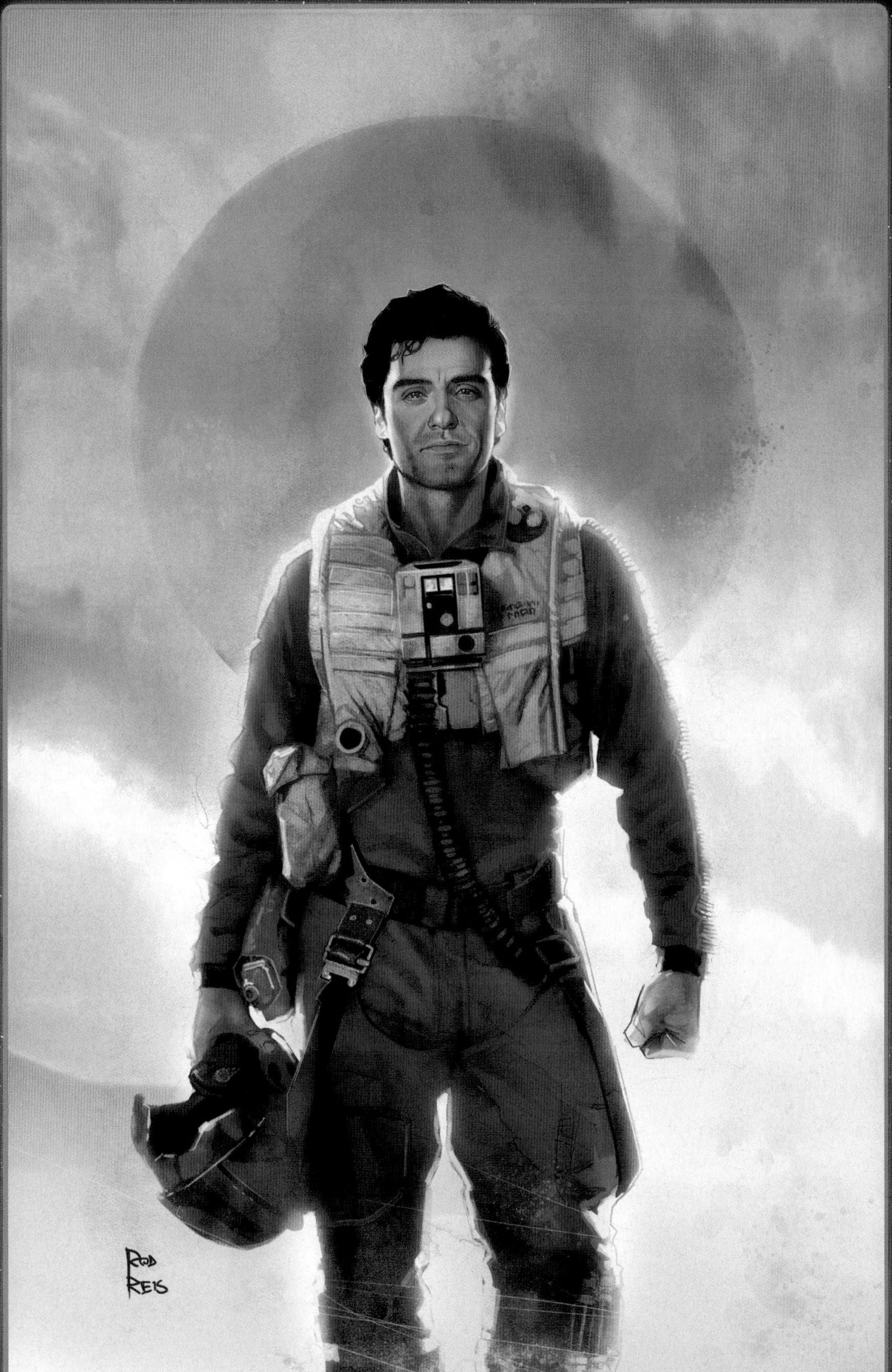
ROD
REIS

ANNUAL 2

POE DAMERON
ANNUAL II

The evil First Order has risen from the ashes of the Galactic Empire's defeat.

In response, General Leia Organa has formed the Resistance to defend the vulnerable New Republic and stem the tide of the First Order's power before it consumes the galaxy. But support for the movement has been hard to secure. Even Leia's husband Han Solo has left the rebel life and returned to his smuggling ways.

Leia now relies on new allies like famed pilot Poe Dameron, his trusty droid BB-8 and the skilled pilots of Black Squadron. Together, they stand ready to defend the New Republic at all costs....

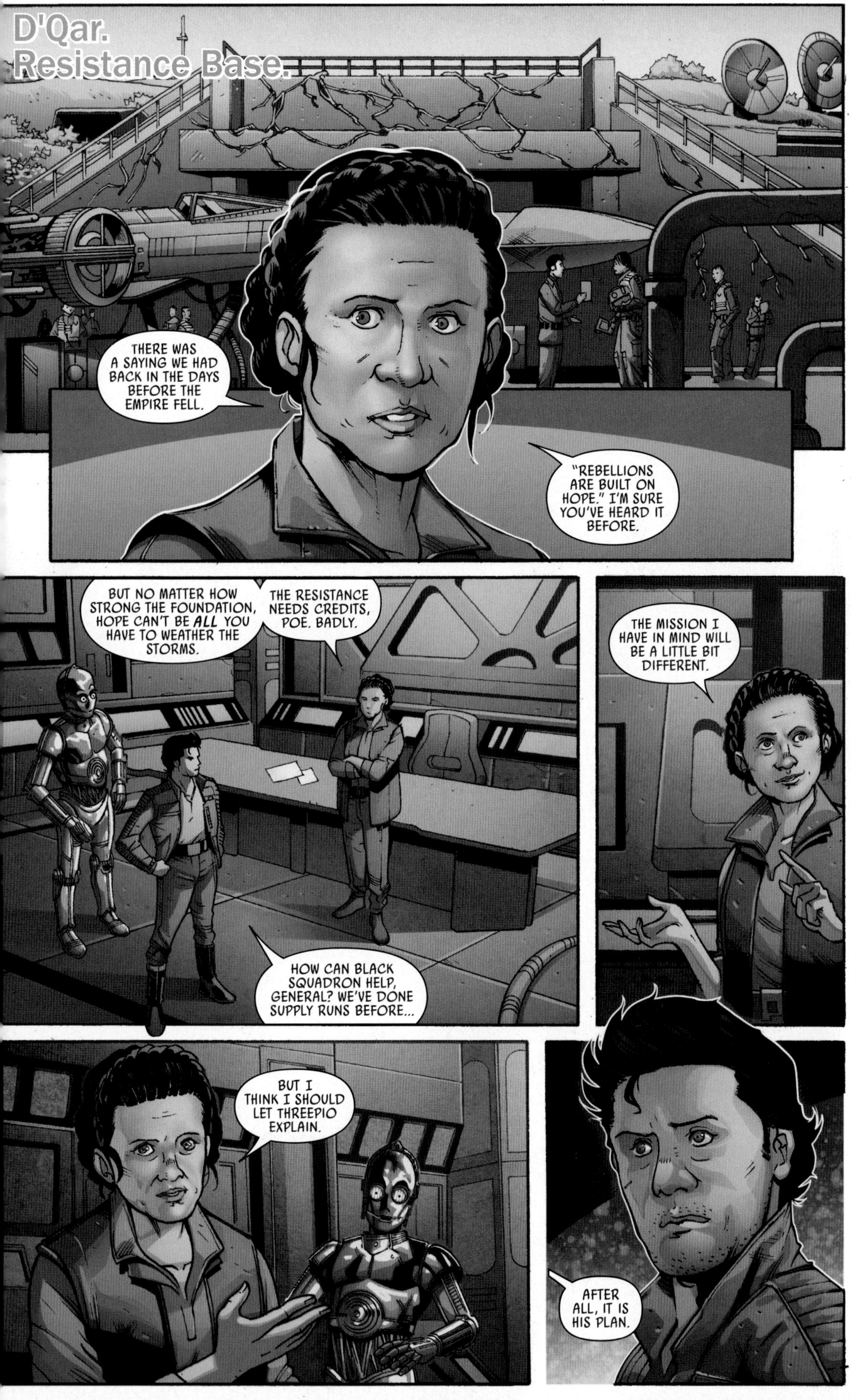
D'Qar.
Resistance Base.
THERE WAS A SAYING WE HAD BACK IN THE DAYS BEFORE THE EMPIRE FELL.
"REBELLIONS ARE BUILT ON HOPE." I'M SURE YOU'VE HEARD IT BEFORE.
BUT NO MATTER HOW STRONG THE FOUNDATION, HOPE CAN'T BE ALL YOU HAVE TO WEATHER THE STORMS.
THE RESISTANCE NEEDS CREDITS, POE. BADLY.
HOW CAN BLACK SQUADRON HELP, GENERAL? WE'VE DONE SUPPLY RUNS BEFORE...
THE MISSION I HAVE IN MIND WILL BE A LITTLE BIT DIFFERENT.
BUT I THINK I SHOULD LET THREEPIO EXPLAIN.
AFTER ALL, IT IS HIS PLAN.

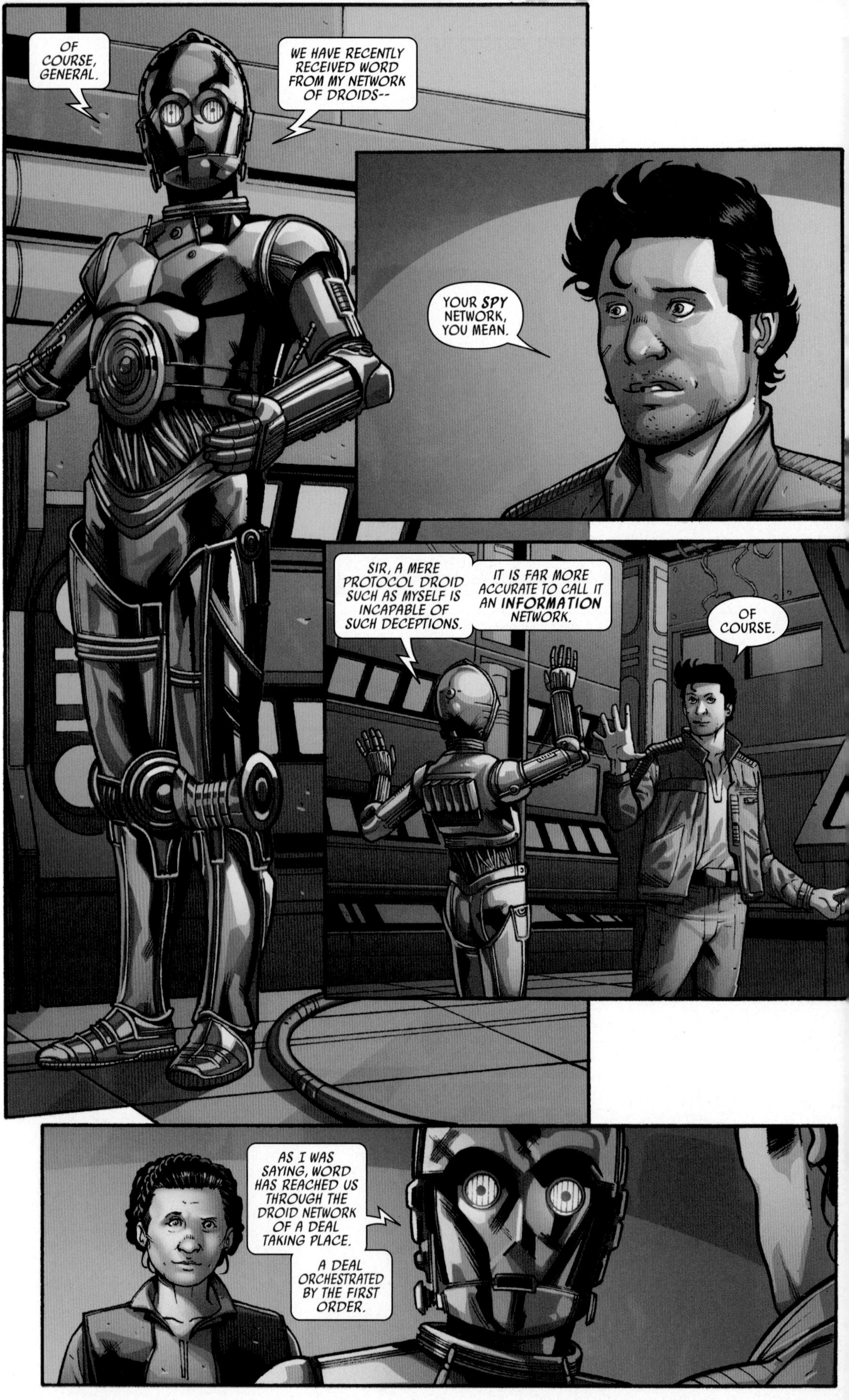
OF COURSE, GENERAL.
WE HAVE RECENTLY RECEIVED WORD FROM MY NETWORK OF DROIDS--
YOUR SPY NETWORK, YOU MEAN.
SIR, A MERE PROTOCOL DROID SUCH AS MYSELF IS INCAPABLE OF SUCH DECEPTIONS.
IT IS FAR MORE ACCURATE TO CALL IT AN INFORMATION NETWORK.
OF COURSE.
AS I WAS SAYING, WORD HAS REACHED US THROUGH THE DROID NETWORK OF A DEAL TAKING PLACE.
A DEAL ORCHESTRATED BY THE FIRST ORDER.

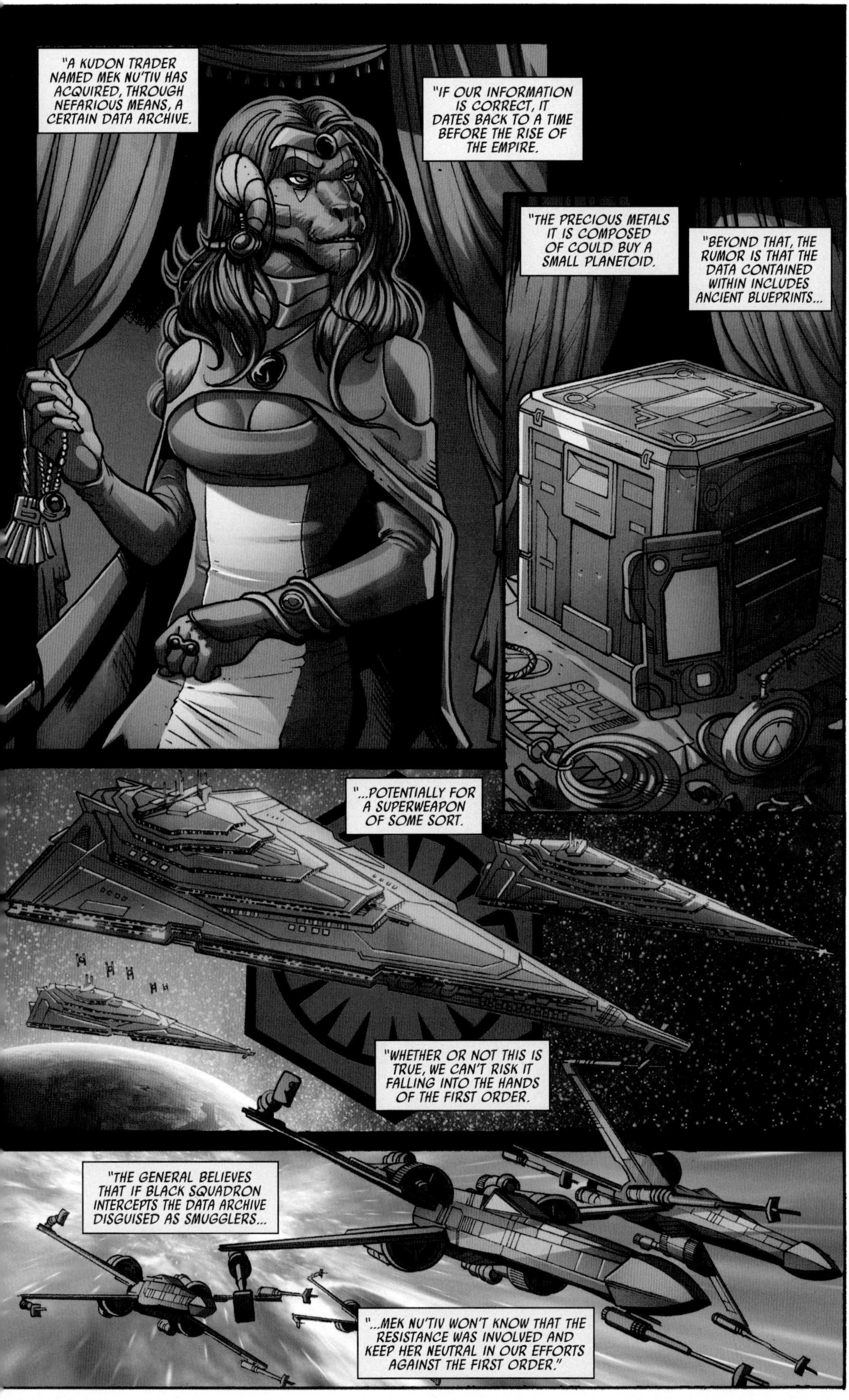
"A KUDON TRADER NAMED MEK NU'TIV HAS ACQUIRED, THROUGH NEFARIOUS MEANS, A CERTAIN DATA ARCHIVE.
"IF OUR INFORMATION IS CORRECT, IT DATES BACK TO A TIME BEFORE THE RISE OF THE EMPIRE.
"THE PRECIOUS METALS IT IS COMPOSED OF COULD BUY A SMALL PLANETOID.
"BEYOND THAT, THE RUMOR IS THAT THE DATA CONTAINED WITHIN INCLUDES ANCIENT BLUEPRINTS...
"...POTENTIALLY FOR A SUPERWEAPON OF SOME SORT.
"WHETHER OR NOT THIS IS TRUE, WE CAN'T RISK IT FALLING INTO THE HANDS OF THE FIRST ORDER.
"THE GENERAL BELIEVES THAT IF BLACK SQUADRON INTERCEPTS THE DATA ARCHIVE DISGUISED AS SMUGGLERS...
"...MEK NU'TIV WON'T KNOW THAT THE RESISTANCE WAS INVOLVED AND KEEP HER NEUTRAL IN OUR EFFORTS AGAINST THE FIRST ORDER."

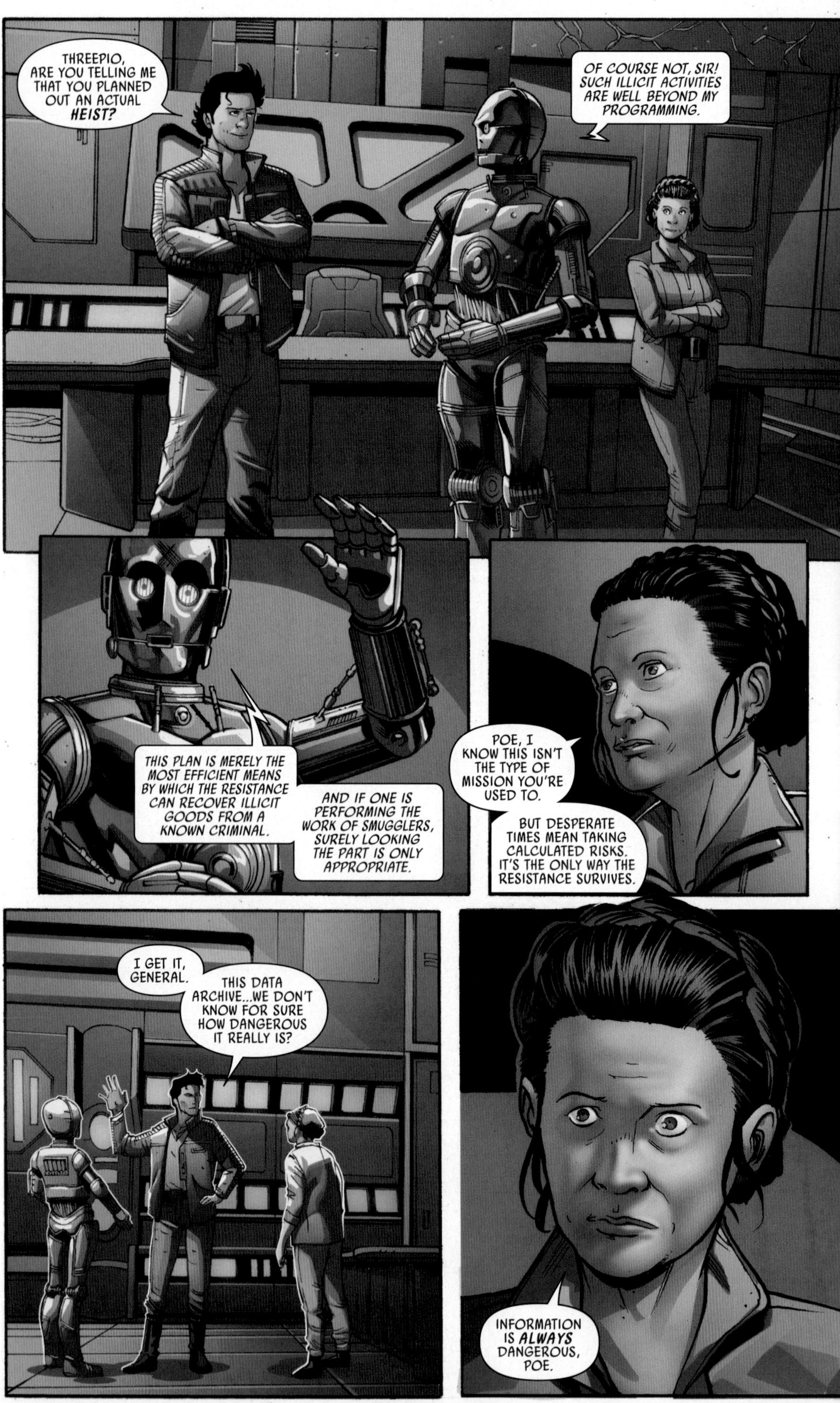
THREEPIO, ARE YOU TELLING ME THAT YOU PLANNED OUT AN ACTUAL HEIST?
OF COURSE NOT, SIR! SUCH ILLICIT ACTIVITIES ARE WELL BEYOND MY PROGRAMMING.
THIS PLAN IS MERELY THE MOST EFFICIENT MEANS BY WHICH THE RESISTANCE CAN RECOVER ILLICIT GOODS FROM A KNOWN CRIMINAL.
AND IF ONE IS PERFORMING THE WORK OF SMUGGLERS, SURELY LOOKING THE PART IS ONLY APPROPRIATE.
POE, I KNOW THIS ISN'T THE TYPE OF MISSION YOU'RE USED TO.
BUT DESPERATE TIMES MEAN TAKING CALCULATED RISKS. IT'S THE ONLY WAY THE RESISTANCE SURVIVES.
I GET IT, GENERAL.
THIS DATA ARCHIVE...WE DON'T KNOW FOR SURE HOW DANGEROUS IT REALLY IS?
INFORMATION IS ALWAYS DANGEROUS, POE.

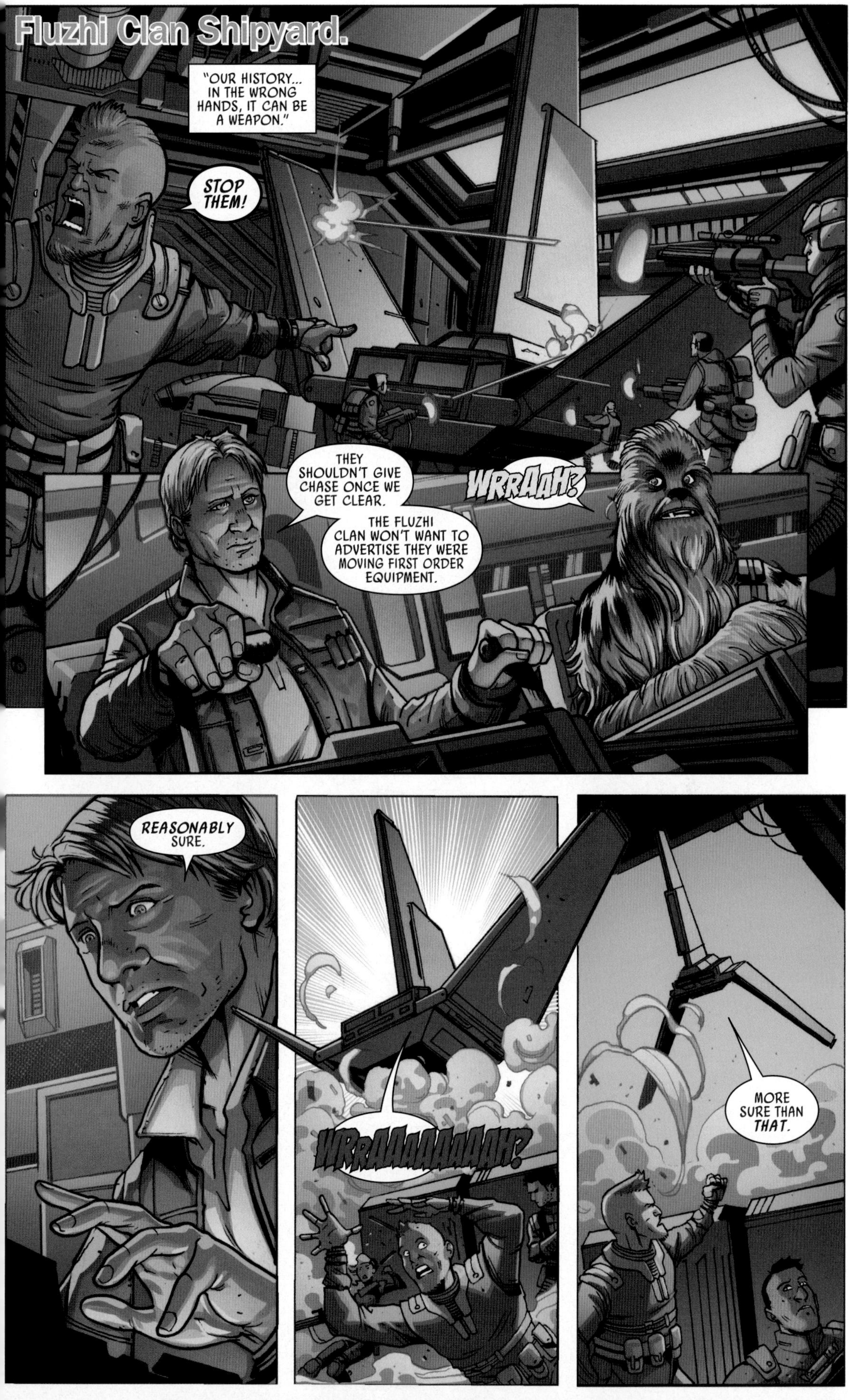
Fluzhi Clan Shipyard.
"OUR HISTORY... IN THE WRONG HANDS, IT CAN BE A WEAPON."
STOP THEM!
THEY SHOULDN'T GIVE CHASE ONCE WE GET CLEAR.
THE FLUZHI CLAN WON'T WANT TO ADVERTISE THEY WERE MOVING FIRST ORDER EQUIPMENT.
WRRAAH?
REASONABLY SURE.
WRRAAAAAAAAAH?
MORE SURE THAN THAT.

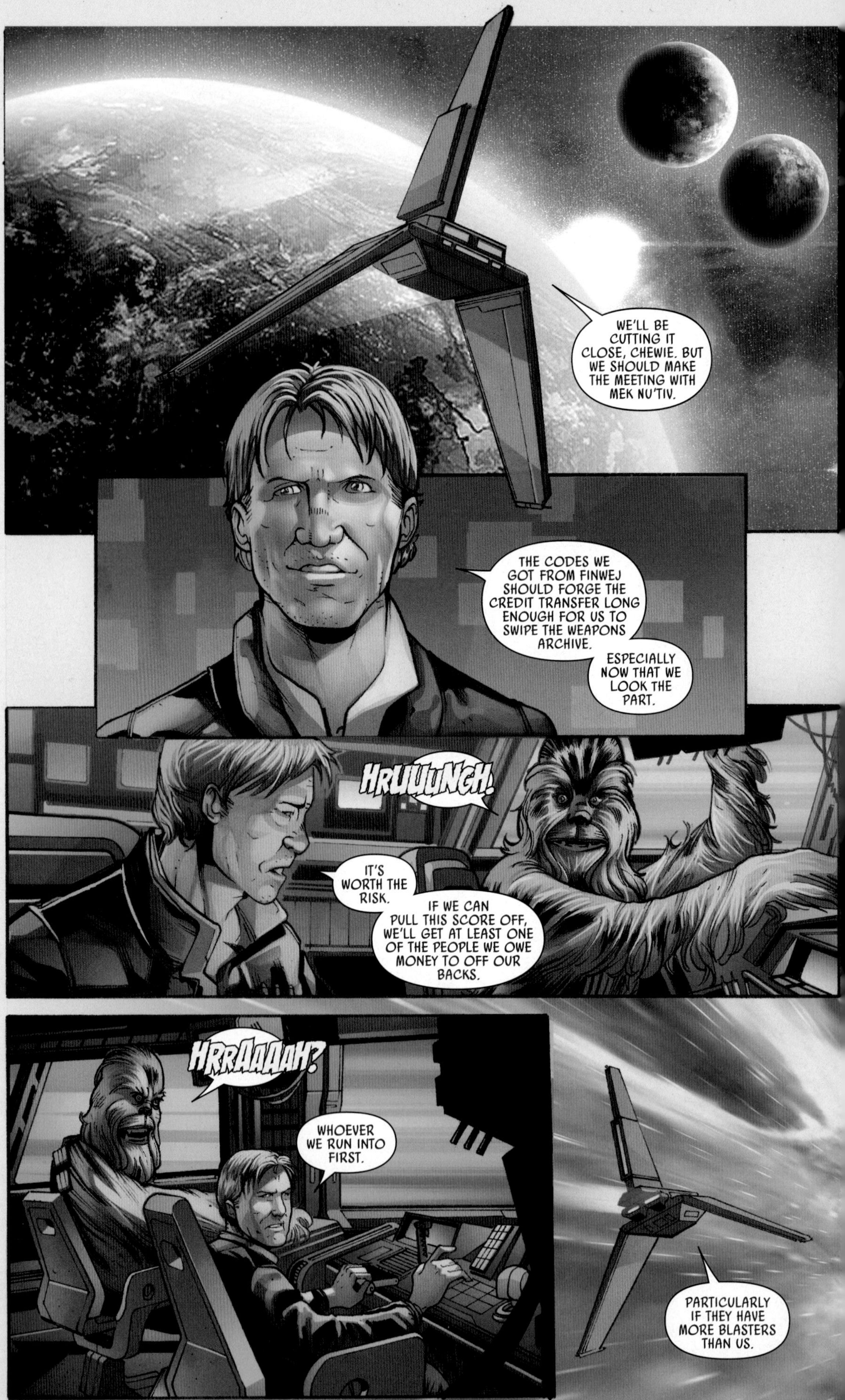
WE'LL BE CUTTING IT CLOSE, CHEWIE. BUT WE SHOULD MAKE THE MEETING WITH MEK NU'TIV.
THE CODES WE GOT FROM FINWEJ SHOULD FORGE THE CREDIT TRANSFER LONG ENOUGH FOR US TO SWIPE THE WEAPONS ARCHIVE.
ESPECIALLY NOW THAT WE LOOK THE PART.
HRUUUNCH!
IT'S WORTH THE RISK.
IF WE CAN PULL THIS SCORE OFF, WE'LL GET AT LEAST ONE OF THE PEOPLE WE OWE MONEY TO OFF OUR BACKS.
HRRAAAAH?
WHOEVER WE RUN INTO FIRST.
PARTICULARLY IF THEY HAVE MORE BLASTERS THAN US.

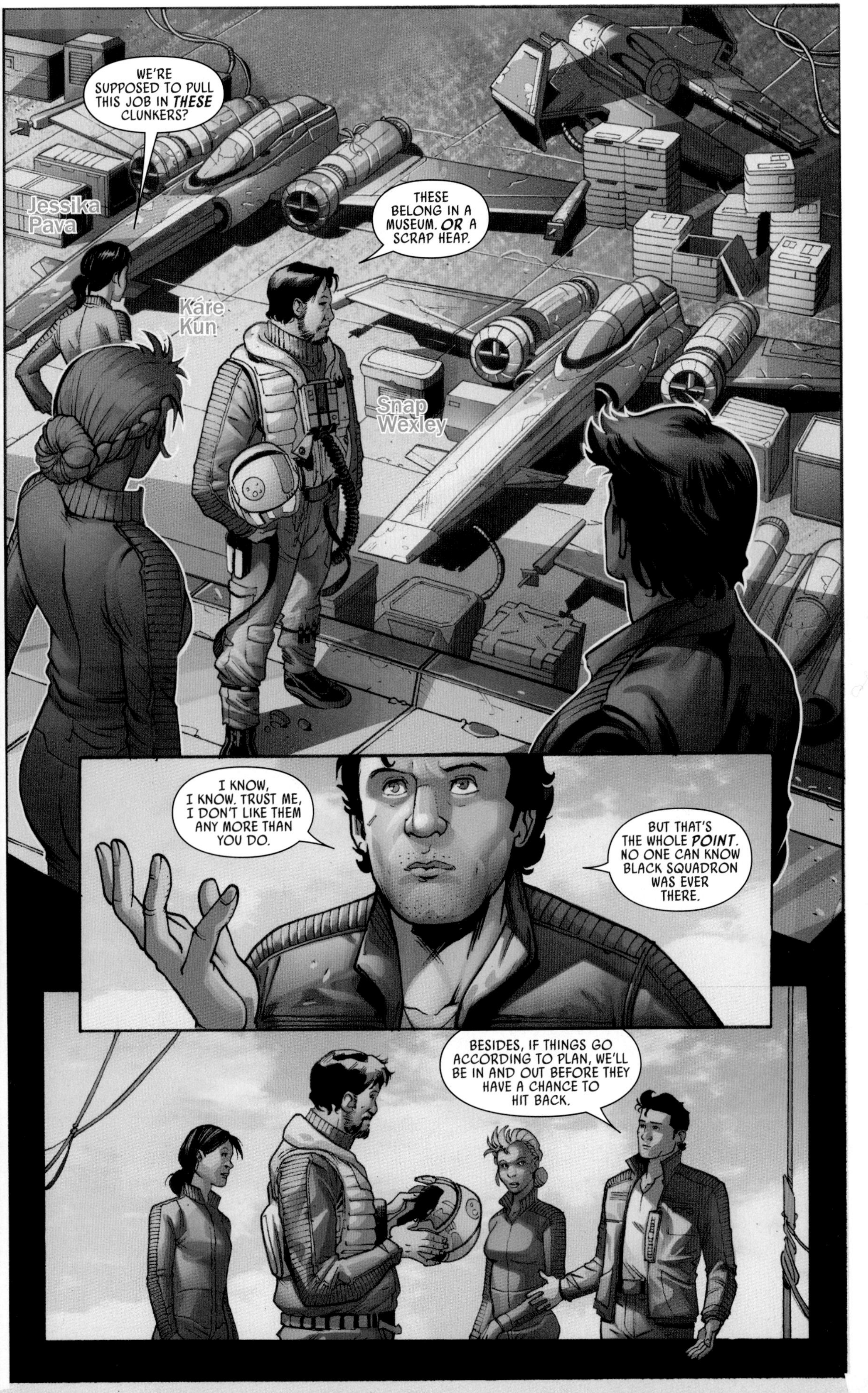
WE'RE SUPPOSED TO PULL THIS JOB IN THESE CLUNKERS?
Jessika Pava
THESE BELONG IN A MUSEUM. OR A SCRAP HEAP.
Káre Kun
Snap Wexley
I KNOW, I KNOW. TRUST ME, I DON'T LIKE THEM ANY MORE THAN YOU DO.
BUT THAT'S THE WHOLE POINT. NO ONE CAN KNOW BLACK SQUADRON WAS EVER THERE.
BESIDES, IF THINGS GO ACCORDING TO PLAN, WE'LL BE IN AND OUT BEFORE THEY HAVE A CHANCE TO HIT BACK.

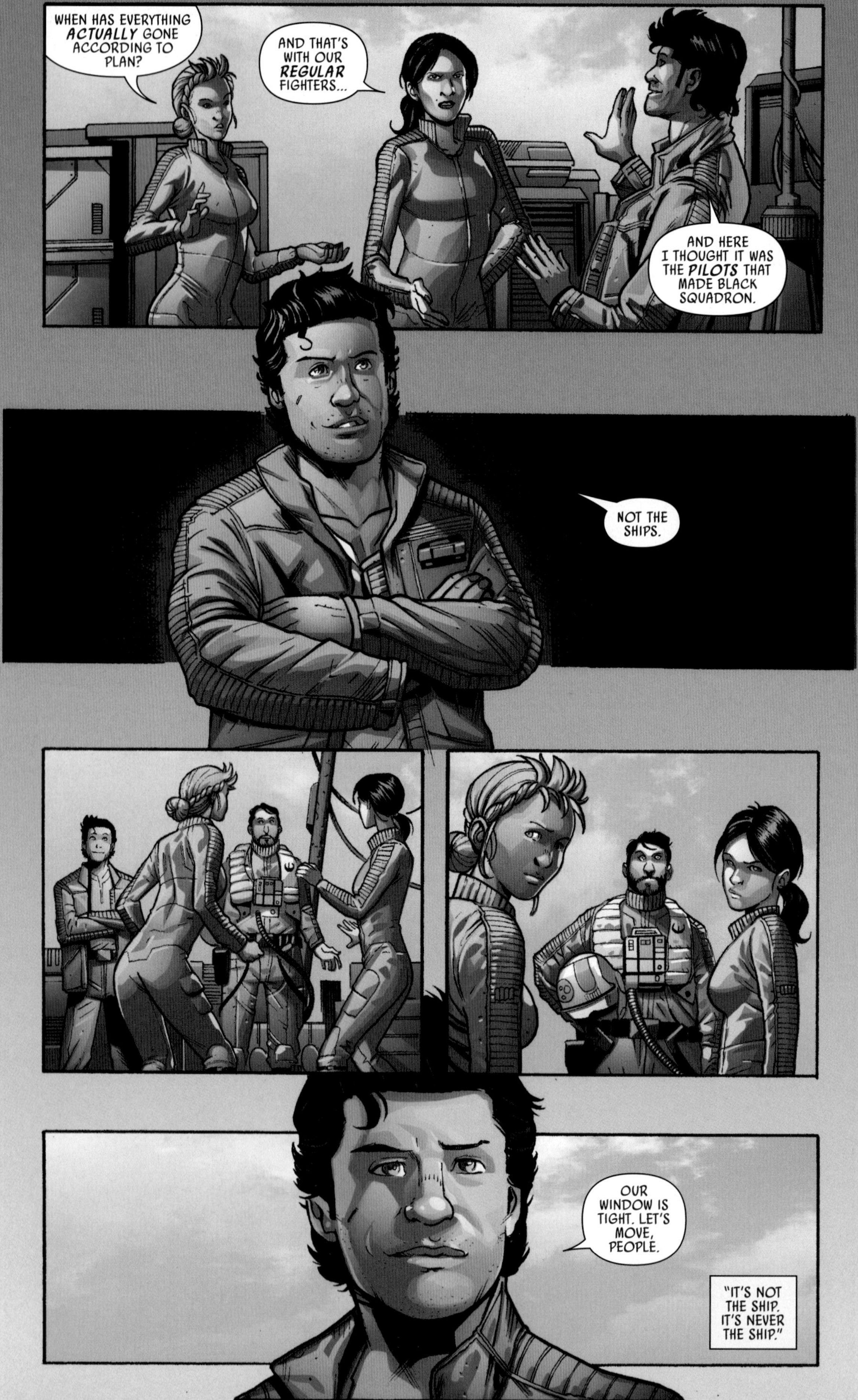
WHEN HAS EVERYTHING ACTUALLY GONE ACCORDING TO PLAN?
AND THAT'S WITH OUR REGULAR FIGHTERS...
AND HERE I THOUGHT IT WAS THE PILOTS THAT MADE BLACK SQUADRON.
NOT THE SHIPS.
OUR WINDOW IS TIGHT. LET'S MOVE, PEOPLE.
"IT'S NOT THE SHIP. IT'S NEVER THE SHIP."

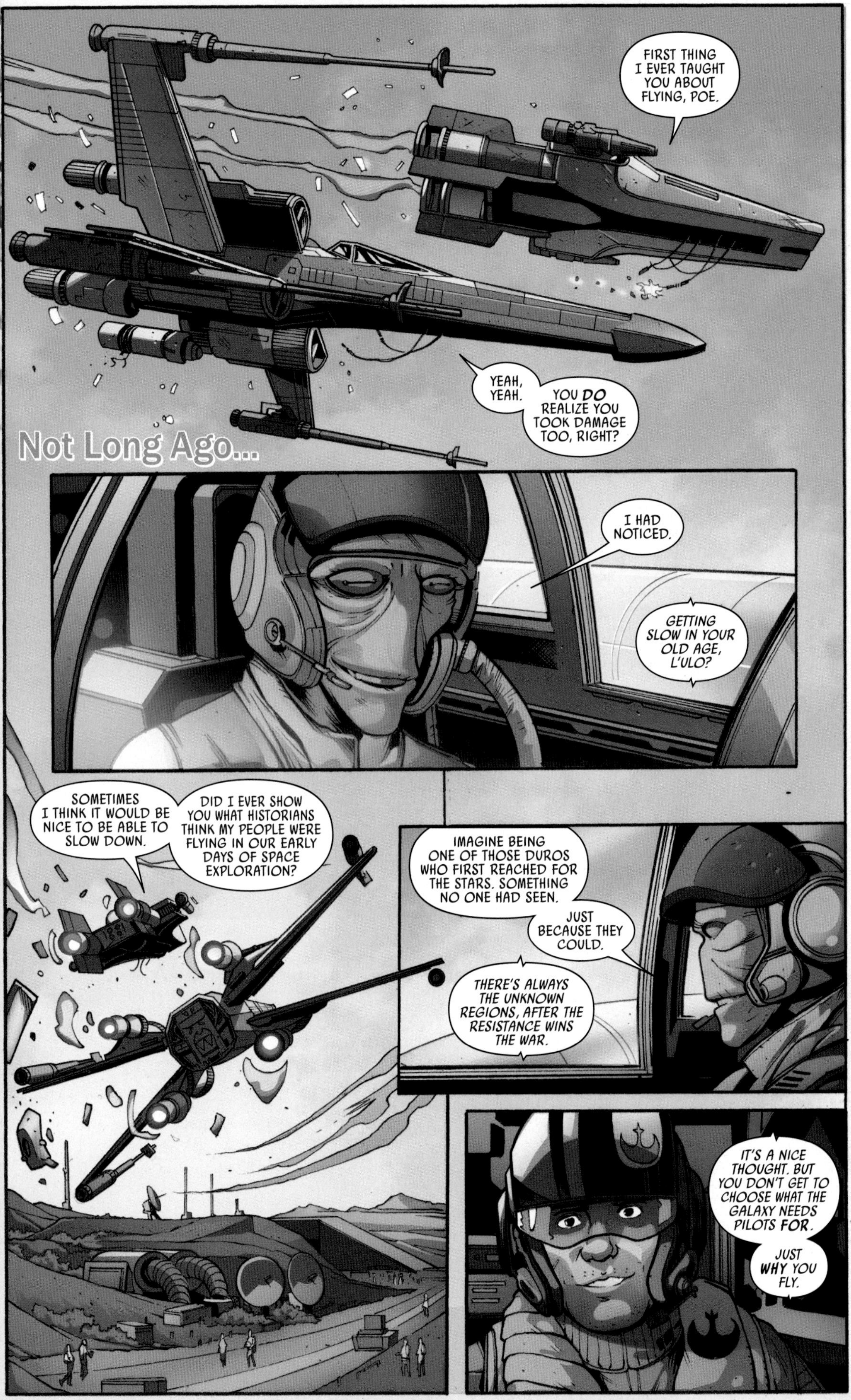
FIRST THING I EVER TAUGHT YOU ABOUT FLYING, POE.
YEAH, YEAH.
YOU DO REALIZE YOU TOOK DAMAGE TOO, RIGHT?
Not Long Ago...
I HAD NOTICED.
GETTING SLOW IN YOUR OLD AGE, L'ULO?
SOMETIMES I THINK IT WOULD BE NICE TO BE ABLE TO SLOW DOWN.
DID I EVER SHOW YOU WHAT HISTORIANS THINK MY PEOPLE WERE FLYING IN OUR EARLY DAYS OF SPACE EXPLORATION?
IMAGINE BEING ONE OF THOSE DUROS WHO FIRST REACHED FOR THE STARS. SOMETHING NO ONE HAD SEEN.
JUST BECAUSE THEY COULD.
THERE'S ALWAYS THE UNKNOWN REGIONS, AFTER THE RESISTANCE WINS THE WAR.
IT'S A NICE THOUGHT. BUT YOU DON'T GET TO CHOOSE WHAT THE GALAXY NEEDS PILOTS FOR.
JUST WHY YOU FLY.

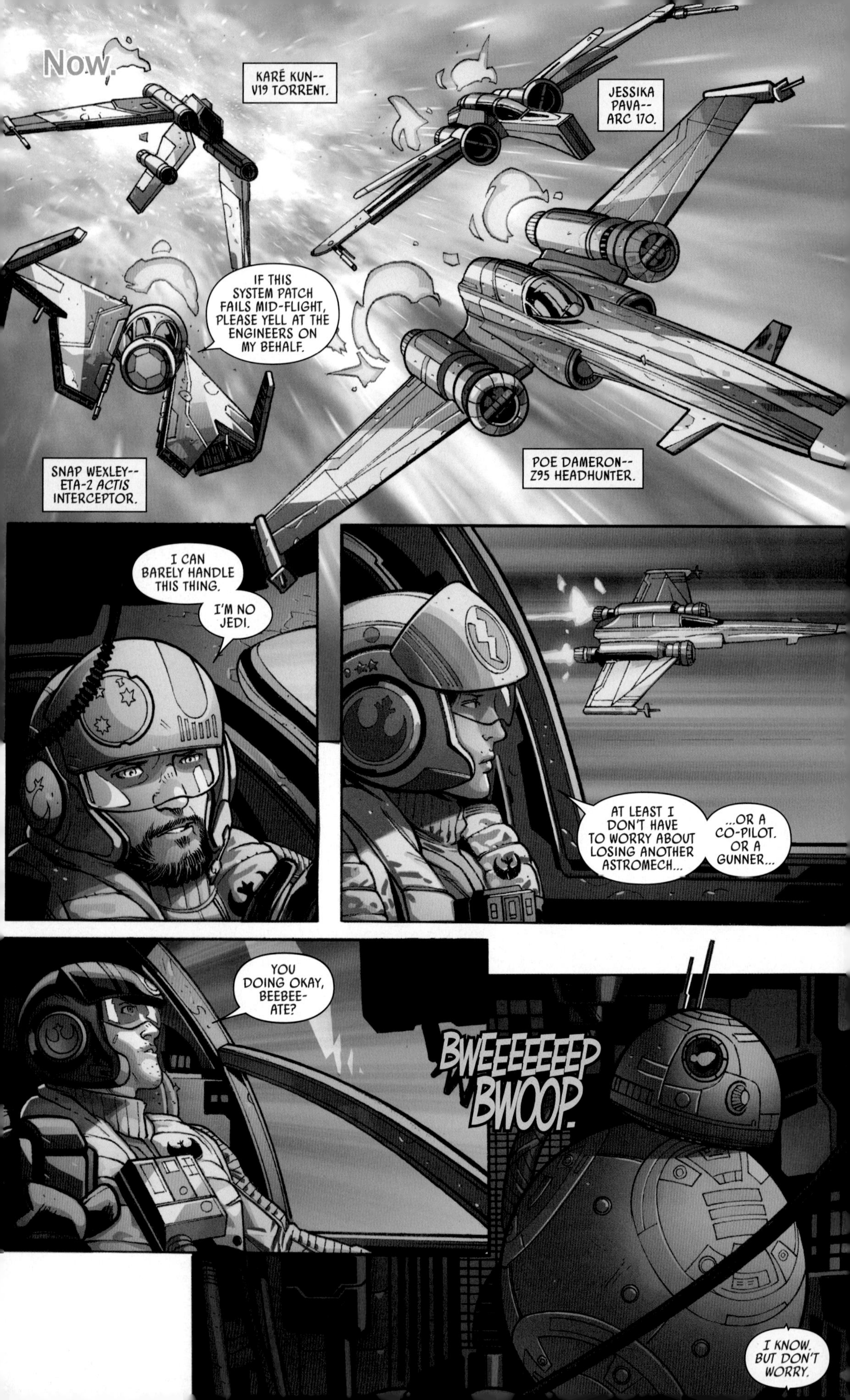
Now.
KARÉ KUN-- V19 TORRENT.
JESSIKA PAVA-- ARC 170.
IF THIS SYSTEM PATCH FAILS MID-FLIGHT, PLEASE YELL AT THE ENGINEERS ON MY BEHALF.
SNAP WEXLEY-- ETA-2 ACTIS INTERCEPTOR.
POE DAMERON-- Z95 HEADHUNTER.
I CAN BARELY HANDLE THIS THING.
I'M NO JEDI.
AT LEAST I DON'T HAVE TO WORRY ABOUT LOSING ANOTHER ASTROMECH...
...OR A CO-PILOT. OR A GUNNER...
YOU DOING OKAY, BEEBEE-ATE?
BWEEEEEEEP BWOOP.
I KNOW. BUT DON'T WORRY.

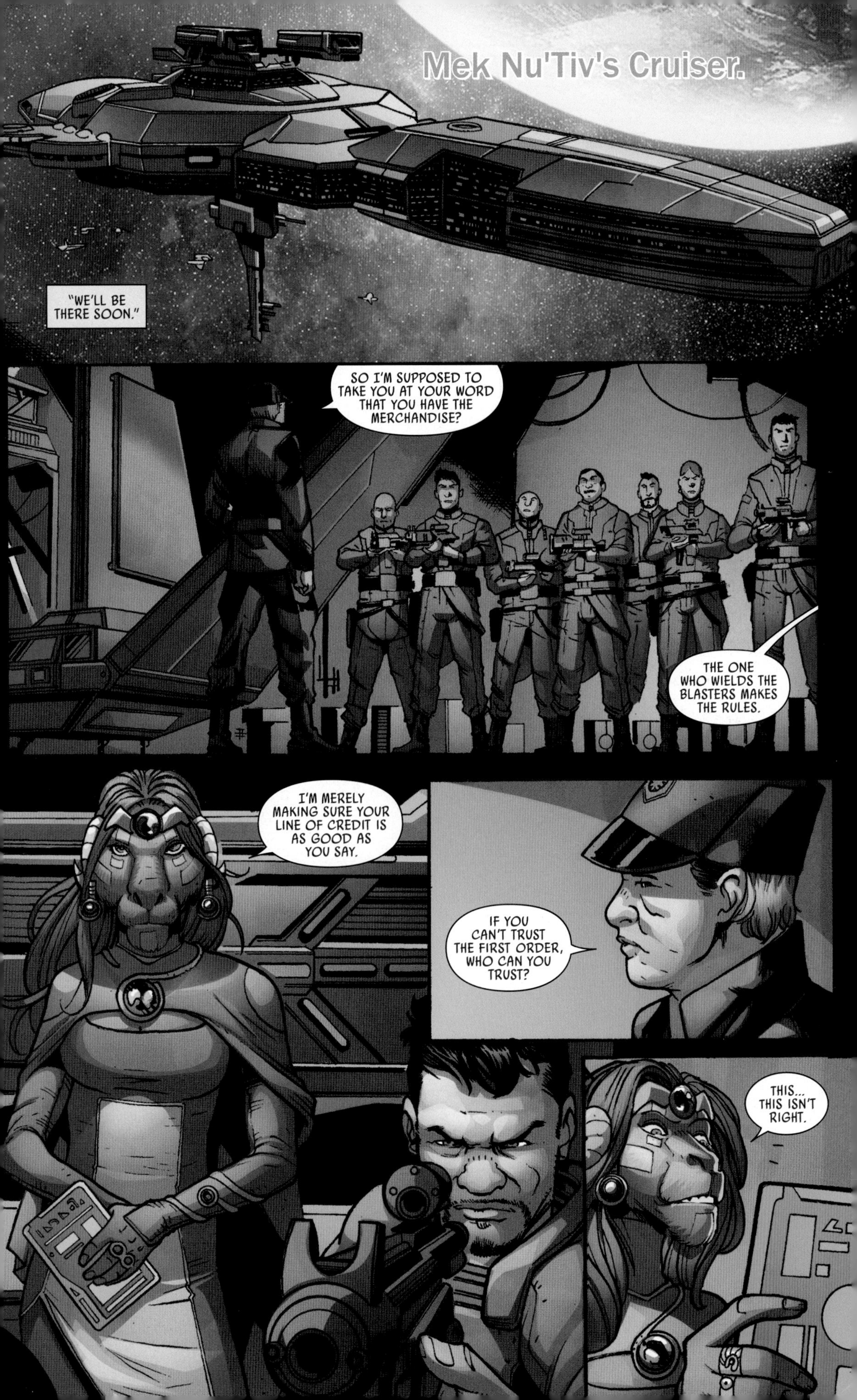
Mek Nu'Tiv's Cruiser.
"WE'LL BE THERE SOON."
SO I'M SUPPOSED TO TAKE YOU AT YOUR WORD THAT YOU HAVE THE MERCHANDISE?
THE ONE WHO WIELDS THE BLASTERS MAKES THE RULES.
I'M MERELY MAKING SURE YOUR LINE OF CREDIT IS AS GOOD AS YOU SAY.
IF YOU CAN'T TRUST THE FIRST ORDER, WHO CAN YOU TRUST?
THIS... THIS ISN'T RIGHT.

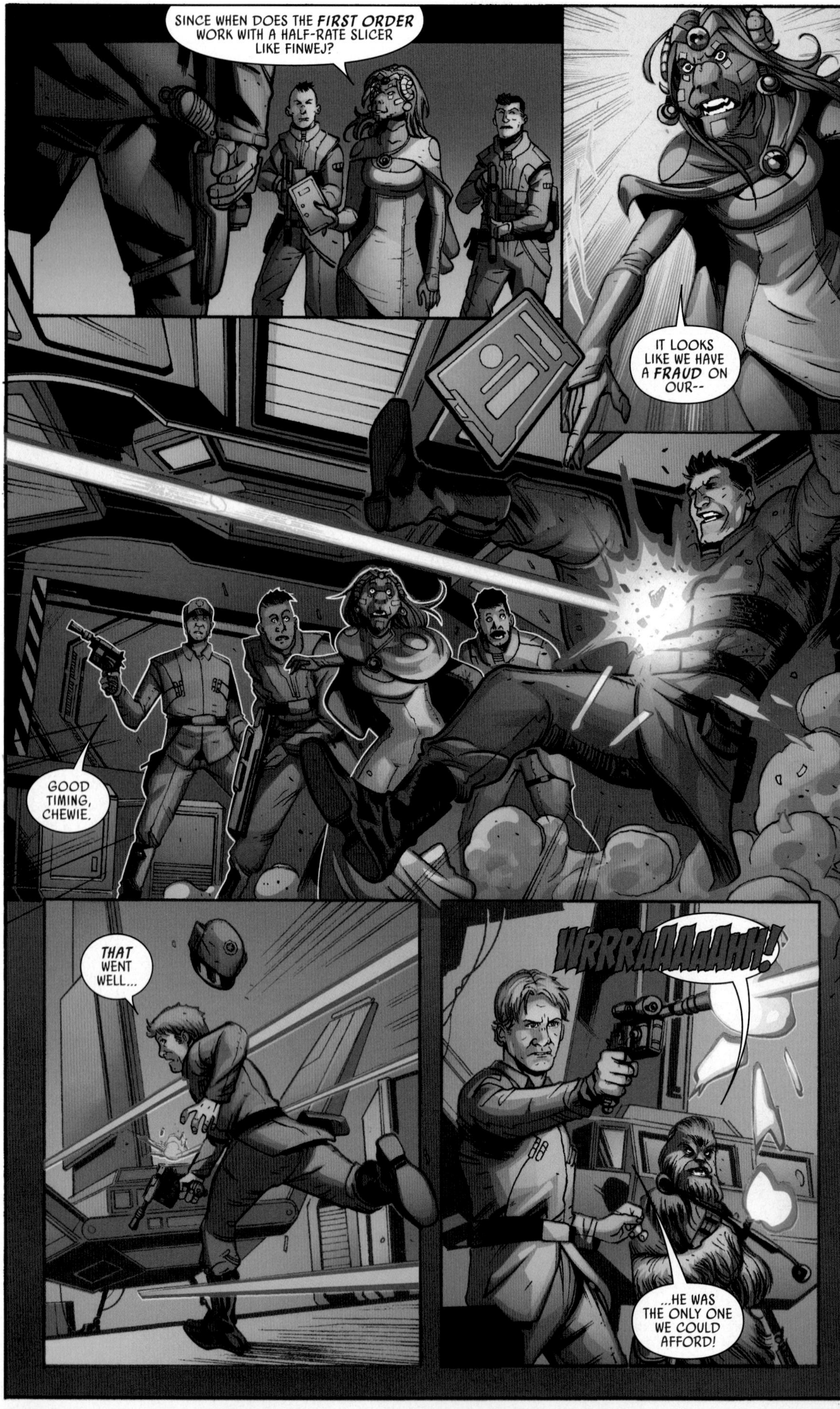
SINCE WHEN DOES THE FIRST ORDER WORK WITH A HALF-RATE SLICER LIKE FINWEJ?
IT LOOKS LIKE WE HAVE A FRAUD ON OUR--
GOOD TIMING, CHEWIE.
THAT WENT WELL...
WRRRAAAAAAHH!
...HE WAS THE ONLY ONE WE COULD AFFORD!

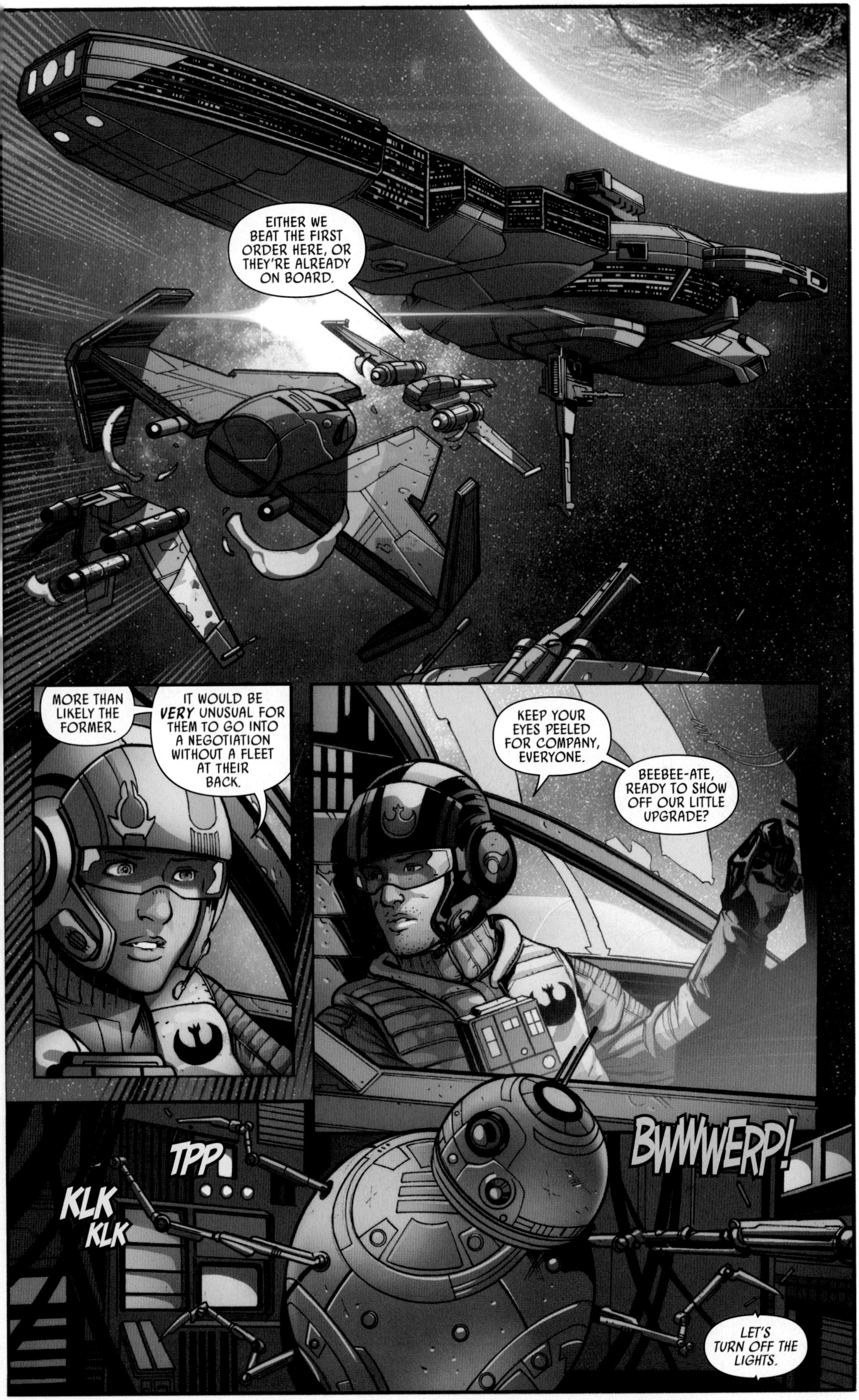
EITHER WE BEAT THE FIRST ORDER HERE, OR THEY'RE ALREADY ON BOARD.
MORE THAN LIKELY THE FORMER.
IT WOULD BE *VERY* UNUSUAL FOR THEM TO GO INTO A NEGOTIATION WITHOUT A FLEET AT THEIR BACK.
KEEP YOUR EYES PEELED FOR COMPANY, EVERYONE.
BEEBEE-ATE, READY TO SHOW OFF OUR LITTLE UPGRADE?
TPP
KLK KLK
BWWWERP!
LET'S TURN OFF THE LIGHTS.

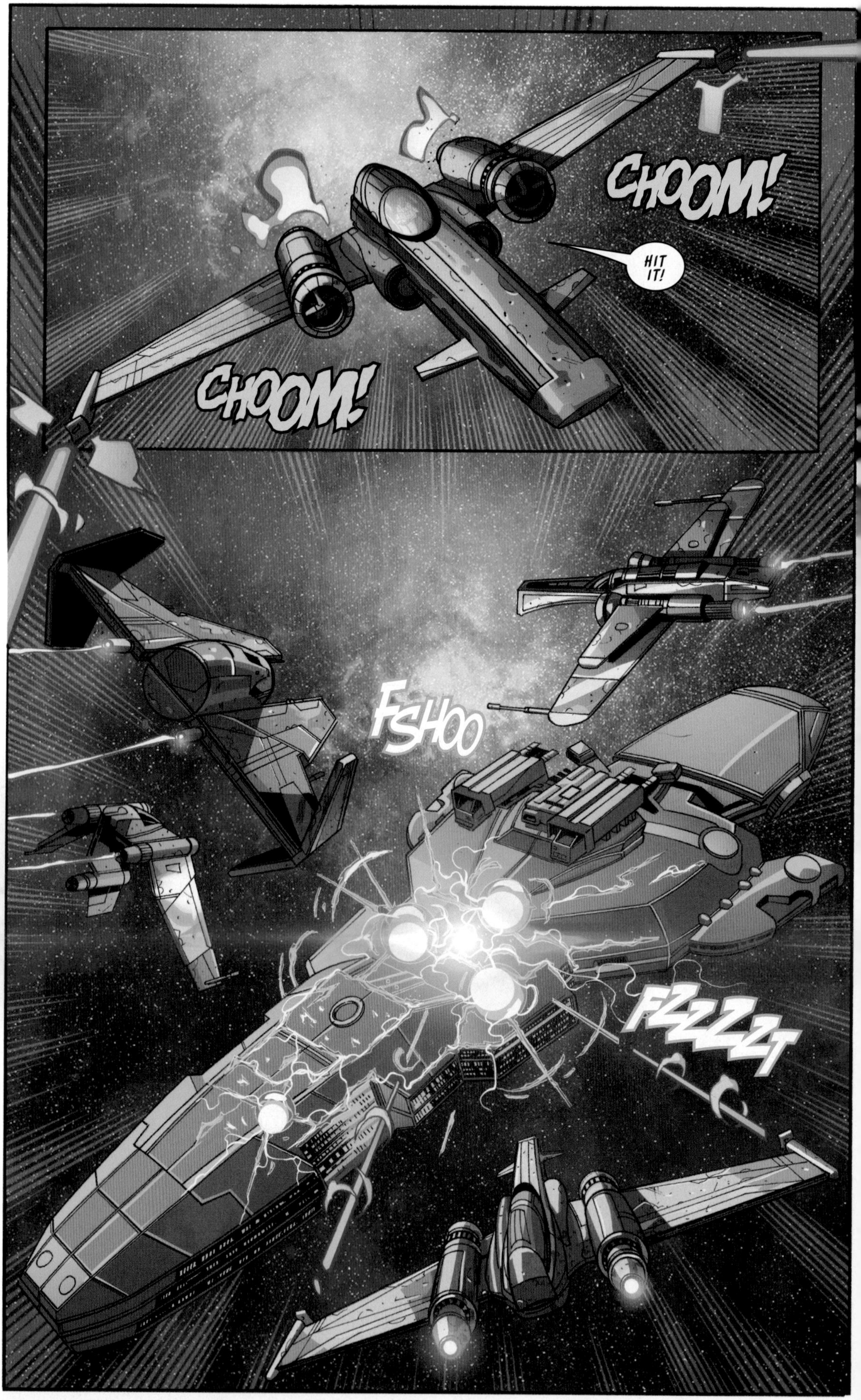
CHOOM!
HIT IT!
CHOOM!
FSHOO
FZZZZT

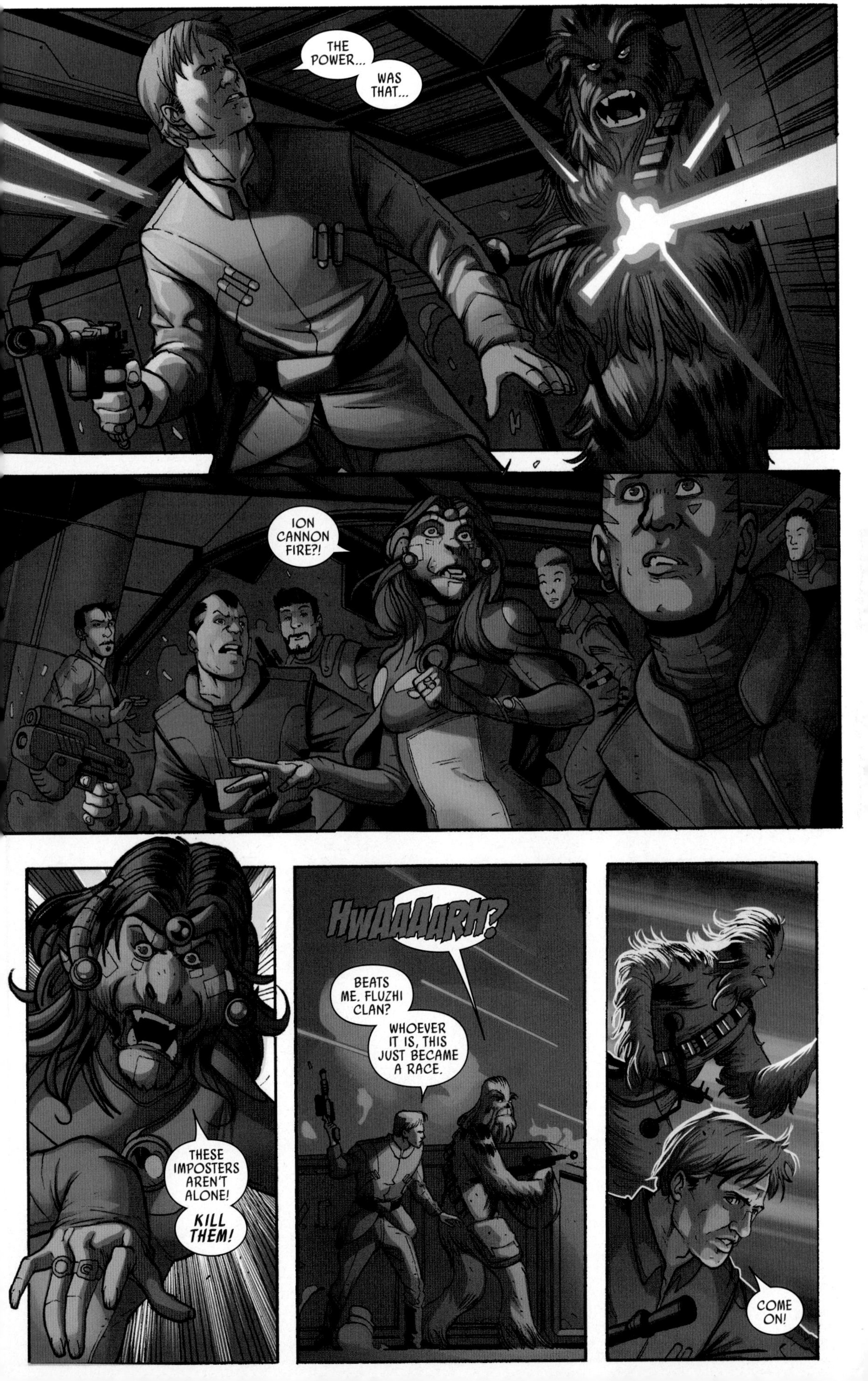
THE POWER...
WAS THAT...
ION CANNON FIRE?!
THESE IMPOSTERS AREN'T ALONE!
KILL THEM!
HWAAAARH?
BEATS ME. FLUZHI CLAN?
WHOEVER IT IS, THIS JUST BECAME A RACE.
COME ON!

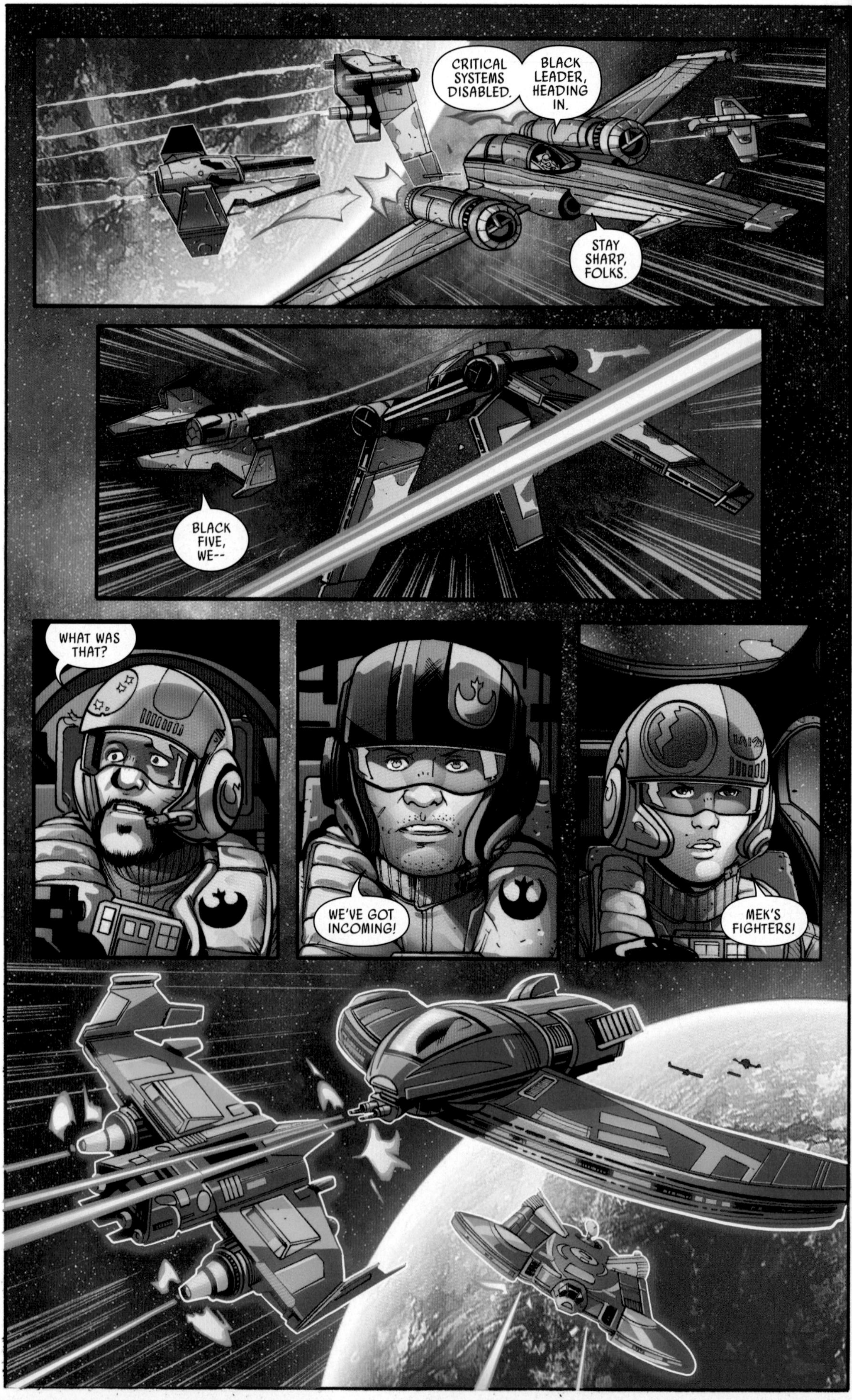
CRITICAL SYSTEMS DISABLED.
BLACK LEADER, HEADING IN.
STAY SHARP, FOLKS.
BLACK FIVE, WE--
WHAT WAS THAT?
WE'VE GOT INCOMING!
MEK'S FIGHTERS!

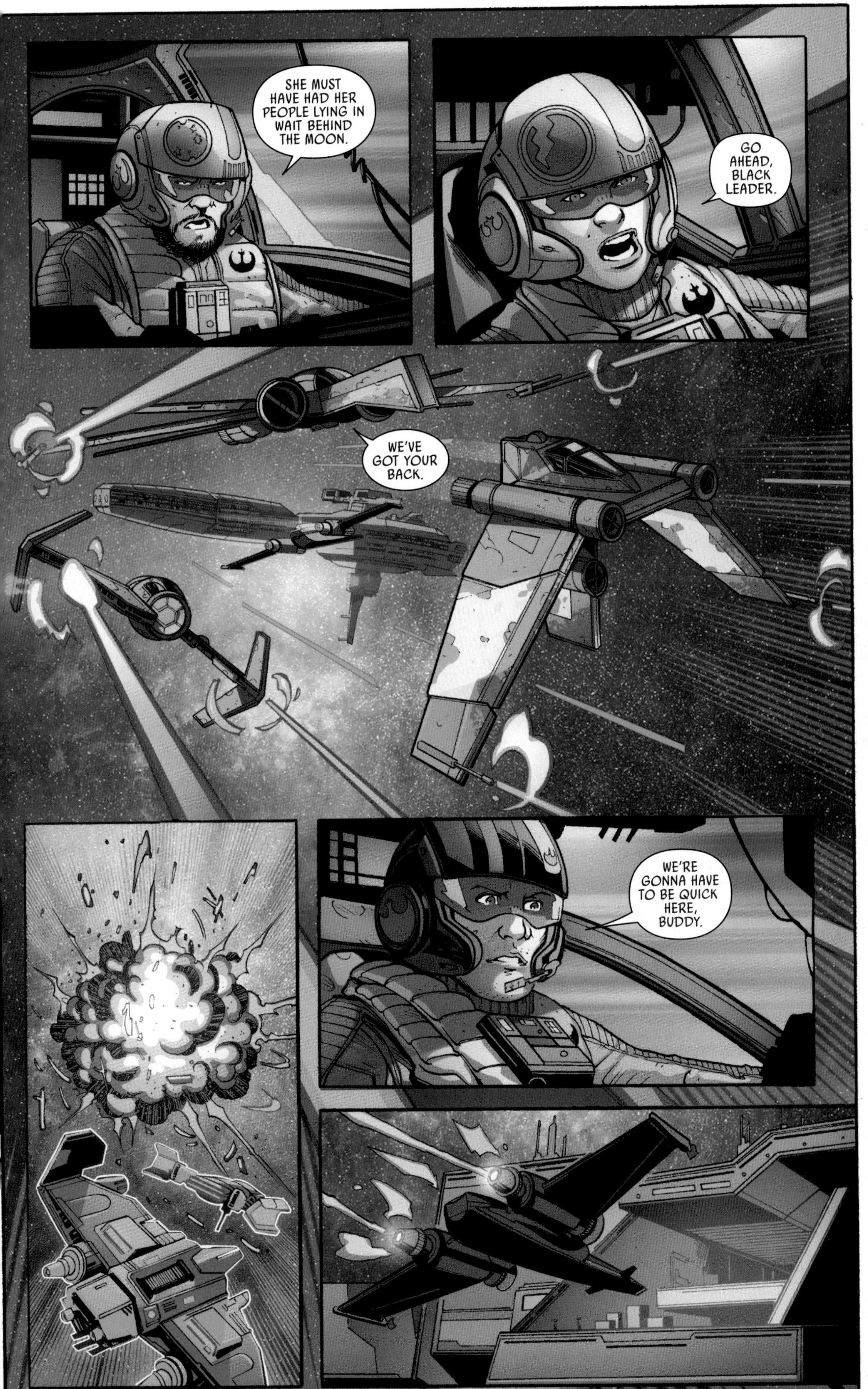
SHE MUST HAVE HAD HER PEOPLE LYING IN WAIT BEHIND THE MOON.
GO AHEAD, BLACK LEADER.
WE'VE GOT YOUR BACK.
WE'RE GONNA HAVE TO BE QUICK HERE, BUDDY.

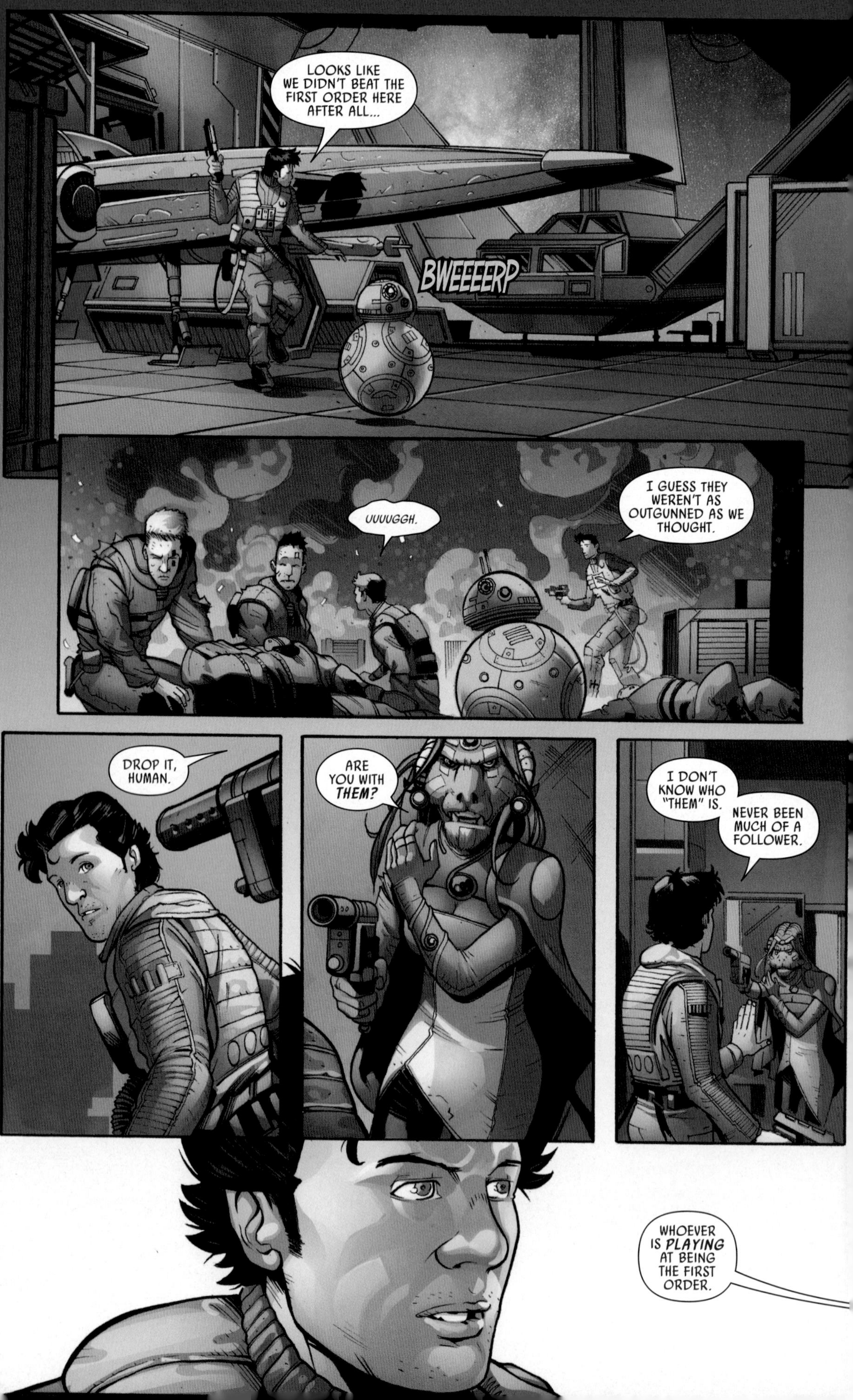
LOOKS LIKE WE DIDN'T BEAT THE FIRST ORDER HERE AFTER ALL...
BWEEEEERP
UUUUGGH.
I GUESS THEY WEREN'T AS OUTGUNNED AS WE THOUGHT.
DROP IT, HUMAN.
ARE YOU WITH *THEM?*
I DON'T KNOW WHO "THEM" IS.
NEVER BEEN MUCH OF A FOLLOWER.
WHOEVER IS *PLAYING* AT BEING THE FIRST ORDER.

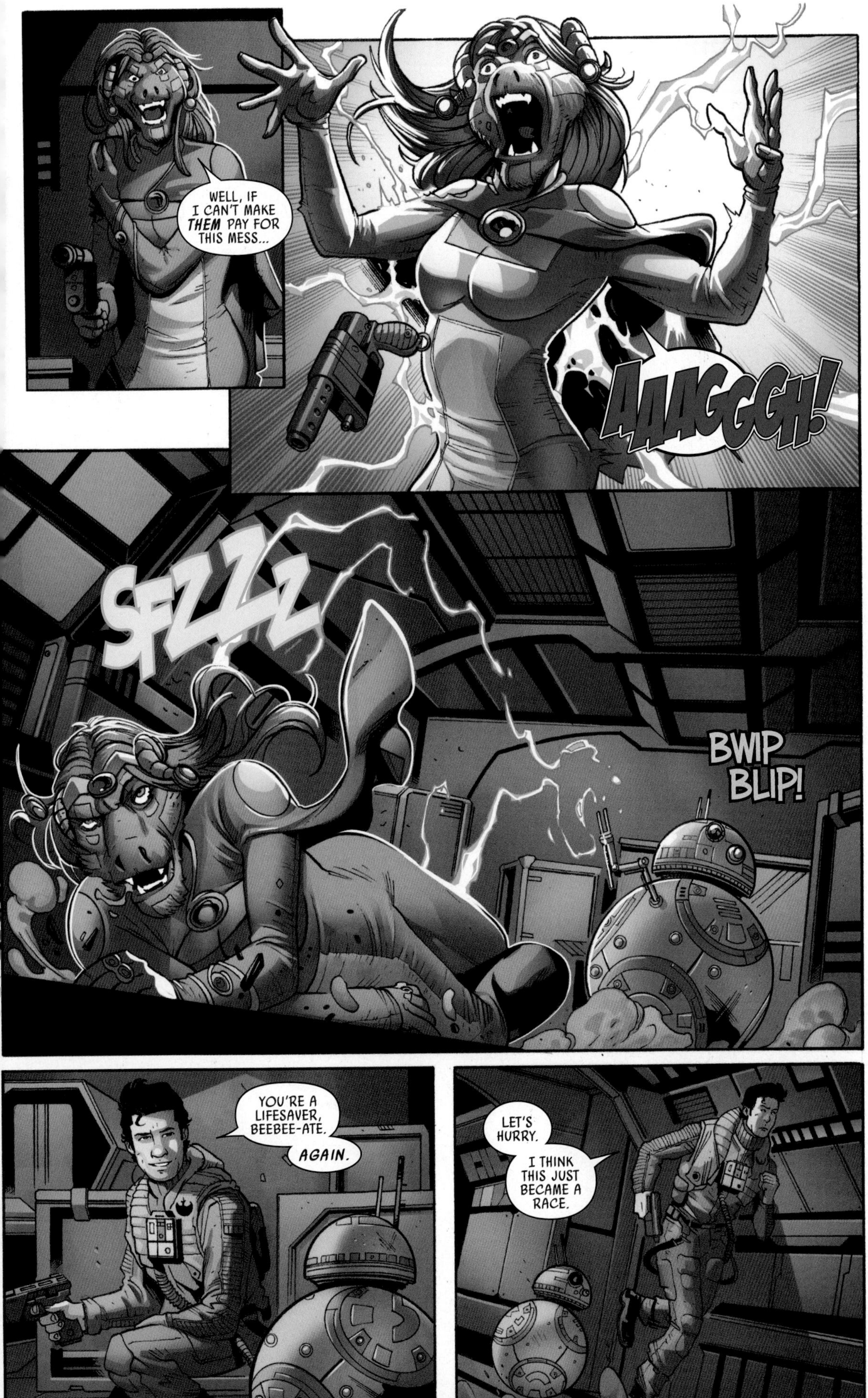
WELL, IF I CAN'T MAKE THEM PAY FOR THIS MESS...
AAAGGGH!
SFZZZ
BWIP BLIP!
YOU'RE A LIFESAVER, BEEBEE-ATE.
AGAIN.
LET'S HURRY.
I THINK THIS JUST BECAME A RACE.

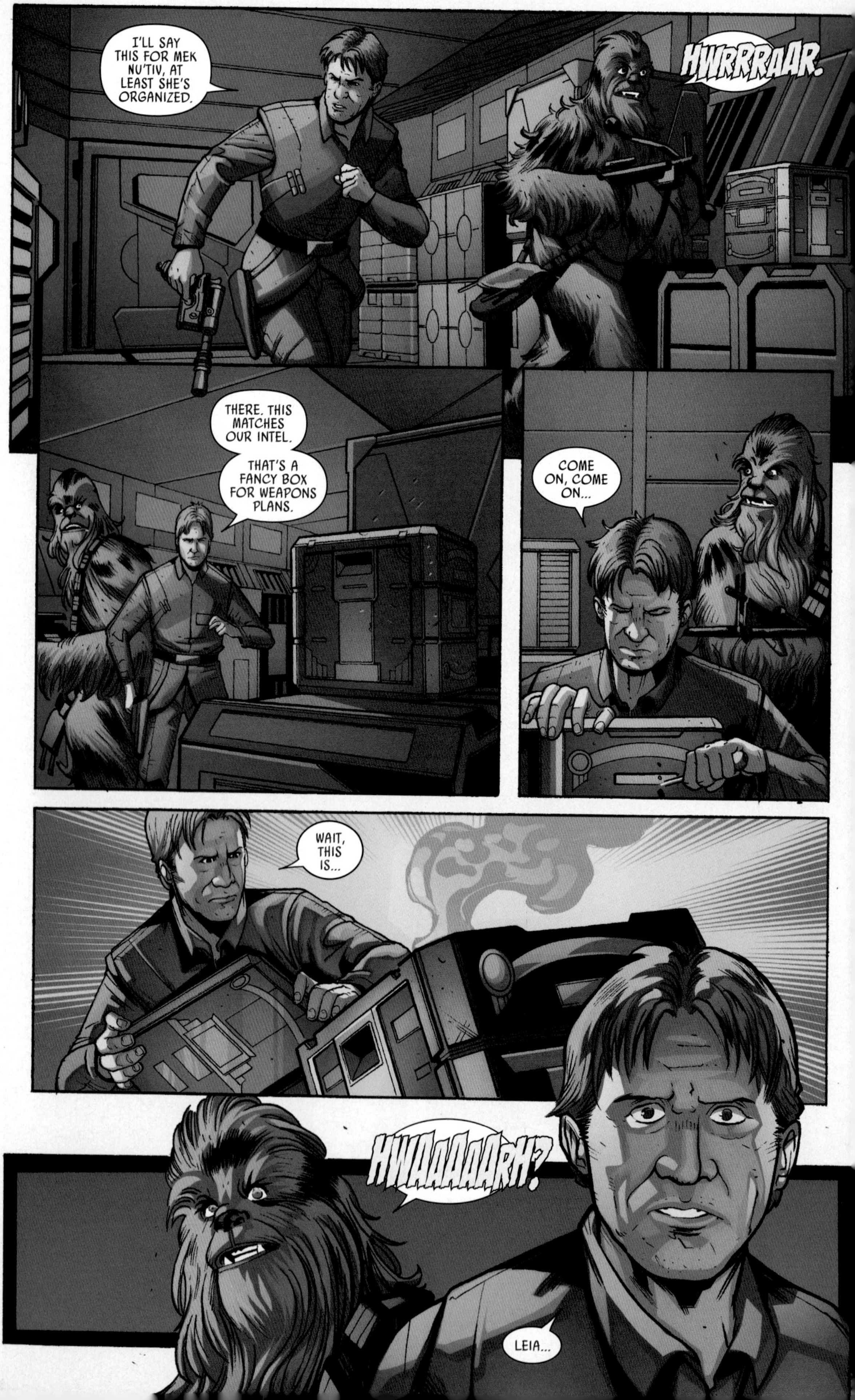
I'LL SAY THIS FOR MEK NU'TIV, AT LEAST SHE'S ORGANIZED.
HWRRRAAR.
THERE. THIS MATCHES OUR INTEL.
THAT'S A FANCY BOX FOR WEAPONS PLANS.
COME ON, COME ON...
WAIT, THIS IS...
HWAAAAARH?
LEIA...

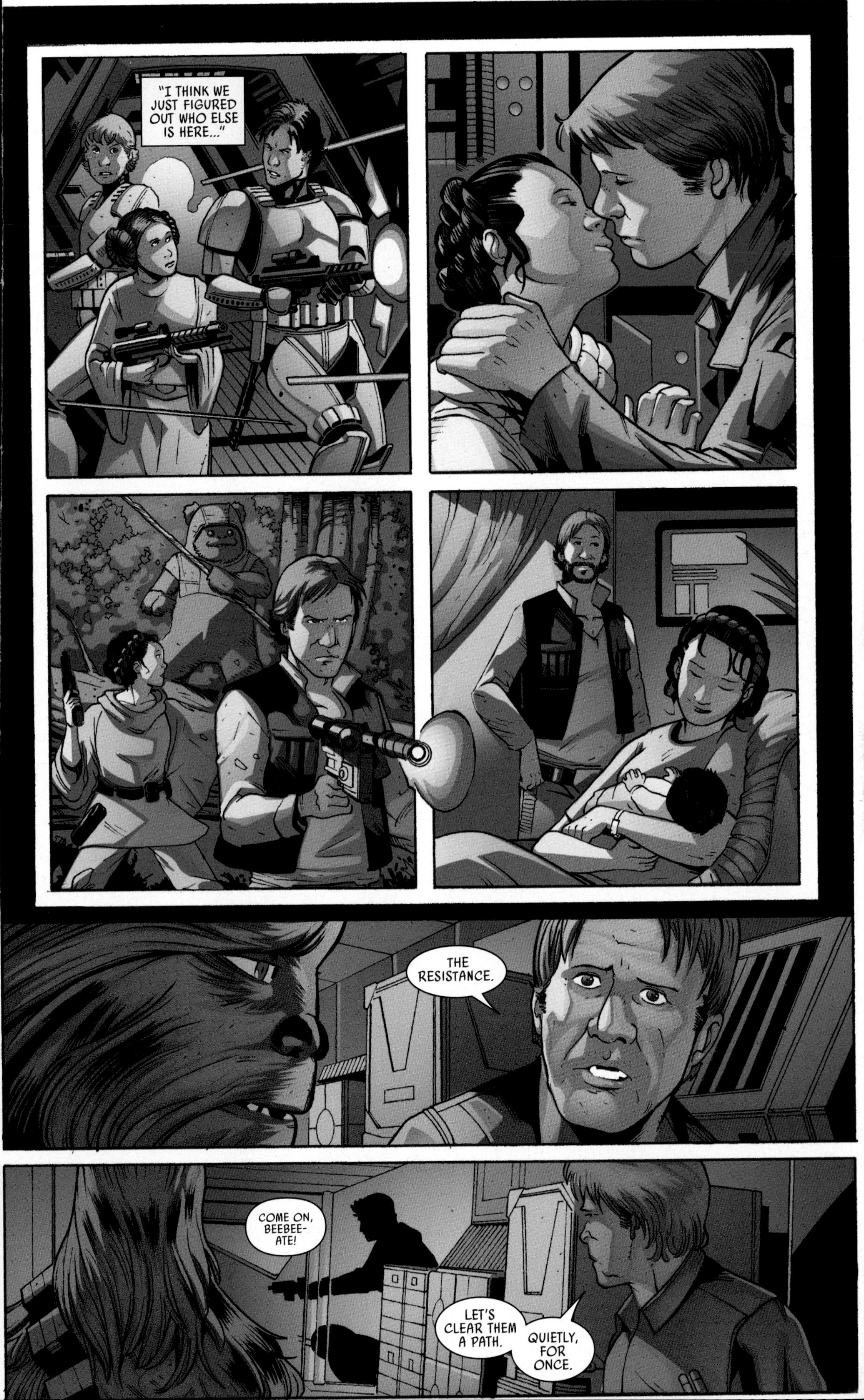
"I THINK WE JUST FIGURED OUT WHO ELSE IS HERE..."
THE RESISTANCE.
COME ON, BEEBEE-ATE!
LET'S CLEAR THEM A PATH.
QUIETLY, FOR ONCE.

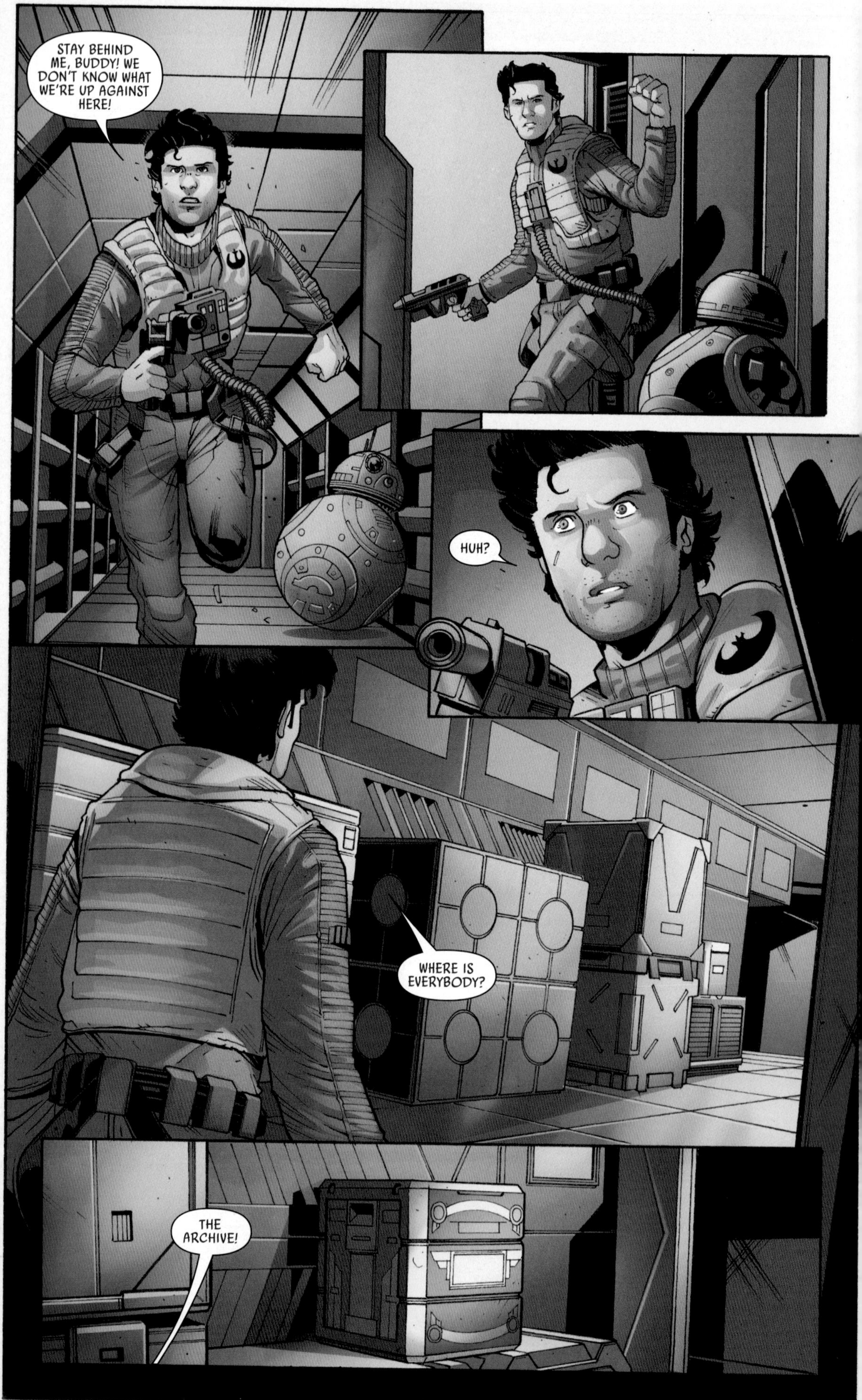
STAY BEHIND ME, BUDDY! WE DON'T KNOW WHAT WE'RE UP AGAINST HERE!
HUH?
WHERE IS EVERYBODY?
THE ARCHIVE!

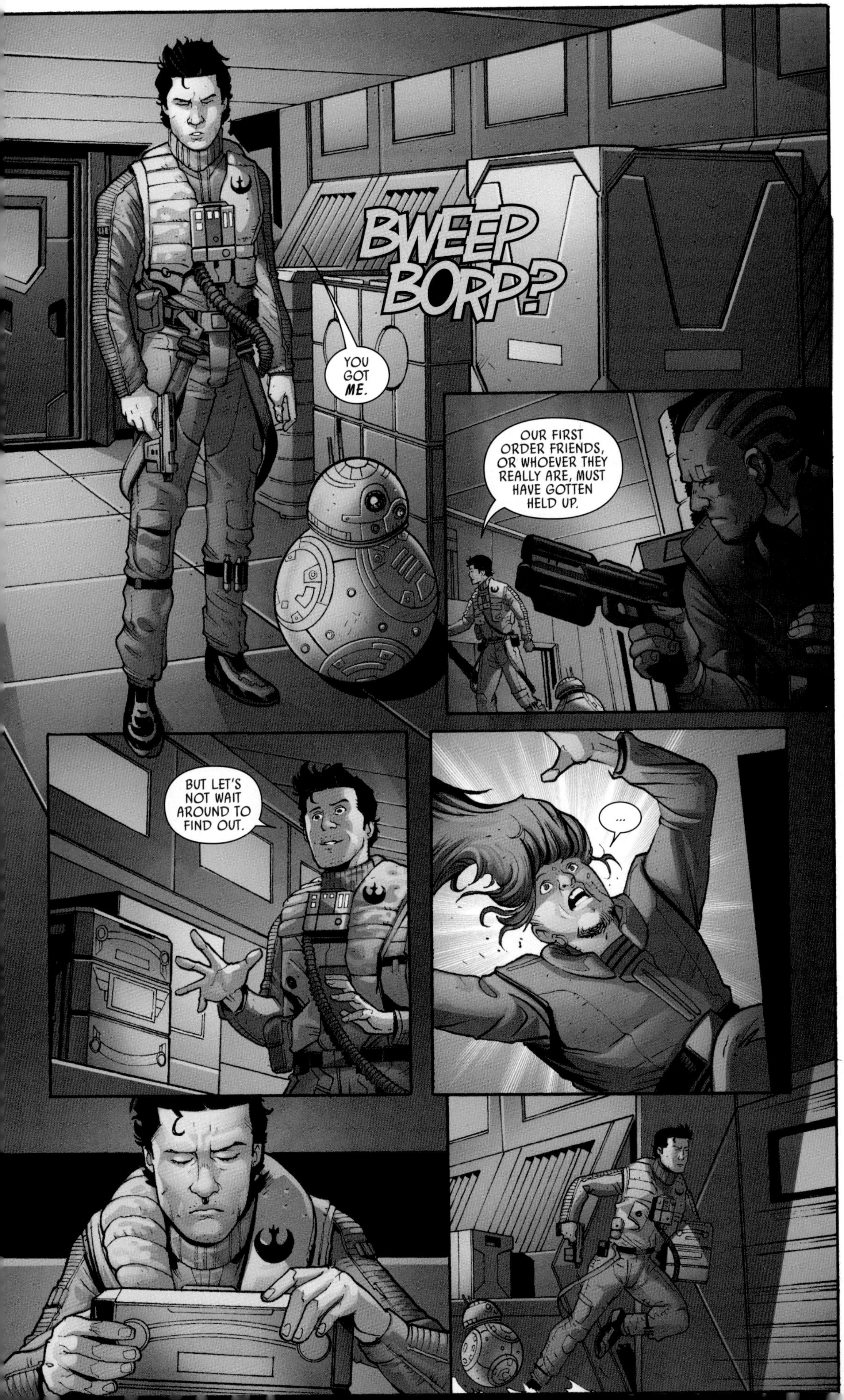
BWEEP BORP?
YOU GOT ME.
OUR FIRST ORDER FRIENDS, OR WHOEVER THEY REALLY ARE, MUST HAVE GOTTEN HELD UP.
BUT LET'S NOT WAIT AROUND TO FIND OUT.
...

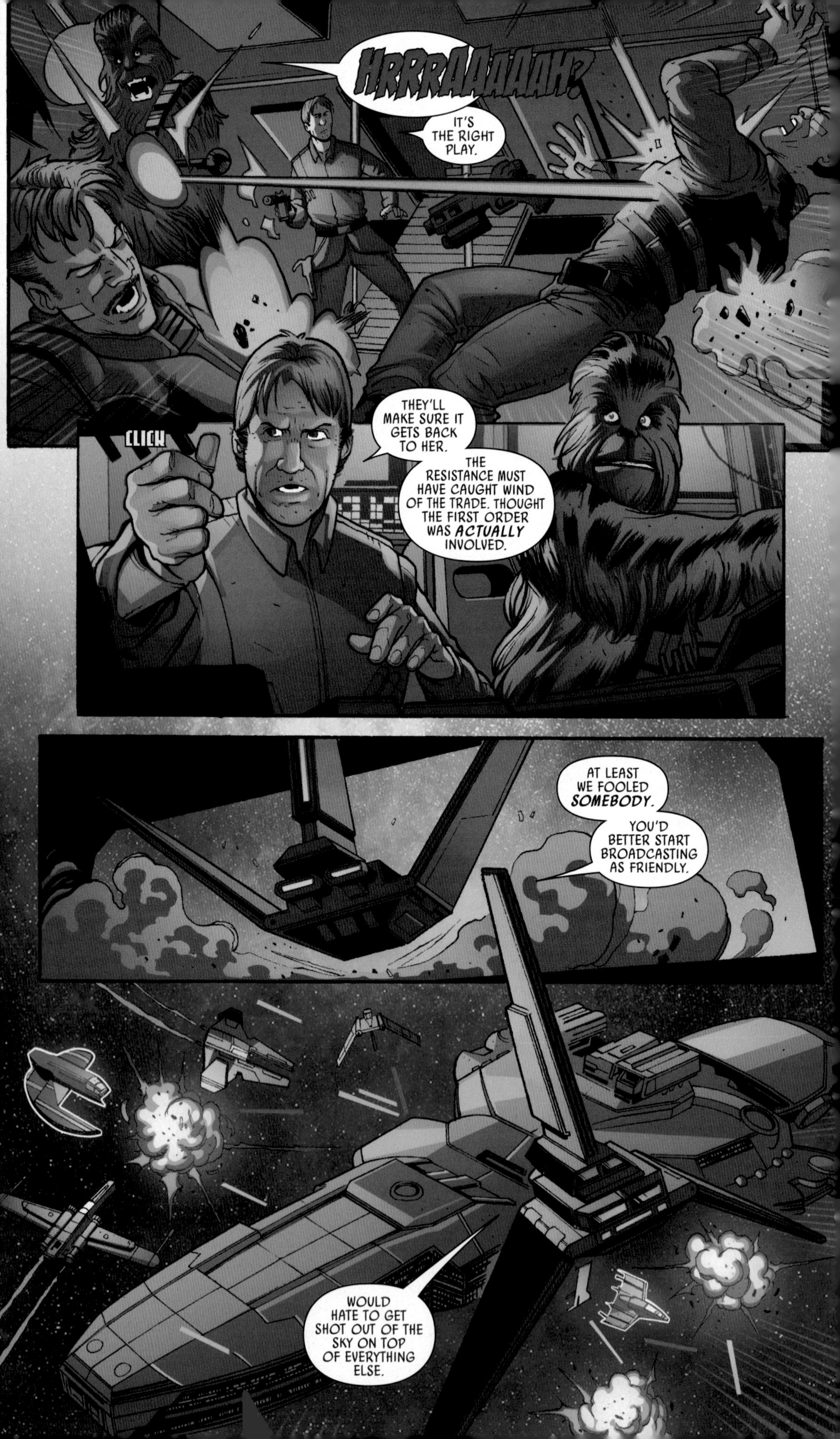
HRRRAAAAAAH?
IT'S THE RIGHT PLAY.
CLICK
THEY'LL MAKE SURE IT GETS BACK TO HER.
THE RESISTANCE MUST HAVE CAUGHT WIND OF THE TRADE. THOUGHT THE FIRST ORDER WAS ACTUALLY INVOLVED.
AT LEAST WE FOOLED SOMEBODY.
YOU'D BETTER START BROADCASTING AS FRIENDLY.
WOULD HATE TO GET SHOT OUT OF THE SKY ON TOP OF EVERYTHING ELSE.

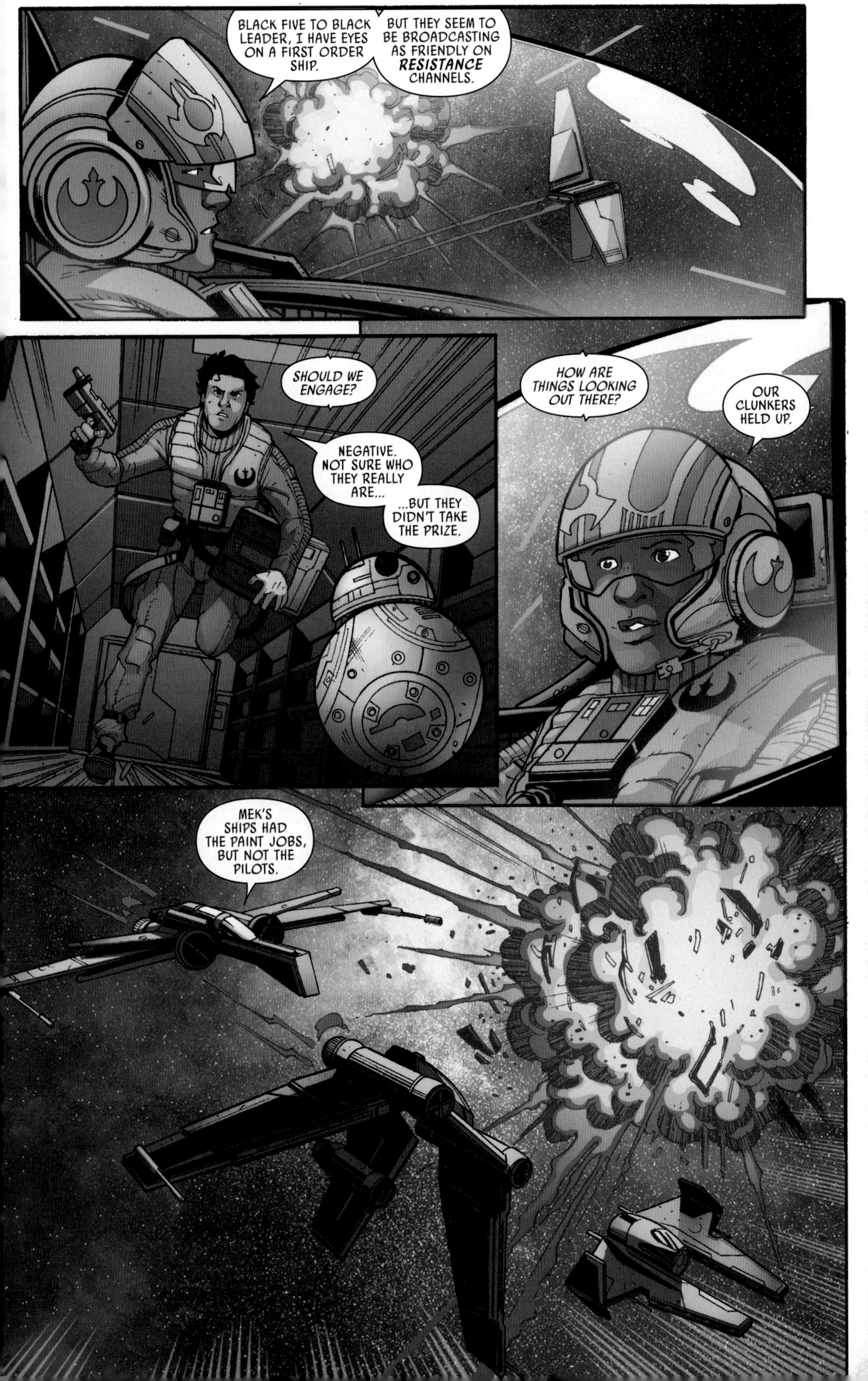
BLACK FIVE TO BLACK LEADER, I HAVE EYES ON A FIRST ORDER SHIP.
BUT THEY SEEM TO BE BROADCASTING AS FRIENDLY ON RESISTANCE CHANNELS.
SHOULD WE ENGAGE?
NEGATIVE. NOT SURE WHO THEY REALLY ARE...
...BUT THEY DIDN'T TAKE THE PRIZE.
HOW ARE THINGS LOOKING OUT THERE?
OUR CLUNKERS HELD UP.
MEK'S SHIPS HAD THE PAINT JOBS, BUT NOT THE PILOTS.

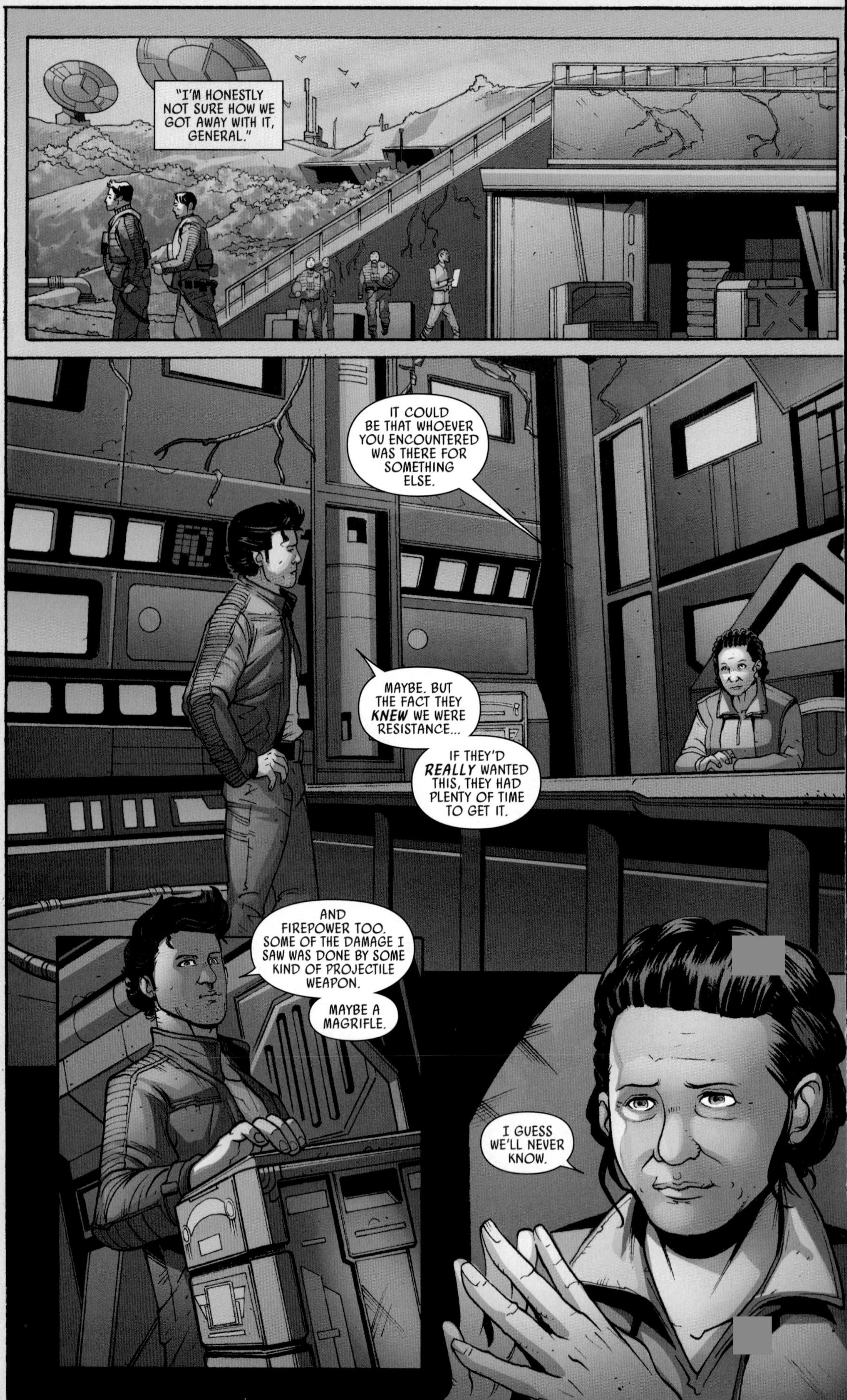
"I'M HONESTLY NOT SURE HOW WE GOT AWAY WITH IT, GENERAL."
IT COULD BE THAT WHOEVER YOU ENCOUNTERED WAS THERE FOR SOMETHING ELSE.
MAYBE. BUT THE FACT THEY KNEW WE WERE RESISTANCE...
IF THEY'D REALLY WANTED THIS, THEY HAD PLENTY OF TIME TO GET IT.
AND FIREPOWER TOO. SOME OF THE DAMAGE I SAW WAS DONE BY SOME KIND OF PROJECTILE WEAPON.
MAYBE A MAGRIFLE.
I GUESS WE'LL NEVER KNOW.

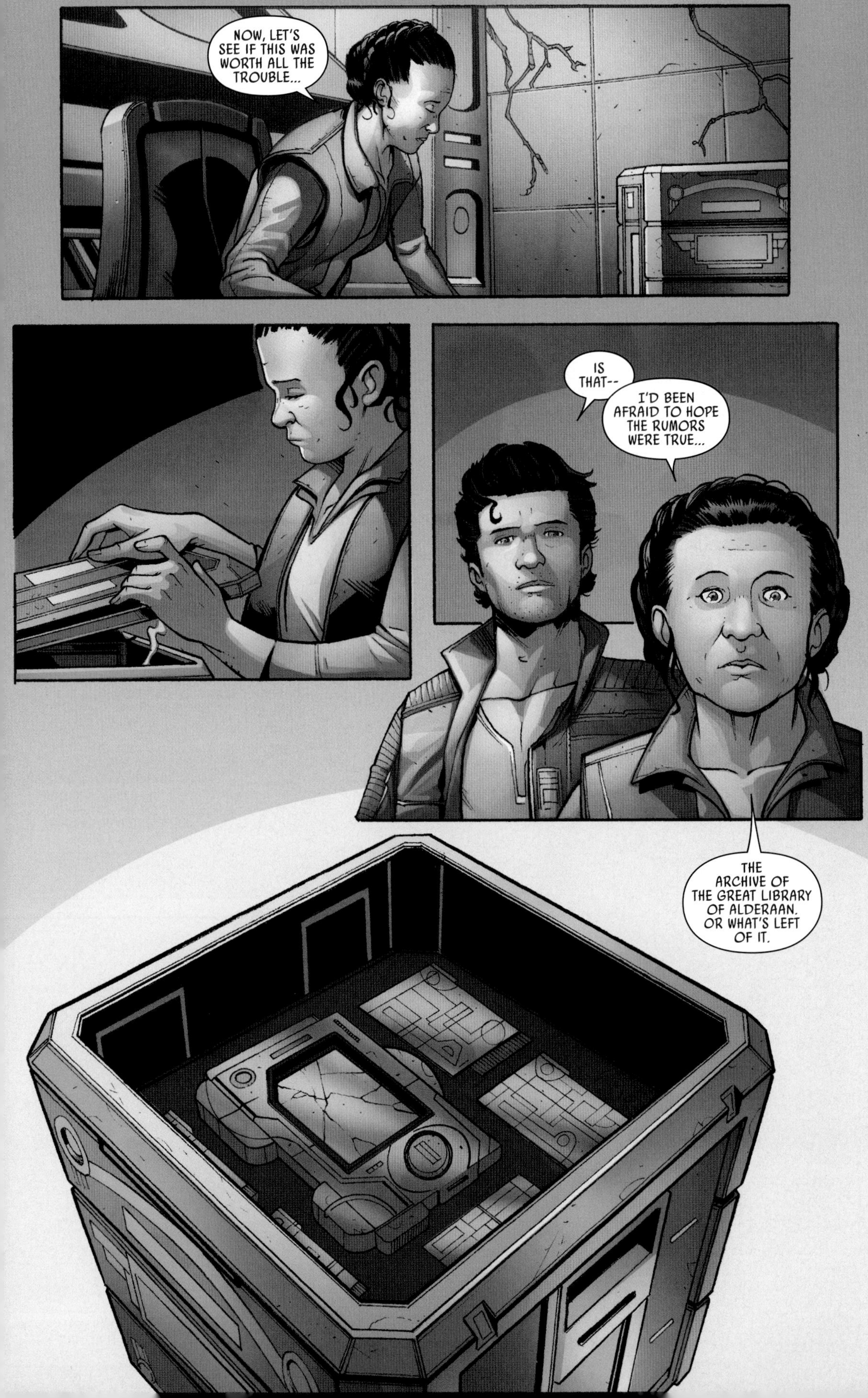
NOW, LET'S SEE IF THIS WAS WORTH ALL THE TROUBLE...
IS THAT--
I'D BEEN AFRAID TO HOPE THE RUMORS WERE TRUE...
THE ARCHIVE OF THE GREAT LIBRARY OF ALDERAAN. OR WHAT'S LEFT OF IT.

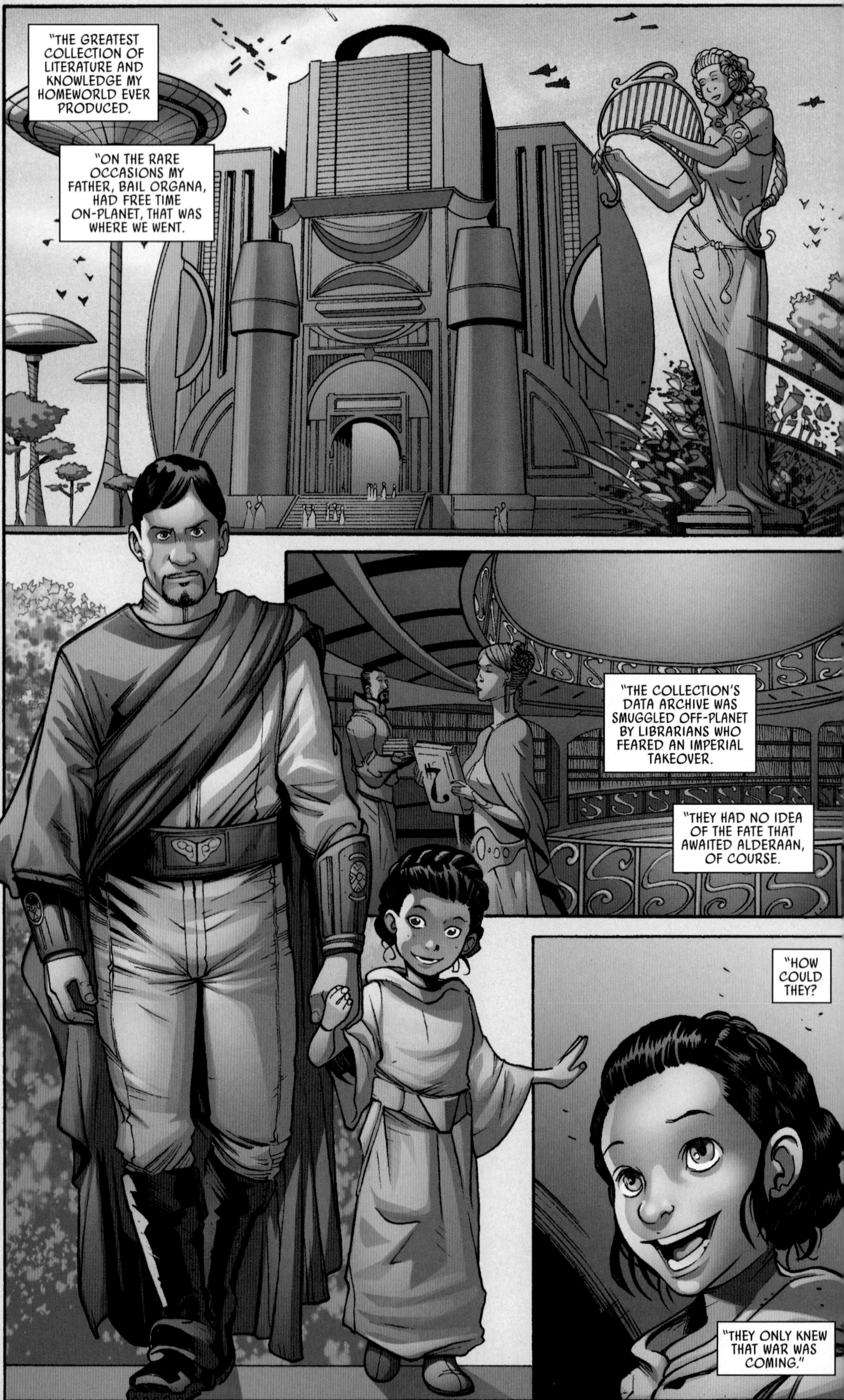
"THE GREATEST COLLECTION OF LITERATURE AND KNOWLEDGE MY HOMEWORLD EVER PRODUCED.
"ON THE RARE OCCASIONS MY FATHER, BAIL ORGANA, HAD FREE TIME ON-PLANET, THAT WAS WHERE WE WENT.
"THE COLLECTION'S DATA ARCHIVE WAS SMUGGLED OFF-PLANET BY LIBRARIANS WHO FEARED AN IMPERIAL TAKEOVER.
"THEY HAD NO IDEA OF THE FATE THAT AWAITED ALDERAAN, OF COURSE.
"HOW COULD THEY?
"THEY ONLY KNEW THAT WAR WAS COMING."

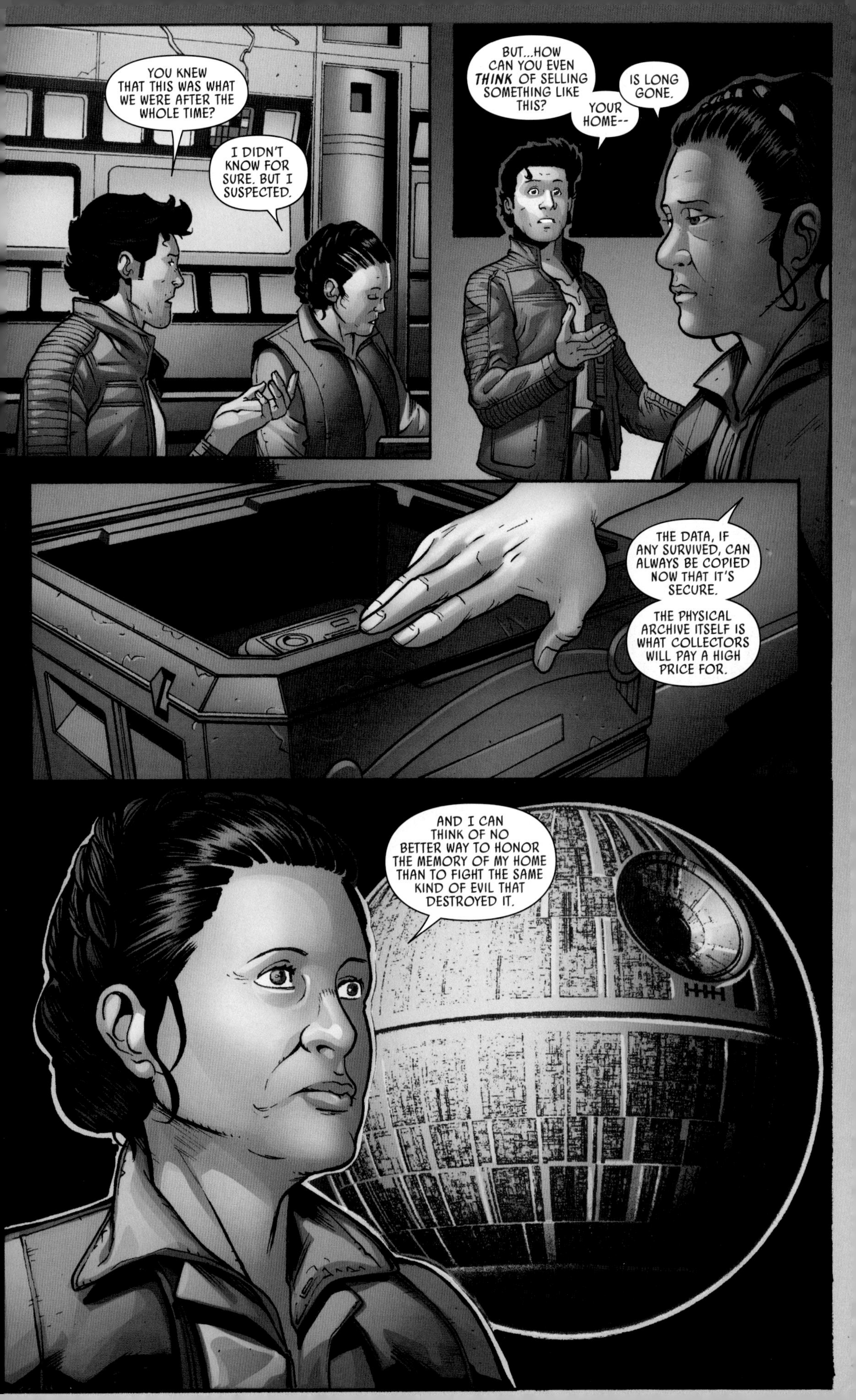
YOU KNEW THAT THIS WAS WHAT WE WERE AFTER THE WHOLE TIME?
I DIDN'T KNOW FOR SURE. BUT I SUSPECTED.
BUT...HOW CAN YOU EVEN *THINK* OF SELLING SOMETHING LIKE THIS?
YOUR HOME--
IS LONG GONE.
THE DATA, IF ANY SURVIVED, CAN ALWAYS BE COPIED NOW THAT IT'S SECURE.
THE PHYSICAL ARCHIVE ITSELF IS WHAT COLLECTORS WILL PAY A HIGH PRICE FOR.
AND I CAN THINK OF NO BETTER WAY TO HONOR THE MEMORY OF MY HOME THAN TO FIGHT THE SAME KIND OF EVIL THAT DESTROYED IT.

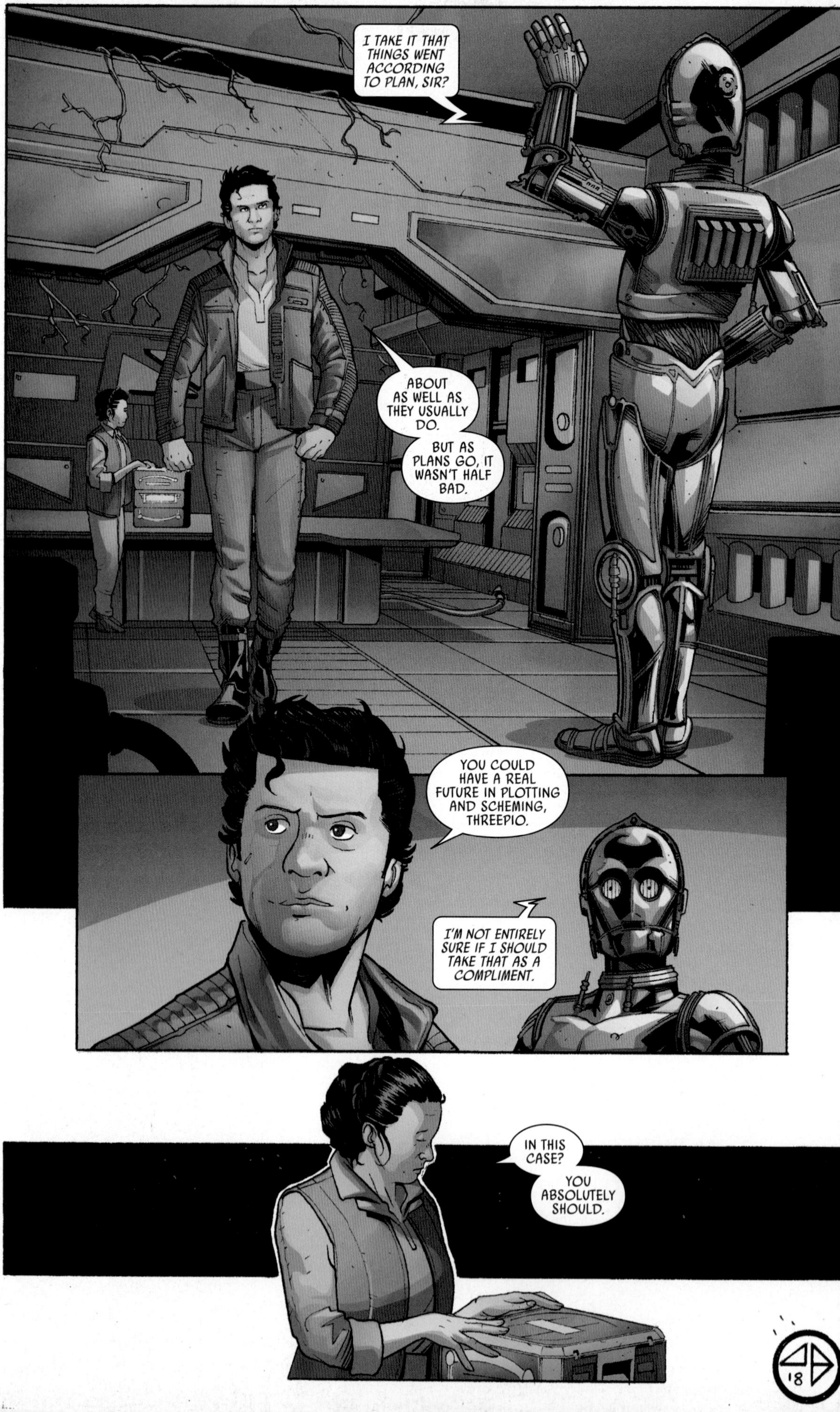
I TAKE IT THAT THINGS WENT ACCORDING TO PLAN, SIR?
ABOUT AS WELL AS THEY USUALLY DO.
BUT AS PLANS GO, IT WASN'T HALF BAD.
YOU COULD HAVE A REAL FUTURE IN PLOTTING AND SCHEMING, THREEPIO.
I'M NOT ENTIRELY SURE IF I SHOULD TAKE THAT AS A COMPLIMENT.
IN THIS CASE?
YOU ABSOLUTELY SHOULD.
18

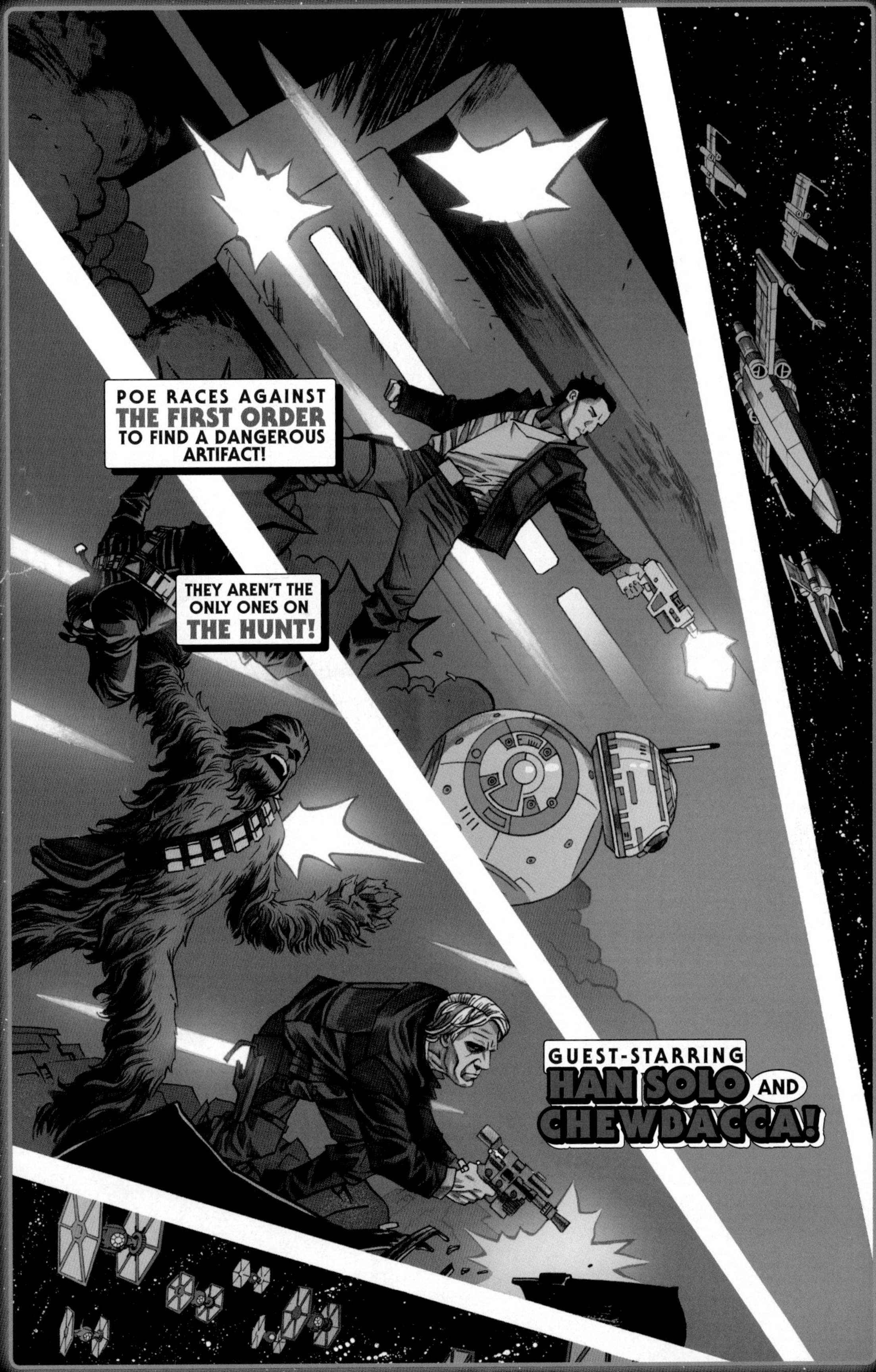
POE RACES AGAINST THE FIRST ORDER TO FIND A DANGEROUS ARTIFACT!
THEY AREN'T THE ONLY ONES ON THE HUNT!
GUEST-STARRING HAN SOLO AND CHEWBACCA!

STAR WARS: POE DAMERON ANNUAL 2 Variant by
DECLAN SHALVEY & TRIONA FARRELL

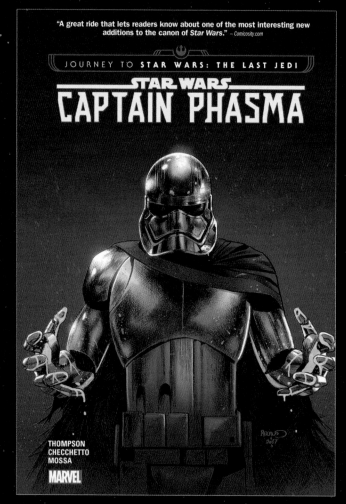